Acclaim for Ted Conover's

NEWJACK

"Nobody goes to greater lengths to get a story than Ted Conover. Immersing himself in his subject to a degree matched by few journalists working today, he has given us a compelling, compassionate look at a terribly important, poorly understood aspect of American society. My hat is off to him."   —Jon Krakauer

"*Newjack* tells the straight skinny on a guard's life inside prison without being overly judgmental or cloyingly sentimental. It's experiential journalism at its best."   —*The Denver Post*

"Ted Conover is a first-rate reporter and more daring and imaginative than the rest of us combined. This book is one of his finest."   —Sebastian Junger

"Profoundly eye-opening."   —*Chicago Sun-Times*

"A devastating chronicle of the toll prison takes on the prisoners and the keepers of the keys."   —*Star Tribune* (Minneapolis)

"This book takes a reader inside one of the many locked doors of America's penal system. It is clear-eyed and sympathetic, intelligent and engrossing. It reminded me of some of George Orwell's admirable journalism."   —Tracy Kidder

"A fascinating and sobering read."   —*USA Today*

"It is hard to know if there has ever been an institution that cost more and achieved less than a prison. And after reading *Newjack*, that statement seems truer than ever."   —*Chicago Tribune*

Ted Conover

NEWJACK

Ted Conover is a writer best known for his participatory investigations: riding the rails with tramps, travelling with Mexican undocumented workers, and working at Sing Sing prison. Two of his previous books, *Whiteout* and *Coyotes*, were named Notable Books of the Year by *The New York Times*. His writing has appeared in the New Yorker, the *New York Times Magazine*, the *Guardian*, and many other publications. He teaches at the Arthur L. Carter Journalism Institute of New York University. Further information can be found at www.tedconover.com.

Thanks to Kathy R., agent nonpareil; to Dan M., early believer; to Nicky D., Bob R., and Estelle G., good readers, advisers, and secret keepers all; to Robert S., Esq., for advice; to Jerry C., Jody and Jenni K., David S., Katie C., and especially, as ever, thanks, Jay.

NEWJACK

3 5 7 9 10 8 6 4 2

Published in 2011 by Ebury Press, an imprint of Ebury Publishing
A Random House Group company

First published in the USA by Vintage Books,
a division of Random House Group Inc.

Copyright © Ted Conover

The Random House Group Limited Reg. No. 954009

Addresses for companies within the Random House Group can be found at
www.randomhouse.co.uk

A CIP catalogue record for this book is available from the British Library

The Random House Group Limited supports The Forest Stewardship Council
(FSC), the leading international forest certification organisation. All our titles
that are printed on Greenpeace approved FSC certified paper carry the
FSC logo. Our paper procurement policy can be found at
www.randomhouse.co.uk/environment

Mixed Sources
Product group from well-managed
forests and other controlled sources
www.fsc.org Cert no. TT-COC-2139
© 1996 Forest Stewardship Council

Printed and bound in Great Britain by CPI Cox & Wyman, Reading, RG1 8EX

ISBN 9780091940959

To buy books by your favourite authors and register for offers visit
www.randomhouse.co.uk

NEWJACK

A YEAR AS A PRISON GUARD IN NEW YORK'S MOST INFAMOUS MAXIMUM SECURITY JAIL

TED CONOVER

EBURY
PRESS

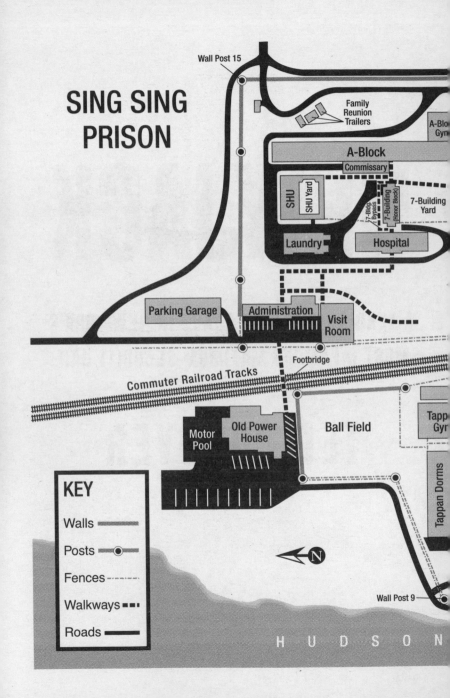

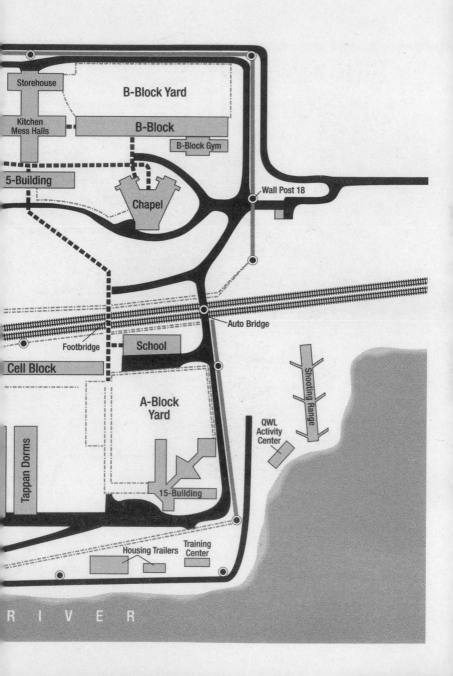

This is a work of nonfiction, describing events that I witnessed and participated in. No scenes are imaginary or made up, though some dialogue was, of necessity, re-created. Like all officers, I kept a small spiral notebook in my breast pocket for note-taking; unlike most of them, I took many notes. Most of the individuals in the book are identified by their real names. But to protect the privacy of certain officers and inmates, I have made up the following names for real people:

Aragon	L'Esperance	Astacio
Antonelli	Michaels	Van Essen
Foster	Rufino	Gaines
Arno	Hawkins	Perch
Dobbins	Wickersham	Pacheco
Bella	Chilmark	Scarff
McCorkle	Duncan	Saline
Popish	St. George	Pitkin
Dieter	Birch	Lopez
Di Carlo	Massey	De Los Santos
DiPaola	Phelan	Garces
Speros	Perlstein	Riordan
Turner	Billings	Delacruz
Malaver	Mendez	Perez
Fay	Larson	Addison
Melman	Sims	Blaine

CHAPTER 1

INSIDE PASSAGE

Six-twenty A.M. and the sun rises over a dark place. Across the Hudson River from Sing Sing prison, on the opposite bank, the hills turn pink; I spot the treeless gap in the ridgeline where, another officer has told me, inmates quarried marble for the first cellblock. Nobody could believe it back in 1826: a work crew of convicts, camping on the riverbank, actually induced to build their own prison. They had been sent down from Auburn, New York State's famous second prison, to construct Sing Sing, its third. How would that feel, building your own prison?

The shell of that 1826 cellblock still stands, on the other side of the high wall I park against; the prison has continued to grow all around it. In 1984, the roof burned down. At the time, the prison was using the building as a shop to manufacture plastic garbage bags, but as late as 1943, it still housed inmates. Sometimes now when inmates complain about their six-by-nine cells, I tell them how it used to be: two men sharing a three-and-a-half-by-seven-foot cell, one of them probably with TB, no central heating or plumbing, open sewer channels inside, little light. They look unimpressed.

I park next to my friend Aragon, of the Bronx, who always puts The Club on his steering wheel; I see it through his tinted glass. This interests me, because, with a heavily armed wall tower just a few yards away, this has got to be one of the safest places to leave your car in Westchester County. Nobody's going to steal it here. But Aragon is a little lock-crazy: He has screwed a tiny hasp onto his plastic lunch box and hangs a combination lock there, because of the sodas he's lost to pilfering officers, he says. Between the Bronx and prison, a person could grow a bit lock-obsessed.

There's no one else around. Most people park in the lots up the hill, nearer the big locker room in the Administration Building. But it's almost impossible for a new officer to get a locker in there, so I park down here by the river and the lower locker room. The light is dim. Gravel crunches under my boots as I head into the abandoned heating plant.

This six-story brick structure is one of those piles of slag that give Sing Sing its particular feel. Massive, tan, and almost windowless, it looks like a hangar for a short, fat rocket. The whole thing is sealed off, except for a repair garage around the corner and a part of the first floor containing men's and women's locker rooms and rest rooms.

The men's locker room—I've never seen the women's—is itself nearly abandoned; though it's stuffed with a hodgepodge of some two hundred lockers of inmate manufacture, fewer than twenty are actively used. The rest have locks on them, some very ancient indeed, belonging to officers who quit or transferred or died or who knows what. Nobody keeps track. An old wall phone hangs upside down by its wires on the left as you enter, the receiver dangling by its curly cord, a symbol of Sing Sing's chronically broken phone system.

Cobwebs, in here, find a way onto your boots. For a few weeks following my arrival, on Aragon's advice I checked the room for lockers that might have opened up. None ever did. All those unused lockers needlessly tied up. This might not be a problem for the officers who drive to work from the north, but down south in the Bronx (I live there, too) you don't want to advertise that you're a correction officer: Too many people around you have been in prison. Officers tend not to stick the big badge decals they pass out at the Academy on their car windows (because they like their windows), and most, like me, don't want to walk the street wearing a uniform. It's just awkward. A locker lets you leave your uniform at work.

My second month, I found one old lock that was so flimsy I could almost twist it off with my hands, but not quite. I brought in a small tire iron and it came off easily. Inside were plastic cups, magazine pictures of women in bikinis, and newspapers from 1983. I've since heard of a locker coming available in the Administration Building, but I'm not pursuing it. I've come to prefer it down here. The feel of neglect is somehow truer to the spirit of Sing Sing.

It's barely fifteen minutes till lineup. I throw on my gray polyester uniform, making sure I've got all the things I need on my belt: radio holder, latex-glove packet, two key-ring clips, baton ring. I put pen and pad, inmate rulebook, and blue union diary in my breast pockets, slide my baton through the ring, lock the padlock, and slam the locker door. I walk past a pile of old office desks and, by necessity, into the men's room. It smells like an outhouse. I sit down, for the second time this morning. Every morning is like this, and it is for the other new guys, too: Your stomach lets you know, just before the shift starts, what it thinks of this job.

A decrepit footbridge takes me over the tracks of the Metro North railroad—Sing Sing may be the only prison anywhere with a commuter railroad running through it—and other officers start to appear. My climb continues, up a wooden staircase that's been built atop a crumbling concrete one.

Here is the Administration Building parking lot, and the main entrance to the prison. Parked in the middle is the "roach coach," purveyor of coffee and rolls. To the right is the entrance to the Visit Room, not yet open. To the left, officers are lined up, waiting to deposit their handguns at the outside window of the Arsenal. For reasons lost to time, New York State correction officers are allowed to own and carry concealed weapons, and most seem to enjoy doing so. However, they can't bring the guns inside with them (nobody is allowed to carry inside)—and few of us have any doubt that prison is the safer for it. I take the last steps to the main gate and flash the badge and I.D. card I carry in a special wallet that I picked up at the Academy. The officer takes a cursory peek inside my lunch bag—the contraband check. I punch my time card and proceed to the morning's worst moment, getting my assignment.

The desk of Sergeant Ed Holmes is the focal point of the lineup room. It's on a raised platform, in front of a window. From up there, Holmes can see everybody in the room and most of those ascending the front steps. His eyes are constantly scanning, never settling on any person or object for more than an instant, moving from an officer to the printout in front of him and back again. The printout tells him what jobs he'll need to fill—who's on his day off, who's got vacation, who's out sick, who's on suspension. He checks off old-timers as he sees them—they've chosen their jobs and know where they're going. It's the new guys, like me, who are at his mercy.

Holmes is one of the tough black officers who have been here forever, a big man who seems to enjoy his distance from the rank and file. Several of his fellow white-shirts spoke to us during orientation, mostly about how the institution runs. Holmes was different. He came only to warn: Don't fuck with me, he said, glancing at the back wall of the room. I'm gonna give you your job assignment, and if you complain, I'll give you a worse one tomorrow. I have no patience. I'm not nice. Don't fuck with me. A few days later, a longtime officer advised me never to show Holmes I was scared—of him or anything else. "Holmes feeds on weakness," she said.

And now the line has moved and I'm next, a small, new officer before the mighty sergeant. I place my time card in front of him— he initials all the cards, to prevent us from punching in for friends—and then he is uncharacteristically silent: Holmes hasn't decided what to do with me. Or maybe he's not thinking of me at all; maybe his mind has wandered to his car or his electric bill or the movie he watched on TV last night. He riffles through his printout. Usually I'm sent to A-block or B-block. These are massive human warehouses, two of the largest prison housing units in the world, containing over a thousand inmates between them. I live for the exceptions: an easy day in the wall tower, the barbershop, or the hospital. That's the root of my dread—the hope for something else.

"Two fifty-four B-block," says Holmes finally, glancing to my left. Holmes could tell us the job instead of just the number, but if it's in the blocks, he won't. He wants to leave us guessing, as if we're still at the Academy. I turn and walk back among the eighty-odd officers milling around the crowded room, looking for someone who might know what job 254 is. I ask Miller; he shrugs. I ask Eaves; he thinks it's an escort job. That would be good. Escort officers spend a while in the mess hall and then get to leave the block for chunks of the day, taking groups of inmates to other buildings in the prison. Eaves has written down all the jobs in his union diary but hasn't yet found the number when a different sergeant shouts: "On the lineup!" As we assemble in rows, I pray it's true that it's an escort job and not a gallery job. Gallery officers run the galleries, the floors on which inmates live. Galleries are understaffed, and the officers on them, surrounded by inmates all day, are put at risk and run ragged. It's an awful job. I often get it.

We form into six or seven files, facing the white-shirts, most of whom are sergeants. As we're called to attention, it's interesting to watch the heavy ones try to squeeze between our narrow rows as they make a cursory check for violations of uniform—missing collar brass, whiskers, an earring inadvertently left in. Then a lieutenant, often the watch commander, speaks, telling us what has gone on in the prison since we left the day before. Today it's Lieutenant Goewey.

"Okay, it's been pretty quiet. They had one guy cut in the leg, in the tunnel from A-block yard. No weapon, no perp, the usual. Then we found three shanks buried in the dirt there in B-block yard, two of 'em metal, that we found with metal detectors. You think they're just sitting around out there, but these crooks are always conniving." In other words: one inmate stabbed, assailant unknown, knife not found; three homemade knives found; no officers hurt. A fairly typical day. Then a new sergeant steps forward: "Remember, there's no double clothing allowed during rec, for the obvious reasons. Inmates with two shirts on or two sets of pants should be sent back to their cells and not allowed in the yard or gym." Double clothing is understood to be both a defense against getting "stuck" and a way of quickly changing your appearance if you stick someone else.

Often we'll hear a moral message at lineup, too: a warning that we're not stepping up to the inmates enough or a caution that we need to watch one another's backs better and know the names of the people we're working with or a reminder that our job is "to get out of here in one piece at three P.M."—as if that needed saying. No such message today. There's the schedule of driver's-ed courses, for anyone interested, and a reminder of next week's blood drive, and the announcements are over.

"Officers, a-ten-*shun*!" yells a sergeant. Everyone is quiet. "Posts!" And we're off, not exactly at a run, through the long, rough corridors and up the hill to begin the day.

Sing Sing sprawls over fifty-five acres, most of it rocky hillside. It's flat down where I parked, near the river—the old cellblock and the railroad tracks. The former Death House, site of the electric chair that killed 614 inmates between 1891 and 1963, is down there too. (It's now a vocational-training building.) And so is Tappan, the medium-security unit of Sing Sing, with some 550 inmates housed in three 1970s-vintage shoe box–shaped buildings.

But most of Sing Sing is on the hill, and from the lineup room, we climb there. Getting to B-block is the longest walk; it's the remotest part of the "max" jail. There are a couple of ways to go; both involve a lot of stairs. Officers sip from coffee cups and grip lunch bags as we make the slow march up to work. We are black and white and Latino, male and female. Members of the skeleton night crew pass us in the hall and wave wanly; most have that gray night-shift look. They trade normal diurnal rhythms for the perk of having very little inmate contact—at night, all the inmates are locked in their cells. If I didn't have a family, I might put in for night duty.

The corridors and stairways are old, often in disrepair. When it rains, we skirt puddles from leaking roofs. When it's cold, we have reason to remember that these passages are unheated. The tunnels snake around Sing Sing, joining the various buildings, and at the beginning and end of each—sometimes even in the middle—there is a locked gate. Most of the officers posted to these gates have big, thick keys, but at one gate the guard pushes buttons instead, as they do in modern prisons. By the time I pass through the heavy front door of B-block, there are ten locked gates between me and freedom.

A-block and B-block are the most impressive buildings in Sing Sing, and in a totally negative sense. A large cathedral will inspire awe; a large cellblock, in my experience, will mainly horrify.

The size of the buildings catches the first-time visitor by surprise, and that's largely because there's no preamble. Instead of approaching them from a wide staircase or through an arched gate, you pass from an enclosed corridor through a pair of solid-metal doors, neither one much bigger than your front door at home. And enter into a stupefying vastness. A-block, probably the largest free-standing cellblock in the world, is 588 feet long, twelve feet shy of the length of two football fields. It houses some 684 inmates, more than the entire population of many prisons. You can hear them—an encompassing, overwhelming cacophony of radios, of heavy gates slamming, of shouts and whistles and running footsteps—but, oddly, at first you can't see a single incarcerated soul. All you see are the bars that form the narrow fronts of their cells, extending four stories up and so far into the distance on the left and right that they melt into an illusion of solidity. And when you start walking down the gallery, eighty-eight cells long, and begin to make eye contact with inmates, one after another after another, some glaring, some dozing, some sitting bored on the toilet, a sense grows of the human dimensions of this colony. Ahead of you may be a half-dozen small mirrors held through the bars by dark arms; these retract as you draw even, and you and the inmate get a brief but direct look at each other.

A-block and B-block are aligned with each other, end to end, and span the top of Sing Sing; between them sits the mess-hall building. Both were completed in 1929, and they're very similar in structure, except B-block is twenty cells shorter (sixty-eight), and one story taller (five). Though few civilians have seen anything like them, there is nothing architecturally innovative about the design. It plainly derives from the 1826 cellblock, based on Auburn's "new" north wing, which was the prototype for most American cell-house construction: tiny cells back to back on five tiers, with a stairway at either end and one at the center of the very long range.

From the ground floor, which in both buildings is known as the flats, you can look up and see how each structure is made up of two almost separate components. One is the all-metal interior, containing the inmates; it's painted gray and looks as though it could have been welded in a shipyard. The other is comprised of the exterior walls and roof, a brick-and-concrete shell that fits over the cells like a dish over a stick of butter. One does not touch the other: Should an inmate somehow escape from his cell, he's still trapped inside the building. A series of tall, barred windows runs down either side of the shell. They would let in twice as much light if they were washed. As it is, they let pass a diffuse, smog-colored glow, which crosses about fifteen feet of open space on each side before it reaches the metal, which it does not warm. There is a flat, leaky roof, which does not touch the top of the metal cellblock but leaves a gap of maybe ten feet. If the whole structure were radically shrunk, the uninitiated might perceive a vaguely agricultural purpose; the cages might be thought to contain chickens, or mink.

The blocks are loud because they are hard. There is nothing inside them to absorb sound except the inmates' thin mattresses and their bodies. Every other surface is of metal or concrete or brick.

A crowd of officers is milling around a cell near the front gate of B-block when I get there; this cell is the office of the officer in charge, or OIC. Rooms for staff were not included in B-block's plan, so a few cells near the front gate have been converted for that purpose. Next to the OIC's office, an identical, tiny cell houses the sergeants; two of them are squeezed in there. Next to that is the coat room, which contains a barely functioning microwave oven and a refrigerator that won't stay closed. There's an office for paperwork and filling out forms, and one for a toilet—the only staff toilet on these five floors.

For many years, the day-shift OIC has been Hattie "Mama" Cradle, a fifty-something woman five feet tall and just about as big around. She's got a clipboard in her hand and horn-rimmed reading specs on a chain around her neck. Officers give her their

names and job numbers; she tells them where they're posted. I
hang back a little, but then there's no more stalling: "Conover, two
fifty-four," I say. She gets the spelling off the tag on my shirt, then,
already poised to jot down the next name, says, "R-and-W."

My heart sinks. It's as bad as it could be. I am the first officer
on the second-floor galleries, known by the letters *R* and *W*.
I've worked there a few times before, including my very first—
horrifying—day of on-the-job training, when I accompanied a
novice officer, or "newjack," who barely knew what he was doing.
Today I'm that newjack, going it alone.

I crowd into Cradle's office and look for my keys—four separate
rings of the big, heavy "bit" keys, which work cell doors, with
center-gate, end-gate, and fire-alarm keys thrown on for good
measure. I attach these to my belt, and feel the weight. My heart is
pounding, but there's nothing for it. I find a fresh battery for the
floor's portable communications radio and grab a sheaf of forms
that I have to fill out during my shift. Last is the list of "keeplocks." I copy mine from Cradle's bulletin board, noting that there
are two new ones in the past twenty-four hours. Keeplocks are inmates on disciplinary restriction. In the old days there were few
such inmates, and often they would be sent to solitary confinement, known as the Special Housing Unit or the Box. But now
their numbers overwhelm the Box, so they stay put, mixed in with
the general population—except they can't come out of their cells.
One of our main responsibilities as gallery officers is to keep the
keeplocks locked up. Because we're always in a hurry and often
don't know the inmates, this is harder than it sounds. It's easy to
unlock the wrong door.

I pass through two more gates on my way upstairs and relieve
the night officer on R-and-W. Since the galleries are all locked
down at night, mainly her job is to check, every hour or so, that
every inmate is still breathing. It's not a bad job, and if an inmate
does die, it's no problem—unless he's found with rigor mortis. In
that case, she will lose her job, because of the cold, hard proof that
she wasn't really checking. The night officer hands me the radio
and some other keys. Does she know what the new keeplocks are
in for? I ask.

"I don't know, I don't care, they're not my friends, and I don't
like them," she says with a suddenness and finality that I find kind
of funny. She hands me the radio, which I attach to my belt. She's
left some wrappers and tissues around the desktop, but I don't

mention it; she looks tired. I envy her as she puts on her coat: She's going home and doesn't have to deal with the inmates any longer. "The cells are all deadlocked," she adds before leaving, which means that not only is the huge bar, or "brake," in place which locks them all at once but the cells are locked individually. Inmates are not at large at night, swarming around you on their way to chow, arguing with you when it's time to "lock in," calling you names, stressing you out. Pandora's box is closed. My first job of the day, with breakfast less than an hour away, will be to open it.

CHAPTER 2

SCHOOL FOR JAILERS

> When the recruit arrives he is plunged into an alien en-
> vironment, and is enveloped in the situation 24 hours a
> day without relief. He is stunned, dazed and frightened.
> The severity of shock is reflected in 17-hydroxycortico-
> steroid levels comparable to those in schizophrenic pa-
> tients in incipient psychosis, which exceed levels in other
> stressful situations. The recruit receives little, or erro-
> neous, information about what to expect, which tends
> to maintain his anxiety.
> —Peter G. Bourne, "Some Observations on the
>   Psychosocial Phenomena Seen in Basic Training,"
>   *Psychiatry,* Vol. 30, No. 2 (1967), 187–196

When the appointment letter from the Department of Correctional Services arrived, Arno had been managing a Burger King in
Syracuse. Chavez was working the floor buffer machine in the
lobby of a Manhattan apartment building. Davis was pounding
fenders at his upstate body shop. Allen and Dimmie were supervising teenage boys in youth detention centers in Westchester.
Brown was a plumber in Keeseville, near the Canadian border.
Charlebois worked distribution for Wal-Mart in midstate. Others
hadn't had jobs for a while. I had been working for several months
on a story for *The New York Times Magazine.* The letter gave each
of us two weeks or less to drop these jobs and report to the Albany
Training Academy, where we would enter state service as correction-officer recruits.

I tried to quickly wrap up my work and prepare for the seven
weeks away from home—and possibly much more, if I decided to
stick with the job and work in a prison. Then, on a rainy Sunday
evening in March 1997, I drove from New York City to the Academy. I'd been there twice before, for psychological testing. The
three-story brick structure had a white statue in the bell tower and
looked like a suburban Catholic high school. Later I would learn

that it had once been a seminary. From seminary to corrections academy: a sign of the times. In the foyer, two uniformed officers sitting at a table asked for identification, took my letter, and nodded toward a mountain of luggage nearby.

"Dump your bags there and get in line."

The line of male recruits in suits (and a handful of women in dresses) stretched way down a long hallway and around the corner, out of sight. All stood at rigid attention. As I made my way to the end, carefully skirting an officer chewing out a guy with a badly knotted tie, it dawned on me that I had reported to boot camp.

"You call that wearing a tie?" the officer demanded of the young man. "Button the collar. No. I've changed my mind. Take it off and start over." The man got started but, without a mirror, apparently didn't make much progress. A second officer, assigned to dog the recruits, walked up and laughed at him.

The officers were like sharks, sniffing for blood. This first lesson of the Academy was immediately clear: Don't stand out. I had a sense of foreboding about the recruit who stood three people ahead of me. Blond hair spilled over his shirt collar, and he had an earring. Of course, others stood out, too, like the guy who had chosen to wear army boots along with his coat and tie. But long hair made a different kind of statement.

The first officer stopped and gaped at the man in a stagy way. "What did you think you were coming to, a club?" he demanded. The guy with the hair mumbled something. "*What*?" said the officer, stepping right up into his face. "Did you think you were going out to a nightclub? Were you dressing up for a nightclub? He was dressing up for a club!" he told the other officer, who laughed some more.

My hair was only slightly shorter, but I passed the first inspection. The line advanced slowly. I tried to take in my surroundings with my peripheral vision. On the walls were a succession of old black-and-white photos of New York State prisons and two big display cases. The first case I passed contained objects with hidden compartments in which inmates had stashed things—a false-bottomed Coke can, a hollow-heeled shoe, and a hollow-handled hairbrush. The next one displayed inmate weapons: a sharpened piece of Plexiglas, a filed-down serving spoon, a metal spike. They were riveting; it was hard to keep my eyes forward.

"What do you think this is, a museum?" barked an officer from the hallway behind me. At first I thought I'd been caught, but as the officer yammered on, I realized it was someone behind me who'd been spotted looking at the shank display. "Eyes directly ahead! That's the meaning of *attention*!"

The officer walked by and stopped again in front of the recruit with the tie. The officer gestured at it angrily. "Are you *intentionally* disrespecting me?" he demanded. A few minutes later, perhaps thinking he was over the worst of it, the same man was caught leaning slightly against the wall: a born target. "Excuse me! Does the wall need holding up? Do you think I'm an idiot? Give me twenty push-ups."

"Umm . . . right here?" the recruit stammered.

"Of course right here! You think we're going to the gym?"

The man bent down and awkwardly got started.

"Five! Six! Seven! Eight!" counted the officer impatiently.

I closed my eyes for a moment. That night I'd been scheduled to give a slide-show lecture about Alaska at a club in my neighborhood. My dad and I had been in the north country recently, retracing a 1915 wilderness journey taken by my grandfather. The organizers had graciously rescheduled when I told them something had come up, but I pictured myself there now, finishing my after-dinner talk and glass of wine, waiting for coffee to be served, hands on the white tablecloth. It was a sudden but long-awaited assignment, I'd explained—a trip that couldn't be postponed. That was the first of the thousand dodges and sorry-I-can't-talk-about-its I'd have to make over the next thirty or so months as my life split into two parts, neither of which could know about the other.

The slow shuffle forward continued for nearly an hour. Finally, I was in the foyer again, receiving a bunk-room assignment and some bedding, both of which, it occurred to me, could have been quickly given out upon our arrival. But then no one would have had a chance to yell at us. I retrieved my bags and headed upstairs.

There was no time to unpack or meet my three roommates; we were due back downstairs immediately. The "auditorium" was a former chapel, with marble floors and tall stained-glass windows, dark now at 9:30 P.M. In the back, behind where a priest would have stood to lead vespers, was strung a banner. TOTAL QUALITY, it said, A D.O.C.S. COMMITMENT. A passable slogan for a factory but an odd concept, it seemed to me, for junior prison guards. In any event, I never heard it again. I was just taking a seat in a row of stackable chairs among my 127 classmates when a loud "Ten-*hut*!" brought us all to our feet.

A short, fit, florid-faced man strode in, looking unhappy. This was Sergeant Rusty Bloom, who ran the Academy. He surveyed us silently for a moment through thick glasses. From this night onward we were correction-officer trainees of the state of New York, he began, making $23,824 a year. "And notice I said 'correction officers,' not prison guards. It doesn't take much to become a prison guard. There is no academy for prison guards. You are here to become professionals." We would be joining more than 26,000 other state COs, he said, working for a department with an annual budget of $1.6 billion. More than 18,000 people had taken the civil service exam we took two years before; we were among the first classes to be drawn from the list of those who had passed, because our scores were high. Even so, he said, we didn't look like much. Over the next seven weeks, he and his staff would try to change that.

Like every new class, we were restricted to the grounds for the first week, Bloom explained, though we could return home on the weekends, dressed in our coats and ties, when he excused us Friday afternoon. If we didn't think we could follow the rules that guided life at the Academy, we should leave right now. Personal housekeeping, for example. The guidelines governing display of uniforms and toiletries were very clear; if one guy's stuff was out of compliance, the whole room would be written up for it. That applied on a larger scale, too. Our class of 128 would be divided into four "sessions." If anyone in a session messed up—was late or sloppy or disobeyed any order—the rest of the session would pay. Generally this meant being restricted to the grounds, as we were now, like any new class in its first week. And lest we forget what the job was about, Sergeant Bloom told us, "The easiest way to mess up is to leave a lock open." We had brought padlocks, as instructed, for the lockers in our rooms. "And I'll tell you right now, if I find anyone's lock open—and I promise you I will—that session's going to be held accountable."

Bloom told us to look on either side of us—one of the two people we saw would no longer be in the Department in twelve months' time. It was not an easy job; it was not for everybody. That sounded kind of ominous. But the next thing Bloom said broke his own scary spell. "And if you decide to quit during the Academy—I can guarantee you some will—please, please, let me know you're leaving. Don't just walk out."

Hearing the sergeant implore us was sort of funny, and a relief. Bloom wasn't just a terrorizing demon; he was also a bureaucrat at the mercy of paperwork. I suspected that recruits left the Academy without saying good-bye fairly often, and the thought of it cheered me considerably.

The job, he said in conclusion, was about *care, custody,* and *control.* "The gray uniforms are the good guys, and the green uniforms are the bad guys. That's what it's all about." And in twenty-five years, we'd have a pension.

We were given notebooks, a training manual, and a tall stack of forms to fill out. One officer got angry when recruits started asking him for pens—few people had brought them, because we hadn't been told to. "Well, what did you think you were going to be doing here tonight?" he demanded inanely. Everything was delayed while he went to look for pens. When he returned, he discovered he hadn't brought enough. He tossed the last handfuls of them angrily into the air above our heads. I would later find that of the several assholes on the Academy's training staff, this officer actually wasn't one of them; it was just his act for opening night.

Next stop was the quartermaster's room, where we were issued an armload of uniforms and insignia, and then, at 11 P.M., it was up to our room on the second floor to hem trousers and sew on American flags. "Did anybody bring scissors?" "Can I borrow your Magic Hem?" "Where'd that iron go?"

I had a feeling of dread—born of fatigue and aversion to military discipline—that I tried to disguise. But at least one of my three roommates seemed completely charged up by the experience. He was Russell Dieter, an ex–Marine aircraft mechanic who had been working as a production welder and, since his divorce, living on the family farm, midstate. I would grow to dislike Dieter, and he would grow to hate me, but we were, for the duration, bunkmates—I, unfortunately, in the bed above him. Since this was the first night, a sort of cordiality reigned. Dieter had been through several boot camps and was no stranger to abuse. His hair was already shaved to the skull. His small brown mustache was closely trimmed. And he was prepared in other ways: Though nobody had told us to, he had brought along an iron and ironing board, even spray starch. I watched as he bent over his new gray shirts, pushing his glasses up on his nose while applying a precise military crease to the middle of each breast pocket.

Also in the room were Chris Charlebois, the former Wal-Mart employee, and Gary Davis, an Air Force vet in his fifties, who had barely been making ends meet at his body shop in Ticonderoga, New York. Like me, they had taken a civil service test nearly two years before and then not heard a word until January 1997, when we'd all been summoned to Albany for physical and psychological testing. Charlebois had been given only three days' notice to report to the Academy. He'd even taken a cut in pay, he said, but he felt it was worth it in the long term for the pension, the health and dental insurance, and the paid leave—basically, a month per year.

It wasn't until 1 A.M. that we had our uniforms prepared, toiletries displayed on our tiny closet shelves, and extra stuff stashed away in lockers. Housed above us, on the third floor, were members of the class in front of ours, and sometime around midnight one of those more seasoned recruits ventured by and offered a tip: "Short-sheet your beds. That way, you don't have to make them again every morning," he explained. Huh? The logic was that short-sheeting gave you an extra sheet. This you could keep in your locker during the day and throw onto your apparently perfectly made bed every evening. With an extra blanket that you brought from home, you could then sleep comfortably on top of your bed and not waste time making it in the morning. It was idiocy, I thought, the military bed-making fetish, but the wisdom of the advice was immediately clear. Making the precise corners and folds required for bed display took a long time. Dieter, in fact, was already planning for it: he announced that he had set his big alarm clock, which had bells on top, for 5 A.M. We didn't need to report to the classroom until 6:30 A.M., so I groaned. Nobody else said anything, though, so I kept quiet and went to sleep.

––––

I was here, basically, because the Department had told me I couldn't be. The Academy, they said, was off-limits to journalists—no exceptions, end of conversation. Now, why should that be? I wondered. With prisons so much in the news, costing so much money, and confining such unprecedented numbers of people, it seemed to me that their operations should be completely transparent.

I have been fascinated by prisons for a long time. There is little,

I think, that engages my imagination like a wall. A small town in Minnesota that I've passed through countless times en route to family reunions has a prison with a massive brick wall and turret-like guard towers, which I have spent hours thinking about. Every old prison I've seen since, from the Tower of London to Philadelphia's massive and abandoned Eastern State Penitentiary, has inspired a similar fascination.

Tightly knit cultures or subcultures, such as that of the police, represent a different kind of locked door. By combining journalism with anthropology, I've tried in previous writings not simply to observe but to participate in the lives of railroad tramps, illegal Mexican immigrants, Kenyan truckers, and even the elite of Aspen, Colorado. Sometimes these worlds lie behind an open door through which no writer has thought to pass for a while. Other times, the door is locked, and getting in takes some extra effort.

That challenge is something I relish. Getting in can take patience and resourcefulness. Often it involves overcoming my fears—as it did in this case. Punishment is frightening, and confinement, the modern punishment of choice, frightens in a particular way. When I was a kid at camp, older boys once shut me in a locker until a friend let me out; those brief moments filled me with a terror I'll never forget. Maybe as a result, I'm made uneasy by the sight of birds in cages, fish in tanks, large dogs in small apartments. I treasure tales of escape, be they from Alcatraz or Nazi concentration camps or the dungeon in which Dumas's Count of Monte Cristo was unjustly imprisoned for fifteen years. I've always felt that a special ring of hell should be reserved for kidnappers who place their victims in the trunks of cars.

But how to learn about prison? Short of becoming an inmate, I thought, how could you ever learn what that world was like? Most of the accounts in contemporary nonfiction are by prisoners—inmates from the radical (Eldridge Cleaver, George Jackson, Mumia Abu-Jamal) to the establishment (former New York chief judge Sol Wachtler, Boston politician Joseph Timilty) to the hard-core (Jack Henry Abbott and Sanyika Shakur). Documentary films, as well (such as the excellent *The Farm*), tend to focus on inmate life.

But prison, it occurred to me, is actually a world of two sides—two colors of uniforms—the "us" and the "them." And I wanted to hear the voices one truly never hears, the voices of guards—those on the front lines of our prison policies, society's proxies.

What most civilians believe about guards is what they learn

from the movies. *Cool Hand Luke, Brubaker, The Shawshank Redemption,* and many others paint melodramatic pictures of prison life that have some common denominators. Among their lessons: while a few inmates are very bad, many are actually reasonable people, wrongfully imprisoned; middle-class white men face a high likelihood of rape; wardens are often corrupt; and guards are uniformly brutal.

This stereotyping of guards was particularly interesting to me. Was it true? And if so, was that because the job tends to attract tough guys predisposed to violence? Or were guards normal men who became violent once enmeshed in the system? If the stereotype was false, why did it persist?

All of this seemed urgent because of what can be called America's incarceration crisis. While crime rates fall and the economy prospers, far more people than ever before are getting locked up, mainly due to mandatory sentencing for drug crimes. Huge resources are diverted as a result: California, where prisons are already at double capacity, must build a new prison every year to keep up with the flood of new inmates. But while other priorities—health care, education—suffer, there is little evidence that this mass jailing provides either a cure for crime or a deterrent to it. Since the dismantling of apartheid in South Africa, the former number-one jailer, the United States has run neck and neck with Russia in the race to become the world leader in rates of imprisonment. We lock up six times as many citizens per capita as England, for example, and seventeen times as many as Japan. By early 2000, United States prisons and jails held nearly 2 million people, meaning that one out of every 140 residents was behind bars. The number of inmates has tripled in the last twenty-five years, and rates of incarceration keep climbing. In the 1990s, while Wall Street was booming, one out of three black men between the ages of twenty and twenty-nine was either behind bars or on probation or parole. Young black men in California are now five times as likely to go to prison as to a state university. Through knowledge, political will, and perhaps some luck, we seem to have tamed inflation and the budget deficit. But our response to crime remains a blunt and expensive instrument that more often seems to scar the criminal than reform him.

Incarceration, the best punishment we have been able to think up, has itself become a social problem. One of its unintended results is the growth of so-called prison culture. The baggy low-slung pants popular among inner-city (and white suburban) teenagers are a fashion thought to have originated in prison, where inmates are issued ill-fitting clothes and, sometimes, no belts. Same with the sneakers-without-shoelaces look, a psych-ward regulation. So common is confinement among the older brothers of young minority-group men I have met in New York City that a prison term seems practically inevitable to many, almost a rite of passage. That prisoners should have such an influence on civilians is just one of the indicators that prison has unwittingly given rise to its own empowering culture, theorists suggest, one that keeps inmates resentful and resistant to the "reformative" goals that prison authorities once pursued and still pay lip service to.

At first, I didn't consciously think about becoming a guard myself. In 1992—having been rebuffed by the state in an effort to discuss guards and prison in general terms—I got in touch with the New York State guards' union, Council 82 of the American Federation of State, County, and Municipal Employees. Its executive director, Joe Puma, was initially wary, but we ended up having two long conversations. Puma was a guard himself, and a former Teamster, from Brooklyn. He told me that prison guards had the highest rates of divorce, heart disease, and drug and alcohol addiction—and the shortest life spans—of any state civil servants, due to the stress in their lives. They feared not only injury by inmates but the possibility of contracting AIDS and tuberculosis on the job. (One officer had recently infected his family with prison-contracted TB; another had died of a resistant strain.)

Puma reinforced my sense that the work was awful, that prison guards were the dentists of the law enforcement world. "I'd take a cut in pay for some more respect" was how he put it, still chafing that New York governor George Pataki had recently referred to his rank and file not as "correction officers" but as "prison guards"— as did most newspapers. "It has always killed me how fast the criminal goes from being a bad guy at his trial to some kind of victim once he's in prison, according to public perception," he added. "We officers hate that, because we're the good guys." He agreed when I suggested that some of the officers' persistent image problems were of their own making: They shunned publicity because so often it was bad. "But we're coming out," he insisted. "We're going to tell our story." Puma promised that we would talk again soon and that he would introduce me around. Then, without explanation, he stopped returning my calls. I pestered him for months, and finally, through the press liaison, I was invited to attend the union's initial bargaining sessions for its new contract with the state. There I became friendly with a handful of union reps, including Rick Kingsley, of Washington Correctional Facility, a medium-security prison in Comstock, New York.

Kingsley and I ate dinner near the Quality Inn in Albany. He'd been a dairy farmer for years, he said, before switching to corrections thirteen years earlier, succumbing to economic inevitability. His brother, once in car sales, had become a CO, too; and many family members lived nearby. He was divorced, with a son he was putting through college, because, as he put it, "Officer after officer will tell you: There's no way in hell you'd want your kid to be a CO."

Kingsley startled me by admitting that probably 90 percent of the officers he knew would tell strangers they met that they worked not in a prison but at something else—say, carpentry—because the job carried such a stigma. Sure it had its advantages, like the salary, the security, and, with seniority, the schedule: Starting work at dawn, Kingsley had afternoons free to work on his land and rebuild his log cabin. But mainly, he said, prison work was about waiting. The inmates waited for their sentences to run out, and the officers waited for retirement. To Kingsley, it was "a life sentence in eight-hour shifts."

He invited me to visit his prison and even asked me to stay in his trailer when I did. Getting permission to visit was hard, so I was thrilled to finally be inside. I knew from the first half hour, though, that I was seeing only surfaces. Conversations stopped when Rick and I entered a lunchroom, and officers in the parking lot stopped talking when we walked up. I was like the guy in the loud shirt who steps off a big cruise ship into the commercial district of some tropical port—the locals would show me what they wanted to show me, and two hours later I'd be gone and their real life could resume.

This feeling was never stronger than when Rick took me to the yard and I met some of his officer friends. They told me the rules they followed to prevent trouble: breaking up gatherings of more than six people; forbidding martial arts practice, group worship (Muslims wanted to pray together and kneel toward Mecca), and contact sports; frisking inmates as they came in. I asked if there was ever trouble despite all the precautions. They looked at each other and then at Rick, whose expression I didn't catch. No, they replied after a split-second but telltale delay; there really wasn't. It was a tight ship.

Bullshit, I felt like saying. But I couldn't.

Rick had told me about the Academy, and it seemed like a great subject to write about: the place where the values of the profession were first imparted, where guys from the sticks first learned the ways of the prison guard. He thought my idea of profiling a new recruit, following him all the way through, was a good one. I set about trying to make it happen.

But DOCS turned me down flat. They offered no explanation and were not interested in hearing my reasons. It just wasn't done. I was disappointed. And it made me want to know about this world more than ever.

I saw that the only way into the Academy was to enter as a recruit, like anyone else. In 1994 I put in an application to take the next correction-officer exam and, several months later, I sat down with a test booklet in a large room full of people desperate for a job. Then, for months, I waited.

———

Our session gathered the next morning in a classroom in the basement, near a lounge and the mess hall. The Academy's instructors were all correction officers with a training credential. Ours, luckily, was Vincent Nigro ("NY-gro," he was careful to tell us), a CO from a downstate maximum-security prison called Eastern Correctional Facility. A jolly round man with a buzz cut, Nigro said that inmates had nicknamed him Abbott, after the partner of Costello. One of his training specialties was chemical agents, he said, explaining with a wink that "chemical agents make you fat." He seated us alphabetically around the room—our session contained people with surnames from A to F—and then gave us a mock quiz. "What's the first three things you get when you become a CO?" he asked. We waited. "A car. A gun. A divorce."

Thus began our education in the ways of the Academy. Our days would start before he arrived in this, our "homeroom," Nigro said. Having left our dorm rooms spotless, we would gather in the classroom and check one another's uniforms: collar brass had to be straight, name tag placed just so, a single pen in our breast pocket, wallet pocket buttoned, shoes perfectly shined. Then we'd proceed, silently and in single file, to the mess-hall queue. There was a prescribed way to turn corners: You had to pivot on the ball of your inside foot, not interrupting your stride. Breakfast was to be eaten in silence. We'd regroup in the classroom at around seven forty-five and he'd be there by eight. Then, every day, two different officers would count the class, as if we were inmates, and present the completed count slip, along with a fire and safety report, to Sergeant Bloom. Nigro acknowledged that Bloom was a little scary and said he'd try to help us steer clear of him.

Each instructor had a specialty, and Nigro explained that each would lecture us before we were through. The subjects would range from report writing to the use of force, from penal law to "standards of inmate behavior," from tool and key control to drug awareness. There would be tests every Friday, on which we'd have to score 70 percent or better; if we didn't, we could take the test only two more times. That, along with first aid and CPR, was the academic stuff. In addition, we'd have two hours of physical training—PT—every afternoon, and we'd have to pass a physical performance test in our last week. We'd learn how to use a baton and how to fight hand to hand in a course called Defensive Tactics. We'd have to qualify on a shooting range. Finally, we'd be exposed to tear gas ("CS gas" or "chemical agents," they insisted on calling it) and learn how to fire gas guns.

Among the things we could get fired for, Nigro advised, were arriving at the Academy late or drunk—once we were allowed to go out, that is—or, oddly enough, sleeping in class. I had thought one of the advantages of corrections work was the chance for a bit of shut-eye now and then. But Nigro said that if we felt ourselves falling asleep, we were to stand up and walk to the back of the class. In future days, the number of recruits trying to remain conscious against the back wall would be an accurate indicator of the deadly dullness of a given lecture.

Nigro questioned the class, in roughly alphabetical order, about what we had done before coming to the Academy. The Antonelli brothers, handsome identical twins from the Buffalo area who were into bodybuilding, ran a landscaping business, which they had temporarily entrusted to their brother. Don Allen, one of three black men in the group, had worked in detention centers for the state's Division for Youth (DFY). Tall and thin Aisha Foster, one of four black women, had been a guard at Rikers Island. Her Academy roommate, bubbly Tawana Ellerbe, had worked a clerical job for the New York City Police Department. Dave Arno, though he had a four-year-college degree and part of a master's, had managed a

Burger King, unable to find any other job in the Syracuse area. Cleve Dobbins was a scatterbrained former Army M.P. in his forties. Carlos Bella had been a guard/counselor for New Jersey's juvenile detention services department. Felix Chavez, a courtly Puerto Rican from Brooklyn, had worked as assistant to a building's super. I too had managed an apartment complex, I could answer truthfully, and had also driven a cab. Peter DiPaola had worked as an accountant for a vending machine company. Matt Di Carlo, a Navy veteran and CO's son, had run a gas station and, for the present, was still doing so on weekends. Diandre Dimmie was another former DFY guard; judging by his sharp suits, it made sense that he had also worked in a men's clothing shop. Brian Eno was an intelligent, pear-shaped former emergency medical technician. Diminutive Anthony Falcone had recently finished his hitch with the Army.

To see if any of us were going to have trouble with the physical-performance test, Nigro hung a whistle around his neck after lunch and marched us, four abreast, across the Academy parking lot to the gym. The gym was set up for a run-through of the test, and the first thing I noticed when we came in was the heavy gray dummy dangling limply from the high ceiling by a noose around its neck. He was going to be part of the test. Another dummy lay next to him on the floor. Nearby stood a large track-and-field timer sign and a lot of other equipment.

Nigro explained that there were ten stops on the circuit, and we had to complete all of them within two minutes and fifteen seconds. Every task simulated an actual situation we might have to deal with as correction officers. Nigro said we'd better clap and cheer as our classmates ran through the course. A dozen preceded me; suddenly I was next. Nigro blew the whistle.

I grabbed a big silver fire extinguisher and, awkwardly, sprinted about thirty-five yards with it (to put out a fire set by an inmate, of course). Turning, I pushed with all my might against a movable wall (simulating an inmate barricade) and then climbed up and down a ladder attached to the side of the gym (simulating a wall tower). The 160-pound dummy—a stand-in for a suicidal inmate—was next: I wrapped my arms around his middle and lifted him up to relieve the pressure around the neck. Presumably, during the time I was holding him, another officer would be cutting him down. A whistle blew after I'd held him there for ten seconds, so I let him down gently ("Don't break his neck!" Nigro shouted) and quickly went to the lying-down dummy. This, apparently, was the dummy who didn't make it. The job here was to drag him about fifty feet.

I was breathing hard when that was done, but right in front of me lay an eighty-pound barbell to raise from floor to standing position and hold for several seconds more—here I was carrying my end of a stretcher. The next stop was a gymnastics horse to vault (just to show we were not too out of shape); to my dismay, I wiped out on the far side. But my classmates cheered anyway, and in a flash, I had staggered to my feet and was threading my way around three quarters of the gym through a red-cone slalom course and then running up a staircase to the gym's second floor and back down. Finally, to simulate pulling together the arms of a struggling inmate in order to handcuff him behind his back, I squeezed together a pair of calipers representing fifty pounds of resistance. And was through.

As I stood aside panting, the next recruit took off. Several more of them fell while coming over the horse, and two of the women had trouble squeezing the calipers. But everyone made it around in time, and Nigro, who might have had trouble negotiating the course himself, looked relieved.

———

New York's seventy-one prisons are scattered across the state. Among them are famous maximum-security prisons—Sing Sing, Attica (in western New York, near Buffalo), Auburn (midstate), and Clinton (in the northern Adirondacks, near Canada)—as well as a variety of mediums and minimums, and work-release and mental-health facilities. (State prisons hold people with sentences of a year or more. Inmates awaiting trial or those serving shorter terms stay in local jails, such as New York City's giant Rikers Island complex, near La Guardia Airport. Federal prisons generally house criminals convicted of federal crimes—often, drug dealers.)

Fifty of the state's seventy-one prisons were built in the last twenty-five years, a period in which the number of inmates has increased nearly sixfold, from 12,500 to over 70,000, due mostly to mandatory sentencing laws for drug offenses. The majority of these inmates are young men of color from New York City. Because the state government is based in Albany, however, and the state senate is dominated by politicians from rural precincts, nearly all the prison construction has been outside of and away from New York City, where job-hungry communities clamor for it.

A state salary goes far in small-town New York—correction officers, after eight years, make nearly $40,000 and enjoy numerous job benefits. Reflecting the demographic makeup of the state's small towns, the officer corps is overwhelmingly white. As inmates are overwhelmingly minority, the racial hierarchy at most facilities resembles that of South Africa under apartheid.

Both inmates and younger officers tend to be on the move. Inmates are often shifted, with little notice, between facilities, according to obscure agendas of the Department. Officer recruits leave home to go to the Academy, then typically spend the next few years trying to get back: often, their first posting is Sing Sing, which always needs staff because of its chaotic reputation and location in pricey Westchester County. (Because of the prison's proximity to New York City, the regular staff of Sing Sing is predominantly minority—an exception to the statewide rule.) The more desirable prisons have seniority-based waiting lists of up to several years. Until they get where they really want to be, most correction officers will hit the road for home at the beginning of two days off, even if it means a six- or seven-hour drive. And they'll play hopscotch, transferring upstate from one "jump jail" to the next, until they can finally live at home again. Thus most of my classmates, starting with their seven weeks at the Academy, were becoming a kind of migrant worker.

———

Sergeant Bloom hoped to weed out the unsatisfactory recruits as soon as possible. With that goal in mind, he explained to us later, he sent our section on a field trip the second day, to a real prison called Coxsackie.

It was about a forty-minute drive from the Academy. We didn't know another thing about it until the driver of our state schoolbus, CO Popish, pulled up to the old complex of brick buildings ringed with tall fences and swirls of razor wire and shut off the engine. There were a few bare trees around, and some snow gusting over dead brown grass. Popish swung around in his seat. He was chubby and pale, and the other instructors didn't seem to respect him much; driving the bus was, apparently, a chump job. But when Popish began to speak, our nervous chatter quickly stopped. Coxsackie, he said, was "a prison for youthful offenders." Things had been rough here lately; there had been attacks on guards, he added. With that the bus grew completely silent. It rocked slightly in the wind. Two officers had been slashed in the head, Popish said; one was now on disability. Two years ago, the Box was attacked, and the guy in the control booth held hostage. Popish described having seen the baton of a CO who came face-to-face with a shank-wielding inmate; the baton had a large slice cut out of it.

Our guide here, Popish said, would be McCorkle—one of the officers who had harassed us on the night of our arrival at the Academy. When he wasn't training officers, he worked as a CO at Coxsackie, which he called "Gladiator School," or "the Whack." All I associated with *Coxsackie* was the respiratory virus that had first been discovered in the town, and named for it.

Once McCorkle's bus arrived, we circled around the facility to the "sally port," or vehicle gate. Normally a prison of this vintage would have a wall around it, not a fence, I was thinking; later I read in a DOCS newsletter from 1949 that Coxsackie had begun life in 1935 as a state "vocational institution" that aspired to "reformation rather than punishment" of youth through "care, supervision, and training." (In the newsletter photo, there appeared to be no fence at all.) But those goals seemed to have slipped a bit. We were told to get out of the bus so that guards could search it, and then we were all scanned with metal detectors. It began to rain. We slogged through mud to a rear entrance, showed our I.D.'s, passed through another metal detector, and then marched down a long gray corridor.

We peered into cells and the mess hall and watched young inmates pass us, walking in double file with their hands in their pockets (as required), as we went by the metalwork and woodwork shops. All the inmates were male, and almost all were black or Latino teenagers. (Now and then I spotted older men—they were thrown in, our guides said, to lend a bit of social stability.) They all wore the dark green pants issued by the state, but a surprising amount of individuality was expressed by their shirts— they were allowed to wear any color but blue, black, gray, or orange, which were *our* colors—and by their haircuts, beards, and mustaches. Some looked at us briefly as we passed by, but apparently we were not a particularly unusual sight. The officers were almost all white men, middle-aged or older.

Yellow lines on the floor indicated traffic patterns for inmates, telling them where to line up and where to wait. McCorkle pointed out overhead video cameras, which had been installed in prisons all around the state to provide a record of altercations and other incidents, and said we might be smart to remember where they were. Then, conspiratorially, he offered to show us a place that we couldn't tell anyone, particularly Sergeant Bloom, we had seen: the Box, or Special Housing Unit. We reached it via an isolated, unheated corridor. "This can be a long, cold walk for an inmate who's assaulted staff," said the officer who escorted us, noting with a wink that there were no cameras in the corridor.

We passed through a heavy door and into the Box. Suddenly the atmosphere felt close, like in a bunker; the light was all fluorescent. On our left was an officers' room and on our right a windowed control center; an officer standing inside it pressed a button and we continued on, into a larger room ringed with solid cell doors, each with a small clear window. A few inmates appeared at them to examine us. At a signal from our guide, the control officer remotely opened an empty cell so that we could take a look. It had a cot bolted to the wall, bedding, a sink, a toilet, and nothing else. When they first arrived, the officers told us, inmates segregated here received no privileges beyond an hour of daily exercise—no reading or writing materials, no personal property. In fact, the most intransigent got fed "the loaf" for the first few days. Nigro had told us about the loaf—a nutritious but awful-tasting bread invented at the Great Meadow maximum-security prison solely for the purpose of feeding the worst inmates. Supposedly, the facility's superintendent rejected an early recipe because it tasted too good. The current version would keep you alive—if you could get it down. There was a slot in the door through which guards passed food to the inmates; inmates leaving their cells put their hands behind their backs and stuck them out through that same slot to be handcuffed.

We peered through windows into other cells. The men inside either glared back or ignored us in a way that suggested mental illness or depression more than sullenness. We had heard that the Box here was always run by the same bunch of officers—a group of guys who were all related, cousins and brothers—but the men who showed us around didn't look related. They walked nonchalantly and talked tough, explaining how the hour-long recreation period was mandated by the courts. "What if they won't come back in?" one of our group asked the officer. He looked surprised by the naïveté of the question and offered a wry smile. "Oh, they'll come back in, all right," he assured the recruit. I tried to imagine the scene in his mind's eye just then, the little movie replaying, the recalcitrant inmate being "encouraged" to return to his cell . . .

Back outside, our guide told us how in 1988 inmates had smashed through the reinforced glass of the control room (now replaced with Lexan) and taken hostage an officer who was attempting to escape to the roof by a ladder. Other officers were beaten and held hostage as well. I guess it would have been bad form to bring that up while we were inside.

The Box was spooky, but I was scared more by the sight of a sergeant who stopped to chat with us in the corridor. He was a union official, a deputy of Joe Puma's, with whom I had had a two-hour lunch two years earlier, when I was first exploring this subject. I'd forgotten he worked here. Either he didn't notice me now or he had forgotten me altogether. Maybe my wearing the uniform helped; once in uniform, I suspected, a person seemed more standard-issue, less an object of curiosity.

Next we visited a keeplock gallery. The Box held only around thirty inmates, a fraction of those who were under disciplinary restriction. The remainder, because there wasn't enough room for them in the Box, were "keeplocked" in their cells or placed on the special gallery we were now visiting. They were locked in for twenty-three hours a day, just like Box inmates. We walked out to the exercise courtyard, where these inmates were placed in large chain-link cages to exercise several at a time.

As we assembled in the courtyard, a barrage of catcalls began raining down. The inmates whose cells surrounded the courtyard were shouting obscenities at us through their windows. They knew we were fresh meat, and in this setting there was no accountability. We couldn't see them, so we couldn't figure out who they were. Even if we'd been able to, there was nothing we could have done. Those recruits who stood out—the fat guys, like the smart but funny-looking Eno; the short guys, like Falcone, five-foot-one and pugnacious as hell; the women; and the blacks—caught the worst of it. "Hey, Shorty," "Yo, Uncle Tom," "Black bitch—yeah, you. Come suck my dick!" The yard was not large, and it had brick buildings all around it, so the noise was amplified—it was loud and intimidating.

Over the noise, our tour guide told us that earlier in the morning, the guards had had to break up three fights in these cages, which were being used to hold inmates on a tier that was being fumigated for roaches. "And tell 'em how you broke it up," suggested McCorkle to his colleague with a slight smile. I moved closer, because it was hard to hear. "Well, you wait for backup," the officer replied. People couldn't hear. He raised his voice. "You sure as hell ain't going in there alone. In fact, two or three may not be enough. You wait until there's a lot of you, and then you all go in together. And by the time you do, who knows?" He smiled too, now. "Maybe they've stopped fighting."

As we walked back into the building, a tiny folded bundle of paper dropped at our feet; it was an inmate's tobacco envelope, which had somehow fallen en route to a neighbor's window overhead. McCorkle opened it, smelled it, paused, and looked up . . . then emptied the contents on the ground. Howls of protest issued from above. One of the Antonelli twins looked around, wide-eyed. "They're animals," he said.

It dawned on me, as we ate lunch in the prison auditorium, that there had been no particular need for us to go into that yard, or to linger there. Seeing those cages was hardly crucial. Instead, from a comment I heard from a portly CO with a candy bar sticking out of his shirt pocket—"How'd they like X-yard?"—it became clear that our taking the abuse out there was part of the initiation. The old-timers wanted to see how we'd handle it, wanted to cull the faint of heart. If nothing else, the experience was good practice in the cop art of being stony-faced, of not tipping your hand. Certainly, all the guards we passed in the halls had adopted blank, tough expressions that betrayed no weakness or curiosity, no disgust or delight. I wondered: Was this only about closing the blinds on your own soul so they couldn't see in? Or was it also about self-control, staying on top of your feelings, repressing those that got in the way of an emotionally difficult job? If you could make your face do it, in other words, maybe the rest would follow. Maybe.

Sergeant Bloom debriefed us soon after we returned to the Academy. He looked around the room as he asked for our impressions, trying to see if anyone had flipped out. (Nobody had, visibly.) But he also shared with us his surprising view that even at the most tightly run prisons, "we rule with the inmates' consent." There were several times every day when inmates, if they were organized, could take over most of a prison, he said. But the fact of the matter was, inmates were almost never that organized. And it was during disorder that they were most likely to get hurt, particularly by each other. In an orderly situation, they were relatively safe. Therefore, as a group, he thought, they quietly conspired to keep things calm.

Once Sergeant Bloom left, CO McCorkle openly disagreed with his thesis: "Maybe the inmates run things on Rikers Island, maybe they run things at Sing Sing, but not where I work. Not at my facility, Coxsackie. And not in the rest of the state system, either, from what I hear." For him, this question of control was a matter of considerable importance—as it would be for the many officers I'd come to know later. Many judged themselves and their peers on the degree of control they were able to maintain over inmates. To McCorkle, Sergeant Bloom had sounded a bit off-the-wall, a maverick theorist selling out the program.

That night on the dorm floor, there was much recapping of the day's events, particularly the abuse we had received in the Coxsackie yard. In our room, Gary demonstrated a technique for polishing his gleaming dress shoes, the same pair he had worn in the Air Force many years before. I paid close attention, because my black Doc Martens were one of many pairs of shoes Sergeant Bloom had accused of lacking sufficient shine during a spot inspection. Across the hall my bunkmate, Dieter, was exchanging military insults with Di Carlo, a Navy veteran whom he now called Commodore; Di Carlo in turn recited the shortcomings of jarheads he had known. "Being a Marine is like having a lobotomy," he said. They warmly attacked each other. And they assured those of us who hadn't been in the service that the Academy was "nothing like" a real military boot camp.

DiPaola, the vending-machine accountant, and Colton, the lieutenant's son, spoke of how DOCS was a stopgap until they heard from the state police or federal law enforcement groups, such as the U.S. Border Patrol and the Treasury Department police. The Antonellis had just withdrawn from the Florida Highway Patrol academy—which, they said, was much harder than this—when family trouble called them home. For all those other jobs, you needed some college, but not to become a correction officer. "I know a guy from back home who got through this academy and he's as dumb as this post," said one of the Antonellis, whacking the pillar of his bunk.

Finally we started turning in. Gary, a quiet sort who seldom offered his opinion of anything, unbidden, said as the lights went out, "My son's almost as old as some of them, and the worst trouble he could get into is a fistfight or drugs." He was speaking, of course, of the young inmates in Coxsackie, most of them violent repeat offenders. Who knew what world they came from? No one said a word in reply.

———

Classes started in earnest the next day, and among the many sleep-inducers—Note-Taking, Tool and Key Control, Cultural Awareness—were a few that made everyone sit up and take notice. A good-natured, shaved-headed, bullnecked older black man named Kirkley taught a class called Use of Force, in which we learned when it was okay to lay our hands on somebody. You had to wade through a pile of handouts—"Article 35," "Directive 49," "Employee Manual 8.2," "Chapter V," "Correctional Law 137–5"—to figure it all out, but the bottom line was that you could "lay hands on or strike an inmate" if necessary "for self-defense, to prevent injury to a person or to property, to quell a disturbance, to enforce compliance with a lawful direction, or to prevent an escape." The requirements seemed pretty tough until you focused on the second-to-last one: "to enforce compliance with a lawful direction." That was the clincher right there, 99 percent of what you needed to know. If the inmate wasn't doing what you told him to, as long as it wasn't "Shine my shoes," you could use physical force on him.

Deadly physical force was okay to use in three instances: to prevent an escape; in self-defense; or to prevent arson. Arson? "Arson is serious because an inmate could burn a whole building down, maybe one with people in it," said Kirkley. Well, yes. But it was hard to imagine the scenario. An inmate, perhaps surrounded by empty gas cans, stooping to light a match. "Stop or I'll shoot!" we could yell. And if he didn't stop, we could kill him.

In one of the asides that probably prepared us for the job better than any of the approved curriculum items, Kirkley said that occasionally officers *did* have to act in self-defense. Usually, it was the result of a sudden flare-up—say, an inmate who was angered by something you had said or told him to do who went on the attack. It was even possible that we COs would be victimized in more deliberate ways. Early in his career, Kirkley related, while patrolling on a walkway inside a prison, he was jumped by five hooded inmates, who took his wallet. We were amazed that this could happen *inside* a prison. And Kirkley was a big man. But self-defense, in this case, was a moot point. "I was completely outnumbered," Kirkley said, so his attackers got away with it. So much (in this case, anyway) for officers being in control.

Another officer, Voltraw, taught us Legals, a class that involved mostly memorization—the difference between larceny third degree and larceny fourth degree, for example, and the legal precedents of Miranda warnings—but also informed us about the powers we were about to possess. Among these were the rights to purchase a gun and carry it concealed and the power of arrest: on duty or off, we could make arrests for any felony or misdemeanor we witnessed. (Even if we did not witness it, we could still make an arrest for a felony.)

All this was due to our status as state "peace officers." New York had sixty-three different kinds of peace-officer agencies, ranging from park police to state-university police to local police—but DOCS, with a budget that was one quarter of the state's General Fund—was by far the largest. "The Department doesn't want you to enforce the law—it doesn't train you to do that," Voltraw said. "There are liability issues, and actually, they're unhappy that we can make arrests. But legally we can do almost as much as police officers."

A couple of days later, Tom Testo, the director of the Department's Bureau of Labor Relations, warned us against abusing these powers. His office revoked officers' firearms permission several times a week, he said, for infractions such as being caught drinking while wearing a gun, menacing somebody with it, or having it stolen. Currently, the Department was being sued by a stockbroker who had been pulled over and then chewed out by a correction officer for speeding, Testo told us, sounding tired. Then there were guys who glued numbers under their badges so that they would resemble those of New York City Police Department detectives, and undertook their own "investigations." Doing these things would get you fired, Testo said; and one in ten of us would receive a notice of discipline from his office sometime during his career. Not that the pressures weren't understandable to Testo; he knew, he said, that inmates were "the lowest of the low, the scum of the earth. And we have to be with them every day." But that didn't excuse our abusing our authority.

On that first night at the Academy, Sergeant Bloom had asserted, unexpectedly, that "the most important thing you can learn here is how to communicate" with inmates. In the two or three weeks that followed, I had started to understand what he meant.

Corrections was, albeit in a rarefied macho way, a "people-skills" profession. Much of our success and well-being as officers would depend upon how we carried ourselves and interacted with inmates.

But the Department's idea of how to develop these skills was given to us in a short series of classes, Interpersonal Communication (IPC), taught by a would-be comedian. He had actually done stand-up comedy in clubs, Officer Speros told us, and for the first day we were less his class than his audience. Speros's extemporaneous opening act was to decide which figures from popular culture we looked like: DiPaola was Bart Simpson, Chavez was Zorro, Dimmie was a soul singer from the 1970s. Somebody complained afterward to Sergeant Bloom about the racial overtones of Speros's jokes, and Bloom, another trainer told us gravely, chewed him out for it. The next day the communications instructor, acting hurt, was all business.

By communicating effectively with inmates, Speros began, we could keep problems from escalating, build relationships with inmates, manage them better. In addition, he said with a wink, listening carefully would enable us to get information out of inmates, get them to tell us things "when they don't even know it!"

Speros used graphs and charts and handouts to detail the cutely named stages and progressions (The Basics, The Add-Ons, Taking Charge)—the fashions of business-management training had spread to corrections. But what everyone left with was a funny method that we watched in a film and that Speros made us try. He called it Responding to Content. We called it What You're Saying Is . . . The point was to show an inmate that you were listening to him by keeping quiet until he was through, then rephrasing his point so that he knew you had heard him—even if you then disagreed or were not persuaded. It was a good technique, I suppose, but it made for hilarious exchanges at dinner that evening ("So what you're saying is, you want more Salisbury steak?") and in days to follow, when we imagined how it would sound in a place like Coxsackie: "So what you're saying is, I'm a skinny white motherfucker and you wish I were dead—is that it?"

Strangely enough, in view of this class, we had been told never to communicate with the handful of inmates who worked in the Academy. Some were there every day, ladling out our food in the mess-hall line; we grew to recognize their faces. Others came as work crews from Coxsackie to vacuum and dust the lounges or clean up the filthy rest rooms. These crews—always, in my experience, made up of young black men—were watched over by tough-looking armed COs wearing wide-brimmed hats and leather boots, their pants tucked in at the top. They looked like something out of a southern-chain-gang movie. The inmates kept their eyes down as they did the scut work, emptying ashtrays and wiping the urine from toilets. Never talk to them, we were ordered. Do not engage them in any way. So we recruits ignored these inmates, tried to treat them as if they didn't exist. It was an odd way to begin a job that supposedly depended upon communication techniques. When, at training's end, I suggested in a feedback session that some inmates be brought in to talk to us, maybe to participate in IPC workshops, everybody looked at me as if I were nuts.

———

Every few days we were subjected to a surprise inspection by Sergeant Bloom, who would march us out of the classroom and into a corridor and then review us—first from behind and then from the front—while we stood at strict attention. He was particularly interested in the shine of our shoes, but he could find something wrong with just about anything else: a name tag infinitesimally askew, hair touching the ears, a spot missed while shaving, an inadequate crease. If enough recruits disappointed him, he'd make us all do twenty or forty push-ups, right there in the hall. If we continued to disappoint him, he warned us, we'd be put on restriction and forbidden to leave the Academy at night.

Similarly, Bloom trolled the halls of the dorm floor every morning looking for anything out of place. My room was written up one day because there was still a scrap of paper at the bottom of the trash can after it had been emptied; another time, we had left on the tiny light over the sink. Records of these transgressions, Bloom warned us grimly, went straight into our personnel folders.

Therefore it was always a relief, every afternoon, to march out the Academy's back door and across a dirt parking lot to the gym for Physical Training. Those who had trouble completing the unimaginative, unvaried course of calisthenics did not always agree, but I was ready for any break from the tedium of the classroom. And after calisthenics, there was always a run of a mile or two, consisting of laps around the Academy. As we ran, some of the instructors would chant military songs adapted to corrections, and we would call back every line:

> I've got a dog, his name is Blue
> Blue wants to be a CO, too.

Or

> We're mentally able and we're physically fit
> If you ain't corrections, you ain't it!

Just to make sure there was an easy way to get in trouble during Physical Training, too, the authorities had forbidden us to wear watches. In our haste to change out of our uniforms and into exercise gear and get over to the gym by the specified time, it was easy to forget this rule. Usually, roommates noticed and warned each other; one day I caught my own watch transgression as we marched into the gym. There being no other place to hide it, I dropped it into my briefs. I said a prayer of thanks when, at afternoon's end, I found it still there.

Felix Chavez was not so lucky. Chavez, the former assistant building superintendent, was one of my favorite classmates. He lived with his wife and kids in the nongentrified part of Park Slope, Brooklyn. There was something dashing about Chavez, with his small mustache; he said he hadn't been bothered at all when Speros nicknamed him Zorro. He was very upbeat, optimistic, and excited about being there, and he wanted to do a good job. But he could never remember to take off his watch. The first time they noticed it, the PT instructors gave him a warning—wear it again and not only will you suffer; your whole session will suffer. We stopped the forgetful Chavez a couple of times after that on the threshold of the gym. But one day during an unusual PT morning session, nobody noticed. The instructor—an especially humorless, muscle-bound type—stopped all 128 of us mid–jumping jack when he spotted Chavez's watch. Instead of chewing us all out right there, he told our session he'd see us later.

It was after lunch when the instructor showed up at our classroom door. "Uh-oh," mumbled Bella. We were sent to a hallway upstairs and told to line up. There, as we stood at attention, the muscle-bound instructor told us he could put us on restriction for what had happened, then commanded, "Down on the floor." We put our hands down and got into push-up position. "Give me fifty, all together," he ordered. This was out of the range of most of the group. He counted, sometimes repeating a number or even backing up if he thought somebody hadn't done a good job. At around twenty, recruits started dropping in exhaustion. He ignored his threat to begin at zero if anyone did that and made do with berating them. Then he kept counting. Trembling, those of us who were able to go on did so, until our arms could no longer lift us. After that, we lay on the floor in our pressed uniforms. He told us to stand up.

"No, not you," he said to Chavez. Chavez lay back down.

"Give me twenty more."

I'd never heard Chavez complain about anything at the Academy, with the exception of the pain that push-ups caused his one bad elbow. This must have been killing him. Sweat poured off his face onto the floor. His uniform was soaked. He started shaking so badly I couldn't bear to look. "Eight!" screamed the instructor. Tears now mixed with sweat on the floor under Chavez's face, which seemed to delight his tormentor.

"You think inmates are gonna care if you cry? Inmates ain't gonna care." What inmates had to do with this, I had no idea. Maybe the instructor was just saying he didn't care either. Maybe he was saying that forgetfulness and shows of weakness or emotion wouldn't fly in prison. Maybe he simply believed, along with a number of his colleagues, that abuse was a perfect preparation for prison work.

When it was clear that Chavez had no more push-ups to give, the instructor told him to stand up and then dismissed us.

———

"Ah, so you were studying CPR, eh?" asked the instructor as he arrived in the room after lunch, looked at the chalkboard, and noticed what we'd been taught in the morning. "So who here can tell me how to do inmate CPR?" We were quizzed so frequently that everyone thought the question was serious. "Nobody? She didn't teach you that? Then I'll show you."

The instructor placed his boot on the chest of an imaginary prone inmate, pumped five times, then straightened up, looked down, and blew five times loudly toward the floor. He repeated it—to titters, then laughter.

———

Other sessions had taken Chemical Agents before us; we'd see them in the mess hall at lunch with gas masks around their waists and apprehension in their eyes. Or we'd talk to them at night in the lounge after they'd been to the range, hearing tales of how they'd been exposed. ("We had to hold hands." "This cloud of smoke rose up from the ground." "I was crying so hard my shirt was soaked." "He had this huge booger hanging out of his nose.") Then it was our turn.

Chemical agents (call it *tear gas* and you had to do ten push-ups) were an important part of most prison arsenals and came in many different kinds of containers. We learned about them in a class. First were the handheld aerosols, beefed-up versions of the little canisters found in women's purses. This "irritant dust" was most likely to be used in small situations with one or two recalci-trant inmates. For larger groups, there was a variety of handheld grenades, and many prison mess halls had a special kind of car-tridge installed in the ceiling, for quick remote activation in case of disturbance. All-out riots called for cartridges shot out of a gas gun, which looked a bit like a sawed-off shotgun. The instructors passed around spent cartridges that smelled slightly of citrus; one had enough residue left inside that my nose started to run after I sniffed it and the skin on my forehead burned slightly.

But the lecture and this small sampling paled in comparison to the main event of our chemical-agents education—the practical class. Again we boarded a bus, this time to a National Guard "mil-itary training range." We were somewhat nervous as we walked a path alongside a stream, gas masks bouncing on our hips. We knew we were going to "get it" up there, but didn't know exactly how or when; other sessions had been taken to a different spot. The streambed opened onto an expansive grassy firing range, with an observation tower and berms at the near end and hillocks at the far end. Some civilian observers, maybe bureaucrats from the De-partment, stood by as several of us fired grenades onto the range using the gas gun. As each one landed, it emitted a thick cloud of white smoke, which hung malevolently in the air. Part of our job was to memorize the different types of "delivery devices." One of the most impressive was the Federal 515 Triple Chaser grenade, which exploded into three parts upon landing, each piece spewing smoke. Then there was the Defensive Technologies ("Def-Tec")

No. 2 Continuous Discharge grenade—"the Department's work-horse," an instructor called it. He explained that this one, like many others, gets hot as it combusts, which gave me new respect for the 1960s student activists I remembered from TV, who would run up and hurl smoking gas grenades back at the cops.

The instructors ushered us down to a small shack off to the side of the range, near the woods. We all went inside, whereupon the lead instructor asked for four volunteers. He got only two, Dimmie and Falcone. He "volunteered" Bella and Dobbins to stand with them in a row, facing us. Peering in from a window behind them were some of the civilians. This was it. The instructor produced a handheld aerosol. "Do you want me to tell you when I'm going to do it?" he asked. While they thought about that, he sprayed them, one at a time, in the face. Each in turn screwed shut his eyes, turned red, and started to tear and sputter and bend over. "Do you want to fight?" the instructor demanded. All of them tried to say no. "Will you come out of your cells?" A couple succeeded in nodding. The instructor assigned others to lead them outside, where they could recover. (Dimmie would later liken the burning sensation to "bobbing for french fries.")

Next we were all told to don our gas masks. Half the class was ushered outside. The instructor shut the door and told the drill to those of us remaining: We were to lock elbows and move in two concentric circles around him, one clockwise, the other counter-clockwise. When he dropped the grenade, our movement would churn the gas up into the air, and we would see how effective the masks were. And then we would remove them. We would attempt to say, "Correction-officer recruit," and our name and Social Security number, during which time we would presumably learn how effective the gas was. After that we could leave the room. "But if one person leaves early," he warned, "you're all going to have to do it again."

It was dim in the shack with the door closed and a gas mask on. I remember looking down toward the instructor's feet as we circled him, seeing the white smoke as it began to swirl over the wooden floorboards. And then it rose. It seemed a miracle that it could obscure my vision but not cause me to choke: The gas mask worked. I remember glimpsing a big bureaucrat whose face filled one of the windowpanes and thinking, Maybe he ought to come in here and try it himself. We walked in our circles. And then, on the instructor's order, I remember overcoming my every instinct for self-preservation and pulling off the mask. There were a couple of dreamlike seconds before anything happened, and in this space a cacophony of names was shouted, and I got to "Correction offic—" before my throat clamped shut and a wall of fire crossed my face. Tears burst from my eyes and, squinting, I saw that the door had opened and others were filing out. I staggered that way and was quickly grabbed by my classmate Anthony "Big Buck" Buckner, a 275-pound man from the Bronx, who walked me out into the open. There I joined some twenty others, all of whom were gasping, with red, wet faces, as the pain sharpened. Streams of mucus issued from our mouths and noses and dripped to the ground in long strands. My eyes didn't hurt too badly until someone said to open them. And then some more stabbing irritant flowed in, sharp and prickly. They said that holding your eyes open made it pass sooner, and everyone tried to. Water was splashed in our eyes by a strange piece of equipment designed to do just that, but it didn't seem to help. Finally, I just stood there shaking, and Officer Popish, whom others considered an asshole, held my arm and I felt deep gratitude.

Fifteen minutes later the roles were reversed, and I was holding the massive arm of one of the Antonelli twins as he sputtered and teared. Nearby, as Arno recovered, someone pointed out that the cap hanging from his belt was covered with puke. Brown sheepishly confessed that he was responsible. For a while, Bella was spitting up blood. We took off our shirts and shook our hair, since the chemical agent lingered in both. The instructor handed out garbage bags for us to place our uniforms in and offered us the rationale for this ritual of suffering. It was necessary, he said, so that we didn't panic if it occurred inside a prison. He painted a scenario: Chemical agents were released into a mess hall containing unruly inmates, and officers too. The inmates would soon be rushing outside to the yard, hopping mad and "looking for the first uniform they can find" to beat up. If we officers could calmly remain inside the mess hall, we would be more likely to remain safe.

This was just barely plausible. Who said the mess hall would have an exit to the yard? And that it would be open? Our afternoon on the range made more sense to me as a rite of passage that might bring us closer by making us feel we'd endured something awful together. In conclusion, the officer assured us that the chemical agent, "once you're out of it, will be nothing more than a painful memory."

At chow that evening, somebody commented that the exposure had caused "the worst pain I ever had." I thought about that, and about the instructor's remark—kinds of pain, kinds of bad memories. For a pain of fifteen-minute duration, this was probably the worst. But I'd had worse pain, duller and more long-lasting, from various injuries. And how did you compare these nerve-related pains with heartache, or with the pain—call it soulache—of imprisonment, the kind of pain, no one seemed interested to observe, that we were going to administer in our chosen profession? It hardly seemed right to use the same word for all of them.

———

Concomitant with the rise of imprisonment, there were 239,229 correction officers nationwide at the beginning of 1998, up from 60,026 just sixteen years before. In large areas of New York and other states, corrections is the only growth industry, the most likely profession for thousands of young people. But how odd to devote yourself professionally to confining others in a small space.

"You're just a forty-thousand-dollar baby-sitter," one instructor told us in summary, after describing the misbehavior of inmates. Only, most baby-sitters can't get away with the use of force, and most are not seriously endangered by their charges.

"You leave here and become a boss," another instructor asserted. "You're automatically a supervisor, because supervising inmates is your job." This instructor, Turner, who was not very good at telling a joke but clearly intended one, proceeded to read us a passage from *The One Minute Manager:* " 'Take a minute out of your day and look at the people around you—they're the most valuable resource that you have!' " He put the book down and cleared his throat. "Of course, that doesn't really apply in a correctional setting," he said. "Get rid of these, and there's ten thousand more out there waiting."

In one sense, Turner said, prisons were like little towns—with infirmaries their hospitals, commissaries their department stores, chapels their churches, exercise yards their parks, gyms their health club, mess halls their restaurants, and we a special sort of police department. If our job title, "correction officer," suggested a role in setting people straight, though, Turner suggested we think again. Because in reality, he said, "rehabilitation is not our job. The truth of it is that we are warehousers of human beings." And the prison was, above all, a storage unit.

Turner offered this opinion after the warning that was issued in two thirds of classes at the Academy: "What's said here doesn't leave this room." That was always a signal to pay close attention, because we were about to learn something of actual value. Police work must be like this across the board: There's the official line and then there's what you really need to know, and the invaluable instructors are the ones who can cut through the crap and, perhaps at their peril, tell you the truth.

We learned many things this way. To be attentive to the location of surveillance cameras, as in our Coxsackie tour, was one of them. One instructor said that in past years it was true that a team of COs would patrol the blocks and "adjust" individual inmates who had been causing trouble, but that it really didn't happen anymore; on the other hand, the Antonellis had heard there was a room in Attica where troublesome inmates would still "get a tooth through the lip" as encouragement to change their attitude. We learned that you probably wouldn't get in big trouble for showing up at work slightly drunk or unshaven, or even for falling asleep once in a while, but call in sick or punch in late one too many times and you were history.

At the same time, the Academy seemed to embrace an institutional denial that what we were being taught to do had a moral aspect. The moral *weirdness* of prison was never discussed—the racial inequality and the power inequality; the them and us; the constant saying no.

I thought about this during "range week," one of the most enjoyable periods of training because of the time we got to spend away from the Academy, at a shooting club. We learned all about the Department's three standard firearms—the Smith & Wesson Model-10 .38 Special revolver; the Colt AR-15 semiautomatic rifle; and the Remington 870P 12-gauge pump-action shotgun—and their ammunition, and we practiced loading, unloading, cleaning, storing, and, by far the most fun, firing them. The concentric circles of the targets were set inside the shape of a dark human torso, but I was so busy working to get my qualification card and trying to outscore gun-nut Dieter (owner of seventeen pistols) that I hardly noticed. What finally got my attention was the shotgun instruction. In the event of a riot in the yard, one instructor said, simply stepping outside the wall tower with a shotgun held high or pumping it near the microphone of your public address system could be enough to get inmates to stop. Similarly, he added, shooting at the ground in front of rioting inmates, rather than directly at them, could be highly effective, as it sprayed buckshot at several individuals instead of giving only one man the full force of a blast. We were firing our shotguns into the ground in front of a high bank of dirt to see how this worked when I faced the fact that this class was essentially about killing and wounding inmates.

Sergeant Bloom called us into the chapel at the end of our last day on the range to read us some announcement. I don't remember what it was; I only remember thinking it was strange to have spent so much time learning details about firearms (on our weekly test we were asked about the range of the different kinds of buckshot the Remington could fire, the direction in which the crossbolt safety button had to be pushed to enable the gun to fire, and a zillion questions of nomenclature) while never once being asked whether we thought we could shoot somebody. Or never discussing what shooting someone meant, in an ethical sense—how officers might be not only legally but morally justified in doing it. Probably, it was true in all of the police agencies, as well as the armed forces, that training had its own physical and intellectual momentum and the spiritual side was left to the student. A Black Muslim inmate would later opine to me that this kind of denial was the very reason for military discipline; it was necessary, he said, in order to make men do something unnatural, something they ordinarily wouldn't do. Maybe that was true; or maybe it was more a matter of needing to have strict control over the behavior of those who held life-and-death power over other men.

In any event, here we were in the chapel, illuminated by stained glass of men who had aimed to do right by God, and our job as correction officers, it seemed to me, was to think about those godly things as little as possible.

————

With four weeks to go, Dieter was really starting to get on my nerves. (I'm sure it would delight him to read this.) Now nicknamed Sarge by many in our session, he had in the first week been elected session leader—our group's liaison to the instructors and Sergeant Bloom. This was, in large degree, because he knew how to march and had other military training that could keep us out of trouble. Even I had voted for him; he seemed conscientious and responsible. He was elected over his own objections: He was too impatient with people, he freely admitted, and was basically a misanthrope. "I'm best off by myself," he said one day.

His new authority seemed to give freer rein to his mean streak. Dieter had a sixth sense that told him I was somehow out of place in the Academy, and he didn't like things that were out of place. He would ride me in a joking way in the room, criticizing my housecleaning or the way I wore my uniform.

I can't remember having met a person who was more unlike me than Dieter. Our every habit was opposite—he rising at the earliest moment, I catching a few winks; he enamored of the martial life, I skeptical or oblivious of it; he in love with firearms and hunting, I indifferent; he a smoker and drinker, I doing little of either; he fond of gay jokes and full of violent fantasies about liberals and women, I counting among my friends many who are gay, liberal, or female or all three.

One night, when we had turned the lights off, he flat-out asked what I was doing in the Academy. I flat-out asked him back. "My job didn't pay too good," he said. "Not much security." "Well I could say the same," I retorted, with less than total candor. No other officer, in my entire state service, would ever ask me a question about my past, whether employment or education; the lack of curiosity surprised and relieved me. Previously, I'd vaguely told two or three classmates that I'd been involved in publishing and printing. Dieter now suggested I tell people I'd been working a job they'd understand. "Tell 'em you're a ball-joint chromer," he suggested. "Sure," I said. "Tell me how that goes."

Dieter would accuse me of shaking the bunk bed when I turned over; he joked that if I didn't stop, he'd bring in one of his guns and shoot me. That left me no choice but to murder him before the weekend, I retorted. Then he started saying he'd shoot me whenever I did anything to irritate him—like when I wouldn't move quickly enough out of his way when he was headed for his locker, which was directly beneath mine or, later, when I caught a cold.

I'm pretty sure Dieter gave me the cold. He came back from home with one on a Sunday night. By the end of the week, I had it. As his subsided, he treated me as if I had the plague. He wouldn't touch anything I'd touched, whether it was a doorknob or a faucet, and he winced whenever I blew my nose. We always tried to sit apart in the mess hall, but sometimes seating arrangements were out of our hands, and one night we found ourselves across the table from each other. I had a stuffy nose and was sniffing. "Don't you blow that thing!" he warned, in what surely sounded like a joke to the woman sitting next to him; she smiled. But I knew, in the way I knew Dieter at some level *did* think about shooting me when he merely joked about it, that he was serious. I tried not to blow my nose, just for the sake of peace. But finally there was no other option. I took a napkin, turned away from the table in my seat, and blew my nose.

"Fuckin' asshole!" Dieter muttered, throwing down his fork and standing up to clear his tray. He stormed away. The woman looked at me. "Was he serious?" she asked.

"He's a different kind of guy," I answered.

That night, when Dieter was telling Gary about how he had murdered his little brother when the kid sneezed at the dinner table, I knew we were near the point where something was going to give: Dieter was in abuse mode nightly. He threatened to shoot me in the top bunk as he shot the birds on the roof of his barn, made jokes about "fucking bitches"—indeed, about skinning them as you would skin a deer you'd shot—and about smashing the heads of toddlers. They were I'm-sick-and-I-like-it kinds of jokes. Would we fight, I wondered, or would I go to Nigro or the sergeant?

In the end, we were saved by a Howard Johnson's motor lodge. So desperate was the state for new COs, they had started another training session before ours was finished; for our last three weeks, we were given rooms at a HoJo so that newer recruits could move into our dorm rooms. The motel rooms were doubles, and to my profound relief, my roommate was mild-mannered Gary.

———

Monday morning, and Colton and I had drawn the chore of reporting the count to Sergeant Bloom. Toward the beginning of our stay at the Academy, this job scared everyone, because of the likelihood that Bloom would find some fault in the presenters; you had to say things just right, look just right, move just right. But now we'd had a lot of practice, and neither Colton nor I had run badly afoul of Bloom. Also, Colton seemed among the most capable of my classmates. He had a degree from the John Jay College of Criminal Law in New York City. He scored well on our weekly tests. And he even had a sort of preppie, arrogant air about him: If I'd run into him wearing tasseled loafers in some uptown real estate developer's office, I wouldn't have blinked an eye. Here, he seemed supremely overqualified. Nigro went over the drill with us as we left the classroom, but I felt we hardly needed a refresher. Colton and I were bulletproof: We were going to blow Bloom away.

We checked each other's appearance and then smartly wound our way through the halls. Coming upon the open door to Bloom's office, we slowed, then halted, Colton in front. We could hear Bloom on the phone. Wait, or proceed? Nigro had been late arriving, so we would certainly be the last session to report—and it was getting later by the minute. We waited at attention for a while and then, consulting each other in whispers, decided to proceed. Colton reached around the doorway and rapped on Bloom's door. Bloom kept on talking. Finally, we heard the phone being slammed down. "Come in!" he roared.

Spinning on our toes as required, we stepped into Bloom's office and then stood side by side at attention before his desk. Bloom rose and approached to get a close look at us. "Correction officer recruits Colton and Conover with the seven forty-five A.M. count, sir," said Colton. "It's twenty-seven total, twenty-six in, one out." I handed him the paperwork.

Bloom looked at the clock on his wall. "It's eight-fifteen," he said accusingly. We stared straight ahead, not responding. He glanced at the count slip, the classroom inventory and, finally, the meal evaluation form. (We had learned the first week never to criticize any of the food. After our class gave the inedible pea soup an "unsatisfactory" rating, Bloom angrily demanded of the messengers why they hadn't taken it up with the kitchen staff before complaining to him.) The meal evaluation we gave him now was for the preceding Friday. Bloom noticed that we had rated Friday's dinner "good" and barked out that we hadn't eaten dinner at the Academy on Friday—we'd gone home.

"It's a false report!" he yelled. He paused as we stood still. "Well? Get me another one!"

Colton and I beat our retreat to the classroom and filled out a new form. Nigro rolled his eyes when we told him the mistake. In a matter of minutes we were back before Sergeant Bloom. He scrutinized the new report and acidly noted that we had neglected to sign it. Caught in some continuing confusion over whether to carry pens in our shirt pockets or hide them in our pants pockets (there was no official Academy policy; all that mattered was that everyone in a session did the same thing), Colton and I realized that we did not, at the moment, have pens. We had taken them out before coming to see Bloom, since none of the other sessions carried pens in *their* breast pockets. Bloom stared at us as we realized our dilemma.

"May we borrow a pen, sir?" Colton finally asked, with trepidation. Sighing loudly, Bloom handed Colton his. Colton signed and handed the report to me; I signed and returned it to Colton, who said, "It's the sergeant's." I smiled and, with a little laugh, handed the pen back to Bloom.

"Why are you laughing?!" Bloom thundered, reddening. ("Because who on earth could ever take this seriously?" I wanted to say.) He was now beyond his usual ruddy color—he'd gone deep crimson. "I have to buy these!" That was even funnier, I thought, but the sight before me took care of my smile. Colton decided that our duty was done. We slunk back to the classroom and assured Nigro that our second trip had gone just fine.

———

Things were getting worse at Coxsackie. We'd heard rumors of disturbances there since our visit, the first week of March. Colton came back one Sunday night in early April and said he'd heard through his father that two officers had been stabbed there the week before. Later that week Chamberlain, whose father was a sergeant in the department (and had, incidentally, been Sergeant Bloom's roommate when both of them were at the Academy), said he'd heard that three more had been hurt. Finally, on a Monday morning in mid-April, Nigro asked us if we'd seen the papers: Eight Coxsackie COs had been hospitalized on Saturday, and two more on Sunday. And, related or not, another large group of officers had been hurt at a midstate medium-security facility called Mohawk. The journalist in me wanted details: Where in the prison had the attacks occurred? What had instigated them? How unusual were they? But as I was learning, part of being a CO was appearing indifferent to such details. Curiosity, perhaps, was not very macho. I prayed that somebody would ask Nigro for more information, but nobody did; and there the discussion ended.

But it cast a pall, this news. The very place we'd visited was in turmoil. Experienced officers, not newjacks, which we'd soon be, were getting badly beaten up. Despite the silence, I knew everyone was thinking the same thing: Would we be next? The feeling must be somewhat similar in the military among troops about to be dispatched to faraway trouble spots: Some of us are going to get hurt. And yet the nature of both jobs was that, ceding the decision making to commanding officers, you went anyway. In this agreement to go, there was solidarity.

During the pain from chemical agents, the classroom boredom, and—especially—my conflicts with Dieter, I had always consoled myself with the knowledge that my career as a guard might easily end after seven weeks, with graduation from the Academy. My real life was still waiting for me, and there was plenty of work out there.

But some group feeling was overtaking me. More and more, the thought of leaving now was unimaginable. Everything so far had been prelude: From what we'd been told, you could be a star at the Academy and then fall flat on your face inside a real prison. There was no true preparation for the main act—you just had to do it. I wanted to see if I could; I wanted to see what would happen to all of us. The group had momentum, and a probable trajectory—Sing Sing. Down that road lay fear, but the deal was that we went anyway, together.

Later that week, we heard that two more Coxsackie officers had been hurt, bringing the total to seventeen. A lieutenant attached to the Academy was dispatched, telling us at the end of a lecture on another subject that somebody had to go "and straighten things out down there." We officers said nothing—just swallowed hard.

———

The pace of training seemed to accelerate in our last two weeks. There was more physicality, for one thing, and that always helped: We received instruction in the use of the baton and in a variety of martial arts and other tough-guy methods, cumulatively labeled Defensive Tactics. Because the gym was in use, we cleared the chairs off the marble floor of the chapel and had baton training there. Our instructors were two somewhat scary blond guys, one who had patrolled our afternoon Physical Training sessions with a baton hanging from a belt around his gym shorts (was he going to strike the slackers?), the other a huge, primitive-looking bodybuilder, named Malaver, with short, spiky hair. Malaver taught while chewing tobacco. (Nigro, who ran a part-time business as a party disk jockey, was putting together Malaver's bodybuilding competition tape for him.) Never hit an inmate on the head with a baton, Malaver cautioned matter-of-factly—"that's a big no-no."

It was not going to fly, on your use-of-force report, to say that you had been aiming for his ribs when the inmate suddenly ducked. Best was to aim low—for the shins or for various vulnerable points in the torso, such as the lowermost ("floating") rib. "I've heard those ribs crack," said Malaver with satisfaction, and nobody wondered who had done the cracking. Malaver and his partner drilled us in various jabs and parries. And they showed us how two partners could hold opposite ends of a baton to create an impromptu chair for an injured CO or inmate. "Or if the inmate's real skinny," Malaver said, joking, "you can just stick the baton up his ass and carry him that way."

The penalty for dropping your baton during these exercises was doing push-ups on your knuckles on the marble floor, hands wrapped around the baton. Eno, the dufus, dropped his soon after the warning, so we all had to get down on the chapel floor on our knees and knuckles, like penitents.

The batons were made of hardwood, Malaver explained—usually, oak or ash. Members of local CERT teams—the acronym stood for Corrections Emergency Response Team, and every max facility had one—were sometimes issued special black plastic batons because, Malaver told us, "the wood ones can break. You heard about what's been going on at Coxsackie?" he went on. "One of those officers was hit three times on his head and shoulders with a baton. The third time, it broke. You know how hard you have to hit these to break them?" Malaver struck a table with a baton, hard. Again. And again. It didn't break.

The rest of the Defensive Tactics course was a bit more involved. Drawing from sources as diverse as aikido and barroom brawls, the instructors taught us ways to tangle with an attacking or resisting inmate that you weren't likely to see in, say, a John Wayne movie. This wasn't about fistfights; it was about saving your ass in whatever way possible, or about coercing a misbehaving inmate in ways that wouldn't cause death or other lasting damage.

The first exercise, learning how to fall, was conducted in the gym on a big expanse of mats. Essentially, it was a hazing ritual: Despite the instructors' claims, I could see no real connection between repeatedly falling flat on your face and self-preservation inside a prison. The idea was that if you learned to land on tensed forearms and elbows, you wouldn't hurt yourself—wouldn't break a wrist, wouldn't bang your nose on the floor, etc. So, endlessly, we repeated what we had learned not to do around age two: tipped ourselves forward, bodies straight, feet still, until we landed with a *bam*.

It was perhaps the only time during my work in corrections when being small and light was an advantage; aside from a little pain in my neck, I didn't get hurt. But those who were heavy and tall had it rough. The muscular Antonellis rubbed off all the skin at their elbows. Our stout classmate "Big Buck" Buckner, a big man with a big appetite, kept landing stomach first—it was physically impossible for him to land any other way—his limbs and head crashing down a split second later and the whole mass pitching forward till it seemed that most of the fall was taken by his head. Finally, and worst, tall and thin Aisha Foster was hurting so badly that after the fifth or sixth time she just curled up on the floor and cried. Sergeant Bloom walked in by chance, stared at her for a while, asked the instructors something, and left.

Next came lengthy instruction in "pain compliance." We learned that if you could get hold of an inmate's hand or wrist, several inventive ways of twisting it would drop him to the floor with you on top. We practiced with partners. The worst for me was the painful aikido grip where you placed your thumb between victim's pointer finger and middle finger, grabbed his thumb, and twisted his hand up under his armpit. I gravitated toward gentle Cleve Dobbins, a forty-something former military policeman, who was as disinclined toward suffering as I was. That worked fine until the instructor ordered us to rotate to the next partner in the circle. "Now, switch positions," he said. "Those who were the inmates are now officers. It's payback time!" Those who had been abused now got to wreak vengeance, and some did it with gusto. A tubby, mild-mannered recruit named Emminger, harshly flipped onto the mat, suffered torn ligaments in his shoulder and was sent off to the emergency room of a local hospital.

It reminded me of Philip Zimbardo's famous experiment at Stanford—now recounted at every police academy and introductory psychology course—where the students who were assigned to "guard" fellow students who were playing inmates often acted with excessive zeal, even with brutality. The experiment seemed to demonstrate the way even seemingly decent people could be corrupted by undue authority. Zimbardo has since accepted some criticism of his methods and admitted that the experiment was "clearly unethical." But given the scene around me and my own tender wrist, I wondered whether his study wasn't valid after all.

Of course, grabbing a hand or arm isn't always possible. And some inmates in a brawling frame of mind need additional persuading. For these situations, we were taught how to cause pain through "pressure points"—places where clusters of nerves lie just under the skin. Most of these are around the head: under the nose, in the mastoid process (near the jaw joint), under either side of your jaw near the windpipe. ("Do any of you fish for bass?" the instructor asked.) We also practiced karate-chopping each other on the sides of the neck and four inches above the knee. And through it all we were urged to be creative. "Pain's a wonderful thing," an instructor told us. "The floors and walls can be your friend."

But the most dramatic moves—which we did not practice on each other—were saved till the end. Jabbing an inmate with straightened fingers in the windpipe (the "trachea poke") or the eyeballs (the "eye poke") was said to be extremely effective. And in the case of the latter move, there was a good chance it would not even cause blindness. According to the instructor, "You can poke into the eye sockets about two to three inches and a few seconds later, they'll be looking at you and saying, 'What happened?' "

———

The schedule showed something unusual on our last day of regular course work: a class called Stress II, to be taught by Sergeant Bloom. As he was the master of causing stress, I assumed he was well prepared to address the subject, but it was strange, because there had been no Stress I. And the sergeant's expertise turned out to be completely different from what I expected.

Bloom, who seemed somehow more approachable and human than before, began by talking about the most stressful scenario a CO could ever possibly face: being held hostage. This situation was a complete turning of the tables between officer and inmate— payback time to the highest degree. Bloom didn't say so, but I knew from talking to the recruits and others that if a hostage situation did not end quickly in death, it usually involved torture of some kind, including rape. As a result of an inmate takeover of the Coxsackie Special Housing Unit (SHU) in 1988, Council 82 had initiated hostage insurance—a payment of half a year's salary to any member held hostage for more than eight hours. ("If they're gonna release you after seven and a half," a Council 82 rep had quipped to us, "tell 'em to go make a pot of coffee.") Bloom now wrote on the chalkboard a list of all state-prison hostage incidents since 1970, when records started to be kept. There were eleven, including the big one at Attica (seven guards and thirty-six inmates killed) and an extended one at Sing Sing in which seventeen officers were held hostage in B-block. Not included in this list were incidents in which civilian staff members—a psychologist, for example—were held hostage.

Bloom told us the warning signs of prison disturbance: inmates stockpiling food in their cells, unnaturally quiet cell blocks, inmates wearing heavy clothes (often with magazines or newspapers tucked underneath, to deflect knife thrusts) in warm weather, inmates who were normally well behaved trying to get keeplocked so they wouldn't have to mix with the general population.

An officer on the verge of being held hostage should, if he could see it coming, get rid of his keys and radio, break the television sets (so inmates couldn't watch the local news), and "destroy cutting torches if possible." That last suggestion seemed odd, but Bloom explained that during a bloody riot at the New Mexico State Penitentiary at Santa Fe in 1980, inmates in possession of a torch had not only cut their way into other cell blocks, spreading the riot, but had tortured living inmates and mutilated the dead. "They had a barbecue," he said.

The Academy had a video on this subject, but it would be more useful for us to ask someone who had been there and could talk about it. "So go ahead," Bloom said.

The stunned silence lasted several seconds. Bloom could only mean one thing.

"You?" somebody asked.

Bloom nodded. He had been working the Coxsackie SHU in 1988. As inmates came in from exercising outdoors, one slugged him in the jaw—he didn't even see it coming. Four other officers were overpowered as well, and thirty-two SHU inmates, the worst men in the prison, were soon out of their cells, terrifying their captives and destroying the Box's control center.

To me, it seemed that an officer held hostage might not tell his fellows everything that had happened to him, because it was either too painful or too humiliating. Bloom, though brave enough to stand up there in front of us, offered information only in response to our questions, and even then not a lot. One inmate had wanted to cut off his ring finger, he said, because it was too swollen for the inmate to remove his wedding band, but another inmate had talked him out of it. The inmate who started it all had a fifteen-years-to-life sentence and apparently felt he had nothing to lose. His name was Rafael Torres, and he was now in Sing Sing's SHU. The incident had lasted fourteen and a half hours. Bloom went back to work three and a half weeks later, "after the stitches came out." What stitches? someone asked. Bloom explained that he also had been struck on the head with a baton. What else happened to you? I wanted to ask. But you couldn't ask—that much, I had learned. Couldn't he have retired on some sort of disability? someone asked. "If the horse throws you, you gotta get back on," Bloom replied.

He had, however, become a training instructor soon after, "in order to get a different kind of work." Then two years ago he became a sergeant and head of the Academy. He no longer had nightmares, Bloom said, but he did still dream about it.

A short while into the crisis, the prison chaplain had called Bloom's home to inform his family. His wife wasn't there, so the chaplain had given the news to Bloom's twelve-year-old daughter. Bloom wanted us to know that he thought talking to our families, and soon, about the possibility of being taken hostage was a good idea. He asked how many of us would do that and, slowly, about half the class raised their hands. Mine was not among them. Families would know this at some level anyway, I thought. In my journal, trying to further justify my stance, I wrote, "Clearly, the odds are against it."

The staff saved another frightening thing for the last week of our Academy session: prison video. Nigro showed footage of yard disturbances taken from a wall tower at Eastern Correctional Facility. In one film, two inmates tried slashing each other while the surprised and nervous tower guards tried to zoom in with the video camera; in another, a large mass of inmates tried to catch and punish an inmate who had been a snitch. The pictures of the mob reminded me of news footage from some besieged African capital. You could hear the report as the tower guards fired the gas gun, and then watch inmates disperse as the clouds of tear gas drifted toward the prison. Though officers were nearby in both cases, none of them, surprisingly, appeared to be in much danger. What the films did reveal was the frightening power of crowds.

Another batch of film, shown to us by an assistant district attorney from an upstate county, hit even closer to home. He pointed out, entirely correctly as far as I knew, that movies featuring prison guards portrayed them as cold and brutal, without exception. "Anybody seen *Cool Hand Luke*?" he asked. "Well, these movies are going to show you something different."

We watched still-mounted camera footage of urine flying out of a cell and drenching an officer as he walked, unsuspecting, down a hallway. This was a special crime: As we had learned, the number of incidents of this sort had skyrocketed in recent years, to the point where the union had recently pushed for—and gotten— "antithrower" legislation which added a mandatory three to five years to such inmates' sentences. But we had also learned that many D.A.'s saw attacks on correction officers as low-priority prosecutions, since the criminals were already in jail. It went without saying that this was a strong argument for taking retribution into your own hands, but the prosecutor pleaded that we not do so. "And don't wash your uniform if you get shitted down," he advised. "We'll need it for evidence."

On the TV screen, we watched as another unsuspecting officer opened a cell and was coldcocked by an inmate; he crumpled to the floor. There was also footage of about six white officers subduing a flailing black inmate in an office. Just when it appeared they'd gotten him handcuffed and pushed against a wall, he whirled around and took them on again. In the melee that followed, the camera was briefly pointed at the floor, walls, and ceiling. The next thing we saw, the officers had piled on top of the man.

But most riveting of all were slides of the upper body of a CO who'd been slashed all around the neck and face and back. An inmate had lured him into a kitchen basement for the attack.

The picture that emerged from all these images was of a group of men who could be only reactive, not proactive, and who spent day after day, as one officer said, "waiting for the other guy to take the first swing."

The room was silent as the prosecutor turned the projector off.

"Everyone's got to do their time in the bottom of the barrel," the union rep had said to our class regarding the likelihood of our initial assignment to Sing Sing. A list handed out to us on our last day by the personnel department showed that it was purely a matter of numbers. Clinton, in the Adirondacks, had 219 officers waiting to be transferred in; that translated to four or five years' wait for officers like us, with no seniority. Ogdensburg, a medium-security prison even farther north, had 279 awaiting transfer. Attica, near Buffalo, had 140—maybe a three-year wait. Of the seventy-one facilities in the state, only two had no waiting list at all: Bedford Hills, a women's max in Westchester, and Sing Sing.

Sing Sing, Bloom confirmed to us on Thursday, was where we would all report on Monday. For a few lucky ones, this assignment might last only days or weeks. For others, it was an indeterminate sentence of months or years. That afternoon, we were handed "dream sheets," the requests for transfer. Most of my classmates would hand one in on their first day at Sing Sing, and most started filling them out immediately.

Rick Kingsley, back when he was showing me around the Washington Correctional Facility, had remembered Sing Sing as the worst nine months of his life, his stint in Vietnam included. "Yeah, it's a rough place," an instructor who'd recently worked at Sing Sing told our class. "But," he said, "you'll learn more in six months at Sing Sing than in two or three years someplace else." Sergeant Bloom, addressing us in the chapel on the eve of our graduation, asked for a show of hands from everyone in the room who was scared about starting work on Monday. Everyone knew what the "right" answer to this question was, given what we now knew about Sergeant Bloom. But in this case, I thought, the right answer was probably also the true answer. All of us raised our hands.

———

Howard Johnson's, the Academy annex, served as the site of graduation. And the night before, there was celebrating to do. Our session voted to begin the evening at a nearby Hooters; later, back at "800-block," as one instructor had nicknamed the HoJo building with room numbers in the eight hundreds, matters escalated considerably. Some of my classmates had to be carried back to their rooms in various states of drunkenness; I saw Arno, a total straight-arrow up to this point, passed out on the floor of an upstairs conference room. At one point, urine streamed past the window of our second-floor room, where Gary and I were getting ready to sleep. But it was probably the fact that motel management phoned the police that led to our being called on the carpet in the chapel the next morning before the ceremony. "I hear that some of you decided to be prison guards instead of correction officers last night," Sergeant Bloom chastened us. A captain we'd never seen before came in and threatened us, swearing he'd track down and fire the worst offenders. (Nothing, to my knowledge, ever happened to them.)

To my surprise, almost all my classmates had family members packed into the motel's conference room, where, in dress blues, we were presented with diplomas and badges. It had only been seven weeks, but relatives came in from hundreds of miles away. An assistant deputy commissioner spoke a few words, and our class valedictorian (who, I heard later, decided to seek other employment the following week) said that trained by great eagles, we had learned to soar. My classmates from upstate left for one last long weekend home with their spouses and kids before joining me, down in the bottom of the barrel.

CHAPTER 3

UP THE RIVER

The safety of the keepers is constantly menaced. In the presence of such dangers, avoided with such skill but with difficulty, it seems to us impossible not to fear some sort of catastrophe in the future.

—Alexis de Tocqueville and Gustave de Beaumont, writing about Sing Sing in *On the Penitentiary System in the United States and its Application to France,* 1833

Criminals used to travel to Sing Sing by boat from New York City "up the river" to "the big house," some thirty miles north. That's how both phrases entered our language. The prison's unusual name was borrowed from the Sint Sinck Indians, who once inhabited the site. It may have meant "stone upon stone," which describes the rocky slope rising from the bank of the Hudson that the prison is built upon.

Once a lonely outpost, Sing Sing now occupies fifty-five acres of prime real estate in suburban Westchester, one of the priciest counties in the United States. The town that grew up around it, once called Sing Sing, is now called Ossining. Up until the 1960s, prison employees could afford to live in and around Ossining, and in many ways they set the tone for life in the area. Now, however, though the town is slightly tattered—Ossining is far from the most desirable address in Westchester—housing prices have pushed out practically all state correction officers. In 1995, the average two-bedroom rental in Ossining cost $1,525 a month, and the average price for a three-bedroom house was $241,000. Away from "the city," as many recruits think of Westchester County, the same apartment would cost $350 (in Dannemora, New York, near Clinton Correctional Facility) and the three-bedroom house around $64,000 (near Auburn). The department's "location pay," meant to help compensate officers assigned to Sing Sing, is considered a joke—about fifteen dollars a week.

In some upstate towns, the prison is the main event, visually speaking: Clinton's imposing wall runs along Dannemora's main street. But even though it is huge, a visitor to Ossining will have to look to find Sing Sing. And once there, all she is likely to see is a portion of its immense wall. This main wall, some twenty-four feet high, is punctuated by twenty-one distinctive wall towers but is otherwise as blank as a cop's face. The longest stretch, atop the hillside, runs roughly parallel to the riverbank, a few hundred feet below; extensions at either end angle down the hillside. No single spot on land offers a good vantage point of the whole facility; you can't even see the main entrance from the street.

But I wasn't thinking in these larger terms as I drove "up the river" at dawn on that Monday in late April, my first day at Sing Sing. I was just thinking of the one Sing Sing story I'd heard at the Academy that had really stuck with me. I'd been told it three times, and though details varied, the gist was the same: A trainee from the class ahead of ours, a guy I'd met, had walked up to an inmate smoking a cigarette during his second week in Sing Sing. "There's no smoking here," he said. "Better put it out." The inmate ignored him. He repeated it until the inmate told him to get lost. Then the new CO reached over and took the cigarette from the inmate's mouth, whereupon the inmate struck him on the head or broke his shoulder bone with the CO's own baton or punched him in the mouth—the versions varied. He was badly hurt over a cigarette.

The story had stuck because the lesson was vague. Apparently, it wasn't a good idea to pull a cigarette out of an inmate's mouth. I suppose I already knew that. But what were you to do in such a situation? Write the inmate a ticket for disobeying a direct order? Walk away and lose face? In how many ways would my authority be challenged inside the prison? And how would I react when it was?

Given wrong directions at the Academy, I parked at one end of the top wall, as far as I could possibly be from the corner of the prison where I was due to report. It took fifteen minutes to hustle down a crumbling cement staircase lined with a rusty railing to the main gate and then down more steps, over the railroad tracks to the flat terrain by the river. Outside the prison walls, just a few feet from the Hudson River, are three low, white buildings that contrast with the rest of Sing Sing in their newness and cheap construction. Two are small prefab bunk rooms for officers and sergeants. The third is the Quality of Working Life building, or

QWL, a conference room with sliding glass doors and a wooden deck used for training, meetings, and parties.

Here began the four weeks of on-the-job-training (OJT) that would qualify us to become regular officers (though, technically, we would continue on probation for a full year). I was nervous but excited: Sing Sing, storied and mysterious, was exactly where I wanted to be. And I was glad to be living at home again. For most of my classmates, however, Sing Sing was even farther from home than was Albany. Expecting postings in the lower Hudson Valley, my classmates had begun looking before graduation for cheap, small apartments they could share. Davis, DiPaola, and Charlebois had found one in a bad neighborhood in Newburgh, about an hour north of Sing Sing. Arno, Emminger, Falcone, and some others had found a rooming house—"really, it's more like a halfway house, with recovering addicts and all," Arno said—around Beacon. Dieter was staying with Di Carlo and his family. Others moved into the few spaces available at Harlem Valley, a former state mental hospital about forty-five minutes from Sing Sing that was now used to house correction officers. A year before at this former asylum, a drunken CO had shot and killed his girlfriend, also a CO, and a female roommate, over unrequited love. But at twenty dollars a week, the price was right.

We were told to set up enough folding chairs and tables to accommodate the 111 people who remained of our class in four or five long rows. There was a lectern at the front of the room; rest rooms and a kitchen were off to the side. Wearing the same dress-blues uniforms we had graduated in the Friday before, we stood at our tables and snapped to attention when the training lieutenant, Wilkin, entered the room.

Wilkin, a laid-back guy, told us all to take a seat, put our brimmed "bus driver" hats on the table in front of us, and just talk to him for a while. Rumors about Sing Sing abounded at the Academy, he knew. "What have you heard?"

It took a while for anyone to raise a hand.

"That officers here sell drugs," someone finally ventured.

"Uh-huh," said Wilkin. "What else?"

"That it's totally crazy and chaotic," said someone else. "That inmates run the place, and nobody follows the rules."

"Mm," said Wilkin. "What else?"

"That some of the officers are real buddy-buddy with the inmates," said one of the Antonellis, seeming emboldened. "And that they won't always cover your back." It was black officers I'd heard thus disparaged at the Academy, but Antonelli left that out.

Instead of laughing, shaking his head, and denying all this, Wilkin, to my surprise, was circumspect. "No officers, to my knowledge, are selling drugs," he said. "When they have been in the past and we have learned of that, we have arrested them.

"And inmates don't run this place—officers do. You will see that with your own eyes on Wednesday.

"And as far as following the rules . . . we are not an upstate prison. We try to follow them to the letter, and we will expect you to. The new administration is committed to tightening security at this prison. But we are a training facility, and not everything is exactly the way we'd like it to be."

"Training facility" was not an official designation, the superintendent would later explain; it was just the way things had worked out. New recruits came here to answer the chronic shortage of officers, and they had to be trained. Five thousand had started out at Sing Sing since 1988, sixteen hundred of them in 1996 alone. The department had an unprecedented need for new officers right now, apparently due to higher-than-usual rates of retirement and attrition.

A training officer named Hill told us that our job would be unusually difficult, because "OJTs irritate inmates." Inmates appreciate a constant set of keepers, he explained; they don't like having the rules enforced differently every day. Not that it was necessarily a snap being an old-timer, either; one longtime employee had had his nose broken during a scuffle in the yard just the previous weekend. Sing Sing had between 700 and 750 "security employees" at a given time; 34 percent of these officers had less than a year on the job.

We broke for lunch, and afterward, we were each issued a baton. Down the row from me, someone noticed that his had dried blood on it. Next, we lined up to have our pictures taken. First, we faced the camera while holding up a little piece of paper displaying our name and Social Security number and the date, and then we turned for a profile shot—just as if we were inmates being processed at a jail. These were "hostage photos," one trainer told me, for our permanent files, to be released to the press if something happened to us—such as being taken hostage. I laughed, thinking the man had a dark sense of humor. But he was unsmiling and, I slowly realized, serious. As unsettling to me as the photos' purpose was the fact that they weren't called something else—say, employee contingency portraits, or some other euphemism. Calling them hostage photos was like saying we were "guards" in a "prison."

In the afternoon, we learned more about the inmates. Sing Sing is the second-oldest (after Auburn) and second-largest (after Clinton) prison in the state, and at this time it had 1,813 inmates in the maximum-security prison and 556 in Tappan, the medium-security portion. Of the total—2,369—1,726 were violent felons; 672 had been convicted of murder or manslaughter. In other words, between a quarter and a third of the inmates had killed somebody. Other violent felons had committed rape (93) or sodomy (38) or a variety of crimes including robbery, assault, kidnapping, burglary, and arson. Eighty percent were from the New York City area. Forty-three percent were ages 25 to 34. African Americans made up 56 percent of the inmate population, Hispanics comprised another 32 percent, and whites around 10 percent.

Sing Sing is unusual for a large max in that it has few vocational or other programs for inmates. Inmates are still required to work for their GEDs, but almost all college-level programs ceased in 1994 and 1995, when state and federal lawmakers ended the funding. "Now there isn't much to take away," the programs director admitted candidly during his brief presentation after lunch. "We're pretty much down to the bare minimum. We have trouble finding things for all the inmates to do—there are only programs for three or four hundred men." The gap was filled with recreation: unstructured time in the yard or gym. Up to sixteen hundred men might be in recreation at a given time.

The superintendent had less than a year on the job, too. Charles Greiner, who was fit, white-haired, and soft-spoken, stood before the lectern and told us he had come up through the system, starting upstate as a CO. We'd been told he was more security-minded than his predecessor (who, old-time officers complained, was overly concerned with housekeeping and appearances) and interested in tightening up the prison. He told us that he had reinstituted assigned seating in the mess halls, so that inmates couldn't sit wherever they wanted. He had tried to make sure inmates were more securely escorted from cell to mess hall and back. Other reforms were in the offing but would be instituted very slowly, "so as to only create a tiny ripple back." Situated, as we were, on the bank of a huge river, the metaphor suggested the prison was a big body of water and we were all in it together. Create too big a wave, and we would swamp ourselves.

The atmosphere inside the prison was apparently stressful at present. Five inmates had committed suicide within the past five months. An inmate-grievance system had been instituted after the Attica riot; Sing Sing inmates typically filed about twenty-five grievances a week against the administration, but recently that number had gone as high as seventy-five. Two months ago, the entire facility had been locked down in Code Green emergency status, meaning that an area (B-block) had gone out of control. Still, said the first deputy superintendent for security, Sing Sing was "no more out of control than anywhere else." Yes, he conceded, there had been "lots of cutting lately." But, he added, "That's true everywhere."

On Tuesday, our second day, we learned more about emergencies. Many of us, depending on our post, would be furnished with radios equipped with special "emergency pins." In case of attack by an inmate—or any violent situation we could not control—we were to pull the pin out of the top of our radio by tugging on the lanyard. This sent a signal to the arsenal, where an operator would identify the radio's location and broadcast a special message to all the other radios. The "red dots," specially designated officers on standby for an emergency, would then run there to offer aid. Other free officers in the area would join them. The response was immediate, we were told, and usually impressive.

If things got so wild that the local red dots couldn't handle it, red dots from down the hill at Tappan (or up the hill at Sing Sing, if it was Tappan that had the emergency) would be summoned. If they couldn't control things either, the Code Green would be called and supervisors were to send all available officers to the trouble spot. A milder state of emergency, Code Blue, called for ceasing all inmate movement and locking down the whole jail. A Code Blue would be called if, for example, the count came up an inmate short and finding him was the top priority. No officers would be allowed to leave the building; wall-tower officers were to step out onto their catwalks with rifles in hand. Everything would be frozen until it was certain that no one had escaped.

Later that day, we were shown a movie produced by the Department, called *Games Inmates Play*. The film, starring state COs, was a primer on how not to let inmates manipulate you for their own ends and make a fool or a criminal out of you. It dramatized three situations that, we were told, had actually occurred in the past two years. In one, an inmate "porter" (trusty, in more common parlance) sweeping the floor around the officer's desk became privy to his football pool and collected evidence from his wastebasket; when the CO wouldn't help the porter set up his own pool, the porter threatened to turn him in to his supervisors; the CO did the right thing and fessed up to his sergeant and lieutenant. A second CO didn't come clean soon enough, though. After working near one congenial-seeming inmate for a long time, he'd become so comfortable talking to him that he'd confided to the inmate about some problems at home and a shortness of cash. The inmate offered to help him out by paying him a hundred dollars just to bring in a package from his brother. After hemming and hawing for a while (inmates are forbidden to possess cash, which is almost always connected to drug traffic), the officer finally agreed. The final scene of the vignette showed him pulling into his driveway that night and being arrested in front of his disbelieving wife and kids.

Finally, there was the tale of the civilian teacher who allowed an eager inmate to help her grade papers and confided in him when her boyfriend dumped her. He asked if he could take her out when he was paroled in six months. Yes, she indicated, but then he told her he couldn't wait; they were caught by an officer having sex in a storeroom, and she was fired.

The moral was: Don't confide in an inmate about your personal life. And don't be tempted by bribery or other offers. The moment an inmate gets anything on you, he'll have power over you and is certain, eventually, to sell you out.

After all these warnings, a training officer finished our second day with one more. "By the way," he said, "we've had a problem lately with brown recluse spiders in the facility." Three COs had been bitten by the venomous spiders, he said; one officer got so sick that he required chemotherapy. "So just make sure to shake out your jackets if they've been hanging up, or look around a desk before you sit down."

Spiders—on top of everything else.

<hr/>

It had been driving me crazy to be right next to Sing Sing but unable to go inside. On Wednesday that changed.

As our tour group walked the perimeter fence to the main gate, I noticed that we looked slightly different. No longer was everyone so obsessively concerned with his uniform. Sing Sing, it was clear from watching the training officers, did not care much about the polish on your shoes or the crease in your shirt or the length of your hair. Instead of everyone wearing the long-sleeved gray shirts prescribed by the Academy, some had slipped into the short-sleeved version, despite the still-cool spring weather. Other officers now spurned their black oxfords for more casual boots, especially the lightweight Bates and Hi-Tec brands, which were popular among police. And our belts, newly laden with batons, had begun to spring key clips and latex-glove holders, though no one had told us to put them on yet. A new groove had been set, and officers were sliding into it.

We passed through the front gate and several more as we made our way up the hill. Our group felt very white to me compared to the on-duty officers we passed—and particularly compared to the inmates we saw. But the real revelation came in one tight corridor when our group passed an inmate group of nearly equivalent size. As we tried to squeeze into half the hallway, arms and shoulders didn't just brush, they rubbed. This wasn't like the small group of subservient workers we'd known at the Academy or the double-file inmates from the roomier halls of Coxsackie. This was something with mass and energy, something . . . unnerving. I was thinking how easy it would be for someone with a knife to do some damage to us—and get away with it. Ahead of me, one of the Antonelli brothers suddenly turned around and gestured to us, trying to subtly point out one of the inmates—a transsexual, complete with breasts: nothing you wouldn't see on any given day in Greenwich Village or on the city subways, but decidedly exotic if you were from rural New York. Bella and Chavez seemed more at home with the mix. As we turned the corner, Bella commented, with some satisfaction, "It's just like the city!"

Ahead of us, a Plexiglas sign hanging from the ceiling announced HOUSING UNIT A. Underneath, there was a barred gate with a solid-metal door behind it. Our guide pushed a doorbell and we heard ringing on the other side. Finally, an officer inside pulled open the door to admit us to A-block and our first glimpse of the great cavern, so drab and yet so stunning. We stood slack-jawed, trying to make sense of the railings, the fences, the bars, and the spaces, both tiny and immense. Our training officer commented on the fame of the building, how corrections officials from around the world came to visit it. It was hard to hear him, due to the din. Heavy gates were being slammed; shouts echoed. We moved closer. When he stopped talking, we followed him up the center stairs and walked a long gallery or two, attracting a couple of epithets—someone called out, "Clarence Thomas!" to Dimmie (meaning Uncle Tom), and we heard a few cries of "Newjack!" But it was nothing like our experience at Coxsackie: Even these hardened inmates, who so outnumbered us, were intimidated by a large detachment of officers.

A-block had a big gym but no adjacent yard. In another quirk of Sing Sing, the yard was way down the hill and across the tracks, next to Tappan. Before heading that way, we visited 7-Building, the "honor block," with space for eighty-six inmates who had gone several years without being cited for disciplinary infractions. And then we went to 7-Building's opposite, the Special Housing Unit, a two-story structure that housed sixty inmates; it was larger and grimmer than the one at Coxsackie. While 7-Building's yard contained a running path, benches, vegetable gardens, and a great view of the Hudson River, the SHU had a bare blacktop courtyard divided in two by a chain-link fence. Down a dogleg corridor from the SHU was the State Shop, where inmates on their way in or out of the prison were processed and given clothes and bedding. On the first floor of the State Shop building were a fourteen-chair barbershop and a shower room (rows of individual stalls without curtains, and lookout points for supervising officers).

On the way to B-block we passed 5-Building, a small cellblock (housing 272 inmates) with floors devoted to distinct groups: recent arrivals to Sing Sing, including transfers and absconders (former inmates captured after parole violations); mess-hall workers; and inmates with mental health problems. We saw the laundry, one of the few freestanding buildings in the maximum-security section, and the mess hall, with its busy nexus—"Times Square"—which sat right in the middle of the dining rooms for A-block, B-block, and 5-Building. The chapel building, opposite B-block, was used mainly to show movies, but it had churchlike worship spaces for Catholics and Protestants and areas in its basement for Muslims, Jews, and Quakers.

Sing Sing's maze of corridors, gates, and staircases had grown organically over the years according to the demands of the particular era; no master plan had guided the development. Looking out from some high windows, you could see a dozen red-brick walls facing different directions and the roofs of the many connecting corridors. Some of the beautiful slate shingles of these roofs were missing, and decaying soffits hung down from them, too. There seemed to be a score of little courtyards, half of them abandoned and overgrown. The whole area was dotted with small sheds, and the buildings themselves had a mishmash of additions. The gyms of A-block and B-block, for example, had been oddly appended years after the original construction. The interior of most corridors was painted brick and cinder block. No one could memorize this layout in a day—perhaps not even in a week—and yet we weren't allowed to bring our maps inside; they were thought to be a security risk. Still, we didn't need them to wonder what had happened to 6-Building or 3-Building or 4-building, the gaps in the number sequence, buildings perhaps constructed but then abandoned or renamed.

The most startling corridor—my favorite, actually—was the long, semi-open one connecting the max facility to the school building and Tappan, across the railroad tracks. The walls of this corridor were a series of barred arches, through which rain and icy winds blew in bad weather. With its peeling, chipped paint and water stains, the interior had the air of a colonial ruin. Past the school gate, the corridor was fully enclosed and, for reasons I still do not understand, partially unlit. At one staircase, if it was bright outside, the contrast with the gloomy tunnel dazzled you so much that it was hard to see the steps; you had to feel your way down with your toes. Set into the wall by these stairs was an old, rusted gate, and an inmate would later ask me if that was where the Death House used to be. Certainly it looked like it.

But it wasn't. The Death House, 15-Building, was an old brick structure down by the river. It had been converted, following the abolition of the death penalty in New York State, to a vocational building with modest print, drafting, woodworking, welding, and small-engine shops. Old Sparky, the electric chair, had been removed to a museum in Virginia; Death Row, converted into an orientation classroom. Six hundred and fourteen people (including Julius and Ethel Rosenberg, convicted of selling atomic-bomb secrets to the Russians) had been executed here, but there were no plaques; the only links to the past were the memories of officers like the one who showed us where the chair had been, and the switch, and the so-called Dance Hall—I thought I recognized it from a James Cagney movie—through which condemned inmates passed on their way to the chair.

Tappan had a much different feel from the Sing Sing max. Its three-story cinder-block buildings had large, open dorm rooms, containing up to seventy-five inmates each. The dorms were divided by waist-high partitions into single or double cubicles. There was freedom of movement within the dorms except during the three daily counts; inmates washed their own clothes and could cook their own meals, and there were television rooms. A single officer sat near the entrance to each room at a large desk, and it was a sought-after job, for though some of the inmates had committed crimes of the same violence as inmates "up the hill," they were in the last five years of their sentences, tended to be older, and were often on track for parole. Tappan had its violent incidents, but much less often than the max facility.

Outside the three dorm buildings was a large gym, built by Warner Bros. as thanks for use of the Death House and other prison sites in its gangster movies of the 1930s. And outside the gym were a weight-lifting area and a lawn, tended by inmates who, on warm days, reclined there.

We'd been up the hill and had come back down. Before we climbed back up to the main gate, we were given a closer glimpse of the fence that substituted for a wall along the riverfront and on either side of the sunken railway corridor. It was a double fence, actually—two high chain-link barriers topped with spirals of gleaming razor ribbon and a kind of no-man's-land in the eight or nine feet of ground between them. In this zone, infrared sensors checked for movement, with strands of taut wire and electromagnetic green wire providing redundant protection. It was the sort of thing squirrels and birds could wreak havoc on, our guide said, which was one reason for the system of zoomable, rotatable cameras mounted along the top, which were monitored in the arsenal. The entire system had cost about $12 million, he said. As we showed our I.D.s to leave the prison—a safeguard against inmates walking out the front door—I decided that if I were an escaping inmate, I'd stay away from the fence.

As we walked back to the QWL building, we spoke among ourselves of how run-down Sing Sing was. But in the debriefing by Lieutenant Wilkin, the focus was on how chaotic it was, how so many of the rules weren't respected. Several times, by now, we had been quizzed by the training staff on the contents of the *Inmate*

Guidelines booklet. There were ninety-nine guidelines, all of which we had to memorize, governing the minutiae of inmate life. For example:

31. You will be allowed to carry a maximum of two (2) packs of cigarettes on your person. Only a maximum of six (6) cartons of cigarettes will be allowed to be stored in cells/cubes. [An inmate in possession of more than this was likely a "mule," collecting or paying off some illicit debt.]

36. Visibility into the cell . . . must not be obstructed by . . . furniture, clotheslines, clothes, bedding, or towels.

24. Pictures, photographs, newspaper clippings, and one small national flag (10″ × 12″) . . . are to be . . . taped or fastened at the top only on the cell wall in the [designated] 2 × 4   area. Other symbols not authorized will be confiscated.

25. Display of pictures or photographs of nudes will only be placed where they cannot be seen from outside the cell or cubicle (above cell door, or inside locker).

Metal hangers weren't allowed. Music could be played only through headphones, not speakers. Beds had to be made before inmates left their cells.

But we told the lieutenant we'd seen many of the rules broken: sheets hanging from the bars, hard-porn girlie shots staring us in the face, music blaring from radios, a dozen cigarette cartons lurking under a table. What was the deal?

The lieutenant gave a little smile. "As I said, this is a training facility. Not everything is exactly as it should be. We'll need your help to make it that way. In fact, we'll demand it: Your job is to enforce the rules." The lieutenant was a man stuck in that kind of bureaucratic crack where you have to pay lip service to the way things should be yet at the same time acknowledge the reality or appear to be an out-of-touch fool. I just wondered if they were really planning to make *us* enforce the rules when nobody else did.

One of the female officers then asked an eminently sensible question: "But are we supposed to talk to them?"

The lieutenant didn't get the question. He apparently didn't know that in the Academy, we had been ordered not to talk to the inmates around us. But the idea of not talking to them here was so preposterous to him that he had a hard time grasping the concept.

"Of course you have to talk to them!" he finally said. "You'd better talk to them. How else are you going to let them know what to do and hear what they need from you? Oh, yes! The job is all *about* talking to them. That's really what it's about."

That echoed what Sergeant Bloom, head of the Academy, had told us. And yet it seemed to be a point of pride among Bloom's instructors that the training was about *us,* not about *them.* We'd been taught that worrying about inmates' concerns was tantamount to pandering, that it almost demeaned an officer. Let *them* worry about how to communicate with *us* was the more common attitude.

As we walked out to the cars, the Antonelli brothers were muttering that others might not enforce the rules (the wimps!), but they sure as hell were going to. We passed under one of the watchtowers along the river, and someone noticed a familiar face—a recruit from the class ahead of ours, the guy who had taught us to short-sheet our beds.

"Hey, how'd you get that job?" someone asked him as we all craned our necks skyward.

"I think it's because I was the high scorer on the range in my section," the man answered. (I'd later learn that this was highly unlikely; Sergeant Holmes was oblivious of our scores.)

We told him how chaotic it seemed to us inside the prison. "Any trouble getting them to do what you say?" asked a recruit.

"I just swear at 'em," he replied. "It's the fastest way to get the job done."

———

The following Monday morning, we began training inside the prison. I threaded my baton through its ring on my belt, trying to imagine a scenario in which I might have to wield it. Before joining regular officers in the lineup room, our group had a separate lineup at which we received our assignments. Mine was the floor of B-block containing galleries R and W, and I was to assist the officer on duty there.

On our long hike up the stairs, minutes behind the regular officers, few of us had anything to say. We trainees were strangers here. Our heads were filled with rules and anecdotes, but we lacked any real knowledge of how to perform the job that was ours as of today. Now separated, we would each face our fear alone. Our main problem, it seemed to me, was that the state had

certified us as lion tamers before ever leaving us alone in a cage
with a lion.

Our group got smaller the farther into the prison we went, with
groups breaking off at the hospital building and at every side corridor. One particularly large contingent exited at A-block. The dozen
of us remaining strode off down the dark hallway to B-block,
listening to the sound of our shoes hitting the concrete floor.

Like A-block, its fraternal twin, B-block was a massive structure. We clustered near the gate like a small herd of doomed sheep,
looking at the galleries above. Inmates who were out of their cells
on the galleries gazed back down on us. *OJTs*, we heard ourselves
called again and again, and *newjacks*. Officers around us were
smoking, though nobody was supposed to. We heard gates slamming, music playing, men yelling, and showers running as though
B-block were one immense locker room.

We stood on the flats, ground-floor corridors that encircle the
tiers of cells. The cells are arranged with two galleries, or rows,
back to back on each tier. From top to ground level, they are:

> U and Z
> T and Y
> S and X
> R and W
> Q and V

The Q-and-V galleries are on the flats. The Q-R-S-T-U galleries
comprise the "front side," or river side, of B-block; V-W-X-Y-Z,
the back. B-block's letters were what was left of the alphabet after
the galleries had been named in 5-Building (A, B, C, D), 7-Building
(E, F, G), and A-block (H, J, K, L, M, N, O, P). The anonymity of
it all was telling, I thought. Every other public building in the
country was eagerly associated with the glory of a leader or, in recent years, a corporation: the John F. Kennedy Center in Washington, D.C., the Alfred Murrah Federal Building in Oklahoma City,
Houston's Hobby Airport, 3Com Park, Coors Field. But there was
no Microsoft Men's Correctional Facility, say, and no Reagan Center for Juvenile Detention. Prisons were usually named after
places; their buildings, after letters of the alphabet.

The officer in charge (OIC) appeared, warned us not to let out
any keeplocks, and then ordered us up the center staircase to our
assignments. To get to the top, we had to pass through a locked

staircase gate on every single floor. R-and-W was just one floor up, but it took a long time to get there. "R-and-W, center gate!" we yelled again and again. Through the mesh we could see a lot of inmates milling around, apparently arriving on the gallery via some other entrance. Finally, a gray uniform appeared among them, and an officer in his early thirties plodded up, stuck a key in the gate, and pulled it aside. We passed through, my fellow trainees quickly disappearing up the next staircase. I held out my hand. "Conover," I said. "Here to help you today."

"Okay, here's your keys," said the officer, passing to me two of the four heavy rings on his belt. His name tag identified him as Fay. "And here's the keeplocks." He dug in his shirt pocket for a scrap of paper with the numbers of a dozen cells on R and as many more on W. As I began to copy them down, he said of the regular inmates, "They're just coming back from chow."

Around us was pandemonium. Inmates were crossing from the R side to the W side and back again through the center passage, which I had a feeling they weren't supposed to do. Fay, instead of trying to impose order, appeared distracted by the succession of inmates presenting him with special requests. One wanted him to make a phone call; one wanted a form; one wanted a new bed. Fay was tall, round-shouldered, and bald, and wore a baseball cap with a state corrections emblem. He looked like he could be a deacon in a conservative black church. He himself had finished his training just a few weeks before, he would tell me later in the day, and did not have much experience on the galleries. He was, I would ascertain, not especially smart, and his slow wits and mild manner were no match for the chaos swirling around him. I watched helplessly, awaiting further direction.

"What do we do now?" I finally asked.

"Get them into their cells," said Fay.

"And how do we do that?"

"You just tell 'em," said Fay. "Why don't you take that side"— he gestured to W gallery—"and I'll take this." I took about five steps and looked both ways down W. It was 425 feet long and three and a half feet wide. At the exact center of it was the staircase, where I stood. The view to either side was of a sort of tunnel with cells defining one wall and a mesh fence overlooking the flats the other. Of the sixty-some inmates who lived on the gallery, fifty must have been out of their cells. The narrow space outside the cells was stuffed with inmates. Many of them were engaged in shouted conversation with inmates down on the flats. Maybe seven out of ten were black, another two Latino, and the last one white. The greatest number seemed to be young, well muscled, and in their twenties.

On our tour and during the twenty-five minutes or so I'd been in B-block, I'd heard officers yelling a line that seemed appropriate to a situation like this, so I started: "Gentlemen, step in, please! Step into your cells."

Most ignored me, or seemed to. But I persisted, and in five minutes maybe half the inmates had disappeared from the gallery, presumably into their cells. I made my way from one end to the other, saying "Excuse me" to inmates in the way, and repeated my mantra. "Step in, guys—time to step in." One of them imitated me but then smiled when I stared at him. I began to grow irritated at a handful who continued to ignore me; at an upstate prison, I knew, this would never be tolerated. I decided to make it personal with one, who I felt was making a show out of ignoring me.

"Time to step in, pal. Five minutes ago."

"Pal? You're not my friend."

"Step in anyway. It's time."

"Time for you, maybe, not time for me."

"No?" I said, on the verge of anger.

Suddenly he grinned. "Chapel porter, CO. I was just leaving."

"Chapel porter?"

"Yeah, I go every morning. The regular officer knows. Or you can call Officer Martinez over in the chapel."

"Maybe I will," I said, jotting down the name.

He'd either bamboozled me or had a little fun, neither of which was the outcome I'd hoped for. I had just decided to approach the next guy who was still out when an inmate called to me from his cell.

"CO! CO! They didn't call me down for my medication."

"Yeah? What are you supposed to get?"

I waited half a minute while the man doubled over with a deep chest cough. He started to speak again, then coughed in my face.

"TB pills, man, gotta take my TB pills every day."

I wiped my face. He didn't seem to have coughed on me intentionally; he was just heedless. "What's your name and cell number?"

He told me his name and then pointed out the cell number painted by the door lock. "You're new here, right, CO?"

"How can you tell?" I said ruefully.

"You know who you look like? You look like that guy on *Three's Company,* CO. Know who I mean?"

I nodded.

"Anybody ever tell you that?"

"No," I said. "I'll get back to you."

I went to ask Fay about the chapel porter and the medication when I realized, through the din, that somebody had been shouting "R and W, center gate!" a number of times and that I probably had the key. I fumbled with my rings, tried a likely candidate, and was pulling open the gate when I realized it was inmates on the other side—about four of them—not officers. I hesitated, and stopped with the gate open two or three inches.

"What are you going down for?" I asked.

"OIC porters, CO, come on!"

"I've never heard of OIC porters," I said—which, I would learn, was a mistake. You were never supposed to betray your ignorance to inmates.

"Oh come on, man, you're new. We do it every morning."

Without closing the gate, I told them to wait. I'd check it out. I threaded my way down R-gallery, which seemed to have even more inmates on it than W, and finally found Fay, who said to let them through and to call the hospital about the TB pills. But when I returned, the gate was wide open and they'd let themselves through—a significant offense, I thought. Certainly it was one of the ninety-nine rules—inmates were never to touch gates, apart from the doors of their own cells. Or was it my fault for leaving the gate open? I was debating whether to follow up on this when I heard the phone ringing inside the cell used by R-and-W officers as an office. I signaled to Fay over the heads of several inmates, and he indicated I should answer it. Finding the right key took about twenty rings, and at first there was no one on the other end of the line. Then a voice demanded to know why we hadn't responded to the page over the public address system. The inmate in W-21 had a visit. I hadn't even heard the page, I confessed. The OIC sounded exasperated. "Are your galleries clear yet?" she demanded. "No, not quite," I said. "Well, clear 'em up now!" she ordered, and slammed down the phone.

I went to ask Fay what to do about the visit, and he told me to let the guy out. Since I'd never succeeded in locking everybody in anyway, that would be easy, I thought. I went and told the inmate he could go. "I know that," he said. "But now what about my shower?"

"What about it?"

"You gonna let me into the shower?"

"It depends. Why should you get a shower?"

The inmate's impatience reminded me of the OIC's. He sighed as though trying to keep his blood pressure under control. "When you get a visit, you automatically get a shower," he said in a patronizing tone. Fucking newjack.

I let him into the shower, allowed two officers and an inmate through the center gate, and then returned to the task of trying to clear W-gallery. Every inmate still out claimed he was a porter—an inmate employee who swept, mopped, or cleaned up the common areas at a designated time. There were maybe seven of them. I couldn't imagine that we needed more than two. I went to ask Fay, who said there should be a list posted somewhere.

"Like where?"

"In the office somewhere, maybe."

I walked back to the office. The phone was already ringing. A lieutenant wanted me to check the logbook for an entry written three weeks earlier, something about when an inmate had been keeplocked. The logbook was a maroon tome that the first officer—Fay—was supposed to keep current all during the shift, noting who the keeplocks were, what time chow was called, when inmates returned from chow, who went out on a visit, and so forth. Fay hadn't written a line since signing in an hour and a half ago. I turned back to try to help out the lieutenant, but the handwriting on the day in question was illegible. I apologized, but it was no comfort to the lieutenant, who slammed down the phone. I resumed my search for the porter list. What I found seemed ancient, but I copied down the cell numbers for A.M. porters anyway and returned to W-gallery.

An inmate was standing outside the shower cell I had unlocked for the inmate who had a visit. He was wearing only a towel. "Why are you here?" I asked.

"Gym porter, CO. I can't take my shower in the afternoon, so I get it now."

"Says who?"

"The regular officer—he always lets me do it."

"But you haven't done any work yet."

"And I won't do any work, either, unless I get my shower. You can call over there, CO. Ask for Officer Ebron."

I decided I would do just that, but then I remembered the more pressing matter of inmates still outside their cells who were claiming to be porters. In the next ten minutes, I managed to anger or amuse most of them, or so it seemed, by trying to enforce my hopelessly outdated porter list. Then I heard new calls to open the center gate. "Sanitation porters," said three Latino men with plastic garbage bags in their hands. I let them through.

"Who the hell gets to go through the center gate?" I demanded of Fay when I saw him, my stress making itself plain.

"Only those who are authorized," he answered.

"And who's authorized?"

"Well, you know, officers, certain porters, inmates on a visit . . ." His voice trailed off as he reached the limit of his knowledge.

It was barely two hours into the shift, and already I felt I was near the end of my rope. Fay and I weren't coming close to making the inmates do what they were supposed to do, and I was uncertain about whether I should use my power to compel them. Refusal to "lock in" was considered a petty offense. Tickets, officially known as Inmate Misbehavior Reports, were the means by which we had an inmate keeplocked: After locking him into his cell, we filled out a form, got a sergeant to sign it, and sent it off to the Adjustment Committee. The inmate, once "written up," faced three or four days of constant confinement until his hearing, and then possibly weeks or months more if the Adjustment Committee agreed that he was guilty. Apparently, there was a way around the paperwork for a petty offense. If I understood the talk, an officer could "mistakenly" deadlock the cell of an intransigent inmate just long enough to make him miss his morning or afternoon recreation. But I wasn't prepared to try that on my first day.

Before my despair could deepen, the OIC started calling the program runs over the PA system—chapel run, school run, commissary run, State Shop run. Since my inmates would soon be leaving, there was no longer any point in trying to clear the galleries, which was both a humiliation and a relief. At this moment Konoval, one of our training officers, showed up and asked how it was going. "Could be better," I confessed.

Blithely unaware of how bad things really were, Konoval led me down the gallery and asked, "How about the cell compliance?" This referred to the rules about how inmates kept their cells—making their beds, not placing objects on the bars, porn on the wall, fabric over their light fixtures, etc. It was the last thing I was worried about, but Konoval strode purposefully ahead, grunting his displeasure at the number of sheets inmates had hung up, the music being played through speakers, even the smell of cooked garlic coming from one cell. (Inmates weren't allowed to cook.)

"118.21, fire hazard," he said balefully, pointing out a pile of papers. We moved down the line. "118.30, cleanliness and order-liness. Write these cell numbers in your notebook."

We passed over to Fay's side. A few cells down, to my amaze-ment, a young Latino inmate was out on the gallery cutting an older man's hair with electric clippers. The old man was sitting on an upended box; on one side of his head, the hair was quite short; on the other, still shaggy.

"No, no, no," said Konoval. "A haircut on the gallery? Pack it up."

"But, CO!" protested the young barber. "I just need a couple more minutes!"

"Sorry. Now."

"You gonna make him stop when he's only halfway through?" the old man asked Konoval.

"That's right."

The men grudgingly complied. I was relieved to see an officer command a modicum of respect and wanted Konoval to stick around, despite his tsk-ing over housekeeping. But he had other galleries to check. I let him into the office to sign the logbook—he expressed shock at the lack of entries—and then let him out through the center gate. I turned to wend my way through the large number of inmates responding to the announcements for gym and yard runs—I hadn't even heard them—when a tall, lanky black in-mate in a muscle shirt yelled, "Hey, CO!" As I turned to face him, the short, bulky man at his side went through nine tenths of the motion of landing an uppercut on my chin. He stopped maybe an inch away, and as I jumped reflexively backward, the two of them dissolved into laughter and strolled off down the gallery. 102.10, I thought, threats to an officer. But was it a threat if they were only kidding, if they were just trying to make a fool out of me? I tried to calm my pounding heart and wondered if I should have pulled out my baton. I wondered how I'd last five more hours.

———

They placed us on different shifts for the next three weeks, and every day I was at a different post—thank God. The idea was that the regular officer at each post would teach us what he or she knew. But even if the regular officers were there (and not on their day off), in practice they were often sick of constantly explaining things to OJTs and tended to ignore us.

This was the case later that first week, when I was assigned to the State Shop along with DiPaola, Davis, and Colton. Apparently, some days in the State Shop were busy—the shop provided blue jeans and button-down shirts to inmates with court dates and inventoried the belongings of inmates on transfers—but this was not one of them. Still reeling from my experience on the gallery, I was mainly relieved to have some downtime, but the others were on edge and found the lack of activity excruciating. We stood around waiting while the regular officers took all available chairs in the tiny dayroom and drank coffee. Finally, a senior officer instructed us to do a Fire and Safety Report—a daily form for which you count and check the readiness of an area's fire extinguishers, fire-alarm pulls, emergency lights, etc. We discovered that the faucet handle for a fire hose was missing—you wouldn't be able to turn it on in a fire—and duly noted it on the form. "Oh, I've got that in a drawer somewhere over here," the officer said when he read it. "It's to keep any inmates from turning it on. They did that once. Hey, don't worry about it. Write up a new form."

"Without mentioning it?"

"Right."

I pictured Sergeant Bloom, red in the face, saying accusingly, "False report!" We might be held liable if the State Shop burned down! But we rewrote it, because we didn't want the officer to hate us. Reality had set in.

Three more hours passed with nothing to do. DiPaola finally said, "I didn't think prison work was going to be anything like this. I don't want to just stand around and play with my fuckin' dick all day." Another hour passed. It was now Friday afternoon. Three newly arrived inmates were placed in a holding cell near us, awaiting their issue of clothing, and one started watching Davis.

"Be drivin' home up north to visit the missus this afternoon, right, Davis? Countin' the minutes?"

Davis ignored him. But it was unnerving. Inmates had little to do but watch the officers, we'd been told in the Academy; "you're like their TV." From careful watching, they'd read his name tag; from Davis's wedding band, they knew he was married. From our behavior and the way other officers talked to us, they knew we were OJTs (and therefore that we had the weekend off). Statistical probability told them that Davis was from upstate; maybe something in his bearing betrayed it, as well.

Finally, four inmates arrived who had to be strip-frisked before being placed in a holding cell. This was Nuts and Butts, in officer parlance, a very specific procedure that had to be followed to the letter. (Blurred, laminated photocopies of some court order regarding this search were posted in bathrooms; apparently, inmates had won some redress in court because officers had conducted the searches disrespectfully.) We'd quickly been taught the procedure at the Academy, but Davis had spent the entire previous day doing strip-frisks outside the Visit Room: All inmates had to submit to one after a visit, to make sure they hadn't been passed any contraband (primarily cash or drugs) by a visitor. So Davis went over it with us.

My inmate, Ortiz, was clean-shaven, slope-shouldered, bespectacled, and out of shape; he looked like a college student. He handed me cigarettes and matches from his pockets before entering a small cubicle with a curtain for a door. Then he passed me out his glasses and clothing as he removed them: T-shirt, trousers, socks, shoes. I ran my fingers over each item, hung them all on pegs, and stepped inside.

He stood naked facing me on a small square of carpet, briefs in his hand. He offered them to me, and I checked them quickly. There was some blood in the seat. "You okay?" I asked. He nodded, and I began directing him through the obligatory motions. But he knew them better than I did and was always a step ahead.

"Hands through your hair. Pull your ears forward. Mouth open. Put out your tongue, pull out your lips and cheeks." I looked quickly under the tongue. "Arms up." I checked the armpits. "Turn around." He did, and immediately bent over and spread his buttocks so I could see his anus. "Fine, thanks."

I left the booth so he could dress. That was my first strip-frisk, and I hated it. I hated Ortiz's pliant submission. I almost wished he had resisted more, caused me some trouble—I didn't enjoy his servility. I didn't enjoy the visual memory of his anus and dick and the blood on his underwear. (" 'Roids," DiPaola would suggest later.)

Half an hour before we left, an inmate who was being trans-ferred to another facility (on a draft, in the lingo) came in with his personal property to be inventoried. His state-issued clothing was all clean and immaculately folded: six T-shirts, three pairs of green trousers, three green short-sleeved work shirts, one white dress shirt, one green sweatshirt, one zippered winter coat, six sets of underwear, "Felony Flyer" sneakers, and leather half-height boots. He had a Koran and a couple of spare kufis (skullcaps). It took us all of five minutes.

"Enjoying yourselves?" asked a black officer who I assumed was an old-timer. He'd been out of the Academy only a few months, it turned out, but had already been assigned several times to the State Shop. His take on the boredom was that it "beats working a gallery." But a given day could bring either one—hair-pulling overwork on a gallery or absolutely nothing to do in a place like the State Shop. I thought of myself as a fairly flexible person, but not knowing what each day would bring was nerve-racking. What were you supposed to do—shut down your brain when you walked into the prison or drink extra coffee and prepare to go into overdrive?

"I just try to make myself go numb," he said.

———

Ten days later, after I'd spent some time in A-block, Davis, DiPaola and I worked together again, this time in B-block. DiPaola was on the U-and-Z galleries, at the very top, and Davis on S-and-X, in the middle. My job, by comparison, was humdrum: I was posted at the front gate, the main passage into and out of B-block. Several times an hour, when I heard the doorbell ring, I'd stick a key into the heavy metal door, twist it, and give the door a big shove to let an officer or inmate with a pass in or out. It didn't close easily; you had to open it wide and then use its momentum to swing it shut. In an emergency, I was supposed to step outside the block into the corridor and lock the door from there. That way, any disturbance that got out of hand could be contained.

But the job was so dull that I was almost dozing off and could hardly respond when the radio of a nearby officer loudly blared out the emergency tone. An alarm had been pulled on S-and-X galleries, a voice advised. All red dots were to respond.

Half a dozen officers rushed upstairs through the center gate. Shaking myself into wakefulness, I let another half-dozen red dots in through the front gate before stepping out, locking it, and leaving B-block to its fate.

Ten minutes later, the emergency was over and I went back in. The red-dot officers were coming down the stairs with two inmates in handcuffs. One had a deep cut across his face and was bleeding profusely. He was taken to the Sing Sing emergency room. The other, who had attacked him, was locked into an empty shower cell. Apparently, an officer on U-and-Z had mistakenly unlocked a keeplock's cell. Taking advantage of this error to settle a grudge, the keeplock had walked out of his cell when the brakes were opened to let inmates go to their programs, descended two floors to S-and-X, burst into the cell of his unsuspecting enemy, and slashed him.

Fifteen or twenty minutes later, sergeants were interviewing DiPaola and Davis—they had been working on those same galleries—as well as other officers who had been involved. Within an hour, rumors were circulating among our class that DiPaola had been the one who let the inmate out. He denied it, and of course, there was no way to know for sure. Keys were passed back and forth between officers all the time. Still, regular officers reflexively blamed OJTs when there was a screwup, and often they were right. Before our shift the next day, the training officer underscored the seriousness of what had happened and said that the injured inmate was very likely to sue the Department. A lieutenant entered the room just as this comment was being made.

"I don't give a shit about the inmate," he said, unexpectedly. "An officer could've been cut. Who here could live with that?" We were quiet. I don't think anybody had expected the case to turn into a lesson about protecting our fellow officers.

———

Keys were power. And they were responsibility—because many, many bunglings could be traced back to a set of keys and the person who had been entrusted with them. When to lock and when to unlock was, by one reckoning, what we were here to learn. "You are never wrong, in prison, to lock a gate," a sergeant had reassured us at lineup one day. But it was more complicated than that. Gates had to be unlocked for the prison to function smoothly—and then, at the right moment, to be locked again. Sing Sing was a place of, probably, over two thousand locks, many with the same key. The cardinal sin, the one thing you were never, ever to do, was lose your keys. A lost key could fall into inmates' hands. A lost key was a disaster.

I was back in B-block a few days later, responsible for half of Q-gallery, on the flats, as well as the center gate—the main access point from the flats to the galleries above. To learn this job, I had to handle the keys. But while the regular officer, a fat, powerful-looking cigar chomper named Orrico, was at pains to explain the job, he was not handing me the ring of keys. Instead, he played with them, twirled them around a big finger, caught them in his meaty palm. There were several, I could see: the cell key, the brake-padlock key, a gym-door key or two, an end-gate key, a center-gate key, a fire-alarm key, and at least one other, all of them different. The pewter-colored cell key was the biggest, its shaft as thick as a Mont Blanc pen, with a silver dollar–sized handle at one end and skeleton key–like chiselings in a tab at the other.

In case of a red-dot emergency, Orrico was saying, I was to get to the center gate as soon as possible. It was the main passage to the upper floors, and I would need to let through all the officers who had to pass, then lock it back up. In no case was I to follow the responding red-dot officers upstairs—even if my best friend worked up there, even if I heard officers screaming out in agony—because control over the gate was essential to the block's security.

Concluding his lecture, Orrico left to pursue a cup of coffee and handed me the keys. No sooner had he disappeared than the red-dot alarm sounded. Officers were dashing toward the center gate, arriving before me. I rushed through them to open the gate, then realized I had no idea which key to use. My heart rate soared as I stood there fumbling with the key ring while more and more officers shouted at me to hurry up. "Somebody just take it!" I heard someone say.

I had just stuck the right key into the lock when the officers disappeared behind me. The alarm wasn't upstairs, they'd realized, but through the short passage, to V-gallery. I peered around the corner and saw them massing in two huge piles, evidently on top of inmates. Then *bang bang bang*—on the center gate again. This time, officers were on the other side of it, responding from upstairs. Among them was my classmate Don Allen. "Come on, Conover, let's go!" he yelled excitedly. I found the key again. I turned it. A second flood of officers pushed by me.

A few minutes later, everyone was back on his feet, including three mashed-looking inmates, who were handcuffed behind their backs. Each inmate had an officer holding the chain of his cuffs and marching him back to my gallery. First came a young black man with some swelling over his brow and a lot of blood flowing down the left side of his face. Next was a long-haired Latino with no shirt. Finally, there was another young black man, bleeding from gashes around the temple. They were to be locked in empty shower stalls on Q-gallery, and for that they needed keys.

Orrico appeared. "Where are they?" he demanded, holding out his open palm. I checked my belt. They weren't there! I looked in the center-gate keyhole—not there either. My heart sank. "What?" Orrico demanded loudly. "You don't have them?" This was the cardinal sin. Orrico called out to the milling officers, "Anybody got the center-gate key?" From the throng of officers came some questioning looks. Finally, Don Allen emerged holding—God bless him—my keys. Orrico snatched them away in disgust.

"You dropped them," Allen said quietly. I had no idea how it had happened. Allen quickly and kindly changed the subject. He had seen part of the incident from above, he said. Apparently, the attacker was a V-gallery porter who had been sweeping the flats with a push broom. When another inmate appeared, walking down the flats, the porter attacked him, first breaking the broom handle over his head and then trying to gouge his face with the splintered ends. How the third inmate got involved, Allen didn't know.

Allen had already seen a lot of action. "You heard about the guy who hung up yesterday?" he asked me. I'd heard it mentioned at lineup, a minor news item; for seasoned officers, this was a mundane occurrence. "I was there when they cut him down," Allen told me. "He'd tied his shoelaces up high on the bars, but I guess not high enough to kill him, so he's there all pale going *gaagaa-gaaghh*." Allen, a natural comedian, was so funny making this sound with his eyes bugging out that I laughed despite myself. "We cut him down, then we carried him to the infirmary. My God, this place is crazy." Allen, who had previously worked in juvenile detention for the Division for Youth, knew from crazy.

He left me to my thoughts, which mainly concerned my own adequacy. There would be no official repercussions—no sergeant had seen what happened, and Orrico hadn't turned me in. But the incident troubled me. Was I up to the job, to the frequent emergencies?

A couple of days before, while hustling up a staircase to back up an officer who was arguing heatedly with an inmate, I'd slipped and my baton had popped out of its ring, bouncing loudly down the metal stairs to the hands of officers below—a total embarrassment. And now this. During various crises in my prior life, I had responded well, keeping cool when a friend broke his leg skiing or when a girlfriend lacerated her leg in a fall from a motorcycle or when something in the oven caught fire. I was the guy who, when someone tripped over the cord, caught the falling lamp.

Somehow, that didn't seem to translate to prison work. I wondered about the reason. During those other incidents, my starting point was a calm, which was then interrupted. The starting point in prison, however, was stress, much of it born of hostility. Early indications were that I didn't handle it so well.

———

With a seasoned officer named Martinez, I spent the next day on guard at the foot of the tunnel leading up from Tappan. The gate was outdoors, but there was a little shack next to it where I sat with Martinez. He was short and seemed tough. Around us were the abandoned original stone cellblock, boarded up but looking solid enough to last till eternity; the A-block yard, with a weight-lifting area and handball courts visible to us behind high chain-link fences; and a garden, which stood between us and the Tappan dorms. Martinez told me to watch out for inmates who were carrying more than they should be. A lot of contraband was passed between Tappan and Sing Sing, and most of it probably came through here, he said. As we chatted, he told me about a softball game he'd witnessed in which inmates from the two opposing teams went after each other with the bats. "Compare your baton to a baseball bat, and you'll know why we didn't rush in there to break it up," he said.

We were relieved early and walked over to the chapel, where Martinez sat notarizing inmate legal documents for an hour. His brother, who looked just like him, was in charge of the chapel. Things were quiet, and Brown, a new officer from up north, offered to show me around the inmate-programs area in the basement. Reading a newspaper in the Hebrew Affairs Office was one of Sing Sing's more celebrated current inmates, Dr. Charles E. Friedgood, a Long Island surgeon serving twenty-five years to life for murdering his wife—the mother of their six children and a stroke victim—with a massive overdose of Demerol. A week after he had sworn on her death certificate that she died of another stroke, a relative alerted the police that Friedgood was about to leave the country for London. They stopped the plane on the runway at Kennedy Airport and removed the doctor, who was carrying some $650,000 in negotiable securities, and jewelry that had belonged to his wife. He was headed to Europe, police said, to join his Danish mistress, a former nurse, with whom he had had two children.

Friedgood liked Brown, and had apparently spoken to him before about Judaism. "Yes, Mr. Brown, we'll see about you!" he said, smiling, as we left. "Have to have you circumcised one of these days!"

Outside in the hall, I said, "Circumcised, huh?" But Brown seemed embarrassed, whether about the idea of circumcision, an inmate referring to his privates, or the suggestion that he had discussed conversion, I couldn't tell. He didn't say anything.

Martinez was the subject of our pre-shift OJT briefing two days later. Apparently, he had stopped an inmate passing through the gate and asked to see what he was carrying. When the man resisted, Martinez had wrestled him to the ground but was by no means in control of the situation. Two OJTs were among six officers standing nearby who, Martinez had complained to the union steward, did nothing to help him out. Finally, the officer driving a van that ferries disabled inmates and others around Sing Sing jumped out and helped subdue the man. Our training officer was angry, and during the regular lineup we were chastised by a lieutenant.

"You OJTs—and a lot of other officers—need to get more confrontational with these inmates," he said. "If it means you need to get bloody, then get bloody."

The next day, when I was working in A-block, a group of my fellow OJTs was ordered to pat-frisk inmates leaving the block. This was a common activity, which occasionally netted contraband such as marijuana, cash, or a weapon. Inmates had to place their hands up against the wall and spread their legs while we patted them down from collar to socks. Removing a hand from the wall before the frisk was complete constituted aggression at most other facilities, though at Sing Sing it usually prompted merely a warning. "You fucking OJTs are a pain in the ass," an inmate apparently told one of my classmates while up against the wall.

"What?" the officer said.

The inmate took one hand off the wall and began to repeat the phrase but was immediately jumped by the frisking officer and several others. When I heard about it, I was proud, because it showed we weren't wimps. The trainees who had failed to help Martinez probably just didn't realize what was going on or what was expected of them. Certainly none of us, I now felt, after the lieutenant's lecture, would hesitate to help a fellow officer in trouble.

———

I worked a day in Tappan with Officer St. George, who was waiting to be transferred up north. He was slow and flaccid, with the kind of world-weary negativism you might find in employees behind the counter of a fast-food restaurant at a highway rest stop. Though Tappan was a good post by most measures—relatively low-stress, relatively low-danger—he hated life at Sing Sing so much that at 3 P.M. he would hit the road to spend a single day off at home, which was six hours away, on the Canadian border. He'd take a nap the next day and then start driving again at midnight in order to make lineup at 6:45 A.M.

"What town?" I asked, and he shushed me—rightly: He didn't want inmates to know anything about him. This was the reason we didn't have our first name on our tags—only an initial—and didn't reveal other personal information. The reasons for this were best summed up by a story, possibly apocryphal, that I'd already heard at the Academy but which St. George recounted again: A CO pisses off an influential inmate in his block. Three days later, the prisoner hands him a manila envelope. Inside are photos of the CO's daughter at play on her swing set.

Most of the day, St. George sat at a desk facing the door to a stairwell and argued with inmates. He argued over whose turn it was to sweep and mop the floor. (The names were listed on a chart, so there didn't seem to be grounds for disagreement, but the inmates could see that St. George had an endless capacity to argue, and probably figured they should take advantage of it.) He argued over when the television could be on, when inmates could cook in the kitchen, and whether someone could leave a box of personal stuff in a common area. And, in the day's most interesting incident, he argued with an inmate who came in after working in the mess hall with his shirt stuffed with stolen food.

If the inmate hadn't been greedy, I thought, he might have gotten away with it. But the buttons on his shirtfront could barely contain everything he had taken: two loaves of bread, twenty-four frozen waffles, and a ten-pound bag of apples. St. George made him take it all out and put it on the desk. Leaving the mess hall with food was theft of state property, an offense right out of the book. But St. George couldn't decide what to do. Instead of writing the guy up, he proceeded to argue with him, and a dozen other inmates who gathered around, about the fate of the contraband. With the fervor of lawyers, the inmates tried to convince St. George that mess-hall workers were paid so little they *deserved* any extras they could find. ("That's a good point, you know," he told me.) One proposed that the officer simply divide the food evenly among the seventy-five inmates on the floor. "Nobody would tell," he asserted with a straight face. Yet another, tired of arguing, tried simply to intimidate St. George. "You think it's a good idea to piss off this many people with just you here, CO?" Not only did St. George fail to write this inmate up for making a threat; he later concurred with him, telling me, "You really could get a knife in your back at any time around here." Of course you could, I wanted to say, but that wasn't the point.

Still undecided, St. George called the mess-hall officer to fill him in. The man appeared to be about as concerned over the theft as St. George was. Certainly, he didn't care about reclaiming the food. "Just write him up for 116.10," I suggested. "That's what the training officer told us to do." St. George seemed alarmed. I think he had just remembered that the training officers debriefed the OJTs every day and reviewed the actions of regular officers. Suddenly he appeared to be afraid that I was going to tell our superiors about the incident. He placed all the food in a locker and told the inmates that he'd decide later what to do about it. When I got my lunch bag from the locker a while later, I saw that half the waffles were no longer there, and asked about it. "Aw, I gave them to him," St. George said. "But don't get me wrong about these guys," he added. "I wouldn't piss on 'em if they was on fire."

At 11 A.M., a blustery Neanderthal named Melman showed up on the floor to help with the count. He was annoyed because he had just come back from a drive home to discover that a pot of stew he'd put into the communal refrigerator at the Harlem Valley Psychiatric Center had been eaten. He had a bad temper, he admitted, telling how last week he had drawn his baton on an inmate in the tunnel leading up from Tappan. He couldn't wait to transfer, because, he said, "I don't want to work at a place where you tell them to step in, and they say, '*Fuck you*, CO!' " I found myself sympathetic to that idea, to the sentiment that officers deserved better than they got here.

Like our training officer, this man was fond of referring to inmates, out of their presence, as "crooks" and "mutts." The conversation left me thinking about the many reasons that an officer might come to regard inmates as savages. If a savage dissed you, what did it matter? And if a savage got hurt (particularly due to an error on your part), who cared?

———

On-the-job training lasted four weeks, and I'd had several difficult days on galleries by the time, on my second-to-last day, I was assigned to work B-block's V-gallery with Officer Smith. (V. SMITH, it said on his name tag—I didn't learn his first name until I noticed it on his time card weeks later; and even months later, when we had become friendly and were swapping shifts, I never used it. That's just how it was in prison.) The days on the galleries had been uniformly dispiriting. It was an impossible job, was the thing—it would probably take months for an officer to gain any real measure of control. Some of them were too lax, some too brittle, some careless, some too firm, some inconsistent. A gallery was such a huge challenge that it didn't take long to see the ways in which an individual officer didn't measure up. I wasn't sure it was even possible to be a truly competent gallery officer.

Smith had at least three advantages over the others. His gallery was half the size of most—only one side of the cellblock, down on the flats. He was in charge of about sixty inmates. Also, he had chosen the gallery. Although he had only ten months on the job, nobody more senior had wanted it, so it was his regular post. He knew the inmates, and the inmates knew him. Last, it seemed to me that Smith succeeded because he viewed the inmates as human beings and was able to maintain a sense of humor in the face of the stress of prison life—traits that are two sides of the same coin.

With his shaved head and muscular build and his habit of holding his arms crossed in front of his big chest, Smith looked like a black Mr. Clean. He was married and lived in Harlem. He moonlighted as a dry cleaner: He collected dirty uniforms in the parking lot at the end of the day and brought them back pressed, for which he charged $3.50 apiece. He'd graduated from a public high school in the city and worked summers as a lifeguard.

Smith was talkative and tried to answer all my questions. He gave me the keys to the south end of the gallery, and he took the north. Our first order of business was to take individual cells off nighttime deadlock for the morning chow run. (The cells would still be held shut by the brake.) I turned the big cell key in more than thirty locks and finished before Smith; he was stopping at several cells to say good morning, I noticed. During the next hour, we listened as gallery letters were called over B-block's public address system, which squawked so unintelligibly. Smith explained that on weekdays, the order was, roughly, top to bottom; Q and V galleries would go last.

Finally, V chow was called, and Smith and I each pulled a brake lever, releasing our respective sides. Hungry inmates emerged up and down the gallery, closing the cell gates behind them in a chorus of metal-on-metal thumps. Many inmates greeted Smith as they passed. This was so unknown, in my experience, that I wondered if he was too soft, if he gave them too much free rein. The real test, I knew, would come upon the inmates' return from mess hall, when they'd have to do something they were never keen on doing: lock back in.

While we waited, Smith talked. He himself had had a use-of-force on his second day of OJT, he told me, down in Tappan. It was much like the one I'd heard about in A-block a few days before: An inmate took one hand off the wall during a pat-frisk, was warned by Smith, and then did it again. Smith crunched him against a wall, and a shelf of the inmate's books came tumbling down in the process. His sergeant wasn't quite as celebratory as ours had been. "He wrote that I was 'excessively aggressive,' " Smith said, sounding a bit offended.

He told me about a few of his inmates. Two had murdered policemen, and one supposedly was set to inherit a chunk of the World Trade Center but had murdered his brother ("He's got clippings"). These guys were in for drugs; that guy did some kind of computer extortion. I loved hearing these histories, because officers were not supposed to know them. The idea was to protect inmate privacy and to ensure that officers treated all inmates the same—that we weren't unduly harsh to the cop killers or child molesters or anyone else whose crimes might strike a nerve. Of course, there were unofficial ways of finding out, and sometimes the inmates themselves would tell you (though you couldn't always believe them—the child molesters, for instance, always claimed they had done something else). But to my surprise, most officers seemed to have little interest in inmates' histories. Smith was different. V-gallery was, for much of every week, his neighborhood, and he wanted to know who lived there.

A gate swung open at the gallery's end, and the inmates began to return from breakfast. We took up positions among them, keeping our eyes open. Some went back into their cells promptly and voluntarily, but many talked, traded cigarettes, or even jogged away from their own cells to pass something to another inmate at the other end of the gallery. Smith waited a couple of minutes, then rapped his baton on a gate and shouted, "Lock in!" Half a minute went by, and he repeated the cry. By now, only a few inmates were out. Finally, Smith lifted up an arm and yelled "Lock in!" a final time before indicating that we should pull the brakes. The remaining inmates entered their cells, and the gallery was clear.

In four weeks, I'd never seen that, and I told Smith so.

"I thought it up in the car driving home one day," he said. "I call it Presto. I tell them, 'I'll give you three warnings, but then it's on you.' If anyone's still out, I write down his cell number, and"—Smith made a key-turning motion with his hand—"I lock 'em in." Because this was the first step in keeplocking, it always got an inmate's attention. Most knew that an officer wasn't likely to fill out a misbehavior report over slowness to lock in, but they could never be sure. Smith, in a gesture that I would later realize earned him stature among inmates and yet accomplished his goal of discipline, would let them back out for rec if he felt he'd made his point.

After lunch, true to his word, Smith locked the cell door of an inmate who was late stepping in—but the inmate was taking such a long time that Smith locked it before he even got there. The guy was stranded out on the gallery, alone. He came over to plead his case with Smith, who, arms crossed and with a small smile on his face, heard him out. "I'm not convinced," he finally announced. But an inmate down the gallery was waving his arm out between the bars. He wanted to plead his friend's case, explain the extenuating circumstances. "Sometimes I'll let 'em use a 'lawyer,' " Smith explained to me as we walked over there, "but if the lawyer doesn't change my mind either, sometimes I'll lock them both up." That might be an interesting reform for American courtrooms, I thought. As Smith stood listening to the lawyer's explanation, I heard him say, looking bemused, "If you're gonna give me bullshit, at least give me good bullshit." In the Case of the Lone Lingerer, the lawyer didn't convince him, either. But this time, Smith didn't lock him up.

Things hadn't always worked so smoothly for him, he told me. At the beginning, the inmates had been difficult, and some sergeants had given him a lot of "ass-chewings." But worst of all, surprisingly, had been other officers. One, named L'Esperance, who had worked V-gallery before Smith, disapproved of the way he ran it and, upon becoming gate officer stationed at the north end of Q-and-V, let everyone know about Smith's supposed short-comings—to the point of taking OJTs aside and telling them. Smith would leave at the end of the day with pain in his face and neck, which he only later realized was due to stress.

The model of an officer in total control was a lie, Smith said. "Did they tell you in the Academy about the guy who's in such tight control of his gallery that you can usually find him with his feet up on his desk?" he asked. "Well, that's a myth." Even the best officers, he said, had to scramble around to put out fires; it was just a question of degrees.

Officers critiqued the permissiveness they perceived in each other more than any other quality. In a profession that placed a high value on control, that made sense, but I also could see how, in a case like Smith's, permissiveness was a charge that a stupid and unimaginative CO might level against one who was effectively flexible. To me, Smith didn't seem permissive. But sometimes he achieved his ends by engaging in a dialogue instead of simply say-ing no. Later that day, for example, when the keeplocks were re-turning from "keeplock rec"—the hour they were allowed each day in a fenced-off section of the yard—and passed briefly through the south end of V-gallery, two of them wandered up our way. They were not supposed to. Together we approached one, who begged to be allowed to pass by us in order to go speak to a friend, but he was refused by Smith. "Come on, man!" the inmate im-plored. Some discussion ensued. Near the end, Smith said, "I know you got to do your twenty-four hours; just let me do my eight." The man said okay and left.

The other keeplock was standing at the bars of a friend's V-gallery cell, chatting away, when Smith approached. Not saying a word, Smith moved closer and closer, acting as a party to the conversation and entering the inmate's personal space until he stepped back in frustration. "They can't stand it when you do that," Smith said with a wink as the keeplock retreated.

Smith kept explaining things to me up till the very end of the shift. During the last hour—often a "freebie" period, when most inmates were out at rec or at their programs and their cells were deadlocked—most gallery officers found a chair and another CO to chat with. But Smith waved at me to join in a conversation he'd started with one of the few inmates left in his cell. He was Big D— Dominick Dwight, the computer embezzler. Smith had told him that I had some questions, and Big D, Smith said, might have some answers. I raised an eyebrow at what would have been considered heresy in the Academy—we're going to listen to an inmate's thoughts on how we should do our job?—but Smith said to go ahead.

This wasn't his first bid, Big D explained. (Inmates used the same slang word for *sentence* that we used for *elected post*.) He had also done time at Attica, Clinton, and Wende. Even though he knew it made inmates nervous when there was a corrections bus outside waiting to take them to one of those places, he said that he and most others preferred them to Sing Sing because they were more orderly. Sing Sing was chaotic, he thought, largely due to its proximity to New York City and the number of recent transfers from Rikers Island. "They come in from HDM [a unit of Rikers] and they're all full of it," he said. With time and distance, men cooled down.

If inmates preferred to live mainly by the rules, I asked, then why did they give new officers like me, who were trying to enforce them, such a hard time? Why didn't they appreciate a strict CO?

"Being a hard-ass just doesn't go with the system here," said Big D. "You're not going to change everything." And if you tried to make individuals do something they weren't used to doing, he said, they'd feel unfairly singled out.

"You'll get shitted down," said Big D. "And the smell of that shit will stay with you a long time."

On the other hand, he said, we couldn't let them run all over us. "You give an inmate an inch, and he's got a mile." Smith said the trick was to be firm without being nasty or egotistical. Otherwise, you'd have simmering rebellion.

I left work that day happier than I'd been since starting at the Academy. After weeks of hanging out with senior officers who seemed to bring little more to the job than machismo and forbearance, who would say things like "If they're happy, you're not doing your job," here was a guy—Smith—who saw gallery work as an art, something you could perform creatively. Interpersonal skills were a big part of it, though nothing like the IPC skills the Academy had described to us. Smith melded toughness with an attitude of respect for his inmates. In turn, he was respected back. What he seemed to understand was that at the root of the job was the inevitability of a kind of relationship between us and them— and that the officer played a larger role in determining the nature of that relationship.

At the Academy, this principle had never been mentioned. The job, we heard over and over, amounted to *care, custody,* and *control:* We gave the orders, in accordance with the rules, and inmates were to follow them. Simple as that.

In reality, of course, the jailer-inmate relationship was anything but simple. And traditions governing it, if in fact they existed, were vague. Take as simple a matter as saying "Good morning" to an inmate. One senior training officer, who happened to be black, had suggested that there was nothing wrong with such a greeting and that we ought to get in the habit of using it with our inmates. I had immediately flashed back to the Academy, where Officer McCorkle, describing his own gallery work, pointedly avoided saying "Please" or "Good morning" or any other pleasantry, and who, when greeted by his own inmates, informed them, "This 'Good morning' crap will cease!"

"They're only nice to you because you've got the keys," McCorkle had told us. Well, and they're only jerks to you because you've got the keys, I'd thought. They're the way they are and you're the way you are because you've got the keys. Now, where could you take it from there?

Many rap and hip-hop songs had lyrics referring to the "overseers," meaning any kind of cops. The term derived from the days of slavery, when plantation overseers made sure that the work was done and the discipline maintained. Lots of officers, I thought, liked to think of themselves as overseers, as enforcers. A training officer had mentioned that several of us had already been the target of inmate grievances, and one officer had even received two. Di Carlo smiled—he was the guy, I knew, and he was proud of it.

Getting grieved wasn't my goal. But neither was it to make the inmates like me. Another trainer, Luther, told us he once stepped up to a fellow officer whom he had seen give an inmate five and then walk down the hallway, arms over shoulders, with him.

"Hey, man, it's a black thing," the officer had told Luther.

"Bullshit," Luther had replied. Referring to each side's state-supplied clothing, he told us, "It's a gray thing and a green thing, and nothing more complicated than that."

Somewhere between those poles lay the way I wanted to be.

———

Two days after my time with Smith was Conversion Day, when we became regular officers. We had to don our dress-blue uniforms again for the occasion. I talked with Arno outside the QWL building. He'd finally abandoned his efforts to wear long hair and had cut it all off—he was clean-shaven, right down to his skull. He looked good but tired: He'd worked the three-to-eleven shift the night before and had only had a few hours' sleep. But, he said, it had been an interesting shift. He'd been working the first floor of the Hospital Building when an officer in B-block was struck on the head with a broom handle by an inmate. Officers had brought the prisoner down to the Hospital Building, which also housed the disciplinary offices and the watch commander's office, where most of the white-shirts hung out. There, from a room near the ER, Arno said, he and many others, including inmate porters, had heard a white-shirt shout, "You think it's *funny* to hurt an officer?" and the guy responded with prolonged cries of pain. Arno said this went on for about twenty minutes. A month earlier, I would have reacted negatively to a story like that. But now, seeing how outnumbered officers were and feeling more like prey than predator, I found in the tale a grain of comfort.

The superintendent was coming down to speak with us, but first they wanted to show us a video the Department had made of our training class in Albany. It all seemed so long ago, and so transparent now too, as I watched us getting yelled at in the Academy halls and on the floor of the gym—the breaking us down in order to build us back up. And though military boot camp had been the model, it was arresting this time around to see how much it really was like prison.

There we were, in only a slightly more upscale way, doing all the things that inmates had to do: receiving our uniform allowance, waiting in endless lines for chow, getting counted, wearing numbers on our T-shirts during rec, getting sprayed in the face with chemical agents, enduring a nearly single-sex environment and constant supervision, and living by a zillion mindless rules. There was DiPaola marching in the funny mincing step we learned just for graduation—I remembered the day we discovered the note from Sergeant Bloom, penalizing our room for a tuft of fuzz left at the bottom of the trash can. "If he comes by here now," Deep suggested, "let's shit him down."

Now, however, we were at the ceremonial crossroads between our infantilization and our investiture with life-and-death powers. Soon we'd be holding the keys. Lieutenant Wilkin conducted a brainstorming session with us in which he wrote on a big art pad our suggestions for improving CO training. To my surprise, maybe a third of my classmates thought the training should be longer (training for the state police lasted something like five months, we learned). No doubt the prospect of real work around the corner— many, like me, had to return at 6:45 A.M. Sunday morning—led to some sentimentalizing of our Academy days. Others suggested that a longer Academy would not be necessary if short classes weren't booked into long class periods, leaving us to practice pool shots in the lounge for a couple of hours each day.

Our trainers got in the last word, telling the older women in our class that they'd better get used to being called Grandma and the black officers that they should become accustomed to hearing "You been workin' in the white man's house; you a house nigger."

"Good luck" or "Godspeed" were what you might expect to hear at the conclusion of on-the-job training for some other kind of work. Here, our bon voyage had a definite CO flavor:

"You're the zookeeper now," said Officer Luther. "Go run the zoo."

CHAPTER 4

NEWJACK

I still had his collar in my left grip. I pulled his head toward me and swung. No peace officer with any sense, even in dire circumstances, punches where it will leave marks. My right connected above his ear and back from the face.
—J. Michael Yates, *Line Screw,* 1993

The [new] pig was standing in the run with another pig in the midst of teeming inmates going to and fro. Striker pulled up beside the pig and hung about ten inches of that knife into his belly and gutted him. The other pig spun around to face Striker and was hit in the stomach several times as he ran backward to get away. Then Striker turned back to the other pig and stabbed him again with long deep thrusts in the chest area.
—Jack Henry Abbott, *In the Belly of the Beast,* 1981

Lo, the poor guard! In his mind's eye he can see us as we were in the free world; with money, ravishing women, all the sensual delights which must be forever unattainable to him. We have had this. He has never had it, never will have it. Therefore, enviously, gloatingly, he exacts vengeance upon us for the unalterable deficiencies in his own life.
—Victor F. Nelson, *Prison Days and Nights,* 1932

Sing Sing was a world of adrenaline and aggression to us new officers. It was an experience of living with fear—fear of inmates, as individuals and as a mob, and fear of our own capacity to fuck up. We were sandwiched between two groups: Make a mistake around the white-shirts and you would get in trouble; make a mistake around the inmates and you might get hurt.

At the Academy, prison had been likened to a village—a self-contained world with its own school, workshops, hospital, and so forth. But what they didn't say was that prison was also a micro-cosm of a totalitarian society, a nearly pure example of the police state. The military provided the model for the chain of command; enlisted men and women were marshaled daily by their superior officers into a battle of wills with the mass of angry and resentful prisoners. We who were in uniform controlled nearly every aspect of their lives. And prison, more than any place I'd ever been, was about rules.

The Academy had taught us about rules the way a fundamen-talist teaches the Bible in church, taking literally the injunctions about moneylenders and Armageddon and wives who existed to serve husbands. And then the congregation went out into the world, where most Christians were flexible about such strictures but still considered themselves devout, and justifiably so. A good cop, after all, wasn't the one who ticketed you for doing thirty-three miles an hour in a thirty-mile-an-hour zone. A good cop en-forced selectively, using his judgment.

I was intrigued by a Latino officer I'd seen in the lineup room. He was posted to a gallery in A-block. Like the rest of us, he kept his little yellow *Standards of Inmate Behavior, All Institutions* booklet in his breast pocket, but unlike us, he had written FUCK NO in block letters along the top edge of the booklet—the part that peeked out of the pocket. It was his personal message to inmates and, actually, a pretty good summary of the booklet itself. It made me think he was probably a good officer, funny but tough, an en-forcer of the rules. Later, a classmate who would spend a week working with that officer told me how every morning an inmate would fix him his coffee, passing the mug out through the bars of his cell. That made me reconsider. There was no rule against it, but what favors was the officer passing back in the inmate's direction? How could you ever trust an inmate enough to drink his coffee?

This fuzziness surrounding the rules was a strange counterpoint to the solidity of Sing Sing's walls, the seeming immutability of the prison. During that long summer, from mid-May to late Septem-ber, I thought about it as I walked the tunnels and corridors from the lineup room to various buildings up the hill. My classmates and I had been placed in the resource pool and worked all over the prison. Eyes cast downward toward the floor, I'd watch the yellow traffic lines painted down the middle of most hallways to keep op-posing traffic on its proper side. There were broad perpendicular lines at gates, where inmates were supposed to stop and wait for permission to proceed. Of course, they hardly ever did. Had they ever? The lines struck me as wistful suggestions of a stricter time, of rules now observed in the breach, a memory fading like the strict lessons of the Academy.

A-BLOCK

Many times during those first months I was assigned to A-block. The mammoth cellblock required more officers to run it than any other building—around thirty-five during the day shift—but the senior officers there seemed particularly unfriendly to new officers, offering little encouragement and lots of criticism. The best way to fend off their comments, I decided, would be to try and enforce the rules as strictly as I could.

But, assigned to one of the vast eighty-eight-cell galleries for the first time, I found it hard to know where to begin. With the sheets hanging from the bars like curtains? The clothes drying on the handrails? The music blaring from several cells? I decided to start with the annoyance closest at hand: an inmate's illegal radio antenna.

Inmates were allowed to have music. Each cell had two jacks in the wall for the headphones its occupant was issued upon arrival. Through one jack was transmitted a Spanish-language radio station; through the other, a rhythm-and-blues station, except during sporting events, when the games were transmitted instead. Inmates could have their own radios, too, but the big steel cellblock made reception very difficult. Telescoping antennas were forbidden, because they might be turned into "zip guns." By inserting a bullet into the base of an extended antenna and then quickly compressing it, an inmate could fire the inaccurate but still potentially deadly gun. The approved wire dipole antennas were supposed to be placed within a two-by-four-foot area on the wall—where, apparently, they did no good at all.

To improve their chances of tuning in to a good station, inmates draped wires over their bars and across the gallery floor. Some even tied objects to the end of a bare strand of copper wire and flung it toward the outside wall, hoping that it would snag on a window and that they would win the reception jackpot. (When you looked up from the flats on a sunny day, you could sometimes see ten or twenty thin wires spanning the space between the gallery and the exterior wall, like the glimmering work of giant spiders.)

Antennas strewn across the gallery floor could cause someone to trip, and if they seemed likely to do so, I'd have the inmates pull them in. But the inmate in question on my first day as a regular officer in A-block—a short, white-haired man in his sixties—had gotten his off the floor by threading wire through a cardboard tube, the kind you find inside wrapping paper. One end of the tube was wedged between his bars at stomach level, and the other protruded halfway into the narrow gallery space between cell bars and fence, like a miniature bazooka.

"You're gonna have to take this down," I advised him the first time I brushed against it.

"Why's that?"

"Because it's in my space."

"But I can't hear if it's in my cell."

"Sorry. Try stringing it up higher on your bars."

"Sorry? You ain't sorry. Why say you sorry if you ain't sorry? And where'd you get to be an authority on antennas? They teach you that in the Academy?"

"Look, you know the rule. No antenna at all outside the cell. I could just take it if I wanted. I'm not taking it. I'm just telling you to bring it in."

"You didn't tell that guy down there to bring his in, did you? The white guy?"

I looked in the direction he indicated. There were no other antennas in tubes, and I said so.

"You're just picking on the black man, aren't you? Well, have a good time at your Klan meeting tonight," he spat out. "Have a pleasant afternoon. You've ruined mine."

All this over an antenna. Or, rather, all brought into focus by an antenna. In prison, unlike in the outside world, power and authority were at stake in nearly every transaction.

The high stakes behind petty conflict became clear for me on the night during my first month when Colton and I were assigned to work M-Rec, one of the kinds of recreation that Sing Sing relied upon heavily in order to give the prisoners something to do. After dinner, instead of the gym or the yard, inmates could gather at the gray-metal picnic-style tables bolted to the floor along M-gallery, on the flats, to play cards or chess or dominoes, or watch the television sets mounted high on the walls.

"The rule is that they can't be leaning against the bars of the cells," the regular officer said to us, "and the cell gates are supposed to be closed." You could tell from his "supposed" that this rule was not strictly enforced. Still, Colton, a lieutenant's son, seemed strangely zealous. I think he couldn't stand the laxity around us. As we walked along the dimly lit gallery, he challenged one inmate after another. I decided that to keep his respect, I had better do the same. At varying volumes, they objected. "What is this, newjack rec?" asked one older man in a kufi who was sitting right outside his own open cell. I gestured toward the door. He told me that he was *always* allowed to leave the cell door open during M-Rec. Well, not tonight, I said. He yelled and screamed. I closed the gate. He walked right up to me, stood less than a foot from my face, and, radiating fury, said, "You're going to learn, CO, that some things they taught you in the Academy can get you killed."

I would hear inmates utter these exact words several times more in the upcoming months at Sing Sing, a threat disguised as advice. (The phrasing had the advantage of ambiguity, and thus could steer the speaker clear of rule 102.10: "Inmates shall not, under any circumstances, make any threat.") But I hadn't heard those words spoken to me before, and that, in combination with the man's standing so close, set my heart racing. I tried staring back at him as hard as he was staring at me, and didn't move until he had stepped back first.

Some of the conflict we saw, of course, wasn't only a fixed feature of prison life; it had roots in Sing Sing's frequent changes of officers. New officers, as we'd already learned, irritated inmates in much the same way that substitute teachers irritate schoolchildren. To try to lessen these effects, the chart office would often "pencil in" a resource officer to the post of a senior officer who was sick or on vacation. That way, there wouldn't be a different substitute every day.

One day in A-block, however, I was assigned to run the gallery temporarily assigned to one of my classmates, Michaels, whom I knew to be particularly lax. It was Michaels's day off, which made me the substitute for a substitute. I knew before I even arrived that things would be chaotic.

My first problem came at count time, 11 A.M. Inmates generally began to return to their cells from programs and rec at around 10:40 or 10:45 A.M. The officers would encourage them to move promptly to their cells. By 11, anyone not in his cell and ready to be counted was technically guilty of delaying the count and could be issued a misbehavior report. Few galleries, therefore, had inmates at large after 11 A.M.

But on this day, Michaels's gallery had a dozen still out. Michaels had grown up in Brooklyn and, more than most officers from the city, considered the inmates to be basically decent guys, his "homies." He wanted them to like him. Once penciled in to this post, he had quickly learned all their names. I had helped him at count time once before, and when I complained about two inmates who were slow to lock in, Michaels replied that they were good guys. Though I had seen sergeants chew him out for looseness, he had told me privately that the sergeants could "suck my dick in Macy's window" for all he cared.

I liked Michaels for acknowledging the inmates' humanity. He had told me how much he hated A-block's usual OIC, a big, pugnacious slob I'll call Rufino, who told jokes such as "How do you know when an inmate is lying? When you see him open his mouth." But I didn't appreciate Michaels's legacy of chaos that morning.

A group of three or four senior officers strolled by, to my relief—I was sure they'd been sent to help me usher in the stragglers. But they had no such plan. A couple of them glanced disapprovingly at their watches and then at me. They didn't have to help, so they weren't going to. Thanks, guys, I muttered to myself.

About an hour later, a couple of keeplocks returned from disciplinary hearings. The block's keeplock officer, instead of borrowing my keys and ushering the inmates to their cells, called, "They're back," when he came through the gate and then disappeared. One of the keeplocks returned to his cell without trouble, but the second had other plans. It was Tuesday, he told me, and Michaels always let him take a shower on Tuesdays.

"Keeplock showers are Mondays, Wednesdays, and Fridays," I said. "And Michaels isn't here today."

"C'mon, CO, don't play tough. I'll be out in a second."

"No," I said. He acted as though he hadn't heard, grabbed a towel from his cell, and strode quickly down the gallery to the shower stall. I wasn't overly concerned: I always kept the showers locked, just in case something like this came up, and felt confident that once I reminded him he would miss keeplock rec today if he didn't go back, he'd turn around. Then I remembered. On this gallery, the lock mechanism was missing from the shower cell door. The shower was always open. Sing Sing. The inmate was a good foot taller than me and well muscled. I yelled through the bars into the shower that he'd lost his rec. He said, "Fuck rec." I put the incident into the logbook, then wrote up a Misbehavior Report and had his copy waiting in the cell when he got back. He shrugged it off.

"I don't give a fuck, CO," he explained. "I got thirty years to life, right? And I got two years' keeplock. Plus today, I got another three months. When they see this lame-ass ticket, they're gonna tell you to shove it up your ass."

The frustration was, he was probably right. Of all the inmates on a gallery, keeplocks were the hardest to deal with. There were no carrots left to tempt them with, and few sticks—especially for the long-termers. And now it was time for keeplock rec. I tried to match faces with cells as they headed out to the yard on that hot June day—it could help me when it came time to lock them back in. I was in the middle of letting them out when the keeplock officer reappeared. He gestured in the direction I was walking.

"Forty-three cell?" he said. "Hawkins? No rec today."

"No rec for forty-three? Why's that?"

"He doesn't get it today," he said, and disappeared.

I knew there could be several reasons for the inmate not receiving rec. He might have committed an infraction within the past twenty-four hours. Or he might have a deprivation order pending against him; in cases of outrageous misbehavior, a keeplock who was a "threat to security" could have his rec taken away for a day by a sergeant. Or—what I worried about in this situation—he might have pissed off the officer but *not* had a deprivation order pending. In that case, another officer was asking me to burn the keeplock's rec as an act of solidarity. I hoped it wasn't the last possibility and went on down the gallery, passing up forty-three cell.

The inmate called out to me shortly after I went by.

"Hey, CO! Aren't you going to open my cell?" I ignored him until I was on my way back. He stood up from his bed as I approached.

"Open my cell, CO! I'm going outside."

"Not today," I said.

"What? Why not today?"

"No rec today."

"Why not?"

"That's what they told me."

"Who told you that?"

I didn't answer him, but I immediately felt I'd done something wrong. I returned to the office and tried to get the keeplock officer on the phone. I was going to insist on knowing his reason. What was up with this guy? The phone rang and rang. I called the office of the OIC and asked for him. He was outside now; couldn't be reached, Rufino said. But Rufino was always unhelpful. I called the yard. He'd had to go somewhere, wasn't there now. Shit, I thought.

Meanwhile, three keeplocks on their way out to the yard stopped separately to advise me that "forty-three cell needs to come out, CO." I looked down the gallery. He was waving his arm madly through the bars, trying to get my attention. I walked down to talk to him.

"You're not letting me out?"

I shook my head.

"Who said so?" He was angry now.

"I don't know his name," I lied.

"Well, what did he look like?" I declined to help out. "Then what's your name? I'm writing up a grievance." I told him my name. When I passed by the cell again an hour later, he had a page-long letter written out.

Instead of the classic newjack mistake of enforcing a rule that nobody really cared about, I had just enforced a rule that wasn't a rule, for my "brother in gray." I knew that many police admired that kind of thing. But it made me feel crummy. And with the grievance coming, I was going to have to answer for it.

I thought about how the senior officers hadn't helped me during the count, how the keeplock officer hadn't helped me when the two inmates came back, and how the same keeplock officer hadn't explained to me the deal with forty-three, even when I asked. More than once at the Academy, I'd heard the abbreviation CYA—cover your ass. I knew how to do it, though I also knew there could be consequences. In the logbook, I made note of the time and wrote, "No rec for K/L Hawkins, per CO X"—the keeplock officer. And then I waited.

The chicken came home to roost about a month later. I knew it when I arrived at work and approached the time clock. Officer X, instead of ignoring me as usual, gave me a cold, hard stare. His partner, Officer Y, stopped me and asked if I was Conover. Yes, I said, and he gave me the same stare and walked away. It was because inmate Hawkins in cell 43 had slugged Officer Y the day before (as I'd since learned) that Officer X had wanted to send him a message that day.

A sergeant who was unaware of all of this approached me with a copy of the inmate's grievance letter in the mess hall at lunchtime that same day. "Do you remember this incident?" he asked. I said yes. "You'll just need to respond with a To/From," he said, using department slang for a memo. "Do you remember why you didn't let him out? Probably forgot, right?"

"Well, no, the keeplock officer told me not to."

The sergeant wrinkled his brow. "Well, probably best just to say you forgot," he said cheerily, and turned away.

"Sarge," I said. "It's in the logbook. I wrote in the logbook that he told me."

"You're kidding," he said. "Why'd you do that?"

I shrugged. "I was new."

"I'll get back to you," he said.

I wrote the memo the sergeant had asked for, told the truth, and felt conflicted. Days went by. Another sergeant called me in and told to me to see a lieutenant in the Administration Building. My memo was on the lieutenant's desk, and he was poring over it. "So you say you logged this part about Officer X, right?" he asked. I nodded, expecting to receive a stern, quiet lecture on how not to fuck my fellow officer. But the lieutenant just nodded, cogitated a bit, and then picked up the phone.

I heard him greet a sergeant in A-block. "So Officer X remembers saying that to Conover now, is that right? And he's going to write a new To/From? And you'll take care of the deprivation order? Okay, fine." And hung up.

He passed my memo to me over the desk. "Just write this up again, but leave out the name of Officer X," he told me.

"And then we're set?"

"All taken care of."

I was relieved. Officer X was off the hook, which meant that maybe he wouldn't hate me more than he already did. Apparently, a deprivation order would be backdated to cover *his* ass. And I had learned an important lesson: If you were going to survive in jail, the goody-goody stuff had to go. Any day in there, I might find myself in a situation where I'd need Officer X to watch my back, to pry a homicidal inmate off of me, at his peril. The logic of the gray wall of silence was instantly clear, as clear as the glare of hate that Officer X had sent my way when he heard what I'd done.

———

The single most interesting word, when it came to the bending and ignoring of rules, was *contraband*. To judge by the long list of what constituted contraband, its meaning was clear. In practice, however, contraband was anything but.

The first strange thing about contraband was that its most obvious forms—weapons, drugs, and alcohol—could all be found fairly readily inside prison. Some of the drugs probably slipped in through the Visit Room, but most, it seemed, were helped into prison by officers who were paid off. The Department had a special unit, the Inspector General's Office, which followed up on snitches' tips and tried to catch officers in the act; the union rep had even warned us about the "IG" at the Academy. A couple of times a year, I would come to find, a Sing Sing officer was hauled off in handcuffs by the state police.

But even in its lesser forms, contraband had many interesting subtleties. As officers, we were not allowed to bring through the front gate glass containers, chewing gum, pocket knives with blades longer than two inches, newspapers, magazines, beepers, cell phones, or, obviously, our own pistols or other weapons. A glass container, such as a bottle of juice, might be salvaged from the trash by an inmate and turned into shards for weapons. The chewing gum could be stuffed into a lock hole to jam the mechanism. The beepers, newspapers, and magazines were distractions—we weren't supposed to be occupied with any of that while on the job. Nor could we make or receive phone calls, for the same reason. Apart from inmates smoking in their cells, smoking was generally forbidden indoors.

And yet plenty of officers smoked indoors. Many chewed gum. The trash cans of wall towers were stuffed with newspapers and magazines.

A much longer list of contraband items applied to inmates. As at Coxsackie, they couldn't possess clothing in any of the colors reserved for officers: gray, black, blue, and orange. They couldn't possess cash, cassette players with a record function, toiletries containing alcohol, sneakers worth more than fifty dollars, or more than fourteen newspapers. The list was very long—so long, in fact, that the authors of *Standards of Inmate Behavior* found it easier to define what *was* permitted than what wasn't. Contraband was simply "any article that is not authorized by the Superintendent or [his] designee."

You looked for contraband during pat-frisks of inmates and during random cell searches. One day in A-block, I found my first example: an electric heating element, maybe eight inches wide, such as you'd find on the surface of a kitchen range. Wires were connected to the ends of the coil, and a plug was connected to the wires. The inmate, I knew, could plug it into the outlet in his cell, place a pan on it, and do some home cooking. I supposed it was contraband because of the ease with which it could start a fire, trip the cell's circuit breaker, burn the inmate, or burn someone the inmate didn't like. And it must have been stolen from a stove somewhere inside the prison.

I was proud of my discovery and asked a senior officer on the gallery how to dispose of it and what infraction number to place on the Misbehavior Report.

"Where'd you find this?" he asked.

"Cell K-twelve, in a box behind the locker," I said.

"K-twelve—yeah, he's a cooker," the officer said. "Cooks every night. Can't stand mess-hall food. I don't blame him."

"Yeah? So what's the rule number?"

The other officer said he didn't know, so I made some phone calls, figured it out, and did the paperwork during lunch. While I was at it, an inmate porter stopped by and pleaded on behalf of the cooker. "He's a good guy, CO. He needs it." A few minutes later, to my amazement, a mess-hall officer called.

"You the guy who found that heating element?" he asked.

"Yeah. Why?"

"What are you going to do with it?"

"Turn it in."

"Oh really?"

"Yeah. Why?"

There was a long pause. "Oh, nothing." He hung up.

I finished my Misbehavior Report and stepped out of the office to let inmates back into their cells from chow. When I returned to the office, the coil, which I had placed on the desk, was gone.

"Where'd it go?" I asked the senior officer. "Did you move it?"

"What—oh, that heating thing?" he said offhandedly. "I gave it back to him."

"Gave it back? Why'd you do that? I just wrote up a report."

"Look, he's a good guy. Never gives any trouble. I think he's vegetarian. He really can't eat that stuff they serve down there. Why don't you go talk to him?" He made for the door.

I stared at him skeptically. He shrugged and was gone.

Unsure exactly why I did so, I went to talk to the inmate. He did seem like a nice guy, and thanked me profusely for not turning him in. Oh what the hell, I thought.

Not long afterward, I found another heating coil during a cell search in B-block. This time my sergeant, Murphy, saw it in my hands and insisted I turn it in. The paperwork that Murphy told me to fill out was even more elaborate than what I had imagined. Specifically, he said, I'd need to make an entry in the B-block cell-search logbook; to write a contraband receipt for the inmate, with copy stapled to a misbehavior report, to be signed by a supervisor in the Watch Commander's Office, where I would submit all the paperwork and get the key to the contraband locker in the hospital basement, where I would also sign the logbook. Oh, and on the way to the Watch Commander's Office, I should stop and pick up an evidence bag from the disciplinary office, in which to place the burner.

It was the end of my day. I knew that many officers, rather than plow through all this when their shift was over, would just drop the contraband in a trash can by the front gate and be done with it. Sergeant Murphy would never follow up. But some contrarian impulse drove me on. I finally made it to the Watch Commander's Office and waited twenty minutes for my turn with the lieutenant. He looked at the heating element, then at my paperwork.

"Do you think this is a good use of the Adjustment Committee's time?" he asked.

I shrugged and said I supposed it was. My sergeant must have thought so when he told me to write all this up, I added. The lieutenant blathered on about major versus minor offenses, the need to make judgments, and so on, apparently expecting me to say, "Oh, I get it!" and withdraw from his office. But it had been a lot of work. I had stayed late. I was pissed off about this and other things. I didn't move.

"Okay," the lieutenant finally said. "Leave it with me." I stood to leave, wondering how to take this. The lieutenant hadn't signed a thing. A CO at a desk near the lieutenant's translated for me as I walked out. "If in doubt, throw it out!" he said with a big smile. And that was that.

———

No sooner would an officer become savvy as to which rules were commonly ignored, however, than somebody in a white shirt would appear to shake up his whole understanding of accepted practice. That person, for me and many other new officers, was Sergeant Wickersham. While everyone knows that prison can warp or distort the personalities of prisoners, few stop to consider how it can do the same to those who work inside. The most extreme example of this at Sing Sing was Wickersham, who seemed to be on duty every time I was assigned to A-block.

Wickersham, whose full head of silver hair, mustache, and chiseled good looks made him resemble a misplaced Marlboro man, was a rara avis even by Sing Sing standards. For one thing, he was the only white sergeant of the dozen or so there who wasn't waiting to transfer somewhere else. Wickersham had seniority, but Sing Sing was home. Nor was he using his seniority to get a desk job, as were most of Sing Sing's old-timer sergeants, the majority of whom were black. Sergeant Wickersham chose to work A-block, a high-stress post, because he wanted to, because he seemed to feel at home there.

Wickersham's sworn mission, as any new officer knew, was to give new officers a hard time—to ride them, chew them out, dress them down. Most sergeants were more like support personnel, there to set you straight when you erred, but mostly to help when you needed a hand. Not Wickersham. His goal was to put the fear of God into new guys. But not in the manner of a drill sergeant. Wickersham wouldn't raise his voice. He would not smile, would not move his eyebrows. His voice had little inflection, and he always seemed to speak through clenched teeth. This utter self-discipline reminded me of the actor Clint Eastwood playing an unsmiling renegade cop. But behind Eastwood's super-machismo, redeeming it, was always a flicker of dark humor. No such humor appeared to reside in Wickersham. The word among new officers was: Watch out for this guy.

But watching out for Wickersham wasn't easy, because he liked to operate with stealth. He had a public mode, and you'd see him early in the shift or at lunch, with a coffee mug in his hand (he'd clip it to his belt when finished) and a cigarette hanging from his mouth, talking to other sergeants or to a coterie of more senior officers he favored. But once the blocks got busy and officers were rushing from cell to phone to center gate, Wickersham would put down his coffee, pick up the radio, and head out on a solitary patrol, creeping up and down the empty south staircase, peeking around corners to catch us in slipups, blatant or imagined.

My first encounter with Wickersham took place on my first day as a regular officer. I was working on A-block's J-gallery, one floor up from the flats. Someone had asked me to let a keeplock out of his cell, since he had an appointment outside the block. I was, of course, in the midst of doing ten other things, and the keeplock, when I walked down the gallery to get him, was in his boxer shorts and needed a few minutes to get ready. Five minutes later, when I returned to his cell, he still wasn't ready. As I stood outside and waited, I could hear my phone ringing. Slowly, the keeplock emerged. But then, despite my urgings, he dragged his feet; he had things to discuss with the inmate in the cell next to his, and the one next to that. Official procedure was to escort a keeplock down a gallery by walking behind him, but with this guy that was going to take an hour. Meanwhile, my phone rang on. I knew I would see the inmate when he got to the center gate, so I hurried ahead to answer it.

Blocking my way suddenly was Sergeant Wickersham. He hadn't been there a few seconds before. I nodded in recognition, but he didn't nod back. "Why is that inmate out?" he asked in his Darth Vader voice. It looked painful for him to speak.

"Keeplock officer asked for him," I said.

"Why," continued Wickersham, drawing out the word sarcastically, "are you in front of him?"

He'd caught me cutting a corner. Months later, a seasoned officer would advise me, "Always have an answer in corrections. Always have an answer, and you'll do just fine." That day I had an answer of sorts—my phone was ringing, I was in a hurry—but I doubted it would fly with Wickersham. I had no problem with admitting mistakes, however, and thought the sergeant might be pleasantly surprised by candor.

"Guess I messed up," I said. "Sorry. It won't happen again."

"Sorry?" he said. His expression soured ever so slightly, as though he'd just swallowed some grounds with his already-bitter cup of coffee. His anger turned into disgust. He'd wanted a fight and I'd just rolled over. Wickersham now looked at me as though I were beneath contempt. "Huh," he said. And walked away.

Another time, I was taking the count on M-gallery when Wickersham again appeared out of nowhere.

"You afraid you're gonna lose your keys?" he asked.

I had no idea what he was talking about. "What do you mean?"

"You're walking with your *hand* against them," he observed acidly. "Are you afraid somebody's gonna take 'em?"

I looked down at the dozen or so keys hanging near my hip. Sometimes I felt like a horse with sleigh bells when I walked with those things, and when I had enough time to think about it, and didn't want to advertise my approach to inmates who might be doing something illicit in their cells, I would put my hand against the keys to quiet them.

"What's wrong with that?" I asked. This offense, I felt sure, was entirely of his own invention.

"Don't do it."

"Don't? Why not?"

Wickersham walked away.

Another day, I was working upstairs with an older officer named Robinson. Thirty or forty keeplocks were due back from rec, and we had just heard an announcement to clear the galleries of all other inmates in anticipation of this return. As I was clearing O-gallery, a friendly inmate gave me a heads-up: Wickersham was lurking near the end gate. I finished and walked over to K-gallery to see how Robinson was doing. A few inmates were still out but, much more ominous, Wickersham was now at Robinson's end gate, talking into his radio. I had an idea what was about to happen, and I was right. A few seconds later an announcement boomed over A-block's PA system: "Officer on K-gallery, clear your gallery!" chided Rufino. "Keeplocks are on their way! Repeat, clear your gallery!" Wickersham, instead of speaking to Robinson directly, had radioed down to the Officer in Charge. Now everyone in the block knew there was some problem with the officer running K-gallery.

I started helping out the surprised Robinson, but then he caught a glimpse of Wickersham and figured out what had happened. Furious, he stormed down to the gate to confront the sergeant. With only some wire mesh between the two men, their shouting battle raged for five minutes. Robinson returned, sputtering, "I'm forty-four years old, and I will not be treated like a child. I hate that

fucking asshole!" By mutual agreement, Robinson joined the
ranks of officers embargoed from A-block because they couldn't
deal with the sergeant. I envied those officers, but I wasn't the
shouting-match type.

The humiliation tactic was one of Wickersham's favorites, and I
saw him use it again not long after the incident with Robinson. An
OJT named Swiatowy was doing a pat-frisk. He had the inmate
against the wall and properly told him to take everything out of his
pockets and hand it over. During the transfer, the inmate's comb
fell to the floor. Sounding insolent, the inmate told Swiatowy that
he'd better pick it up. Swiatowy was declining to do so when
Wickersham stepped up.

"Do you have a problem with picking this inmate's comb off the
floor?" he asked. Swiatowy just stared at him. ("I think I've still
got the scar tissue on my tongue," he told me later.) Swiatowy said
he would do it, but in the event, the inmate did. Wickersham may
have had a procedural point to make, but humiliating the officer
seemed to be a larger one.

"You can't act afraid of him, though," Miller counseled me one
day in the lineup room. Miller was a recruit from my class who'd
been spending a lot of time in A-block. He told me that it was all
a test, that Wickersham would leave alone those officers who
stood up to him. They'd earn his respect. On my next run-in, I decided, I'd try it.

I didn't have to wait long. It was at the end of a difficult day—
in B-block, actually—during which I'd had trouble getting some of
my porters to follow orders. I was back on R-and-W gallery, which
I had learned was known as a porter gallery, because so many of
its inmates worked somewhere in the prison as porters. The problem with this situation for the gallery officer was that porters, in
recognition of their labor (which, many days, amounted to little),
were usually offered showers in the afternoon, after other inmates
left the gallery for recreation. But some officers would give porters
their showers early, and it was a constant struggle, if you were trying to follow the rules, to keep the shower-eager porters inside
their cells and off the gallery until you had decided showers could
begin.

The largest contingent consisted of gym porters, and because
many were longtime inmates and there was power in numbers,
they were especially demanding. On this day it was a gym porter

who appeared outside the locked shower stall, wearing only a bathrobe and slippers, half an hour too soon.

"No showers till rec," I told him. "You gotta wait in your cell."

"I always get a shower now, CO."

"Not today," I said. "Return to your cell. No porter showers till rec."

Mama Cradle had started "dropping the programs"—calling out inmate destinations, such as law library and commissary, waiting for the inmates to assemble near the front gate and then sending them out with an escort—so I was very busy pulling brakes. The inmate wouldn't return to his cell. I ordered him in again. He was still there the next time I walked by, so I gave him a "direct order," preliminary to issuing a Misbehavior Report, and a moment later, seeing that he was still out, I deadlocked his cell. This way, I figured, he'd be unable to leave the gallery, since he couldn't reach his clothes, and I could deal with him when I had more time.

Then an inmate on my gallery got called on a visit, and he was entitled to a shower. I opened up a shower stall for him. My renegade porter lingered outside it. "You'd better not go in there when he's done," I warned him. But when I next saw him, that's where he was, soaping himself. (Most shower stalls had no curtains.) I can't *wait* to write this fucker up, I said to myself.

Finally, with recreation having been called, most inmates off the gallery, and things settled down, I went to find my disobedient porter and lock him into his cell. He was going to have to stay there today, missing rec, learning that actions had consequences. I was sure I'd find him standing outside it, still dripping from the shower, now feeling a little contrite. But he wasn't there. I checked the other side of the gallery. Gone. Shit. He must have borrowed clothes and shoes from a friend and gone off to the yard with the others. But I knew who he was, and I could write him up anyway. The next officer could lock him in his cell.

By the time I finished writing up the Misbehavior Report, the sergeant for my shift had left. A less helpful sergeant was there in his place. He couldn't sign my report, he said. I'd have to take it to the Watch Commander's Office.

I sighed. The last time I'd been there was on my journey with the ill-fated heating element. After a long day on a difficult gallery, I wasn't in the right frame of mind to go through that again.

But now here I was, back before the same lieutenant. Watching him read this time, I realized he was only semiliterate. I helped him as he stuttered through my report, trying hard to be patient, trying to take a little refuge in numbness. It was only two paragraphs. Finally, he got to the bottom.

"There's too many loopholes in here," he declared, twice. The infraction was so cut-and-dried, and my writing so plain and direct, that I was about to explode from frustration. "I don't understand this," he said finally, dropping the paper on his desk.

"What don't you understand?" I asked, fighting the sarcasm that seemed my only defense against incompetence. Behind me, though I hadn't seen him, Sergeant Wickersham had entered the room. Apparently, he signaled to the lieutenant.

"Get a clean form and meet me in the back room," he said, as though doing me a favor. I got there first, and an officer sitting across the room counseled me to calm down. It had been a terrible day even before the shower incident, and now this. If they tell me when I get downstairs that I have to do overtime, I thought, I'll quit.

Wickersham didn't take the folding chair I set up next to mine. He sat in another chair, farther away. Speaking in such a low monotone (the faux-calm tone) that I could barely hear him, he asked what I had done before becoming a CO. "A million things," I said.

"Answer specifically!" he thundered, glaring.

"Taxi driver, construction," I began.

"Any military?"

"No."

"You keep showing that attitude toward superiors and you're going to have a lot of trouble around here, a lot of trouble," he warned. "Just answer the question, just the *facts*." Now he was the prosecutor.

He told me not to write a single thing on the new form, the implication being that I'd get it wrong. Then he read my report, and red-penned it. My "his cell" became "the cell." "Who do you think it belongs to?" Wickersham demanded. "The inmate? Or the taxpayers who put out a hundred thousand dollars for each of these cells?" He asked me to tell him the whole story, and I actually had to think hard to remember it, because I had been so overwhelmed on the gallery. Upon hearing that I hadn't called a sergeant and hadn't locked the guy in the shower when I saw him there—I'd never even thought of it—Wickersham seethed. "This is an embarrassment!" he pronounced, waving my report in the air. "He's laughing at you now, saying he fucked you! You thought you could avoid confronting him and then come running to Daddy!"

"Sarge, I'm not afraid of inmates. I burned rec for two of them today, and—" I began. I knew at some level that I had mishandled the situation, but Wickersham's approach made admitting a mistake the last thing I could possibly do.

"An embarrassment! Humiliation!" he repeated several times. As he stood and turned, the CO at the table who had earlier told me to take it easy signaled me to relax.

"Can I ask a question?" I interrupted.

"What?"

"Even if I messed up—and now I see that I did—does that change the fact that he did what he did?"

The sergeant didn't answer, just continued mumbling about my crimes and misdemeanors. "An embarrassment!"

Wickersham stood and, with great theatricality, threw all my paperwork into the trash. I tried to catch his eye as he glared at me, but he looked away. So much for earning his respect by standing up to him. Now my day had been an utter failure. Wickersham began walking around the room.

"Are we finished?" I asked.

"*I'm* finished," he said. And left.

A crusty old instructor at the Academy with a flat-top crew cut and a mug of coffee seemingly grafted to his hand told us to learn from his mistakes: He had moonlighted as a local policeman in his off-hours from a prison upstate, and it had broken up his marriage.

"Enough cop is enough," he said. "If you've got to work a second job, do anything besides police work. And my best advice is not to work a second job at all. Exercise, pursue a hobby, work on your car—anything to get the prison out of your system. Don't take it home to the wife and kids."

I was new enough to the job, that evening in June after the encounter with Wickersham, to still believe it was possible to leave prison behind me at night. After I got home, I went for a run, had a beer with dinner, then helped my two-and-a-half-year-old son get into his pajamas. I was doing well at keeping work off my mind until I noticed his younger sister with her hands on the slats of her crib, looking out. Unnervingly, it reminded me of the same view I had all day long. Like an inmate, she was dependent upon me for everything. These two jobs were too much the same, I thought with disgust. My son, tired but rambunctious, didn't want to brush his teeth and, struggling, mistakenly hit me in the eye. I grabbed him angrily and shouted, made him cry. Well, there was one difference between him and the inmates, I thought darkly as I tried to calm us both down. He was destroyed when I got mad; they, on the other hand, seemed energized.

I thought I owed my wife, Margot, an explanation for my temper, but I didn't know how to begin. Certainly, I didn't want to fill her mind with all the unpleasant images from my day. She seemed stressed enough by her own job and the many other things she had to do, and so, avoiding the matter, we both just fell asleep.

I woke up suddenly in the middle of the night, having had a vivid dream. I'd been keeplocked. I'd startled a prison clerk in some grocery store–like setting, and that was the automatic punishment. Whether I was an officer or inmate was unclear, but it suddenly dawned on me, as I sat in my cell, that I'd missed the twenty-four-hour deadline for appealing the charges against me. As a result, I now faced a year of disciplinary confinement. The feeling of terror that seized me was so strong that it woke me up.

A month or two later, Margot and I took a brief vacation by ourselves in Jamaica. My officer friend Miller had, half facetiously, cautioned me against vacation, saying that in his experience, taking time off almost wasn't worth the nausea of reentry. But as I packed my swimsuit, sunglasses, and Walkman, I knew it was the right decision. There was another life out there, a good life.

During my first three days in the tropics, slathered with sunscreen, gazing out over the ocean with a rum drink in my hand, I felt I'd successfully left Sing Sing behind. Then, on my fourth night, I dreamed vividly of Sergeant Wickersham. We were hunting together in the mountains somewhere, on horseback. He was still my superior, but in the dream he was tolerant toward me. Suddenly, he gestured at me to look to the left: Across a ridge, bathed in yellow light, was a tiger. Not an ordinary tiger, but one double the usual size. It looked tame, but I knew it might be very, very dangerous. Shhh, the sergeant said, don't tell anyone there's a tiger up here or all the hunters will come and shoot it. Everyone else thought there were no tigers left. He was letting me in on a CO's secret.

The tiger had smelled or seen us, and I watched as it sniffed out our trail, came closer and closer behind us. I had the feeling that he was not following *us* but following *me*. Wickersham and I, on our horses, rode through a swinging glass door into a room, and soon it was just the tiger and us in there. A trick for you to try, Wickersham said: The tiger's here because we're carrying shrimp in our saddlebags. Chew some up and spray it out of your mouth at him. I did so, and the tiger hesitated, then fled—something to do with the seasoning, it seemed. Then the tiger came back and approached me on my horse. I repeated the trick, but this time only by going through the motions. I made him flee by just pretending I was going to spit! This was such a shock that again I woke up, trembling with happiness. Or was it fear?

I puzzled over that dream several times, and weeks later even wrote to a friend about it. "Seems to me it's about domination, fear, predation," Jay wrote back. "You're caught between two tigers, Wickersham and the mass of inmates; you use an inmate technique—spraying—to defend yourself. The fact that it works is significant: It shows that for all his meanness, maybe you know you're learning something valuable from Wickersham. But at the same time, he's a dominating tiger to you." The tiger coming indoors, Jay suggested, represented prison, a bottled-up wilderness within walls.

That sounded right to me, but while I was in Jamaica, it was much less clear. All I knew then was that even though my body was two thousand miles away, my mind was still trapped in Sing Sing.

––––

Many officers were aggrieved by Wickersham, and I was delighted when one of my favorites, Goldman, from B-block, joined the club. Goldman was from Queens, a streetwise, muscled Air Force veteran in his forties, and I considered him a stalwart. One day I'd been pulling the brake on R-and-W when a high-spirited inmate running down the gallery (a rules violation) crashed into my back, almost knocking me over. It was apparently a mistake, though in the seconds after it occurred I wasn't quite sure. During those seconds, Goldman appeared from the stairwell. As the inmate apologized to me, Goldman sized it all up and awaited my verdict: He was poised to jump the guy if I deemed it an attack. I hardly knew him, but I immediately loved him for that.

Goldman had been on the B-block door one day when a red-dot alarm was pulled inside. Per procedure, he exited the block and locked the gate from the outside. In a few minutes, Wickersham arrived with some red-dot officers from A-block.

"What did you see?" the sergeant demanded as Goldman unlocked the door.

Goldman told Wickersham where he thought the alarm had come from, which officers had been involved, and who had responded.

"You didn't see anything," replied the sergeant, dismissing him with a wave of his hand.

"Hey!" Goldman shouted as the sergeant moved past. "I'm an adult—you can treat me like an adult."

Wickersham had turned and, according to Goldman, said, "It's not my job to baby you."

Offended, Goldman filed a grievance against the sergeant. He'd been treated disrespectfully too many times by him, he complained to some B-block officers a day or two later, and was too old to put up with it.

"Ah, ease up a little," Chilmark, the officer in charge, counseled. "Nobody takes Wick seriously. He's a fuckin' bug."

Bug was prison slang for nutcase. I'd never heard the expression applied to a member of the staff before, only to inmates. But it made sense, in light of the other information that circulated about the sergeant. What was known for certain was there for all to see: several circular round scars on his right forearm. He had been a POW in Vietnam, people said. Upon returning, he had started work as a Sing Sing CO and had been there just two and a half weeks when he and sixteen others were taken hostage and held by inmates for more than fifty hours during the B-block occupation of 1983. Those scars, everyone said, were cigarette burns inflicted by his captors during one of those experiences.

Hearing this story, I checked out some newspaper reports from the time. There was a bearded young Wickersham in a large photo after the incident was over, acting as spokesman for the just-released hostages. Instead of the dominating father figure abusing us for our own good, he was a chain-smoking newjack begging reporters to "bear with me—I'm a little nervous." Being held hostage—suddenly finding yourself prisoner on a volatile inmate-run Death Row—could damage a person in fundamental ways. I thought about odd Sergeant Bloom. What was the legacy of those terror-filled days to Wickersham's psyche?

Perhaps it was the particular context of the B-block riot that had marked Wickersham. In a report to the governor following the incident, a state watchdog gave credence to inmate and officer statements that the sergeant assigned to B-block the night the incident began had arrived at work drunk and had so angered inmates with his inappropriate and abusive orders that they gradually refused to comply with anything the officers said and finally rioted. The backdrop was a prisonwide feeling of rebelliousness: inmates in A-block had been demonstrating during the preceding weeks over prison mismanagement. But it seemed that the one sergeant had set it off.

At some level, I thought, Wickersham hated our innocence and wanted to cure it through abuse. But on another, by keeping new officers on their toes and keeping the blocks running according to the rules—by being a force for consistency—Wickersham may have been insuring himself against repeating the experience. The work inside was never finished. New officers always needed guidance, inmates always had to be listened to but at the same time kept in their place. Wickersham, I thought, probably derived a sense of purpose from obsessively riding herd on us. Part of it may even have been a generous impulse. But it came wrapped up in all sorts of nastiness.

———

In July, I was penciled in for two weeks as officer in charge of the A-block gym. This huge room was filled morning, afternoon, and evening with inmates, and my day shift spanned two of those times. It was regarded as a fairly good post in that you generally didn't have to spend a lot of time telling people what to do. The regular officer, presently on vacation, had had it for years. Its main downside was risk. On a cold or rainy day, the gym could fill with upward of four hundred inmates, and there were moments when I would be the only officer there with them.

Depending on the time of day, eight to twelve porters were assigned to the gym. I had to put through their payroll, I was told, and therefore to keep porter attendance. (The twelve to fifteen cents an hour they earned was credited to their commissary accounts.) Because I knew the B-block porters to be a tight and surly bunch, I thought I'd better let the crew know right away who was in charge.

They arrived before rec was called, supposedly to get a jump on the cleaning. There was a lot to do, because an inspection of the block was scheduled for the next day. The gym had a full-size basketball court with a spectator area around it, a weights area the size of a half court, a table-and-benches zone for cards, chess, dominoes, and similar games, and two television areas. There was also a locked equipment room in front of which sat my desk, on an elevated platform, with a microphone on top. Instead of hopping to work, the porters turned on the TVs and sat down. I turned off the one most of them were watching.

"Gentlemen, I'm going to be here for the next two weeks and I want to talk with you about when the cleaning gets done and who does what."

They sat silently.

"For example, who normally cleans today?"

At first, nobody said anything. There were stares of indifference and defiance. A pudgy inmate whose nickname, I would later learn, was Rerun finally spoke. "Don't nobody normally clean today," he said. "Tuesday's the day off."

"The day off. So when do you clean?"

"Mondays, Wednesdays, and Fridays. We know what to do."

I tried wresting more details out of them, but they wouldn't say more. Firing porters, I knew, was a bureaucratic procedure that took weeks; I'd be working elsewhere in the prison before the wheels had even begun to turn. And evidently the regular officer was satisfied with these men. Wishing I'd never started down this path, I finally had to settle for a plea dressed up as an order. "Those ledges up there? They're covered with dust, and the inspectors will be looking. So tomorrow, make sure somebody takes care of that along with all the rest."

"They don't never check those ledges," came the quick reply as I walked to my desk. And the TVs went back on.

The next day, somewhat to my surprise, six or seven of the porters set to work in earnest upon their arrival. For half an hour, they swept and mopped and picked up trash. As promised, they skipped the ledges. The place looked pretty good, and the inspectors never came.

I began to relax, and as I did, I began to understand the complex culture of the gym. There was, naturally, a big basketball scene—

a league, in fact, with prison-paid inmate referees and a score-board and games that took place about every other day. The games were often exciting to watch—sometimes even a few officers would attend—but also nervous-making, as the crowds that gathered for matches between popular teams were partisan and players would sometimes get into fights.

Weight lifting was also popular, and when I was new at Sing Sing, it was intimidating to be faced with the huge, muscle-bound inmates who took it seriously. But soon I noticed that these purposeful, self-disciplined inmates were almost never the ones who gave us problems, and I came to agree with the opinion, generally held among officers, that the weights and machines were valuable. The only complaint I ever heard from officers was that inmates' weight equipment was much better than what was provided to officers in the small weight room in the Administration Building.

Beyond these activities, the gym held many surprises. On a busy day, it seemed almost like a bazaar. A dozen fans of *Days of Our Lives* gathered religiously every day for the latest installment of their favorite soap. Behind them, regular games of Scrabble, chess, checkers, and bridge were conducted with great seriousness. (One of the bridge players, known as Drywall—a white-bearded man with dreadlocks—came from 5-Building; more than once when he was late, his partners asked me to call the officers over there and make sure he'd left so they could start their game.) At the table next to the games, an older man sold hand-painted greeting cards for all occasions to raise money for the Jaycees, one of Sing Sing's "approved inmate organizations." In a far corner behind the weight area, at the bottom of a small flight of stairs, a regular group of inmates practiced some kind of martial art. Martial arts were forbidden by the rules, but these guys were so pointedly low-key, and the rule seemed to me so ill conceived, that I didn't break it up. In the men's bathroom, inmates smoked—also against the rules but, from what I could tell, tacitly accepted.

A floor-to-ceiling net separated these areas from the basketball court. At court's edge, a transvestite known as Miss Jackson would braid men's hair as they watched the game or press their clothing with one of the electric irons inmates were allowed to use in the gym. She received packs of Newport cigarettes—the commissary's most popular brand—as payment. Miss Jackson seemed a sweet man who was at pains to be noticed: She stretched the collar of her sweatshirt so that it exposed one shoulder, and cut scallop-shaped holes in the body so that it held some aesthetic interest. She often wore Walkman headphones, disconnected, just for the look. She must have been rich in cigarettes, and I wondered how she spent them.

Out on the court one day, just a few yards from Miss Jackson's enterprise, four short-haired, long-sleeved, bow-tied members of the Nation of Islam stood in a close circle, sternly chastising another member of the group, who must have somehow strayed. One of them was also a gym porter, among those most courteous to me. The juxtaposition of such opposites—the ideologues of the Nation and the would-be sexpot—reminded me of street life in New York City.

I walked the floor every fifteen or twenty minutes, making sure no one was smoking too openly, telling those inmates who had put on do-rags to take them off (it violated the rule against wearing hats inside), and making announcements when there was room at the bank of inmate phones that were lined up on the flats near the front gate. (Inmates who had signed up on a list could be excused from the gym to make a call.) It wasn't a bad job overall, and I suppose I should have been sad to see it go. But, as usual, I was simply relieved that nothing awful had happened under my watch.

———

I'd been away from A-block for a while—Sergeant Holmes had been sending me to B-block, which I liked better—but one day a different chart sergeant was on duty and back I went. I was sad to see that Rufino was still the officer in charge. For weeks, it seemed, he had sported a big shiner, courtesy of an inmate he'd angered, who one day had marched straight into Rufino's tiny office and popped him in the eye. Couldn't have happened to a nicer guy, I thought. Wickersham's abusiveness seemed to enable Rufino's; they were a twin star of meanness. Soon after he was punched, Rufino had spotted me chatting at the front gate with Allen while a keeplock I was escorting to the hospital waited to the side. Rufino called me into his office. "Don't you *ever* turn your back on an inmate," he scolded me fiercely.

Unfortunately, in practical terms, it was impossible not to turn away from an inmate occasionally—as Rufino's shiner demonstrated. I didn't point this out.

"Right, right, sure, sure," I said.

The day of my arrival back on A-block, I told Rufino my post number and learned that I was an escort, which delighted me. I would be spending brief periods on a gallery but would also have a lot of time off, accompanying inmates to the mess hall and, later, to the commissary or package room or school building. I relaxed, knowing I wasn't being put in charge of an unfamiliar gallery.

Before I could leave, though, Wickersham emerged from his office and looked over the day's list of postings. L-and-P gallery, on the top floor, had been assigned to a brand-new officer. The guy was so new that he didn't even seem worried about it. Wickersham scanned the group of us milling around the OIC's office. "Switch him with Conover," he told Rufino.

Son of a bitch! Did he have it in for me? I was sure he did, until someone later suggested he perhaps thought I was a competent gallery officer and that things were less likely to go wrong with me up there. I doubted that theory, and in any case, it was small comfort. I was going to be on L-and-P gallery all day.

There were a lot of keeplocks up there, which was never a good thing. P-north, in particular, had a high concentration: ten keeplocks, or one for every four cells. Several of these were in consecutive cells, which concentrated the bad vibe. Most of them left for keeplock rec about an hour into the shift. My problems began when they returned, an hour or so later. When the OIC announced the return over the PA system, my first job was to clear the galleries of other inmates. This was to minimize the chance of trouble—it was chaos enough to have a gallery full of keeplocks at large. The only inmates who were out on the galleries were three or four porters. Two of them were slow to return to their cells and lock in; when I saw the keeplocks arriving—and Wickersham lurking near the end gates—I ordered these two laggards into a shower stall on P-north, next to my office.

"Come on, CO, that's bullshit!" one protested loudly.

"Yeah, CO, the regular never make us do that," the other joined in. I got them in anyway, but the complaining caught on with the two or three keeplocks whose cells were on the other side of the shower.

"Let 'em stay out, CO!"

"You too harsh, man!"

"You want to start a slave revolt, CO? That's what you doing?"

It was too early in the day for this, I said to myself. I walked over to the loudest keeplock, P-49, a somewhat scary-looking guy with unkempt dreadlocks, dirty clothes, and one gray and clouded eye.

"What I'm doing is absolutely appropriate, and you know it," I said, trying to keep my voice low but unable to preserve my sangfroid. "Do me a favor. Shut up and let me do my job."

"Woohoo, 'Shut up!' CO told me to shut up!" he crowed, completely jazzed, as I walked away. Others took up the hue and cry. "CO told him to shut up!" I walked back toward the center gate to start locking the returning keeplocks back into their cells.

And not a minute too soon. The keeplock officers, always eager to avoid extra work for themselves, were beating a hasty retreat down the center stairs.

"Hey!" I yelled after them as they waited for the officer downstairs to open the center gate. "How about sticking around a couple of minutes, help me get these keeplocks back in? I've got thirty of them out and don't know where a single one locks. You going to leave me with that?" Grudgingly, they returned.

At 11 A.M., when it was time for the count, an officer newer than me appeared on the gallery. She was Reid, a tall redhead I had worked with one day when she was in training. The OIC had sent her to do the go-round—a list of where all the inmates planned to be after lunch, so that they could be tracked down in case they had a visit or had forgotten a medical appointment or the like. Go-round forms were filled out at the same time as count forms. To complete one, you stopped at each cell on a gallery and said, for example, "L-3, where are you going this afternoon?"

To let inmates know they'd better be dressed and decent, female officers always yelled, "Female on the gallery!" before setting out. That cry usually occasioned a dozen mirrors thrust out of cells so that inmates could get a good look at her. Sometimes catcalls would issue forth; today, they were especially obnoxious from P-north.

"Hey, Red! Show me that red pussy!" yelled one inmate. "You ain't gettin' enough, are you, Red?" called another. "I'm gonna give it you!" I had misgivings as Officer Reid marched bravely down P-north. She wasn't the tough sort, just a farm girl who needed a job. And with her looks, she was an attention-getter. Some inmates tried to ejaculate on female officers; this had already happened to two of my classmates. I kept an eye on her until my phone rang.

Two minutes later, Reid was back in my office.

"You got a Misbehavior Form?" she asked, flustered.

"What happened?" I asked, handing her one.

"Masturbator," she said.

"What cell?"

She told me. She seemed very tired.

"He's a keeplock already—too bad," I noted, checking my list. "Anything else?" Reid shook her head. I rang the sergeant's office—Wickersham took the call—and let him know. He said to send her down.

I walked down P-north.

"What's your fucking problem?" I demanded of the inmate. He was lying on his bunk, pants zipped up, smiling, looking smug. He wouldn't answer. Upstate, I had heard, this kind of thing didn't happen too often. Upstate, an inmate who spoke a wrong word to a female officer quickly regretted it.

"CO, you call the sergeant yet?" This was the voice of P-49, the keeplock I had told to shut up earlier in the morning. He'd been badgering me since then to get a sergeant upstairs to speak with him. I'd called the sergeant, a man who was working with Wickersham; he knew what P-49 wanted and said that he'd get back to him. I'd already told this to P-49. I repeated it to him again, impatiently, adding that there was nothing more I could do for him.

"Oh yes there is, CO. You can suck my dick!" P-49 proclaimed loudly. There were hoots of approval from the other keeplocks on P-north as I walked away.

P-49 continued to hector me the rest of the day. Unfortunately, his cell was close to my office. "CO, get away from my cell," he'd yell when I walked by. "Homer, get back to the sticks." His neighbor keeplocks would cheer in support; they were his chorus.

"He looks like a puppet, don't he?" he taunted as I tried to keep my temper in check. I knew I had a loose-jointed style of running, but I had never heard it suggested about my walk before.

My nerves were frayed. I'd noticed that he was holding his mirror out on the gallery to keep track of my approaches and also that, against the rules, he sometimes left it balanced up on his bars. Once I had tried to grab the mirror, but he had anticipated that move and snatched it away before I could. Half an hour later, I noticed it was up again. Quietly this time, I walked up and took it. He was furious. "You better watch out when you come back by, CO," he threatened, adding something that I couldn't understand but that I presumed to be about shitting me down. That was an angry keeplock's trump card.

In my eagerness to get the mirror, I'd placed myself on the wrong side of his cell. To get back to my office, I'd have to pass by again.

Another officer was on the gallery, escorting a civilian who was repairing the chain-link fence. "Cespedes, watch me as I go by P-forty-nine," I said. Something told me that a witness might come in handy.

I collected myself and walked down the gallery as I normally would have. I probably should have sprinted past the cell, but I didn't want to betray any fear. As I drew even with P-49, it all happened very fast: a gob of spit flew past my nose, with my cheek catching some spray, and then the keeplock's arm swung out at full length, his fist catching my head just behind the ear. I stumbled forward and then looked back. Cespedes and the fence guy had both seen the incident. The fence guy's mouth was wide open.

My heart was beating fast. I spent a minute calming myself down and then called the sergeant's office. Wickersham answered. I told him what had happened.

"Who was it?"

"P-forty-nine. Folk."

"Bring down your Misbehavior Report," he said curtly. And hung up.

And leave the gallery without an officer? I wondered. That was against rules. But it was only a half hour or so until I was relieved, and it would take me a while to write the report.

Cespedes came into the office with another officer. He asked if I was okay (I only had a little bump) and what had led up to the incident. He turned over the mirror. On the back, in graffiti-style script, Folk had written: *The Universal Don. Da Silva-Back Guerrilla. The Assassin.* I told them about the harassment, told them Wickersham wanted to see me.

"Hey, Wick's a good guy," the other officer said. "He'll take care of you."

"Wickersham's a horse's ass," I replied.

The man looked taken aback. Evidently, he was a Wickersham partisan. "Hey, pal, you're on your own then," he said, walking out.

Though he hadn't said he was going to, Wickersham did send an officer to relieve me. She said things like, "Too bad we can't go in there and show that asshole what the fuck is what." I felt a little better.

When I arrived in his office downstairs, Wickersham glanced up and pointed to the chair beside his desk. I sat. He read my ticket and then went through a reprise of the just-the-facts interrogation he had administered that afternoon in the Watch Commander's Office. This time I didn't even care. He wrote out a new ticket for me in red pen. I watched his right arm as he did, with its six shiny, hairless, cigarette end–size circles. Other officers and a sergeant came in to offer sympathy and read the ticket, many of them assuming I had been shitted down. The nice thing about the finished ticket was that it all sounded worse than it was, containing words such as *assault, unhygienic act, threats,* etc. I did feel an element of shame in being a victim, and heard myself pointing out to everyone that this was the first time it had happened to me. Wickersham asked why I was walking close enough for him to reach me; I said that I hadn't wanted to appear afraid, which he accepted, though he told me an officer should always walk as far as possible from the cells. "It might give you more time to grab his arm and break it," he said, never cracking a smile.

It wasn't really a joke to me, either. This very fantasy had already crossed my mind.

There was more paperwork. Wickersham had to send me to the ER to be checked for injuries. There, a nurse let me wash up with antibacterial soap. She was vociferous in her scorn for my assailant, and I felt warmly toward her, at least until she whispered, "I'll bet he was black, right?" Wickersham entered with a Polaroid camera and took front and profile shots of me—required, I think, in case I made a claim for workmen's comp. I looked at the photos as we walked to the Watch Commander's Office. They were the first time I'd ever seen myself through Wickersham's eyes, as it were. The officer in those shots appeared gaunt and wimpy to me.

The lieutenant who had been my shift commander asked if I was okay. Wickersham had already been in touch with the Box and had reserved a cell for my assailant. This may have spoken to his clout, since there often wasn't room in there. I felt a touch of gratitude. He spoke to a team of officers, who were doing some overtime, about relocating Folk to the Box. "He might not go willingly," he said, which was greeted with nods of satisfaction. I would have enjoyed watching the "relocation," but they would never have let me. And to be honest, all I really wanted to do was leave.

As I walked through the front gate and outside, a sergeant whom I liked, Murray, called out. "Hey, Conover," he said, and made a hawking sound. I smiled weakly.

"So you already heard, huh?" I asked.

"Heard about it in about a minute," Murray answered. The prison was a small world. I wondered if the incident would make the announcements at lineup.

I had a pounding headache—it had been growing all afternoon—and as I pulled my car onto the highway, I experienced a vivid fantasy of A-block going up in flames, all the dross inside being consumed by the fire. And then came dissonant flashes of memory from that same day: the inmate who had tried to tell me a joke as I set up the locking board outside his cell; the inmate who had warned me about Wickersham approaching; the inmate whose classical guitar playing, particularly gorgeous in that setting, had drifted into my office around lunchtime. They weren't all bad, I thought. Just most of them.

THE BOX

> . . . A man is taken away from his experience of society, taken away from the experience of a living planet of living things, when he is sent to prison.
>
> A man is taken away from other prisoners, from his experience of other people, when he is locked away in solitary confinement in the hole.
>
> Every step of the way removes him from experience and narrows it down to only the experience of himself . . .
>
> The *concept* of death is simple: it is when a living thing no longer entertains experience.
>
> So when a man is taken farther and farther away from experience, he is being taken to his death.
>
> —Jack Henry Abbott, *In the Belly of the Beast*

Officially, the dark, squat building was the Special Housing Unit, abbreviated SHU and pronounced *shoe*. But officers called it the Box. It was solitary confinement, a place of punishment within a place of punishment.

The Box had a doorbell and a heavy metal door with a peephole, and a barred gate as well. The structure was compact—redbrick, two-story. Each floor had two galleries, back to back, with fifteen cells. What made it fundamentally different from the other housing units of Sing Sing was that its inmates did not, as a rule, leave the building; in fact, they barely left their cells. Meals were delivered in the Styrofoam "clamshells" that restaurants use for take-out orders; library books, for those granted access to them, were wheeled in on a cart; inmate barbers were brought in to clip Box inmates one at a time at the end of the short galleries; even disciplinary hearings were conducted in the individual cells.

Half of the inmates in the Box, as it turned out—all thirty on the upper floor—were not disciplinary cases but men under protective custody, of which there were two kinds. Those who had asked to be protected were rats or rape or slicing victims who had identified their assailants—people who had enemies and, if left in the general population, might reasonably be expected to be hurt or killed. Among those in the Box involuntarily were victims who had *not* ratted out their assailants, and thus were feared to be either loaded guns, waiting for their chance to get revenge, or sitting ducks, soon to be victimized again. One inmate in there was a suspected gang member whose bed in A-block had been set on fire by a Molotov cocktail; another was a borderline bug convinced that a particular officer was trying to kill him.

Downstairs, by contrast, were the baddest of the bad—almost exclusively, inmates who had assaulted guards. It felt like a dungeon down there, in part because entry to the building was via the floor above, but also because it was darker, with smaller windows and lower ceilings.

The Box had the highest testosterone level in the prison, and somehow smelled like it—close, musty, with an acrid whiff of perspiration. Among COs, working in a max was considered more macho than working in a medium or anywhere else. To work in the Box of a max was—well, the maximum. The officers who chose it tended to be size large. They had a habit of tucking their trousers into the tops of their unlaced boots and rolling even their short-sleeved shirts up over their muscles, the casual SWAT team look.

One was a shaved-headed monster named Perlstein. The day I worked downstairs during OJT, he helped a fellow officer change his shirt; the man was so muscle-bound, he couldn't reach back far enough to get his second hand into the sleeve hole. Perlstein then reviewed for us the pat-frisking procedure used on every single inmate before and after the inmate was released to the Box's small exercise courtyard. "You, get on the wall," he grunted at me.

"Now, if an inmate takes his hand off the wall—if he even looks back at you—you grab him like *this,*" he said, standing behind me and lifting one leg by the shin, "and push him ahead like *this.*" He squished me against the wall like a linebacker, my leg in hog-tied position. It hurt, and Perlstein knew it hurt.

He also reviewed the best places to strike with a baton: the exposed bones of the lower body. As I stood toward the wall, he ran his baton down the front of my shin.

"Ow."

"Imagine if it was more than a little tap," Perlstein said with satisfaction.

Perlstein gave me a lighter and sent me down to the north-facing gallery by myself, with instructions to light inmates' cigarettes. (Like other inmates, they could smoke in their cells, but they were not allowed to have matches.) This was unexpectedly frightening. All I knew about Box inmates was that they were very, very bad. I thought of Agent Clarice Starling approaching Hannibal Lecter's cell in *The Silence of the Lambs.* Downstairs at the Box was the lowest level of hell. The guy who had attacked Sergeant Bloom at Coxsackie had until recently resided here. David Berkowitz, the Son of Sam killer, was in the Box at Sullivan for nine years. The Box at Elmira held Lemuel Smith, who had picked up an unsupervised phone and tricked a young newjack, Donna Payant, into meeting him in a chaplain's empty office at Green Haven Correctional Facility, where he raped and strangled her (and, according to Nigro, at the Academy, chewed off her nipples) in 1981—the last CO murdered on the job in New York State. He was insane, the devil incarnate, as bad as it got. But others here were no doubt almost as bad.

I assumed a confident pose as I passed through the gallery gate and slid it closed behind me. Unlike the Box at Coxsackie, which had seemed a true solitary confinement, with inmates hard-pressed to communicate with each other through solid-steel doors with Lexan windows, the cells here were barred. Some of the inmates had been leaning against their bars, talking; they stopped when I came into view. I held the lighter at arm's length for two who had rolled their own, ready to spring back at any second. Both seemed to watch me closely. I tried not to meet their eyes. I pretended my face was made of granite.

Perlstein had a fair complexion; his pal, Proctor, was similarly proportioned, seemingly more human, and dark-haired. We ate lunch—our own, and sandwiches left over from the inmates' feeding (this was against the rules)—near the exercise yard, and Proctor found it incomprehensible that I had once lived in Colorado. "And you left? I'd die to get out of here." McDonough, as tall as the others but with a potbelly, was, like Perlstein and Proctor, in his late twenties or early thirties. I thought of him as the most arrogant of the crew. One day, in the corridor, when I was working a gate, he had snatched my radio off my belt to make some urgent call. Box officers always acted as though their business was urgent. But McDonough was also funny. One day, as we were leaving for home, he had called out to the chart sergeant at his desk, "*Salaam aleikum!*"—the phrase with which Black Muslims were always greeting each other solemnly.

A fourth officer, Gotham, showed me around another day when I worked the upper floor of the Box. Both floors had cages, or bubbles, in which one officer sat and operated the gates and cell doors by means of an ancient system of brass-handled levers that protruded from the wall. That officer wasn't allowed to leave the bubble before a relief officer came in. (It made going to the bathroom difficult. A friend of mine explained that the downstairs officers sometimes solved the problem by resorting to a door that led from the bubble to the utility space between the cells—there was water in the floor area, and you could add to it.) Most other procedures had to be followed to the letter, many of them having to do with not opening more than one gate at a time, to ensure the strictest control over inmate movement.

Gotham was shorter than the other SHU guys and wore glasses, but he was quick to tell me that he wouldn't hesitate to take down a recalcitrant inmate and that the inmates hated him; "In three years, I've had a hundred fifty use-of-forces," he said. That was an average of about òne per week. I wondered whether he was exaggerating or whether working the Box was just that tough. Gotham had been punched, too, he said. The year before, an inmate had broken a bone in his face and he'd needed six stitches.

Gotham maintained to me that if there was any trouble, pulling the radio's emergency pin would be the wrong response, because "we take care of matters by ourselves here." But he apparently forgot to tell the guys working downstairs. At just past 1 P.M. that day, there was a red-dot alarm called from the exercise yard. Three inmates were fighting; at least one had a weapon. The heavy front door was opened and I pulled wide the gate to the downstairs, standing to the side as some twenty-five to thirty officers responded. That was a lot of meat, and probably several times the number that would be required to subdue two or three inmates (which they promptly did). But emergencies in the Box got everyone's attention.

The environment of the Box produced stunning acts of insanity and barbarism. During our OJT, Officer Luther had told us of a Box inmate nicknamed Mr. Slurpee, who would project a spray of urine and feces at officers—from his *mouth*. One day at lineup, a sergeant held up for display an interesting-looking noose about three feet long. "We think we take everything away that they could hurt themselves with," he said. "And then we find this—made out of toilet paper." He left it out for display after lineup. An inmate had rolled endless yards of toilet paper into tight cords before weaving the cords together into the noose. It was dingy from all the handling and, to judge by my tugging, seemed as tough as a real rope. Impressive, I thought. But, on another level: all this resourcefulness and the end result a *noose*?

One day, on my way out of the building at shift's end, Chavez asked if I'd heard what had happened during the executive team's inspection of the Box that day. No, I said, I hadn't.

"The superintendent found a guy who hung himself up. He even cut him down."

"The *superintendent* found him? Was the guy dead?"

"I don't think so, not quite."

The toilet-paper noose didn't have anything to do with an officer's laxity. Most SHU incidents did. One morning in August, a lieutenant told us during lineup that an SHU inmate had gotten out of the shower stall due to an improperly closed door, grabbed and broken a mop handle, and then smashed fifty-eight windows. (Because the building was old, the large windows were made of many small panes.) When he was finally overcome, a long glass shard with cloth wrapped around it for a handle was found in his waistband. I listened to this raptly, amazed by what it suggested about the man's mental state. But the lieutenant had no interest in the inmate's mental state. He was telling us about the incident in order to reemphasize the importance of strictly follow-ing procedures.

At the next day's lineup, there was more: The day after the window-breaking incident, the officer working the downstairs bubble had had a container of urine chucked at him after a col-league failed to close the gallery gate. Then—this was starting to get embarrassing—a sergeant responding to the incident failed to secure a gate and had liquid of an unknown nature thrown in *his* face. It sounded like the Box was out of control.

"See me after this," Sergeant Holmes had said to me and five others, including my friend Feliciano, shortly before that lineup. We waited, the more senior officers speculating about what was up. A different sergeant pointed us into a separate room. The ad-ministration, he told us, had ordered a second complete search of the downstairs of the Box for contraband, particularly shards of glass, in the wake of the recent incidents. This would be done one cell at a time and one inmate at a time. Some inmates—particularly because it would involve a second strip-search—were expected to resist. We were off to conduct a Nuts and Butts, in other words, with the possible need for a Hats and Bats.

We were each issued handcuffs and a flashlight, and loaded up with Cell Search/Contraband and Misbehavior Forms, as well as three big bags of "cell-extraction"/Hats and Bats gear: helmets with Plexiglas visors, stab-proof vests, knee and elbow pads, and heavy gloves. Box officers joined us, and then two sergeants. A dozen of us marched purposefully downstairs to the Box. There was action ahead, and I felt suddenly excited to have been in-cluded. Despite the ominous tone, and my better instincts, I'd countenanced enough inmate misbehavior and disrespect to feel invigorated by the thought that this is where it all stops. *This is where we draw the line.* We were going to follow the rules, and we were going to have our way.

By the time we'd descended to the first floor, the inmates had be-come very quiet. They could hear us, no doubt, but couldn't yet see us. One of my training officers, Konoval, the first to walk into their view, set up a video camera on a tripod to record the pro-ceedings; I had noticed that the Department often took this pre-caution when a use-of-force was anticipated, probably to protect itself from lawsuits. We all donned latex gloves and then, en masse, poured into the gallery.

Feliciano and I were a team, and there were three other pairs like us. Each team had been assigned a cell. I did the talking to our inmate, a Latino in his twenties. "Good morning," I said through the bars. "We're going to strip-frisk you, then you're going to come out and we're going to frisk your cell."

The man had been through this drill two or three days before, and assented. He didn't look angry or demented, just sort of discombobulated. He handed us his shirt, his pants, his socks, and his underwear, and then he turned, bent over, and spread his cheeks.

"Fine," I said as he dressed. "Now, turn around and we'll cuff you." As the inmate put his hands behind him and through an opening in the door, Feliciano cuffed him.

"Open 105!" I called out to the officer in the bubble. The cell door opened and the inmate stepped out backward, wearing socks but no shoes. Feliciano held his handcuff chain and walked the man toward the opposite wall, where the windows had been broken by the inmate with the mop handle. Feliciano told this inmate not to turn around, then drew his baton and held it in ready position across his torso, what was called port-arms position.

I frisked the cell. It was a pigsty, with roaches crawling over the bunched-up sheets and garbage on the floor. I flipped through his notebooks; the handwriting was unexpectedly lovely. The inmate wrote in Spanish. He had also made a chess set, using toothpaste caps and squares of paper as pieces. (I had seen these games in action. Another inmate had to have a board, too, and they made moves by voice, since neither could see the other's board.) There was a lot of pencil-written gang graffiti on the walls, but no contraband.

The frisk of our second cell, which belonged to a skinny, middle-aged man, was also uneventful. Feliciano turned up only an extra state-issued pillow, which we confiscated. Before this search was over, however, we were distracted by a commotion at the entrance to the gallery. The Box officers, Perlstein, Proctor, and McDonough, had donned full cell-extraction gear. I had seen video of the Hats and Bats outfit at the Academy; it was much more intimidating seen up close. The team was preparing to go in after an inmate named Duncan, who had refused to cooperate.

I recognized Duncan from B-block—a short black man with dreads who apparently was a perpetrator in a recent fracas in the B-block yard in which officers had been injured. Cameras had shown him throwing things at officers and egging on other inmates. He seemed to hate COs. The cell-extraction officers stood one in front of the other, the second and third holding on to the officer in front of him and the lead officer carrying a see-through riot shield. On a signal, they started moving forward in step, like a locomotive gaining speed. "Open 101!" someone shouted. Another officer pulled open the cell door and they went in on one another's heels, the shield used to force Duncan into the back corner of the cell. It was hopeless for him, I knew—like going into battle with a rhino. Three minutes and many thuds later, the team emerged with the inmate in handcuffs and leg restraints. He somehow managed to raise a fist in defiance as they carried him upstairs to do a forcible strip search.

That was when things started getting raucous. Inmates up and down the gallery began to yell. We were "bitch-ass faggot mother-fuckers." We were getting off on looking at them naked. This whole search was just retaliation. They would file lawsuits, because we were not following directive 4910 (which said that sergeants had to be in constant supervision of a strip-frisk). One inmate began pleading to see one of the sergeants but then, when she refused to talk to him, he started berating her and Sing Sing's two black captains as "house niggers."

"Kill all house niggers, kill all house niggers," he chanted, for more than fifteen minutes.

The air of pandemonium made me feel less certain that everything was under control. Somehow, this felt like the first wave of an attack. Feliciano and I were given a third cell, that of a young, thin black man, Lincoln George. I repeated the line about the strip-frisk and asked him to hand us his clothes.

"I'm not going to show you my asshole," he stated without affect as he started to remove his shirt.

"You've got to," I said.

He stopped taking the shirt off.

"I won't do it," he repeated.

I tried to reason with him, in a low voice. "Look, man, you see what they're doing. They'll do it to you. It's not worth it. We'll be done in like five seconds. Let's just get it done."

He shook his head, and said, "According to directive 4910, you could use a hand scanner instead of doing a body-cavity search."

"This is not a body-cavity search," I said. "Nobody's going inside. We're just looking from the outside."

He shook his head. Why on earth, I wondered, would anyone choose cell extraction?

"So you're refusing?"

"I want to speak to a sergeant."

This was every inmate's right. I summoned the male sergeant, who, given the din and the insults, was in no mood for a negotiation. "I'm giving you a direct order to comply with the frisk," he said simply. I couldn't hear the inmate's reply.

"So you're refusing to comply?" the sergeant said. Lincoln George nodded. The sergeant left the gallery and spoke to the extraction team.

They were swift and tough. George made little attempt to brace himself or otherwise prepare for their entrance, so it didn't take long. He was knocked down, flattened, then hauled upstairs to be forcibly searched. We frisked his cell and found nothing.

Meanwhile, the extraction team had brought Duncan back down. They placed him in his cell, unchained him, and were on their way out when he snatched the leg chain from one officer's hand and swung it at him, hitting him hard on the visor. The surprised team completed its exit from the cell and closed the door. Then they turned around, regrouped, and went back in again to get the leg chain. Duncan appeared shortly afterward at the door to his cell, a big scrape on one cheek. No doubt, he had untold other wounds less easy to see. Rather than defeated and injured, he looked thrilled, and once again shouted out his defiance.

The extractors took a break and then bulldozed their way into a third cell. This one I couldn't see, but it took longer than the others and had the officers shouting, "Stop resisting! Stop resisting!" partway through. At the Academy, we'd found out that this phrase was basically a legal requirement that you shouted out to indemnify yourself when you were, for whatever reason, applying a bit of extra force. Konoval was following the team with the camera, but as the officers knew, all he could see was their backs. The inmate continued to struggle as he was carried up the stairs. I picked up half of a shattered face shield after they went by.

And then it was all done but the paperwork. The cell-extraction team came back downstairs, extracted themselves from their armor, and then gave one another hearty hugs and slaps on the back. They were sweaty and charged-up, like victorious football players. I felt the catharsis, too: Prison work filled you with pent-up aggression, and here was a thrilling release, our team coming out on top.

But as the moment faded and I picked up my gear, I paused and looked back down the gallery. It was quiet now—the sound of defeat. No weapon had been found in any cell. Perhaps, I began to suspect, none had actually been expected. It seemed reasonable to conclude that we had been sent in to make a statement about who was in charge. And I had to wonder: With the outcome never in doubt, what had we won? What did it do to a man when his work consisted of breaking the spirit of other men? And who had invented this lose-lose game, anyway?

Vivid to me, and a seeming conundrum, was the refusal of my inmate to submit to a strip-frisk. By refusing this small violation of his privacy, he'd earned himself a big violation. What could account for an action so apparently contrary to his best interests? My idea of his best interests, I later concluded, was colored by the team I was on. Eventually, it occurred to me that self-respect had required him to refuse. His stupidity began to look principled. He was renouncing his imprisonment, our authority, the entire system that had placed him there. If enough people did that together, the corrections system would come tumbling down.

Nearly ninety years ago, Thomas Mott Osborne, a politically connected prison reformer, spent a week in voluntary confinement at New York's other famous historic prison, Auburn. The book he wrote afterward, *Within Prison Walls,* was an exposé of the conditions inside Auburn, and particularly inside its version of the Box, a unit of the prison that was known simply as the jail. By refusing to work in the prison's basket-weaving shop, Osborne got himself sentenced to a night in the "jail"—a barely lit room between Auburn's Death Row and its generator that contained eight metal cells. Prisoners there were allowed only three "gills" of water—three quarters of a pint—per day; they were not allowed any exercise, bathing, mattress, or change of clothes. Osborne conversed with his fellow inmates and soon felt sympathetic and righteous. When the warden, thinking he might have had enough after a few hours, sends the "principal keeper," or head of the guards, to release Osborne, this is how he reacts:

> At the sight of his uniform a fierce anger suddenly blazes up within me and then I turn cold. . . . I am seized by a mild fit of that lunatic obstinacy which I have once or twice seen glaring out of the eyes of men interviewed by the Warden

down here; the obstinacy that has often in the course of history caused men to die of hunger and thirst in their cages of stone or iron, rather than gain freedom by submission to injustice or tyranny.

Sing Sing's SHU has no sweat box of the kind found in *The Bridge on the River Kwai* or *Cool Hand Luke,* none of the dark cells that inmates in "solitary" were subjected to prior to the middle of the twentieth century. Since then, the courts have found the extremity of that kind of treatment to constitute cruel and unusual punishment. Now the cells are slightly larger and slightly brighter, and regular access to showers and recreation, food and water, is guaranteed. But perhaps in part because inmates cannot be "broken" as quickly as they used to be, their sentences in these segregation units now drag on and on, sometimes for years. The process of breaking a man simply takes longer and costs more. Does it represent "injustice or tyranny"? That depends on your point of view: If they are not going to be put to death, the monstrous—the Lemuel Smiths—must be warehoused. Trying to extinguish the spark of the rest—the merely incorrigible, those holding on to civilization by a thread—itself feels like a monstrosity.

LINEUP ROOM

For officers, the lineup room represents the transition between the outside and the inside. There, you can rest a minute with a cup of coffee, talk with your fellow officers about work before actually going in to do it, and prepare yourself mentally. The day after the SHU extractions, CO Konoval showed his videotape in the minutes before lineup. Everyone was eager to see what had happened down in the dungeon. Nervously expecting to be transported back, I instead found the footage sort of dull: Konoval's video, with its poor lighting and bad sound, captured none of the atmosphere of madness, the endless chanting and shouting, the high anxiety. It just looked like tough guys doing a cartoonish job, the kind of thing you might see on a crummy TV show.

In general, the pattern in lineup follows a routine. After 6:45 A.M., when we're called to attention, come the announcements— everything from new parking rules to the schedule for upcoming sergeant tests to reminders about blood drives and retirement parties. Then, sometimes, the day's watch commander, a lieutenant, will step up and say a few words, often a rundown of notable happenings from the shifts before.

There is a strong speechifying tendency in corrections. Another tendency, in the wake of anything gone wrong, is Monday-morning quarterbacking. Someone can always be counted on to tell the victim of some unfortunate incident how he could have handled the situation better.

My favorite watch commander was Lieutenant Goewey. A heavyset man who was somehow more blue-collar than a lot of COs—he could have been the boss of a trucking firm, to judge solely by appearance—Goewey almost always took advantage of his prerogative to speak, and his words were always wonderfully coded. He wouldn't tell you the state police had been at Sing Sing the day before to arrest the longtime CO suspected of supplying drugs to inmates via the package room; he would simply say, "In case you haven't heard, there's a job opening in the package room." He wouldn't say he thought the previous superintendent was an idiot who neglected the security personnel in favor of programs and housekeeping; he'd just say, a couple of times a week, "Security is once again the top priority of this administration." I found it enjoyable to read between his lines.

There was a chalkboard on the wall right behind the front gate, and one morning it read, "CO Diaz had arm broken by a con 8/19/97 and is awaiting surgery." Following up on this, Goewey explained to us that Diaz, a well-liked officer posted to the Adjustment Committee (which conducted disciplinary hearings), had retrieved an inmate from the blocks and was placing him in the disciplinary bullpen to await a hearing when an inmate already in there went after the guy. In the struggle, the gate slammed on Diaz's arm.

Lieutenant Goewey, in his predictably coded way, said, "The incident occurred at about two, and I didn't hear about it until twenty minutes later. When I got there, the guy was just sitting there, happy as a clam." There was a long pause. "Now, these days you can have a use-of-force. Whatever it takes at the time, you can do it. But twenty minutes later . . . I'm not saying it didn't used to happen, but these days you can't just knock all a guy's teeth out and shove 'em down his throat. Twenty minutes after an incident."

He continued: "Now, I know there's gonna be a lot of armchair quarterbacking about this—he should have had another officer there, should have looked, that kind of thing—but it's dead."

In other words, Goewey had just told us: I hope you'll forgive me for not beating the shit out of the perp who did this, and Diaz probably could have prevented it.

PSYCH UNIT

You didn't have to work the galleries long to realize that a large proportion of inmates were mentally ill. The symptoms ranged from the fairly mild—talking to oneself, neglecting to bathe—to the severe: men who didn't know where they were, men who set fire to their own cells, men so depressed they slashed their wrists or tried to hang themselves.

Prison, said the department's assistant director of mental health services at the Academy, was "a hard place to be crazy." He told us that the "last good study," now more than ten years old, had indicated that of the state's 70,000 inmates, 5 percent, or 3,500, were "seriously and persistently" mentally ill—people who would be in a psychiatric hospital if they weren't in prison. But corrections had beds for only 1,000 of them. Another 10 percent, or 7,000, were under the supervision of a psychiatrist, "taking some drugs."

Stress, he said, worsened almost any condition, and prison—obviously—is stressful. "Many people break down for the first time in prison," the official said. In other words, prison not only made crazy people worse; it drove people crazy.

Working as COs, he said, would make us "students of human nature." He gave us thumbnail sketches of people with schizophrenia (and symptoms like psychosis, hallucinations, delusions, and paranoia) and those with personality or mood disorders, like manic depression. Once we got to Sing Sing, however, these distinctions were never made again, at least by officers. A crazy person was a bug—slang used by both guards and inmates. Working a gallery was like sharing a crowded urban street with a higher-than-usual number of disturbed street people. Mostly, you just learned to live with the bugs. Occasionally, however, a bug went off the deep end, and—particularly if he got suicidal—would be sent to the psych unit.

Sing Sing's PSU, or Psychiatric Satellite Unit, occupied the second floor of the Hospital Building. It was run by employees of the state Office of Mental Health (OMH) and by a handful of officers, who were there to provide security.

The door from the building's staircase to the PSU floor was always kept locked. Half of the floor comprised offices for the various mental-health-staff members—psychiatrists, nurses, and social workers. The other half, separated by an iron gate, held the sick inmates.

The worst-off and most dangerous of these men were kept in six special high-security cells. These cells, with bars front and rear, had dense screens installed from ceiling to knee level to keep the occupants from throwing things out. Inmates assigned to them had their clothing taken away and replaced with—in severe cases—paper gowns and hospital slippers. The toilets and sinks were a single stainless-steel unit, such as were found in most newer jails and prisons but not generally in Sing Sing. The remainder of the floor's residents—up to sixteen, who were considered less dangerous—were held in a dormitory room down the hall. They had a TV lounge across the hall, with games and newspapers, and a small room next to that where they received meals.

A very few inmates were transferred from the PSU to the state mental hospital at Marcy. This was a hard transition to make, however, since space at Marcy was limited: they had to come really *close* to killing themselves—slashing their wrists deeper than merely the skin, or "hanging up" in such a way that they came close to death. The only other way I ever saw an inmate get to Marcy was by making a credible threat. "I'm gonna be in here a lot of years, but I'm gonna remember you and when I get out I'm gonna find you," he had said to a female psychiatrist. She must have believed him, because he was shipped out the next morning.

The general understanding among officers was that many inmates played a bug game—worked the system—in order to get themselves into the PSU or Marcy. They did this because life in those places, even though they were surrounded by bugs, was more tolerable than among the general population of a max. In the psych ward, you didn't have to worry about gangs or weapons. You had more room to yourself, and there were more staff looking after you.

For the same reasons, I was always glad when Sergeant Holmes sent me to the PSU after a period on the galleries. It was quiet there, and clean; the inmates were carefully controlled, and there

wasn't much for a CO to do. Most of the time, the PSU was a relief. The most obvious evidence that things were better here was
the presence of longtime officers. Because of seniority, they had
their pick of easy jobs, and there always seemed to be an old-timer
on duty in the PSU.

The one who was there my first day—and many times after
that—was a tall, grizzled guy named Birch. He spent his days
minding the staircase door and the center gate, making sure things
on the floor ran the way they were supposed to, reading religious
tracts, or doing crossword puzzles to pass the time. When I arrived, he was speaking through the screen of a high-security cell to
a tiny Dominican named Colon, who had decorated the cell with
a carpet of shredded pieces of magazine. Tassels of toilet paper fes-
tooned every bar, and some thirty wads of toilet paper had been
stuck to the walls with toothpaste. I knew Colon from B-block—
he had set fire to his cell and destroyed its fixtures once when I was
there. As Birch walked away, Colon angrily scooped water from
his toilet bowl with his hands and threw it out into the hallway.

"Oh, I know that guy," I told Birch. "I wrote him up once for
disobeying a direct order. But when I handed him the ticket, he
told me I was wasting my time. He went and dug up a whole pile
of tickets he'd gotten, which he said were always thrown out because he was crazy."

"There's a lot of guys in here like that," Birch said. "And no,
you can't write 'em up. Keeplocking 'em just makes 'em worse.
Can't write 'em up." He shook his head.

"Guy like you in here yesterday told me he'd written five tickets
so far in his first five weeks. Five! That's more than I probably
wrote in my whole career. I'm part of the old school—we took care
of things without all the paperwork then. Inmates knew that if
they misbehaved, we were gonna fuck them up." That, I should
have realized right away, was how the PSU worked.

At midmorning, Officer Birch told me it was time for the lockdown inmates' interviews with the mental-health staff, and he
handed me a ring of keys. One at a time, I was to escort the inmates into a conference room where the staff was gathered, make
sure they were seated, and then remain standing behind them
ready to protect the staff in case of any outburst. This was a nerve-
racking assignment, as I'd had no experience with any of the
patients. And it was complicated by the fact that the interviews—

with a psychiatrist, social worker, nurse, and two other staff members—were interesting to listen to.

First—carefully, so as not to get wet—I tried Colon. "Will you talk to the committee now?" I asked.

"Fuck, no! Fuck them!" he cried. Birch had told me that this was how he'd reacted for the past several days and that I could skip him if he did that. He'd calm down later.

The next inmate, a tall skittish man, went along without a problem. He described to the psychiatrist how two demon COs were using secret symbols to communicate with space beings who landed on the roof of A-block. The COs intended to jinx him with voodoo. Glancing up at me with a hint of a smile, the psychiatrist suggested to the inmate that he consider taking Haldol (an antipsychotic medication). The man shook his head. "Once you start takin' that shit . . ." he muttered.

The psychiatrist then proposed a drug that was milder, and the others at the big table nodded. Still the man demurred. But then the doctor laid it on: "Wouldn't you take antibiotics for a cold or if you had a small infection?" he asked.

The inmate said he would.

"Well, this is like an infection in your head," said the shrink. The inmate finally agreed to the daily medication.

I had already guarded the next inmate that morning, during a one-on-one interview with a caseworker in her office. He was a heavyset black man who had seemed calm during the meeting. As soon as he left the office, though, he'd begun to speak loudly and incomprehensibly about Mike Tyson. Now, he was calm during his meeting with the committee.

The psychiatrist, reading from a folder in front of him, said he would pretend to do a cross-examination. Was that all right? Sure, said the inmate.

"It says here you sometimes scream when you're all by yourself. Is that true?"

"Yes."

"That you have an entirely new personality lately?"

"Yes."

"That you often feel very angry, and go around yelling at everyone?"

"Yes."

"That you think you're the fifth Beatle?"

"No! That's not true!"

The psychiatrist smiled. "I might have made that one up," he said. Others on the committee chuckled.

"That you break things in your cell."

"True."

The inmate agreed to a new course of medication, much to the committee's satisfaction. This was their main purpose, it appeared: to find a way to manage the inmates such that, with daily meds, they could return to the general population. Guard slang for these meds was *bug juice* or *the cure,* but everyone knew it was not a cure. (Many inmates believed that taking them would addle your brain permanently.) The PSU was a holding tank, not a place where people improved. No one, as far as I could see, improved in prison. It took weeks for an inmate in the general population to get an appointment with a therapist, and the wait between appointments, once a relationship had been established, also seemed to be weeks.

His interview concluded, the inmate left the room. The minute I closed the meeting room door, just as before, he resumed his rant: "Mike Tyson fucked 'em up, and now they'll pay him, they'll turn it around," he bellowed. I was relieved to get him back in his cell.

The next two trips to the conference room passed without incident, but the interviews continued to enlighten me. One inmate, a Latino, seemed candid when describing the drugs he'd done in prison: marijuana, crack, powder heroin, Valium. I was surprised at the variety, but the committee wasn't. And he knew the lines to use to impress them. ("But I know it's important to stop drugs so that I can get my life together and, if I'm fortunate enough to earn parole, be a good provider to my kids.") The next inmate, who was white, seemed more lost. He rambled on about the people who wanted to get him and a threatening letter he'd received. The committee seemed to know all about it. Abruptly changing the subject, a counselor said, "And you know what to stay away from, right?"

"Homosexuals, drugs, dice . . ." he began.

"Gangs, gambling, gays, and drugs," she said.

"Right."

Gays? I wondered. It sounded more like a political point of view than a therapeutic strategy. But I couldn't ask. My radio squawked, as it often did, and the inmate glanced back at me nervously.

"Could you ask him to leave the room?" he said to the committee members. The psychiatrist nodded and gestured for me to leave.

And so the inmates went in and out, doing kind of a shuffle, perhaps a by-product of medication, perhaps because we had confiscated their shoelaces so they couldn't hang themselves. Regardless, they seemed authentically sick to me.

They saved the worst inmate for last. Massey was a medium-size, twenty-something black man who was zoned out, like a zombie. Arriving at his chair, he wouldn't take his seat. "Sit down now!" commanded the psychiatrist strictly and, very slowly, the man did. "Stand right behind him," a female therapist whispered to me. "He might get up." I don't remember much about his interview because I was too busy worrying about what I would do if Massey did get up. I placed one of my hands on the end of my baton. There were general questions about the voices Massey heard, about why he wouldn't take the medication. "That's all for now," said the psychiatrist.

Massey didn't budge.

"I said we're done now. You should leave the room," the psychiatrist directed firmly. I removed my baton from its ring and walked into view of Massey. Slowly he stood. I held open the door. Slowly he moved through it. He seemed unresponsive to normal stimuli, sealed off in his own world. The way to his cell was straight ahead, but he turned right, toward the center gate, which led to the civilian offices. Birch was sitting beyond the gate. "Hey!" I yelled.

Massey bent for a drink at a fountain, then stood up and continued his walk. The center gate wasn't closed as it was supposed to be.

"Stop right there!" I shouted, but Massey plodded on. Birch rose to his feet and stretched his arms across the open gate. *"Go back to your cell!"* he ordered. Massey walked on in slow motion, right into Birch, trying to push him out of the way.

In a split second, Birch had a hand around Massey's throat, and I found myself joining him in pushing the inmate against the wall. Birch punched him in the stomach, yelled angrily, then punched him again. I twisted one of his hands into an ordinarily painful aikido grip, but Massey was oblivious. He stared blankly and struggled to get loose. With difficulty, we began moving him back toward his cell. Just then, a huge keeplock officer from B-block named Phelan appeared—in the nick of time, as far as I was concerned, for Massey was surprisingly powerful. With Phelan, we moved him to the door of his cell, but there progress ceased, for Massey grabbed the bars and held on like a crab. It took ten or fifteen seconds for the three of us to pry him loose, during which Birch's gold watch clattered to the floor. Even after we placed him on his cot, Massey got up and resumed a somnambulant march toward the door.

Phelan lifted him into the air and slammed him against the cell's metal wall.

"Stop all this bug-game shit!" he yelled.

The inmate seemed insensate. No emotion passed across his face, no sign of fear or pain. *Bam!* Phelan slammed him up against the wall again. This time Massey looked more discouraged and didn't try to stand. We locked him in and dusted ourselves off.

"Massey playin' a bug game," said Birch. He'd been in and out much of the past two months, he said, but he wasn't usually this bad.

It was my first use-of-force incident, and the experience was heady. I paused to gather my thoughts. Department policy on this was quite strict. I was in charge of the PSU logbook, so I went to make an entry.

"What're you doing?" asked Birch.

"Logging it."

"Don't log it. That's a waste of time. Won't no punishment come out of it for him, 'cause he's a bug. It's just a lot of paperwork we'd all three have to do. And Phelan's gone now. Forget it."

I held the pen poised above the paper for a moment, then put it down. I didn't want to alienate Birch. What he said was like a lot of things about prison: brutal, but reasonable under the circumstances.

Sitting in chairs alongside the six psych-unit cells most days, twenty-four hours a day, were the officers assigned to two kinds of special watch: suicide watch and drug watch. Suicide watch was clear enough. Inmates thought to be on the verge of killing themselves had to be closely observed until they were deemed out of danger. Drug watch was similar but less glamorous. Any inmate who was thought to have swallowed some drug in a packet—in hopes of not getting caught with it—was placed for seventy-two hours in a cell with the taps and toilet water turned off. He was allowed no underwear, only a paper gown. The observing officer was provided with latex gloves and a tongue depressor. In case of an inmate bowel movement that yielded some "prize," he was to call a sergeant.

I spent two shifts and some overtime watching an inmate from Tappan who an officer had seen swallowing something white during a routine pat-frisk. In trying to stop him, the officer had broken his dental plate, the inmate complained; and all he'd been trying to swallow anyway, he said, was a written note. He'd been in there almost two days when I began, and had completed almost three when I finished, and still no action. His defeat of the system, after seventy-two hours, had much to do with the fact that he wouldn't eat anything from the food trays that were brought to him three times a day. He did, however, drink water, and the area reeked of urine stagnating in the toilet bowl. The job was killingly dull, and I would have been likely to drift off to sleep if not for one fellow officer's warning that an inmate he had once watched had had a movement, all right, but had then quickly reswallowed the packet of contraband before the officer could open up the cell.

Much more often, I was assigned to suicide watch, euphemistically known in the Department as special watch. When you arrived, you received no specific information about the inmate under observation—just the special-watch logbook, the only reading material the officer was allowed to have. One summer day, strung out from the blocks, I settled with relief into the special-watch chair and peered into the cell. My inmate, Morales, was fast asleep. My sole duty was to make an entry, every fifteen minutes, describing what Morales was up to. "Morales asleep," I wrote several times.

The logbook went back two years. I decided to read the whole thing. The majority of entries described inmates snoring, lying on their sides, and turning over. But there were also some startling entries. One officer had accompanied a suicidal inmate to nearby St. Agnes Hospital:

> Inmate is attempting to remove IV from hand. Doctor replaces it.
>
> Inmate Ray is trying to pull tube out of his penis. Nurse Campbell readjusting restraints again.
>
> Straight jacket put on.

Inmate asked, "What would happen if I swallowed my IV?" Then pulled part of IV off. I responded, "We will have nothing but trouble." He then gave me the IV part.

Inmate has swallowed Ensure can poptop lid and bathroom light switch cord ATT. ["ATT" was logbook-ese for "at this time."]

Another series of entries was from the cell next to the one I was watching:

7:00 A.M.	CO J Carmody on duty on PSU special watch cell #20 Inmate Rivera, Richard 94A5932. Inmate appears to be sleeping. All appears secure at this time.
7:30	Inmate appears to be sleeping ATT.
8:00	Inmate appears to be sleeping ATT.
9:00	Inmate Rivera is awake ATT. Inmate state that he is not eating. He is not hungry.
9:30	Inmate states that he is not going to eat or talk to anyone. He states he is going to jump off sink and break his neck on the bed. Inmate is standing on sink. Obeys order to get down.
9:40	Nurse in to talk to Inmate.
9:55	Rivera out to talk to PSU staff.
10:15	Rivera back in cell
10:30	All appears secure ATT
11:00	All appears secure ATT
11:05	lunch served. Inmate Rivera refuses to eat.
11:30	All appears secure ATT.
12:00	All appears secure ATT.
12:30	All appears secure ATT.
12:45	Inmate eating what appears to be feces. OMH [Office of Mental Health] notified.
1:15	Inmate has a pile of feces on the floor and is at times eating it. OMH staff notified.
1:30	All appears secure ATT
2:00	Inmate jumping off sink against the wall. OMH notified.
2:05	Inmate claims he injured his right arm. OMH notified.
2:30	All appears secure ATT.
3:00	All appears secure ATT

3:20	Inmate states to me he wants to fight. States he wants to "set it off."
3:45	Nurse speaking to Inmate Rivera.
3:50	Inmate Rivera eating dinner now.
4:00	All appears secure ATT.
4:20	Inmate jumping off sink onto bunk. Refused order to stop. OMH notified.
4:30	Inmate jumping off sink onto bunk, bounced off north wall, fell on bunk and landed on floor. Claims he can't move. OMH notified. Nurse Dennis and CO's Smith and Copper responded.
4:40	Inmate observed moving his legs and body off floor.
5:00	Inmate continues to lay on floor.
5:15	Inmate stood up and then lay back on floor.
5:20	Inmate makes medical history. He's now cured. Inmate walking around. Inmate threw tray on gallery.
6:00	All appears secure ATT
6:15	Sgt. Carrigan speaking to Rivera
6:30	All appears secure ATT
7:00	All appears secure ATT
7:15	Inmate standing on sink. States he is going to jump onto edge of bed and break his neck. Given order to come down. Inmate complies.
7:20	Inmate standing on sink. States he is going to kill himself.
7:45	Nurse talking to Rivera
8:00	All appears secure ATT
8:55	Inmate issued mattress cover, socks and t-shirt per OMH Nurse Whit.
9:30	All appears secure ATT
10:00	All appears secure ATT
10:30	All appears secure ATT

Morales slept almost the entire shift, rising near the end only to ask for a cigarette. He even slept through the day's only excitement, when an inmate down the hall managed to cut both his wrists with the blade from a disposable razor he'd somehow smuggled in. The officer observing him called a nurse and the sergeant. The nurse, noting that the slashes were only superficial, just had the inmate stick his arms out through the bars so she could clean them up and put on antiseptic and bandages. The sergeant, annoyed to have been called up for nothing, advised the inmate, "Next time, cut the long way. It works a lot better."

By the next day, I'd learned more about Morales. Some of his earlier stays in the PSU had been recorded in this same logbook. He'd frequently been suicidal, and was prone to self-mutilation. A female officer had logged an entry about him masturbating openly. Another officer must have remarked on it to him, she wrote, because when she came back on duty, the next day he was "irate" that she had written it down. Poor guy. He had been observed singing "White Christmas" and dragging a plastic disposable cup top around his cell with a string, calling it his "car." Less benignly, he had pried up and swallowed three pieces of floor tile, and used another shard of the tile to make cuts across his leg and wrist and, apparently, "a blood-filled hole in chest."

I watched the indistinct form of the forty-something Puerto Rican through the screen as he turned in bed and sat up on his mattress. I could tell he had a beard and mustache and a bit of a belly, but all I could really see unobstructed were his feet and pale, thin calves. I didn't know what incident had caused him to be moved from the fourth floor of 5-Building (the psych floor) over to here, but usually it was a suicide attempt. He confirmed this after lunch, when he ran out of matches and I offered him a light. He bent down near the bars to show me the slashes across his right forearm that he had made with a tin-can top. They looked deeper than most. Later, he even lay on the floor so that I could see, below the screen, the still-red scars of previous self-inflicted wounds—a gash near the jugular made with another piece of floor tile, and the now-healed hole in his chest.

It was the pressure of prison, Morales told me, that caused him to hurt himself. Gangs were especially hard on him—they took advantage of the mentally ill by sending them on risky assignments. If they got caught by the COs, their mental status was a kind of indemnity. He said he'd do whatever it took to get out of Sing Sing.

"Including acting crazy?"

"It ain't hard to act crazy when you are crazy, CO," he said.

"Hmm."

"Hey, it wasn't my choice to be here. The guy I killed, you'd probably want to kill him, too. He beat up women. 'Course I was fucked-up at the time."

"What do you mean—on drugs?"

"Drugs and alcohol. But I took the ASAT [Alcohol and Substance Abuse Treatment] course, which I think will help me stay off. You know what I really want, though? Chinese food. Chinese or Thai. I want some fried rice. What I'd do for fried rice."

Two days earlier, according to the logbook, Morales had told his guard that the only way out was to kill himself. There was no way to go home or to see his family. They wanted him to kill himself and even said so, now that his mother had died. He was laughing out loud "for no apparent reason," hitting himself in the head with an open palm.

But sometime between then and now, he'd been told something miraculous: He would be shipped to Marcy in two days. That had calmed him down considerably. During the second-degree murder bid that had started in 1984 and also taken him to Attica and Wende, he'd already been to Marcy four times, he said. It was good there: no gangs, a movie every day, four-man rooms with the doors unlocked during the day, no COs per se. There were punishments—they'd put you in restraints or "stick you in the ass" with a tranquilizing injection—but it was freer there.

"But aren't there only bugs to talk to?" I asked.

No, he said, and he knew a lot of guys there.

He showed me his "inmate accounts" statement—on which inmates keep track of how much they can spend in the commissary—and told me he bet I'd never seen one like this. And I hadn't. He had a negative balance of more than a hundred dollars.

"How can you have a negative balance?" I asked. "They gave you credit?"

"No, man. It's my tickets. I had twenty-three Tier Two and Tier Three tickets in the last year." Each of these serious infractions, regardless of the disposition, resulted in a five-dollar charge to the inmate's account.

"For what?"

"Oh, for drinking paint, for tearing my sink out of the wall, for hurting myself. They're not fair, man. You shouldn't get charged when you're sick in the head."

Drinking paint? Even if you did it with the conscious goal of getting yourself away from the general population, you really did have to be sick to drink paint or swallow shards of floor tile.

I told Morales about the death, the night before, of Princess Diana and about the new MetroCards that were taking the place of tokens on the New York City subways. He asked me for lights for his cigarettes, and when my matches ran low, he showed me how to tear them carefully up the middle, making two matches out of one. Finally, he suggested that we play chess. I found the painted Masonite board and a box of plastic pieces in the lounge; we balanced the board carefully on the cell's food slot, near the floor.

Morales was a competent chess player. We each won a game and then, in excitement, because I was ahead in the third, I bumped the board and tipped it over. Whoops. Birch dropped by, warning me that many sergeants objected to officers playing games with inmates. But then he offered to warn me by rapping on the window if anyone approached. Morales assured me that when he heard the rapping, he'd take the chessboard off the bars and place it under his bunk. I heard a tapping on the window after lunch and told Morales the moment had come. It took a moment for it to register, though, and when it did, *he* tipped the pieces all over the floor of the cell—an instant before Sergeant Holmes rounded the corner. Fortunately, the screen obstructed Holmes's view of the mess. He initialed the logbook and was gone.

Our subsequent games were constantly interrupted by inmate Auguste, in the next cell down. Auguste was a thin black man who greeted every officer that passed, no matter what time of day, with "Top of the morning to you, sir!" In one of the more macabre tableaux I witnessed in the prison, he would stand in the middle of his cell, arms outstretched, head back, singing favorite lines from "New York, New York": " 'If I can make it there, I'll make it anywhere.' " Another time, sounding like one of the homeless men in Manhattan who wait outside fancy restaurants late at night and flatter emerging patrons before asking for a handout, he had told me, "You look like Robert Redford!" To the nurse, I heard him say, "You're a combination of Grace Kelly and Princess Diana!"

Another time, though, I saw Auguste stop singing as though suddenly possessed and then begin to mime savagely beating someone on the floor, as though with a hammer or hatchet. So much for the sweet old nutcase.

Today he was singing, "O beautiful for spacious skies," again and again, until Morales hollered, "Knock it off! Will you fuckin' knock it off?" A long silence followed, while Auguste's brain rebooted. When it came back on-line, he was singing the sixties pop hit "Sugar, Sugar." Then I noticed he was out of his cell. Inmates whom the shrinks judged to be making progress were allowed out for a few hours a day; this was called rec. Auguste came to watch our game.

"The Archies, right?" I asked as he hummed near me.

"Yes, sir. I was their bass player."

Morales tried to cadge some tobacco off Auguste, who obliged, but in return he began to lecture Morales about Egypt and the Pharaohs and how the white man rules but the black man is really in charge because Jesus was black and—

"Stop that bullshit!" screamed Morales.

"Yes, Master, yes," said Auguste, and hurried away.

I wished Morales luck and we knocked knuckles, the way inmates did with each other. I could do it because he was out of there, bound for Marcy, and I'd never see him again.

VISIT ROOM

It was easy to forget when you worked at Sing Sing that all the inmates there were, essentially, missing from someplace else. Outside the walls, however, they were still fathers, sons, brothers, and husbands—mainly of poor people from New York City. In being sent to prison, they had no doubt let people down; some who loved them no longer wanted to see them. But they were missed by many others, and every day of the week these people found their way to the prison via bus, car, train, and taxi. They submitted to searches of their person and property and subjected themselves to long waits in order to spend a short time in Sing Sing's Visit Room.

The Visit Room constituted a sort of breach in the wall between the hermetic world of the prison and the universe outside. In it, an inmate could try to reconnect to the real world and prior life, could try to salve the wound of imprisonment. A visitor could contemplate, with more perspective than any prison employee, the effects of incarceration and the prospects of life after it. The Visit Room was about catching up, reconnecting, and looking ahead, about a woman's touch and a child's chatter.

I worked the Visit Room with Colton, wearing the dress blues that officers had to put on for any post that brought them into contact with the general public. We sat behind a wide desk on a raised platform and surveyed the expansive, cafeterialike space. The back of the room was lined with vending machines, and between those and us were carefully aligned rows of tables and chairs, identified by letters that hung from the ceiling. To our left was an enclosed play area for kids. Behind it were small offices for an inmate photographer, who snapped keepsake Polaroid pictures, and a counselor who could help with matters such as weddings. (Inmates were allowed to get married in prison, with the permission of the superintendent, and thereby qualify for an eventual conjugal visit.) The wall to our right was a series of picture windows—perhaps intended to offer a commanding view of the Hudson River, but now marred by a blue heat-reflective film applied to the glass to keep afternoon sun from overheating the room. Beyond, coils of concertina wire topping a mesh fence further obscured the vista.

To our immediate right was the door through which visitors entered after presenting I.D., checking their belongings, and passing through a metal detector. We pointed toward their choice of seating—either the tables, which were surrounded by four plastic chairs, or rows of chairs near the window, where they could sit next to an inmate. Inmates arrived through a separate door, to our immediate left. Once they had checked in with us, we pointed them to their visitor. If a visitor was still waiting after an hour—this was common—we would call the blocks to learn the reason for the holdup. Occasionally, it was an officer's fault: The gallery officer might have failed to find the inmate and then forgotten to follow up, or someone might have forgotten to notify the gallery officer. But often the problem was with the inmates—they could take forever with showering, shaving, and coiffing, trying to get together the perfect self-presentation.

Colton was in a rotten mood, hardly talking, clearly homesick and hating Sing Sing. "How's it going?" I asked anyway. "I could live without it," he replied. He seemed uninterested in and even averse to the dramas unfolding before us, but I was fascinated. If you'd ever wondered about inmates' lives outside prison, here were some of the missing pieces.

I watched a young woman who came in, found her table, put her head down, and went to sleep while awaiting her beau. He awakened her with a kiss—Prince Charming—and I wondered whether they always did it that way. Then there was another couple whose visit started icily. She practically put an arm up to keep him from hugging her, he settled for a squeeze of the hand, then the two retired to the side-by-side seats in the back of the room. Three hours later, I noticed, they were kissing passionately, the freeze having thawed.

On the other side of the room sat an aging couple, there to

see . . . a son? Almost every visit began with an embrace, but some beginnings were shy or tentative. The son and his parents touched only arms, not chests; he might have given his mother the briefest of kisses. Or was she a foster mother? Was he a stepdad?

One inmate was thronged by three little kids the moment he left our desk. They jumped around him and held on to his legs as he made his way toward their mother—his wife? or was it his sister?—who tried to clear a space for him at the table amidst the crayons and coloring books. It made you happy, this sight, but also very, very sad.

Several regular officers worked the room with us. Since Colton was incommunicado, I began chatting with a regular named Eveillard, who was born in Haiti, he said. Eveillard, balding and with a dirty shirt, had been deflecting the barbs of some of the American-born officers, with limited success. He seemed glad to talk to someone who wasn't going to make fun of him. As he was sealing an envelope, he told me the story behind it. He had just returned from a vacation in Santo Domingo, capital of the Dominican Republic, which shares the island of Hispaniola with Haiti. I had never met anyone who vacationed in Santo Domingo, I said. Got to go! he said enthusiastically. He had met a beautiful woman there and had fallen in love. He spoke some Spanish, and that was how they had communicated, but he could not write Spanish. Fortunately, a porter—he gestured toward a young inmate cleaning the children's play area—had written a love letter for him in Spanish.

Eveillard had me walk around the room with him. A boy was about to follow his father into the inmates' bathroom. "Sorry, that's not allowed," Eveillard told them. You had to keep an eye on them, he emphasized. Though visitors were screened with a metal detector, they could not be pat-frisked unless there was reason to suspect them, and this was one way drugs came into the facility. A woman could have some dope in a packet in her bra, the man could swallow it, and—voilà. And there were lesser scams, too.

"You know they can't have sneakers worth more than fifty dollars, right? Well, their homeboy comes in wearing new Air Jordans. The inmate takes off his old sneakers, and they switch 'em under the table. Maybe we'll catch the inmate on his way out, but maybe we won't." I thought I would probably notice an inmate wearing Air Jordans.

It had also happened that a visitor wearing a double layer of clothes left one layer in the bathroom for his inmate friend. The inmate, dressed in civvies, might try to walk right out of the Visit Room to the street at the end of the day. Of course, there were procedures in place to prevent this—an ultraviolet stamp applied to the visitor's arm when he entered and then checked when he left was one of them—but you had to be careful. An inmate had escaped from the Rikers Island Visit Room that same summer, despite the many fail-safes.

With Eveillard, I stopped at a table where a young woman in a red dress had left her chair and was sitting in the lap of the inmate. "Not allowed!" Eveillard said, making a loud *tsk*-ing noise. Reluctantly, and slowly, she moved. As long as each person stayed in his or her chair, feet on the floor, with no intimate touching besides kisses, we would leave them alone. But the battle against lust required constant oversight: I had to order the same woman off the inmate's lap an hour later. Eveillard told me he'd actually had to interrupt an act of standing intercourse a few months before. The Visit Room had an outdoor annex for warm days, and the couple had been standing behind some of the playground equipment—not exactly family entertainment.

There was also a special sealed-off area provided for no-contact visits. This was the kind of visit space that movies and television made out to be the norm, with partitions, windows, and telephone receivers, and with both parties anguished because touching was impossible. The reality, at least in Sing Sing, was different. Inmate and visitor were kept separated only if one of them requested it. Just the week before, Eveillard said, a woman had arrived and requested a no-contact visit—she was going to tell her husband she wanted a divorce, and feared his reaction. As anticipated, he exploded, and officers had to restrain him.

Another reason to stay alert was that, instead of a disintegrating relationship, an inmate might have an extra one. Every longtime officer seemed to have witnessed a wife arriving when an inmate's girlfriend was already there, or vice versa. Fireworks were guaranteed.

Eveillard had worked the Visit Room for a long time and liked it. I did, too, because I didn't feel as much in prison myself here, and I got to witness positive interactions instead of the customary conflictual ones. But, like a great many other officers who worked the Visit Room, Eveillard found one aspect of this duty really galling: the number of attractive young women who visited inmates.

"You saw the one in the red dress. And look at that one!" Eveillard hissed under his breath. "What does she see in him? What can he do for her? Nothing!"

I found the presence of attractive young women here curious but not vexing. But to Eveillard it was infuriating, evidence of female delusion and divine injustice. "You see her?" he said quietly of a woman holding hands with an inmate at a table. I recognized the inmate from B-block. He was frequently called out for visits. "She comes here after working a night shift, almost every day. To spend her time here! She is doing his time for him!" I knew what Eveillard meant. There was almost no limit to the number of visits an inmate could have, even if he was keeplocked or in the Box. As long as his visitor was there, he could be out of his cell from around 8:30 A.M. to 2:45 P.M., Monday through Friday (and alternate weekends), enjoying the relatively pleasant environment.

He pointed out another woman, this one pregnant, accompanied by a small child and looking very happy to see her inmate. "See her? That's his wife! She met him seven years ago, when she came here with a friend who was visiting another inmate. First they got married. Then they did the FRP [Family Reunion Program—a program allowing for occasional conjugal visits]. And now she's pregnant again. Unbelievable!"

"That *is* strange," I had to agree. "Maybe she just likes having a husband who isn't around."

"But how can he support her?" he asked, exasperated.

Well, there was welfare, and a few inmates had means, but it was mostly a mystery. I wondered what kind of love the woman felt for the inmate. Was it romantic—the desire for something you could never have? Was it practical—a way to raise children without interference? The COs couldn't figure it out, because these men could never *support* the women, and the goal of solvency animated officers' entire lives.

On the other hand, I had gotten to know such a woman while doing research for a magazine article I'd written about a hatchet murderer. The killer had secretly created and then marketed software from within the Minnesota state prison system while participating in a vocational course that allowed him access to the Internet. This woman had had a crush on him since she was a teenager, long before he committed the murder. So strong was her attraction that when the inmate was paroled, seventeen years after his conviction, she divorced her husband (the father of their two kids) and took up with him.

"My whole attitude was, it really didn't matter," she had told me of the murder and conviction, which she considered one-of-a-kind occurrences brought about by a fluky convergence of factors. And practicality, she felt, should always take a backseat to true love.

Since many of the women in the Visit Room were from the ghetto or at least the poor side of town, the absence of loved ones due to incarceration was a fact of life in their world, something they had to accommodate. A line in the movie *Birdman of Alcatraz* seemed to capture this situation exactly. The "birdman" murderer, Robert Stroud, had been transferred to Alcatraz and away from a midwestern woman he had met by mail while in Leavenworth. The woman, whom he had married, showed up one day at Alcatraz to visit him, and Stroud, speaking for every person who had ever puzzled over this question, demanded to know why on earth she had come all that way.

"Because," she said, "you're the only life I have."

———

I returned to sit at the desk with Colton. Both of us were tired. But I got the feeling that exhaustion made him more "cop" and me less "cop." We finished up our paperwork, and at 2:30 P.M. Colton announced through the microphone that all visits had to end; everyone had to be out of the room by 2:45 P.M. As the minutes ticked off, little girls clasped their daddies' necks, lovers hugged as though the embrace had to last through all eternity, and an old woman got teary-eyed. The positive side of visits was made tragic by the truth that prison, over time, eroded or erased practically all relationships. Despite what I had seen in Minnesota, I knew that precious few survived. People on the outside moved or met new people or died. They moved on. Did Colton share any of these thoughts? As we stood up to herd everybody out, I couldn't help myself. I gestured out at the sea of emotion and asked, "Does it make you a little homesick?"

"Oh sure," said Colton wryly. "It's a regular Hallmark card."

———

I stopped at my local garage to get my car inspected on my way home. It was a small place near the tracks in Yonkers. The hard-working owner, Marty, looked upset this evening. As I sat in the waiting room, I overheard him telling another customer that something had happened to an elderly friend of his.

"Harry's retired, and he's walking home with a toolbox last night after doing some volunteer work at his church. And these guys knock him down, beat him up, send him to the hospital. Just to get a couple tools." He shook his head in disgust.

That brought me down to earth, rechanneled some of my sympathy. I know those guys, I wanted to tell Marty—I spend every day with them.

It was all about absence, wasn't it—the absence of imprisoned men from the lives of the people who loved them; the absence of love in prison. And also—what you could never forget—the absence in the hearts of decent people, the holes that criminals punched in their lives, the absence of the things they took: money, peace of mind, health, and entire lives, because they were selfish or sick or scared or just couldn't wait.

WALLPOST

The old chair was comfortable, the view stupendous, the feeling of being left alone delicious.

I was up there by myself—just me, my guns, my newspaper, and the toilet—working Wallpost 18.

It would be satisfying to a closet sniper, this job, because he could spend long hours playing out scenarios of whom he might have to fire at, with which weapon, and under what circumstance. It was satisfying to me because, again, it was a reprieve from the noise and stress of the blocks. The old prison wall was studded with nine of these towers; there was a total of eighteen towers, including the ugly new square ones around Tappan. I loved the architecture: Sing Sing's old octagonal towers were the prison's main emblem, the image on the souvenir history booklet, union key chains, and the coffee cups and T-shirts sold by enterprising officers in the parking lot on payday. Each tower had a catwalk around it, with spotlights affixed to the railing, and the feeling inside was of a cozy bungalow. I loved the breeze blowing through, and my privileged position firmly astride the prison wall, with both sides in plain sight.

All of the actively used wallposts contained a small arsenal. The gun rack, set between two of the eight windows, held a Remington shotgun, a Colt AR-15 assault rifle, a tear-gas gun, and many rounds of ammunition. Around my waist was a belt and holster with a Smith & Wesson .38 Special revolver. Across the room were some chemical-agent canisters in a special vest, next to a riot helmet and megaphone.

There was nothing much to do, and yet you had to stay alert: That was the joy and difficulty of a day in a wall tower. But mostly it was a joy—I had wanted to run up and kiss Sergeant Holmes when he assigned it to me. New officers did not get up here very often. The regular, I found out, was on a two-week vacation.

You enter the wall tower through an ancient gate outside the prison wall. The towers were considered the facility's last line of defense, so they were to be inaccessible from within the prison. To get the key, you presented yourself at the gate and waited for the officer you were relieving to drop the key down in a bucket on a rope. The key itself was marvelous—the oldest I'd seen in Sing Sing, thin and short, with two circles cut out of the grip and the edges softened by a million touches. *Sargent & Greenleaf Co.*, it read on the grip, *Rochester, N.Y. No. 101*. I would later see a similar one in a display case at the retired federal prison on Alcatraz Island, in San Francisco Bay; that one dated to 1909.

Inside the tower was a corroded iron spiral staircase. One complete turn took you up some twenty-five feet to the metal hatch in the middle of the floor above. By the time you arrived, the officer who was headed home had lifted the hatch so you could climb in. You exchanged pleasantries and the key, which he used to let himself out and then placed back in the bucket for you to pull up with the rope. Then you were secure, ready to start your shift.

Sing Sing had three "sally ports," or vehicle passages, to the outside world, and Wallpost 18 sat above one of them. The port had two huge sliding metal gates which, for security reasons, were controlled not from the ground but from my tower. A vehicle entering or leaving the prison would pass through one gate, stop over a submerged inspection bay, and wait for inspection and clearance for passage from officers on the ground, who signaled me when all was clear. Then I would turn one of the big black switches on my control panel, the other gate would open, and the vehicle would proceed. The simple rule I had to remember was to always close one gate before opening the other.

Fortunately, this sally port was used mainly for official vehicles—prison vans, state-police cars, ambulances—and it was a weekend day, so there wasn't much traffic. I could relax a little. Using binoculars, I watched a sailboat regatta down by the Tappan Zee Bridge and saw the slowly moving traffic on the bridge above. I scanned the facility, land of a zillion red bricks. And, resting my eyes, I watched a flock of geese exploring the chapel lawn in front of me. That particular swath of lawn was also pictured in a photograph taped to the wall next to the window. A square yard of it was indicated with Magic Marker. That was where I was to aim any warning shots.

I checked the weapons, counted the ammunition, made the required phone call to the watch commander to say that everything was okay. I flushed the toilet: It was a steel commode/basin combination, just like the ones in the psych unit. A jury-rigged burner and pot also looked inspired by, if not commandeered from, inmate facilities. I glanced into the ambulance log. One seemed to enter the facility every three or four days, on average. A bunch of memos were stuffed into a clipboard. One was headed DISABLING OF HELICOPTERS. First you were to fire into the rear rotor, it directed. Only after that, because of the high risk of explosion, were you to shoot into the engine cowling. Third, after warning shots, you could "fire to disable any inmates who may approach." But only if the exploding helicopter hadn't already wiped all of us out, I supposed.

A second memo, from a captain, seemed aimed at shaking up the tower personnel, who were no doubt a bastion of complacency. "It must be realize [sic] by all staff that the perimeter is the first and last lines [sic] of defense in maintaining the high degree of security necessary for the secure operation of a maximum security Facility," he wrote. "We all must be cognizant of the close proximity of this Facility to NYC which is home to a major part of our population . . ." Blah blah blah.

Another memo, four years old, described the Family Reunion Program, probably soon after its inauguration. Entrance to the family-visit trailers was through the sally port at Wallpost 15, where I would work later. Each unit had an outdoor grill and picnic table, and they shared a swing set; inside, I was told, there was a television, a kitchen, and separate sleeping areas for kids and adults. Married inmates on good behavior were eligible to stay there every few months. The Felon Reproduction Program, some officers called it.

On the memo, a wall-tower officer had penned in a telling editorial change in one sentence. "*Purpose:* To provide for a Family Reunion Program which helps preserve, enhance, and strengthen family ties that have been disrupted as a result of incarceration." The word *incarceration* had been crossed out, and handwritten in its place was the word *individual.* Family disruption wasn't caused by incarceration, in other words; it was caused by actions of the individual that *resulted* in incarceration. The distinction was important to officers, who wanted no personal responsibility for the harmful effects of the system.

Down on the street outside the wall, the roach coach honked its horn. I stepped out onto the catwalk and hollered to the driver: "Pizza and coffee?" I pointed to the bucket on the rope, and he nodded. I lowered a five-dollar bill to him and, soon after, pulled up my lunch and my change.

As I ate, I read *CPO Family,* the magazine of the Correctional Peace Officers Foundation, a group that offered money and support to the families of slain correction officers. (I joined this organization.) The best article was written by a New York State officer.

"What would the average citizen say if it were proposed that police officers be assigned to a neighborhood which was inhabited by no one but criminals and those officers would be unarmed, patrol on foot and be heavily outnumbered?" asked Donald E. Premo, Jr. "My beat is totally inhabited by convicted felons who, by definition, are people who tend to break laws, rules, and regulations. I am outnumbered by as much as 20, 30, and even 40 to 1 at various times during my workday, and, contrary to popular belief, I work without a sidearm. In short, my neck is on the line every minute of every day."

Premo had a good point, I thought, but with the blossoming cynicism of a few weeks in Sing Sing's blocks, I could see he'd understated his case. Twenty, thirty, even forty to one? How about coming to visit me in A-block or B-block? How about 150 to one?

Looking down the hill, I could see a corner of the A-block yard. Guards who worked towers over a yard had a lot of responsibility. The officers on the ground depended on them for support in case of a disturbance, and yards were a frequent site of trouble. Sometimes, as we'd been told at the Academy, an officer could stop a fight just by turning on his PA system and loudly sliding a shotgun shell into its chamber. Some officers were not shy about actually firing. One OJT who'd been at Clinton briefly told me an officer there had recently shot an inmate's finger off, presumably while aiming for something more meaty.

My tower was not responsible for the A-block yard, for which I was glad, because even my partial view of it reminded me of the death of George Jackson, the Black Panther and author of *Soledad Brother*, a collection of letters from prison. Jackson and two other "Soledad brothers" had been accused of helping beat to death a white correction officer at the California prison on January 16, 1970. (Three days earlier, a white tower guard at Soledad had shot and killed three black inmates.) Just before the opening of his murder trial, Jackson was shot and killed by a tower guard at San Quentin, where he had been transferred. The authorities said he was shot because he was armed and attempting to escape. "No Black person," wrote the novelist James Baldwin, "will ever believe that George Jackson died the way they tell us he did."

The trash can on the outside catwalk was stuffed with contraband daily newspapers, I discovered, which made me feel less bad about having run back to my car after getting my assignment, in order to pick up a paperback novel. I had learned about this new book from an advertisement on the chalkboard by the front gate— *Killer,* by Christopher Newman. The author, in his acknowledgments, thanked First Deputy Superintendent Charles Greiner (now the superintendent of Sing Sing), and as I read on, I saw that Greiner must have given Newman a tour and a lot of background information about facility operations. *Killer* was about a New York City police lieutenant who was being stalked by a notorious Colombian gunman who had just escaped from Sing Sing.

The scenario was this: The Colombian knew that his best chance of escape would be during an outside medical trip. With his A-block buddies, he created a fake altercation on his way to supper. Shielded from the eyes of COs by milling inmates, he stabbed himself deeply, purposefully creating a sucking chest wound. It worked. He was driven out of Sing Sing through the very gate I sat astride, in an official van that was soon hijacked by his confederates. In the van with the Colombian was a Sing Sing nurse, who was forced to continue treating him.

Greiner, to my surprise, had authorized a book signing for *Killer* near the lineup room. Any book that postulated an escape, I would have thought, would have been anathema to the superintendent. The fact that it wasn't gave me heart. Maybe Greiner wouldn't be so unhappy when *my* book came out.

UTILITY 1

Occasionally from a wallpost you would see a decrepit Sing Sing van stop somewhere on the road encircling the prison, and out would pile one officer with a chair and five or six inmates with lawn mowers and Weed Eaters. This was Utility 1, a crew of medium-security inmates whose job it was to mow and clean in the area just outside the walls.

One day I had the job of supervising Utility 1, and though it was supposedly a plum, I found it completely nerve-racking: I was terrified that one of these trusted inmates would run off, leaving me to blame for an escape.

This had actually happened recently to Konoval, the training officer, who had taken a different work crew out mowing near a highway in the Bronx. One of the inmates disappeared when Konoval wasn't looking, only to be recaptured a few hours later at his mother's apartment in Queens—luckily for Konoval. Those inmates were supposedly even more trustworthy than mine, and Konoval was supposedly a supremely experienced officer. Thinking of him, I actually felt it was *likely* that it would happen to me.

The inmates and I got into a fight over this anxiety of mine. Apparently, when they mowed the relatively short stretch alongside the south wall of the prison, the regular officer didn't object if those in the lead went ahead and kept on mowing around the corner. But around the corner was out of sight, and I panicked when they disappeared. Two of them told me they would refuse to work if I made them stay back. "What's wrong, CO, you scared? We ain't goin' nowhere—the towers watch us all the way."

"Stay in sight," I said. "If you refuse, I'm writing you up. Or maybe you don't care about your job." This was false bravado—I doubt I could have gotten them fired—but it seemed enough to inspire some hatred of me, if not fear.

We had to go back to a storage shed to swap malfunctioning equipment for barely working equipment. To show the inmates I wasn't a bad guy, I agreed to their request not to take the steep, curvy route that hugged the north side of the facility but to drive a route that was almost as fast, through downtown Ossining. The inmates were mad to see women—any women—and this route was more likely to gratify.

Like several old Hudson River downtowns in the region, from

Peekskill to Poughkeepsie, the neighborhood has seen better days. Parts are a ghetto now, with broken-down stoops, prostitutes at night, and guys playing dice against the curb. There was one corner I had always noticed when I passed on previous occasions. It had a large number of fairly well dressed young men hanging around out front, not drinking or gambling, not visibly occupied with anything except paying close attention to passing cars. The inmates waved at them, and they waved back.

"Looks like a crack house," I commented.

"Of course it's a crack house," said the inmate in the passenger seat next to me. "Been there for months." He seemed to take offense at some condemnation he heard in my tone. "Just guys making a living is all."

I nodded. (Two hundred feet farther on and around the corner was a ramshackle wooden house directly opposite wallpost 15. This was actually a CO residence inhabited by a changing cast of upstate officers I had worked with; with no knowing reference to the real one, *it* had been nicknamed the Crack House.) It struck me as peculiar that the crack trade was flourishing openly perhaps a hundred yards from one of the most famous maximum-security prisons in the world.

It had a little bit to do with jurisdictions, I supposed. The Ossining police probably had several crack houses to deal with, and its proximity to Sing Sing did not constitute a reason to go after that one in particular. In fact, the presence of a crack house was not so stunning alongside what I had seen during a day on another plum job, construction.

Officers on construction detail—like the one who had witnessed me getting slugged in the head that day in A-block—accompanied outside tradesmen doing building or maintenance work inside the prison. Once I spent an entire day on top of the Hospital Building, keeping an eye on a crew of roofers who were removing an old surface laden with asbestos and then laying a new one. Essentially, my job was to make sure they didn't do anything to threaten security, such as drop tools to inmates or leave out dangerous equipment.

During lunch break, I got to talk to a few of them. Like the inmates, they were startled to find that I spoke Spanish. One in particular seemed happy to chat. He hadn't spoken to any white people apart from bosses since he arrived from Ecuador the year before, he told me. The trip had been a difficult one, and it cost him over seven thousand dollars: He had flown from Quito to Guatemala, then taken a boat to Acapulco. From there he traveled overland to the U.S. border, crossed over to Houston with help from a *coyote,* and then finally flew on a commercial airline to New York City.

"So you're still illegal?" I asked.

"Sure," he said, shrugging and looking at the others resting against the wall, thermoses and lunch bags by their sides, *"como todos nosotros."* Like the rest.

Here was a man who had violated federal law—a fugitive, technically—actually working inside Sing Sing. Resting against its very bricks. And not afraid to tell an officer.

TRANSPORTATION

Over four days in my first months on the job, I got to enter another realm normally guarded jealously by senior officers: transportation detail. For people who are in confinement, inmates go a lot of places. They are accompanied outside of prison to court hearings (many, though imprisoned, have additional charges pending), to family funerals, to the hospital, and to other prisons on transfer. Officers on transportation detail get to leave the facility, and because many trips spill over from one shift to another, they rack up lots of overtime pay.

I was sent from lineup one day to work with a transportation officer named Billings. Every trip required at least two officers. If a large contingent of inmates was being moved, even more officers went along. That day, however, Billings and I had only one inmate to transport, a Mexican who had a deportation hearing at an immigration court inside the Downstate Correctional Facility, about an hour's drive away.

We wore sidearms, and it was instructive to witness the lengths to which the prison went to keep guns—even officers' guns—out of the facility. First we walked out the prison's front gate and collected the pistols from the Arsenal's outside window. Then we drove a state van around the perimeter to Wallpost 18, where I climbed out, my arms laden with the pistols, belts, and holsters. I walked to the base of the tower. "Rapunzel, Rapunzel," I called, waiting for the tower officer to appear and lower the bucket. He didn't smile when finally he peered over the railing; COs could be so grim. Then, free of weaponry, we passed through the sally port and went back inside the prison. We placed handcuffs and leg irons on our inmate, helped him into the van, and passed back through the sally port to the outside. Only then, after we had collected our weapons from the wall tower, were we, our guns, and our inmate all finally united inside the van.

The forty-something Billings was an extrovert. He quickly told me about the trouble he was having with his wife due to his extramarital affairs ("I don't think many men my age *haven't* had affairs," he said) and about the tensions at home due to the return of his pregnant, unmarried teenage daughter. We talked about the union's new disability insurance program, about the vocational shop at Eastern Correctional Facility where all the state's highway signs were made, and about an altercation in the B-block yard the night before, during which officers had been injured.

I walked with the inmate into his hearing at Downstate. All morning—from his strip-frisk outside the protective-custody unit to his handcuffing—he had been the soul of civility, and at the hearing he was no different. No, he told the judge, English wasn't his first language; that would be Nahuatl, the Mexican Indian tongue. But he could understand Spanish well enough. Through an interpreter, the judge explained that the hearing was about whether he wished to fight the government's plan to deport him to Mexico as soon as his sentence was finished. No, the inmate said, he would be happy to go home as soon as he could. But there was a favor he wanted to ask. He was serving eight to twenty-five years for manslaughter, he said, and for the past three months, he had been held in involuntary protective custody. This was because his victim had been the younger brother of a leader of Sing Sing's Latin Kings gang and the administration feared that members of the gang in prison would kill him. Couldn't the judge please intervene and have him transferred?

Conveying all this information to the judge through the interpreter took about ten minutes; the judge's reply, about ten seconds. "No," he said. "I'm sorry, but there's nothing I can do." And that was that.

Certainly, I supposed, the matter was outside the judge's jurisdiction. The Department of Correctional Services transferred inmates according to its own obscure agendas. I (probably along with most inmates) was always trying to figure them out—and I made a bit more progress later that night.

My shift was over by the time Billings and I got back. As we checked in, a black sergeant, Brereton, was trying to decide on the racial makeup of a team of evening-shift transportation officers to send on a five-hour drive up to Great Meadow Correctional Facility, the max near Comstock, New York. He didn't want to send "all brothers" to Comstock—it would conform too much to the upstate stereotype of Sing Sing. But his regular white and Latino officers were out. I raised my hand to volunteer, and was selected. It was overtime, he advised me; I probably wouldn't get back until 4 A.M. "That's no problem," I said. This overtime was *easy*.

Sergeant Brereton took me and another officer along to collect the inmate from his cell in 5-Building. This was unusual. Normally, transportation officers collected inmates by themselves. When we arrived at the cell, Brereton was fierce to the inmate: "Collect your bag! Put your shoes on! We're leaving now!" The inmate was a young black guy named Hans Toussaint. He did not seem hostile, but maybe Brereton knew something I didn't know.

"No talking!" the sergeant barked as Toussaint paused at another cell to say good-bye. "Direct order! Walk in front of us now! Stop again and we'll take you down!"

Inmates in neighboring cells snickered at this and imitated Brereton in low tones. I braced myself, knowing Brereton would expect me to do the taking down if in fact Toussaint stopped again. Fortunately, he did not, and Brereton dropped us off at the State Shop, where Toussaint's belongings were to be inventoried before he was shipped out.

A small crowd of six or seven officers gathered around for this routine procedure, and slowly I learned why there was all this interest: Toussaint was one of the gang members who had been involved in the altercation in B-block yard the day before. We had seen videotape of this at lineup: thirty or forty seconds of inmates massing, running and stabbing, attacking and fleeing. The story was that the Latin Kings had a score to settle with the Bloods. Their fighters had gotten to the yard first, armed with shanks, and taken positions along the fence. The Bloods had known a fight was going to happen, known they were outnumbered, but had gone out anyway. They were clustered near the yard door when the Kings attacked, stabbing numerous Bloods and sustaining lesser injuries in the process. As the Bloods fled down a fenced-in corridor toward 5-Building, the video showed Sergeant Murray, his baton out, flailing away to separate the combatants.

I had passed the door where that corridor emptied into the main prison, walked by the large pool of dried blood just inside it. It now seemed likely that some of this blood had been Toussaint's. He had just transferred into Sing Sing from another prison the day before; it had been his first time ever in the B-block yard. The officers were marveling over that circumstance as they sifted through his meager possessions.

"So you knew something was going to happen out there?"

"Everyone knew it was going to happen," said Toussaint.

"So why'd you go?"

"I had to go."

"Where were you stabbed?"

Toussaint lifted up his T-shirt and showed the cut in his back. He would have gotten a "big stick" in his side, too, he said, had it not been for his protective vest of magazines.

"What magazines did you use?" asked Anderson, the female CO who supervised the barbershop downstairs.

"*Ebony* and *Life*," said Toussaint, smiling. He was charismatic, I could see. Officers kept peppering him with questions, but he was talking especially to Anderson. She pointed to three parallel slashes through one of his eyebrows. "What are those?"

He shrugged and wouldn't answer.

She persisted. "Why the big deal about your gang?" The Bloods, originally from Los Angeles, were a growing and feared presence in New York at the time. It was said that membership followed a strict policy of "blood in, blood out": You had to slash somebody—not necessarily a rival gang member, just someone you were robbing, say—to get into the gang, and leaving was impossible without getting cut up yourself.

"Okay, I'll tell you once," said Toussaint. He borrowed Anderson's pen and on a piece of scrap paper wrote B-L-O-O-D in block letters. Then he completed the words he said the letters stood for: "Brotherly Love Overrides Oppression and Distraction." I had never before heard that *Blood* was an acronym. Anderson folded it up and said she'd keep it.

Toussaint had nothing more to his name than an incomplete set of state-issued clothes and a fat envelope of letters from his girlfriend in Brooklyn. ("Dear Sweetie," began one, which an officer had opened. "Your bid's not *that* long.") And, like a bunch of idiot nerd scientists, here we were poring over it all with a fine-tooth comb, grinding along to keep the system going—and the gas in our

SUVs. By comparison, he was like the Rebel, ideals untarnished. His girlfriend would have to write to him at Great Meadow, now. Instead of being placed in protective custody, like the Mexican, Toussaint was being transferred out. This transfer made sense: Toussaint seemed combustible, and getting him out of Sing Sing would help to defuse gang tensions. I felt suddenly sorry for him. These gangs of ghetto kids preyed on the weak, but you had to admit that there was a political element to some of them, a mission of self-help and a drive to maintain pride and focus. Toussaint was not unlike an ambassador from a small, fierce, and backward land.

The only thing I could say on our behalf was that just as everything was finishing up, an officer happened upon a tiny plastic bag with a few leaves of what looked like marijuana in it, enough for just one puff of smoke. The officer held it up accusingly.

"You gotta have somethin' when you goin' out there," said Toussaint, shrugging.

The officer, instead of writing him up, threw it away without comment.

———

We pulled into Great Meadow around midnight. The officers we saw were all white, and they already knew about the altercation in the B-block yard. They, too, seemed eager to see what Toussaint looked like. A sergeant gave him a stern lecture and a pat-frisk, telling him to look straight at the wall, keep silent, hands flat . . . and then offered up a sardonic "Welcome to Great Meadow" when he was done. Actually, Toussaint had told us on the drive up, he'd done time here before.

In return for Toussaint, we received an inmate to take back with us. This game of musical chairs, sort of like a reverse sports draft, was the way of DOCS. Inmates were constantly being shuffled in the hope this would avert volatile situations. You could tell that Great Meadow was tighter than Sing Sing; every time this nervous inmate addressed me, even as I was performing the strip-frisk, he called me sir. The inmate was black. Thinking he had probably grown up in New York City, the same sergeant said to him, "Must feel like you're going home, huh?"

"No, sir," said the inmate. "Actually, it doesn't feel that way at all."

We stopped on the New York State Thruway for gas, within sight of a number of large tractor-trailer rigs. The inmate had been telling me that the farther north you went in the prison system, the less talking there was between officers and inmates. As we waited to pay for the gas, a big rig pulled out ahead of us, then accelerated onto the entrance ramp.

"That's what I want to do when my bid's done," he murmured, "drive one of those things."

It made all the sense in the world to me. He wanted to get behind the wheel and eat up the space, drink it in, make his own choices in that great land without walls. He looked like he would have given anything to do it then and there.

———

One after another, my classmates disappeared. The Department usually gave only two or three days' notice of a transfer, so often there was no good-bye—just the absence of Dieter, Di Carlo, Colton, Davis, DiPaola, Dimmie, Arno, Charlebois, and the rest, usually to the "jump jails" a short drive north. Occasionally, I'd see a big grin on somebody's face in the parking lot and they'd show me the paperwork. Bella and Buckner were on their way to Bedford Hills and Taconic, the women's prisons on the other side of Westchester County. It took a few months, but Miller finally left for the state police academy; Feliciano, for the New York City police academy. A few officers from the city stuck around—Ellerbe, Foster, and Chavez—and I was glad for the familiar faces. I made new friends of more recent OJTs, but reservedly, because they were almost always gone within a few weeks. And I got to know some of the more senior officers better, most of them in B-block, where, shortly, I would be spending a lot of time.

The most dramatic departure was by Officer Mendez, whom I had sat next to against the wall one night at the Academy while waiting for pay phones. Mendez was from up near Buffalo, a strong, articulate, capable-seeming fellow who was still hoping to get into the Secret Service, he told me, and was calling home to see if a letter had come from Washington.

Apparently, Sergeant Holmes had penciled-in Mendez to J-and-N galleries, A-block's version of R-and-W—a chaotic, transient floor that nobody else wanted. One day, it had proved too much. Assailed by uncooperative inmates, Mendez had finally gone downstairs to the sergeants, screaming, "I can't do it! I can't do it!" He wasn't entirely coherent, and apparently the whole block had grown hushed at the commotion. One sergeant ascertained that an inmate had threatened to punch Mendez in the face and demanded to know who it was. He dragged Mendez back upstairs, but the officer couldn't single anyone out. "They were all threatening me!" he wailed.

I saw Mendez in the parking lot the next afternoon, after he'd turned in his badge. He had broken down on the phone with his mother that morning while telling her about it, he told a group of us, and she'd started crying too. He was about to drive home.

"Hey, there's no shame in it," another recruit said, and the rest of us nodded. But obviously Mendez—who probably would have made a great Secret Service agent—felt like a total failure. I looked at him with sympathy, envy, and—because any of us who remained could be the next one penciled-in by Holmes—fear.

CHAPTER 5

SCRAP HEAP

> The progress of mankind from physical force to the sub-
> stitution of moral power in the art and science of gov-
> ernment in general, is but very slow, but in none of its
> branches has this progress, which alone affords the stan-
> dard by which we can judge of the civil development of
> a society, been more retarded than in the organization
> and discipline of prisons . . .
> —Francis Lieber, translator's introduction
>   to Alexis de Tocqueville and Gustave de Beaumont,
>   *On the Penitentiary System in the United States
>   and Its Application to France,* 1833

You feel it along the walls inside, hard like a blow to the head; see
it on the walls outside, thick, blank, and doorless; smell it in the air
that assaults your face in certain tunnels, a stale and acrid taste of
male anger, resentment, and boredom. You sense it all around in the
pointed lack of ornamentation, plants, or reason for hope—walls
built not to shelter but to constrain. In the same way that a murder
forever changes a house, Sing Sing has its own irrevocable vibe, a
haunted feeling surely unlike that of any other prison, one rooted in
the ground and in history: thousands upon thousands of lashings
meted out by my predecessors in the nineteenth century; hundreds
of prisoners executed there by the state while strapped down in an
electric chair built by other inmates; and for the untold numbers of
prisoners who were locked inside, an enforced experience of the
glacial slowness of time. The prison's most famous warden, Lewis
Lawes, called his memoir *Twenty Thousand Years in Sing Sing*—the
number referred to the sum of the length of sentences of all the inmates under his supervision. "Within such cycles worlds are born,
die and are reborn. . . . Twenty thousand years in my keeping. . . .
Will they bring life and purpose to any of our twenty-five hundred
men who are sharing in that tremendous burden?"

The view from some of the wall towers (or from a boat on the

Hudson or from an airplane, the only other good perspective), offers a different sense of the passage of time. You can see pieces of everything from the 1820s stone walls of the original cellblock to the 1980s prefab of the Family Reunion Program trailers and the Quality of Working Life building, as well as the gaps where earlier structures have risen and been razed. Sing Sing is one of those rare American places where enough of the old has been left alone—preserved, incorporated into the present, or simply never swept away—to put one in mind of history. Contained in that 170-year-old architectural hodgepodge are many aspects of the modern history of prisons in the Western world.

A little after my arrival, I found out that the guard who had pointed across the river to a scar on a ridge and told me that it was where the stone for the first cellblock had been quarried was wrong. Sing Sing's site was picked because marble and other stone were already *there,* underfoot. Not only could the material be used to build a prison, the state legislature reasoned, it could be quarried, placed on riverboats, and sold into the indefinite future, helping the prison turn a profit.

The year was 1825. The inmates and their keepers traveled by boat down the Erie Canal from the state prison at Auburn and then by freight steamer down the Hudson, where they landed on the east bank "without a place to receive or a wall to enclose them." In charge of them all and entrusted by the legislature to build the new prison was a cruel but innovative disciplinarian, Elam Lynds. A former Army captain, Lynds had previously been the warden (or agent, in the usage of the time) at Auburn, earning wide recognition for refinements he made in methods for handling prisoners.

The infant country, not even fifty years old, was thinking hard at the time about better ways to punish its criminals. From England and Europe, the United States had inherited a system of mainly corporal punishment for crimes. As James S. Kunen has written, "Before independence, Americans generally flogged, branded, or mutilated those felons they did not hang. Except for debtors and such minor miscreants as vagrants and drunkards, people were held behind bars only to await trial or punishment, and not as punishment." In England as late as 1780, there were still over two hundred capital offenses—among others, "stealing anything worth five shillings, felling a tree in someone's private forest, robbing a rabbit warren, living for a month with gypsies, or picking pockets." Hanging was commonplace.

But generally during this era, throughout the Western world, the nature of criminal punishment was undergoing profound change. The period between the late eighteenth and the mid-nineteenth centuries, wrote Michel Foucault, saw "the disappearance of torture as a public spectacle" and the gradual phasing out of corporal punishments. Less and less did society target the criminal's body; rather, what we wanted to punish was his mind.

The leaders of the American movement to rethink the prison were the Quakers in Pennsylvania. As early as 1682, William Penn's colonial government experimented with incarceration as an alternative to corporal and capital punishment. The Quakers' goals were prevention of further harm to society, deterrence, and, by the early nineteenth century, encouragement of prisoners to engage in "penitent reflection," which could result in their personal reformation. This was the beginning of an American innovation, the penitentiary. Philadelphia's Walnut Street jail, and later, in 1829, its massive Eastern State Penitentiary—the first institution to bear that label—were designed as places for prisoners to spend the day entirely alone, with only daytime work projects in their cells and a Bible for company. The arrangement came to be known as the Pennsylvania—or "separate"—system, and it attracted much attention, both abroad and at home.

Auburn Prison, meanwhile, had been built in the style of Newgate Prison in New York City, with inmates housed in "apartments" holding two to twenty inmates. Thinking that a version of the separate system might be just the thing for its most "obdurate and guilty felons," New York began to build a new north wing of Auburn, composed completely of solitary cells. Elam Lynds became warden of Auburn while contruction was under way in 1821; on Christmas of that year, he moved eighty-three of his worst inmates into the new north wing. The regime he imposed was draconian: He subtracted the labor that kept Pennsylvania's inmates occupied during the day in their cells, as well as the opportunity they had for daily exercise. The system turned out to be too harsh:

> From this experiment results the very reverse of those which had been anticipated, was produced; five of those who had been subjected to this confinement, died within a

> year, one of them had become insane, and another, watching an opportunity when his keeper brought him something, precipitated himself [jumped] from the gallery . . . the rest fell into a state of such deep depression, that their lives must have been sacrificed, had they remained longer in this situation.

The governor pardoned twenty-six of the inmates, and the experiment was abandoned.

But Lynds was not discouraged. He modified the regime into something unique in the United States at the time: Inmates would be kept in individual cells at night but allowed to labor together in prison shops during the day, always in silence. This congregate system, or "Auburn system," as it came to be known, produced more money for the public coffers than Pennsylvania's (which allowed only individual work projects in the cell), and it drove fewer inmates insane. It soon became the leading model for prisons in the United States.

New York needed more prison space, and asked Lynds to build it. Newgate, in need of replacement, was only thirty-three miles from the village of Sing Sing, but Lynds didn't want the inmates from there to build his new prison. He wanted a group from Auburn—men already accustomed to his brand of harsh discipline.

Sing Sing, stone upon stone. Lynds's prisoners, under threat of the lash, put up temporary barracks, a cookhouse, and carpenter's and blacksmith's shops and started filling in shoreline for the prison yard. Then began the arduous work of raising the cellblock. Slowly it grew: four stories; eight hundred cells, 476 feet long. By October 1828, it was finished, Newgate sold, and the prisoners transferred. (Additional stories would be added in 1831—even in those days, the inmate population was growing faster than anticipated—and in 1860, bringing the total to six, with twelve hundred cells.) Tales of Lynds's feat—of inducing inmates to build for themselves the largest prison in the land while unmanacled, uncontained by a prison wall—spread across the country and abroad. Of the foreign emissaries who would stop by to take a look, two Frenchmen were among the first.

Alexis de Tocqueville is famous for his seminal book *Democracy in America,* but what is less well known is his original purpose in coming to the United States. The young aristocrat and his friend Gustave de Beaumont had been dispatched by their government in 1831 with the specific mission of examining America's rumored-to-be-innovative prisons. After their arrival in New York City, the "Mount-Pleasant State Prison," informally known as Sing Sing, was their first stop.

Their first sight of it, on May 29, left a vivid impression, wrote George Wilson Pierson, Tocqueville's principal biographer. "The place was bathed in heat and an unnatural silence, and there was an unmistakable undercurrent of terror in the silence. Mingling with the handful of keepers and watching the inmates at work, the French commissioners themselves became afraid." To the Frenchmen, "accustomed to the fortress-like houses of detention and the old-fashioned walled prisons of France, it was an extraordinary sight." The nine hundred inmates were all around the unfinished cellblock, unrestrained by chains and all engaged in hard labor—and yet, despite the absence of any wall (a few armed guards were stationed around the perimeter)—"they labour assiduously at the hardest tasks," wrote Beaumont to his mother. "Nothing is rarer than an [escape]. That appears so unbelievable that one sees the fact a long time without being able to explain it."

As the prison staff proudly explained to them, it was the separate system and the use of force that enabled the strict control they saw. Whippings, the keepers said, were administered five or six times a day. And, whatever its justification in terms of inmate penitence and self-reflection, the Frenchmen immediately appreciated the administrative power of the separate system. "All strength is born of association," wrote Beaumont, "and 30 individuals united through perpetual communication, by ideas, by plans in common, by concerted schemes, have more real power than 900 whose isolation makes them weak."

Also, they soon saw that the physical force was abetted by a moral one. Soon after their arrival, Tocqueville and Beaumont heard a story that appeared to shed further light on the keepers' ideology. Apparently, Lynds had heard of an angry inmate who had threatened to kill him. Never letting on that he was aware of the threat, Lynds ordered the man to give him a shave in his bedroom. The prisoner lost his nerve and obeyed. When he was finished, Lynds dismissed him with words to the effect: "I knew you wanted to kill me; but I despised you too much to believe that you would ever be bold enough" to do so. "Single and unarmed, I am always stronger than all of you."

The two Frenchmen asked Lynds what quality was the most important for a prison director.

"The practical art of conducting men," he answered. "Above all, he must be thoroughly convinced, as I have always been, that a dishonest man is ever a coward. This conviction, which the prisoners will soon perceive, gives him an irresistible ascendency, and will make a number of things very easy, which, at first glance, may appear hazardous."

Lynds's achievement—the seemingly total subjugation of a large group of violent inmates—is one that would probably dazzle most correction officers and wardens today. The erection of Sing Sing offered a spectacle of total control. And yet by the time they left, Tocqueville and Beaumont had their doubts. In his diary, Tocqueville wrote, "We have seen 250 prisoners working under a shed, cutting stone. These men, subjected to a very special surveillance, had all committed acts of violence indicating a dangerous character. Each, at his right and at his left, had a stone-cutter's *hache* [a hatchet or ax]. Three unarmed guards walked up and down in the shed. Their eyes were in continuous agitation." The prison chaplain, he noted, "likened the warden of the establishment to a man who has tamed a tiger that one day may devour him." And in their final report to the government, Tocqueville and Beaumont wrote,

> One cannot see the prison of Sing-Sing and the system of labour which is there established without being struck by astonishment and fear. Although the discipline is perfect, one feels that it rests on fragile foundations: it is due to a *tour de force* which is reborn unceasingly and which has to be reproduced each day, under penalty of compromising the whole system of discipline. The safety of the keepers is constantly menaced. In the presence of such dangers, avoided with such skill but with difficulty, it seems to us impossible not to fear some sort of catastrophe in the future.

Though they did not say so to their hosts at Sing Sing, Tocqueville and Beaumont were finally dismayed that "whilst society in the United States gives the example of the most extended liberty, the prisons of the same country offer the spectacle of the most complete despotism."

"Do you think one can manage without corporal punishment?" they had asked Elam Lynds.

"I am completely convinced of the opposite," the agent replied. "I regard punishment by the whip as the most effective and at the same time as the most humane, for it never makes a man ill and compels the prisoners to lead an essentially healthy life. . . . I do not think you can control a large prison without the use of the whip, whatever those may think who only know human nature from books."

While a simple brute could never have prevailed over his men the way Lynds did, brute force was certainly indispensable to his rule. In the early years, Lynds was allowed to punish as he saw fit, and a whispered word, a look askance—the slightest infraction— was grounds for a whipping. Once the cellblock was occupied, whippings were administered in an area of the ground floor called the Flogging Post. Two iron rings had been fastened to the wall; hanging nearby were a number of the whips, known as the cat-o'- nine-tails, and—according to one inmate account—a gag. The inmate was stripped, his hands were tied to the rings, and then, to use a modern phrase, it was payback time: The keeper he had offended administered blows to his back.

Levi Burr, an inmate imprisoned for perjury, published a detailed memoir in 1833. Sing Sing, he charged, was a "cat-ocracy." The cat-o'-nine-tails was generally made of six strands of hard, waxed cord, sometimes metal-tipped, that were attached to a hickory handle about a foot and a half long. The cords were "almost as hard as a piece of wire," Burr wrote. While Beaumont had speculated that the fear of upsetting the inmate population would make keepers moderate in their use of the cat, Burr wrote,

It would be an endless task to attempt to enumerate the many applications of this instrument of discipline, or tell the number of blows that are generally applied at one flogging, as they vary according to the will and temper that the keeper happens to be in at the time. The number may, however, be estimated at from twenty to fifty, seventy, eighty, ninety, or an hundred and more. On one occasion I counted an hundred and thirty three; and while the afflicted subject was begging upon his knees, and crying and writhing under the laceration, that tore his skin in pieces from his back, the deputy keeper approached, and gave him a blow across the mouth with his cane, that caused the blood to flow profusely; and then, as if conscious of my feelings at beholding so barbarous a spectacle, turned and faced me with an agitated stare. I averted my head and continued my labor, and directly he walked away without speaking.

In 1841, according to one legislative report, "More than a hundred blows were struck daily. . . . The whipping post was never dry."

Men ate in their rooms, which were a claustrophobic seven feet high, six feet seven inches deep, and three feet three inches wide. There were no windows, no heat, and no running water. A small amount of light and air passed through the pattern of one-inch-square holes in the doors. Inmates slept on straw mattresses atop iron bed frames attached to the wall. (One hundred years after its construction, the original cellblock was still in use. Bank robber Willie Sutton wrote that in 1926, it "had uneven jagged stone walls that sweated moisture all day and all night.") Inmates ate with their fingers; food was doled into a small bucket, called a kid. They were issued a single set of striped clothes, regarded as a humiliation (as well as a visual aid to assist the pursuit of escapees) and washed once a week. From Saturday evening until Monday morning, inmates were locked in their cells; this was the keepers' only time off. Every morning, the keepers marched each gallery's prisoners to an outdoor latrine to dump their tall iron slop cans, or night buckets, which each man carried in his left hand. This march had a special character. It was the lockstep, an Auburn innovation, in which the prisoner's right hand rested on the shoulder of the man in front of him; his footsteps were short and synchronized, and his gaze was straight ahead—upon penalty of the lash.

"There are daily about twenty men on guard," wrote Burr,

with gun, bayonet, cartridges, &c. They form a chain around the quarries, and keep a look-out that none escapes. . . . The guard, as well as the keepers, generally, are in the daily habit of using tobacco; but the prisoners are not permitted to use it, and if seen to have any, they are flogged without mercy. . . . But whenever it was possible, without detection, the men would pick up old quids of tobacco that had been thrown away by the keepers or guard. To prevent this, [the guards] uniformly tread upon [it], and stamp it in the dirt; yet if any part of it can be recovered, the prisoners secure it as quick as possible. . . . I saw a man by the name of Knight, flogged for picking up an old quid of tobacco, and when his shirt was pulled off, the scars of a former flogging for the same thing, were not healed.

Slabs and chunks of marble were transported on carts that were pushed and pulled by prisoners up and down the steep hillside. "Several men grab a chain to pull a cart uphill," wrote Burr, "two men hold ropes to guide it downhill."

But man, who has but two legs, was never made to perform the service of four footed beasts. They cannot hold the cart from running, and are compelled to let it go, and trust their skill in guiding and their speed in running, to keep out the way, until it reaches the bottom of the hill. If a wheel strikes against a stone or other impediment, while in quick motion, it turns the cart with a violent jerk, and often throws them down with more or less injury. Two men have had their thighs broken by this means. They were unable to guide or hold the cart, and the wheel came in contact with a stone . . . [One] will always be a cripple.

The sight of men being whipped as they struggled to move carts prompted consternation among a legislative committee convened to examine the prison in 1832, with particular attention to the system's harsher aspects. Starvation of men as another means of breaking them, and the floggings for which Lynds had been famous, were viewed by the legislative panel as less innocuous than he pretended.

A report from 1839 included the following testimony:

John S. Mattucks, assistant keeper from June, 1832, to May or June, 1836, says . . . he saw a black man punished severely by a keeper named Burr, and John Lent, for raising an axe towards Burr, in the cooper shop; thinks he saw *three hundred strokes of the cat at this time;* the convict was unable to labor in consequence of this whipping; was shut up in his room for several days, and kept on low diet; *says he appeared soon after to be deranged* . . .

Lawrence Van Buren, one of the assistant keepers from September, 1835, to December, 1837, says "that in October, 1837, there was a . . . convict in the prison . . . who he believes was then insane; that this convict was in the habit of talking and making a noise in his cell at night; that for this offence the said convict was taken out, stripped and whipped several mornings in succession; that the said convict was whipped till he was much lacerated, so that his shirt adhered to his back, and his legs were badly swollen . . ."

Daniel W. Odell, assistant keeper for seven years previous to September, 1839, says he "knew a convict by the name of *Judson,* who made his escape, was brought back, tied up, and witness whipped him, he should think one hundred lashes, on the bare back, with a cat [of] six strands; this was on Saturday; *convict drowned himself on Monday morning*" [italics original].

Lynds resigned in 1830, returning to Auburn in 1838. But his aura of heroism had faded. He was asked to leave Auburn a year later, following the death of an inmate whom he had punished for feigning illness. The local coroner held that the death had resulted "from disease, the fatal termination of which was hastened by flogging, labor, and general harsh treatment, imposed by . . . Elam Lynds. . . ."

Still, Lynds was rehired at Sing Sing in 1843. By then, however, he seems to have been a wrecked man. He lasted only a few months before being fired following several escapes, including one in which inmates built their own boat (whose existence had been reported to him) and then sailed away in it. The public had also grown skeptical of the brutality of the Lynds regime. By his own accounting, around fifteen hundred lashings were inflicted per month, not including those he meted out himself. ("His rule was never to forgive an offense, but always punish *and with the lash.*") And there was growing disapproval of his reluctance to allow relatives to visit or to exchange letters with inmates, his conviction that inmates should have no books other than a Bible and a prayer book, and other such harsh measures. One of his own assistants wrote the legislature to say

there is evidence so abundant to establish the fact of the Captain being an inebriate, a tyrant, abusive to the Assistant Keepers, oppressive and contradictory in his order, of his having cursed both the Board of Inspectors and his Excellency the Governor; and also of his having appropriated the property of the State to his own use . . .

I find the decline of Lynds particularly interesting in light of a letter from a former doctor at Auburn, Blanchard Fosgate, who around 1851 wrote legislators a letter to share his observation that the practice of whipping had been wounding to more than just the prisoners.

[The cat-o'-nine-tails] was a means so brutal in its nature that both he who used it, and he who bore its stripes were alike brutalized in its employment. . . . In its application the familiarity it causes with suffering destroys in the breast of the officer all sympathetic feeling, until each ennobling quality of his nature is lost; and the fierce bursts of passion he is often forced to contend against, enkindle, and being oft repeated, strengthen in him a like element only to be appeased in vanquishing all opposition; while in the bosom of the enraged convict, feeling keenly his own degradation, is deeply implanted a spirit of revenge there secretly to corrode until every higher feeling is obliterated.

Lynds's belief that it was impossible to govern a prison without the cat was disproved in 1848, when use of the cat-o'-nine-tails was abolished by the legislature and the prison continued to operate much as it had before. Corporal punishment in general was not renounced, however; other punishments increased in frequency to fill the gap, and the keepers invented new ones: They often attached recaptured escapees to a ball and chain, and might shave half their heads as a humiliation. Others were punished with the yoke, a flat iron bar weighing thirty-four to forty pounds, to which both outstretched arms were attached behind the neck; the pressure against the cervical vertebrae, even to a strong man, quickly became unbearable. ("I think that not one man in a thousand could stand up under the 40 pound yoke for four hours," a keeper named John Ashton told the inspectors. A legislative committee in 1851 learned of one Sing Sing inmate who, punished for poor work with four hours of the yoke, was in such pain that he couldn't leave his cell for two weeks; when he did return to the shop, he promptly cut off the fingers of one hand.) The iron cage, another means of physical punishment, was a round metal construction that the keepers placed over the inmate's head and locked around his neck; it made movements of the head increasingly painful and rest impossible. Darkened cells were a frequent penalty. But the most common, and most feared, new punishment was the cold-water bath.

This procedure, whose contrast with the famously subtle Chinese water torture shows that American justice was perhaps still more interested in punishing the body than the mind, involved stripping the offending inmate and seating him on a bench, with his hands and feet secured in stocks. About four and a half feet above his head sat a barrel, filled completely or partially with cold water, depending on the offense and the mood of the keeper. In the early years of this punishment, the water—which could be icy cold in winter—was released all at once upon the naked inmate, delivering a terrible shock. In later years, it was released with less violence but was often collected in a wooden hopper placed around the inmate's neck, in which it could rise to a level above the inmate's mouth and nose. The keeper controlled the water's release from the hopper, and used it to produce a sensation of drowning. The punishment was popular among prison officials because inmates so feared it and because it left no disfiguring marks.

Auburn physician Blanchard Fosgate attested that while the cold-water bath seemed hardly to affect some inmates, others showed damage both lasting and profound.

> Convict number 4,565, aged thirty-eight years . . . and in good health, was showered with three pails of cold water. He was taken from the stocks in convulsions which lasted some thirty minutes, when he was conveyed to the hospital. When I saw him, about an hour afterward, he had congestion of the brain, accompanied with severe cephalgia [headache]; he was laboring under great derangement of mind, and recollected but little of what had transpired. He said he had been struck on his head, but there were no external signs of violence. . . . He said he felt as though his head was "bound with a band of iron."

> In my presence, convict number 5,458 was showered with one and a half barrels of water. During the operation,

the muscles of the chest and abdomen were severally exercised. When taken out of the stocks his skin was cold and shrivelled; there was no perceptible pulsation in the temporal or radial arteries, and he complained of severe cephalgia . . .

Convict number 5,066, aged about thirty years . . . was brought to the hospital in a perfectly unconscious state and with convulsive twitchings of the muscles. His mouth filled with frothy saliva; no perceptible pulsations in the radial artery; but little external heat and very imperfect respiration. He had been showered, I was credibly informed, with about two pails of cold water. His body was rubbed with stimulants and warmly covered with blankets . . . brandy and other stimulants were administered. In four hours after entering the hospital his consciousness returned.

This individual was so nearly destroyed that he had passed into that calm, quiet mental state that immediately precedes death by drowning. He said that at last he had the delightful sensation of sailing, and then it was all over. He suffered from cramps in his lower extremities for about three months after.

In 1851, Sing Sing's administration reported giving 138 cold-water baths. In 1869, after a huge riot involving several hundred inmates in which many inmates and one officer were killed, a law was passed prohibiting its further use.

Certainly, outlawing barbaric punishments was evidence of progress in penal practice, and perhaps of progress in American civilization as well. But Rev. John Luckey, a Protestant minister who spent at least fourteen years as Sing Sing's second chaplain, saw how it was eclipsed in importance by the character of the guards. Luckey, who has been called "the first social worker" for his research into inmates' family backgrounds, wrote in 1860 that "much more depends upon the sound judgment and humane feelings of the disciplinarian than upon the instrument of punishment which he employs;—hence, a *cruel* man should never enter within the walls of a prison, except as a convict."

The strict disciplinary measures of the nineteenth century served not only order, but profit. Previous systems had been—as they are today—a huge strain on taxpayers; from its beginning, Sing Sing had been conceived of as a moneymaking venture. After the establishment of the marble quarry came the construction of a wharf and of several buildings that housed industrial and craft shops. Over the years the prison shops produced toys, buttons, woven items including carpets and tapestry, cooperage (wooden barrels and tubs), brass, saws and files, boots, saddles, cast iron, cigars, furniture, hats, brushes, windows and doors, printing, knitting and hosiery, mattresses, and, as late as the 1980s, plastic bags. "A big business enterprise," a prominent journalist called it; until 1884, a handful of contractors paid the state set sums for the labor of a certain number of men and then endeavored to get everything out of them they could.

The system was subject to numerous abuses. The agent and the keepers were bribed, in money and in goods, to offer special treatment to certain contractors; inmates were paid on the side to work beyond the prescribed hours, often at risk to their own health. James Brice, another white-collar perjurer who served time in Sing Sing in the 1830s and wrote a pamphlet about it, described contractors gathering in the blacksmith shop when new inmates arrived—they were there to have leg irons removed—to choose the ones they most wanted. Reports showed that at the behest of contractors, inmates were sometimes punished for poor work and that some contractors were even allowed to brandish the whip. The huge demand for inmate labor kept the prison overfull, while Clinton prison, far from downstate markets, was partly empty.

The contractor system was abolished in 1884, due in part to these perennial abuses but also because of the opposition of unions. Prison-made goods had an unfair cost advantage in the marketplace. (The state continued to use inmate labor but restricted it to products that the state itself could use—a practice that continues to this day, with the manufacture of license plates, garbage bags, office furniture, highway signs, and printed materials.)

That abolition made another group happy, too: businessmen in the town of Sing Sing. Ever since the prison had officially changed its name from Mount Pleasant to Sing Sing, shortly before the Civil War, local artisans and manufacturers had felt that the prison goods' MADE IN SING SING labels stigmatized their products. In 1901, in fact, in order to more fully disassociate itself from the infamous prison, the town changed its name to Ossining.

Ironically, in 1970, the state—fleeing a similar historical burden—changed the prison's name to Ossining Correctional Facility. The new name didn't fool anybody, though, and never entered common usage. Besides, the game of name tag was about to come full circle: By the early 1980s, a group of businesspeople decided that the name Sing Sing might attract tourists. Before long, they petitioned the state to change the prison's name back to Sing Sing, and in 1983, the state did.

———

The arrival of the electric chair in 1891 marked the beginning of the grim period for which Sing Sing grew world famous: as a center for executions. From August of that year, when four men were executed in one day, to 1963, 614 people were electrocuted at Sing Sing.

The first execution by electrocution had actually taken place eleven months earlier, at Auburn. Though now considered anachronistic, in the late nineteenth century the chair was thought to be a bold and humane innovation. Electricity harnessed for the human good was making its debut, first in a lightbulb in Thomas Edison's lab and then, gradually, in cities across the land that were equipped by the Edison Electric Light Company with power lines and generators. It was thought to hold promise for medicine, too: Edison marketed his inductorium, an induction coil, as a guaranteed cure for rheumatism, gout, nervous diseases, and sciatica.

At the same time, doctors and scientists were aware of electricity's power to kill. In Buffalo in 1881, Dr. Albert Southwick, a dentist, saw an elderly drunkard touch the terminals of an electrical generator; he was amazed by how quickly and apparently painlessly the man was killed and described the episode to a friend, state senator David McMillan. Also in Buffalo—soon to be dubbed the Electric City of the Future—Dr. George Fell developed a method to help the ASPCA electrocute unwanted dogs. McMillan spoke to Governor David B. Hill, who asked the state legislature to consider whether electricity might somehow replace hanging.

Around this time, in 1887, a New York murderer was put to death the old way—on the gallows. Roxalana "Roxie" Druse, of Herkimer County, New York, had murdered her husband in 1884 in a particularly grisly way. Following an early morning argument, she had enlisted their daughter to help her get a rope around his neck and then fired two shots into him. The bullets did not kill the man, and Roxie somehow intimidated a fourteen-year-old neighbor boy into shooting him again. Still her husband lived. This time she wielded an ax, and despite his cries of, "Oh, Roxie, don't!" she chopped his head off. After further dismembering him, she spent several hours burning the pieces in a stove.

Despite the lurid details, Roxie Druse became something of a cause célèbre—no woman had been executed in New York in thirty-nine years. Petitions arrived in the governor's office, asking him to commute her sentence to life imprisonment. The governor postponed the hanging but ultimately refused to reduce her sentence, and in February 1887, Roxie Druse was hanged in the Herkimer County jail.

The hanging did not go well. In front of a large crowd of reporters and others, Roxie Druse, wearing a pretty dress decorated with roses sent by her daughter, began to moan, weep, and then, when the black hood was pulled over her head, to shriek. When the trapdoor fell, Druse was killed not by a quick snapping of the neck, as was supposed to happen, but instead by slow strangulation as she dangled and writhed, conscious, for fifteen minutes at the end of her rope.

The death of Druse gave new life to efforts to reform New York's capital punishment, and in 1888 the legislature, hoping to burnish the reputation of the Empire State, established "electric execution" (*electrocution* was not in common usage yet) as the state's official method. The law went into effect on January 1, 1889. In March of that year, a Buffalo fruit vendor named William Kemmler, enraged at his common-law wife, murdered her with a hatchet in front of her young daughter, and he soon became the first person in the world sentenced to die by electricity.

By this time, Thomas Edison was locked in a fierce fight with George Westinghouse over their competing technologies: Edison's direct current (DC) was quickly losing ground to Westinghouse's alternating current (AC), which, time would prove, held many advantages for long-distance transmission. Unlikely to win the battle on its merits, Edison devoted considerable resources to trying to discredit AC in the realm of public relations: AC, he and his supporters asserted, was much more lethal than DC.

In Kemmler's death sentence, Edison heard the knock of opportunity. He wanted to make sure that what he called "the executioner's current" would be George Westinghouse's AC. Worried by the plans to use his company's equipment in the execution of

Kemmler, Westinghouse apparently underwrote an expensive legal appeal of Kemmler's conviction, which went all the way to the U.S. Supreme Court, where it was argued that electrocution would constitute "cruel and unusual punishment." Kemmler's appeals were denied, however. On August 6, 1890, he entered the new AC-equipped execution chamber at Auburn prison.

Public excitement and controversy over the execution were said to approach that of a presidential election. Awaiting Kemmler in the chamber were twenty-six witnesses, including six doctors, the district attorney who had prosecuted him, and many journalists; they were arrayed in a semicircle around the electric chair. Kemmler appeared with the warden from a side door, dressed in yellow trousers, a gray jacket, and a black-and-white-checked bow tie. The top of his head had been recently shaved and "had the appearance of a great scar," according to *The New York Times*. "Gentlemen," the warden said, "this is William Kemmler."

Kemmler bowed and said ceremoniously, "Gentlemen, I wish you all good luck. I believe I am going to a good place and I am ready to go." He bowed again and started to sit in a normal chair next to the heavy three-legged oak electric chair. The warden redirected him, then cut a hole in the back of Kemmler's shirt, near the base of his spine, where an electrode would go. He began to attach the electrode, and another, on top of Kemmler's head, with leather straps.

"Now, take your time and do it all right, Warden. There is no rush," said Kemmler, urging the warden to make the straps on the head electrode a bit tighter. "I don't want to take any chances on this thing, you know."

"All right, William," answered the warden. When he was finished, he walked to a door behind the chair and whispered to the electrician working the generator, "Is all ready?" Then he turned back to the room and said, "Good-bye, William," the words being a signal to the technician to throw the switch.

To the horror of the witnesses, the first seventeen-second shock did not kill Kemmler. Doctors thought it had, but then they noticed blood pulsing from a wound where his index finger had contracted and cut deep into his thumb—a sign that his heart was still pumping. Two minutes after the current had been shut off, Kemmler began to gasp and gurgle.

"Great God, he is alive!" someone cried as the witnesses rose from their seats.

"Start the current! Start the current again!" someone else shouted. This time the current was left on for more than two minutes, during which witnesses heard the grinding of Kemmler's teeth and saw blood drops from burst capillaries form on his cheeks. The power occasionally ebbed due to problems with the generator, so Kemmler's body would unpredictably slump, then sit upright again, every muscle straining against the straps. The D.A. ran for the door, gagging. A newspaperman from Washington fainted. The room smelled like cooking meat, and then like feces. Kemmler's head started smoking and his clothes began to catch on fire. A blue flame flickered at the base of his spine.

The power was finally cut. For a long time, the body of Kemmler was left to cool; when finally it was taken from the chair, rigor mortis had frozen it in a sitting position.

Though the doctors later assured everyone that Kemmler had lost consciousness immediately, the newspapers were unforgiving. "An awful spectacle," opined *The New York Times,* a "sacrifice to the whims and theories" of a "coterie of cranks and politicians." "It is obvious that Kemmler did not die a painless death nor did he die instantly," reported the *Buffalo Express.* "It would be impossible to imagine a more revolting exhibition," said *The Times* of London. "The man was really killed by a clumsy stun," reported *Scientific American,* "for which a dextrous blow from a pole ax would have been an expeditious substitute."

Amidst the recriminations and finger-pointing from the doctors, scientists, and prison officials, one might have expected the demise of electrocution technology. Instead, it persisted and indeed at Sing Sing (which soon became the official execution site), the technology was refined. No newsmen were allowed in Sing Sing at the electrocutions of four men on July 7, 1891; prison officials claimed that each was dead within six minutes of entering the execution room. At the following execution, the electrodes were attached to the head and the calf, instead of the small of the back. A witness, though sworn to secrecy, revealed that "on the fourth application of current, the prisoner's eyeball broke and the aqueous fluid ran down his cheek."

Experimentation continued. In hopes of reducing the singeing of hair and flesh, a new electrode system—one originally proposed by Thomas Edison and Harold Brown to demonstrate the lethal nature of AC—was tried on the chair's seventh victim: Instead of forcing electricity to pass from head to leg, officials immersed both of the inmate's hands in a conductive water solution. The first and only inmate to be subjected to this method endured fifty seconds of torture before the power was turned off and he was found to be very much alive. The staff then removed his hands from the water, attached electrodes as previously, and killed him the old way.

Slowly, the problems were solved. Voltage was increased to deal with the highly various resistances of different individuals, amperage was reduced so as not to "cook" the flesh, wet natural sponges were employed to improve the connection between scalp and skin, and diapers were placed on the condemned. In 1958, a New York State Department of Correction (as it was then called) history asserted that "the method of execution has been carefully worked out and standardized over the years." As though in evidence, it offered a degree of detail that could have been of little use to anyone other than an executioner. "An initial shock of 2000 volts is given for 3 seconds, dropped to 500 volts for 57 seconds, built up rapidly again to 2000 volts, dropped again to 500 volts for another 57 seconds, and again instantly raised to the initial voltage. The entire application takes two minutes." Over time, twenty-five states, plus the District of Columbia, adopted the chair. (Lethal injection has since become the preferred method; as of early 2000, only Alabama, Georgia, and Nebraska still use electrocution as their sole means of putting inmates to death.)

Of course, there had to be somebody to run these machines, to check the nuts and bolts of executions, to study it like an art. In New York and New Jersey in the years 1890–1914, it was Edwin D. Davis, a quiet man of "high cheekbones and drooping black mustache" who would arrive at Sing Sing wearing "a Prince Albert coat and black felt hat." Perhaps because of threats on his life, Davis changed his address frequently and refused to be photographed. While electrician at Auburn prison, he designed both the first electric chair and testing procedures for it that involved large slabs of meat. Davis patented the helmet and leg electrodes, and always brought with him to executions a black satchel of secret equipment, which he would let nobody see. In fact, the state tried to purchase his patents and secrets, afraid that he might die before passing them along. The hangman of the age of electricity appears in accounts of Sing Sing history as a character out of the movies, coming in from a foggy night to perform his gruesome work, then leaving without a good-bye.

Davis's eventual successor was his former assistant, an electrician named John Hulbert. Though Hulbert was as close-mouthed as Davis and similarly averse to being photographed, more is known about him thanks to a memoir entitled *Sing Sing Doctor,* by Amos Squire, M.D., who presided over the executions of 138 men between 1914 and 1925, working closely with Hulbert, who actually pulled the switch.

Though Hulbert lived in Auburn and the two were not friends (Squire refers to him as Hilbert throughout), Squire observed him closely. He describes Hulbert as "short and stocky, apparently a man with perfect nerves and excellent constitution," which would seem to be another way of saying that he could perform his job without letting his feelings get in the way. When he read newspapers, Squire noted, Hulbert "studiously avoided all crime news, lest he stumble upon something relating to a person he might afterwards have to execute."

Over time, though, Squire saw Hulbert grow depressed, and says he urged him to stop doing executions. Hulbert replied that he needed the money, the $150 he got for each electrocution. "I never questioned that," wrote Squire, "but I felt that perhaps the very horror of the occupation of executioner had a dreadful fascination from which he could not escape. Otherwise he would have found a way to readjust his life—before it was too late."

The beginning of the end for Hulbert came on a night when, three hours before a scheduled 5 A.M. execution, two inmates escaped from another part of the prison. The escape "upset the entire staff and disrupted routine," a routine upon which Hulbert evidently depended, because, Squire wrote,

> Shortly before the time for the execution I received a call to rush to the death chamber. Hilbert was critically ill. I found him stretched out on one of the spectators' benches, colorless, and his pulse scarcely perceptible. For a while I thought I would have to throw the switch myself. But after working over him and giving him stimulants, I brought him around, so he could go on with the executions—which were delayed half an hour by his sinking spell. He said he was suffering from ptomaine poisoning—but his symptoms indicated a nervous collapse. His condition was so serious I took him into the hospital after he had completed his work that morning and kept him there for a week.

Hilbert eventually resigned his post as executioner—but he had waited too long. Not so long after his resignation, he committed suicide in the cellar of his home.

According to the 1929 obituary in the *Ossining Citizen Sentinel,* John Hulbert used his prison revolver to shoot himself in the chest and temple. His family said he had been despondent over the heart attacks he had suffered recently and the death of his wife the year before. The obituary writer commented, "Mr. Hulbert never could be induced to relate incidents pertaining to the electrocution of criminals. He was averse to notoriety and his comings and goings from the Sing Sing death house were always cloaked in secrecy.

"Whether his work preyed upon his mind no person ever was able to observe from his actions."

Except, perhaps, Squire and others inside the close-lipped world of the Death House. Squire's *Sing Sing Doctor* concerns one of the more interesting periods in the prison's history, the years between 1910 and 1930, which saw the abolition of the lockstep, striped clothing, and the rule against talking at work, as well as the practice of keeping inmates locked in their cells from noon Saturday until Monday morning. This era saw baseball teams organized among inmates, as well as the groundbreaking establishment of an organization of inmate self-government, the Mutual Welfare League.

Squire recognized that readers would want to know about the thing that made Sing Sing increasingly famous as an object of fascination and horror: the Death House. His impossibly conflicted role as prison doctor and co-executioner is an extreme example of the ambiguity inherent in many prison jobs, including guard, but it put Squire in a perfect position to tell the Death House story. His work began with making sure that Death Row inmates stayed healthy—not just for their own good but, perversely, so they couldn't succeed in suicide and thereby "cheat the chair." It continued, on execution day, with his certifying that the inmate scheduled to die was sane. (He excepted only one.) Next, he sat with the condemned man as he was strapped into the chair and gave a hand signal to the executioner, hidden from observers behind a partition, to throw the switch. After a period of time, usually less than thirty seconds, Squire would order the power turned off while he checked for a pulse. As most men still had one, he would then signal for power to be turned back on one or more times, until he judged the man to be dead.

Finally came the autopsy. At the time the electric-execution law was passed, questions persisted about whether electric shock would always prove fatal. Two cases were on record of men having been accidentally electrocuted and then revived by physicians, after several hours' work. To make sure the chair had done its job, legislators required that the brain of execution victims be autopsied.

Grotesquely, the autopsy room was situated in the Death House, next to the cells of Death Row. Inmates there, having seen their acquaintance marched to his execution through an infamous little green door at the end of the hall and then hearing the sounds of the generator, next had to hear the sound of his skull being sawed open. Squire portrays himself as aghast—though he can hardly have been surprised—when one famous condemned murderer, Shillitoni, interrupted an autopsy by going mad in his cell, breaking his furniture, and tearing his bedding to shreds.

Though Squire didn't touch on the larger principle of the Hippocratic Oath (First, do no harm . . .) and the matter of whether doctors should have anything to do with executions, he expressed discomfort about almost every aspect of his work. He regretted that he was "the only member of the prison staff who was compelled to watch the man in the chair every second," and revealed that many times while listening for a heartbeat in the body strapped into the chair, "I have been so overwrought I was alarmed by the thought that what I heard was my own pulse rather than that of the dying man." He conceded that

> Even though I had the respect and cooperation of the prison population in general, there were times when I knew the inmates had a deep, inexpressible feeling of revulsion toward me—owing to the fact that I was about to take part, or had just taken part, in an electrocution. Never with words or overt act would they reproach me, but they did with their eyes—which was worse—and by an unaccustomed silence. . . . It was as if they were accusing me of having betrayed them, after leading them on to believe that I was their friend.

Squire devoted two chapters to arguing against capital punishment ("Each time a person is executed, the effect upon the public is infinitely more degrading than deterrent"), and he told of one sardonic man who on the eve of his execution said, " 'Boys, this is going to be a powerful lesson to me.' " So the reader gets a sense of a man who spent his professional life participating in something that he loathed and that—at least at the end—he did not believe in.

Squire's Hulbertian decline began in a similar way—with disruption of the routine. One of the murderers scheduled for execution had had to be kept constantly in a straitjacket, and Squire, for apparently the first time ever, had sent the governor a letter expressing his doubts that the man was sane. When the day of the execution arrived, the governor still had not responded.

Panicked, Squire boarded a train to Albany to try to speak to him personally, only to learn that the governor was out of town and for the time being unreachable. Two hours later, though, Squire finally got him on the phone, and the governor ordered a two-week reprieve, during which experts reexamined the man and sent him not to the chair but to an asylum.

When I got back home after that experience, I went to bed and stayed there for a month. During that month I lost thirty pounds. As soon as I was able to get out of bed, I went to the Adirondacks to recover my strength.

But a change had come over me. I was oppressed by a feeling of anxiety and menace. I did not realize the trend of my subconscious thoughts until duty took me to the death chamber again and I stood on the edge of the rubber mat, within reach of the chair. On that occasion, just after I had given the signal for the current to be turned on— while the man in the chair was straining against the straps as the load of 2,200 volts shot through his body—I felt for the first time a wild desire to extend my hand and touch him.

Afterwards I subjected myself to severe self-analysis. I decided that my wild and irrational desire was merely a vagrant impulse, and that it would not occur again. But I was wrong. At each subsequent execution the impulse became stronger. It finally got so compelling that I was forced to

grip my fingernails into my palms in order to control it.
Each time I had to stand farther and farther from the chair.
But even then I would feel a sudden, terrifying urge to rush
forward and take hold of the man in the chair, while the
current was on.

Did he want to touch the man to comfort him, I wonder, or to kill
himself?

Having confided in a friend and then his daughter, Squire finally
quit. "If I hadn't," he wrote, thinking of Hulbert, "I might not be
alive today."

The electric chair may or may not have been a more humane
method of execution than hanging—Squire, who had seen two
hangings in Canada, thought it was—but it seems it could not
have been any better for the people who had to operate it. Then
again, the well-being of those who would operate the electric chair
probably never entered the minds of its promoters. I think this
problem—not being taken into account—exists in some degree,
however minimal, for nearly all people who work in prisons. Even
a prison chaplain, one of the "good guys," faces the underrecog-
nized moral dilemma inherent in working in a jail.

Irving Koslowe, Sing Sing's rabbi for forty-nine years (until
1999), attended seventeen executions, including those of the
Rosenbergs, in 1953. The day before an execution, he told the
makers of a historical documentary that aired while I was a guard,
the condemned man was moved from the regular Death Row cells
to a cell near the Dance Hall, through which he would walk on his
way to the chair. His head was shaved. He ordered his last meal.
By the time the guards came for him, Koslowe said, "that man was
half dead." One night after work, I watched Koslowe describe, on
television, the minute-by-minute procedure preceding execution,
heard how he told inmates he'd "be there" for them—"on a rubber mat, but I'll be there."

Could one really "be there" and stand on the rubber mat? I admired Sister Helen Prejean (*Dead Man Walking*) for her pastoral
work among Death Row inmates. But the problem with being an
official prison chaplain, it seemed to me, was that one had to accept the values of the system and could not, as a matter of practicality, question anything. Anyone holding the job was hopelessly
compromised as any sort of moral example. Like Rabbi Koslowe,

you had to agree to stand on the rubber mat. The documentary showed a sign over the door in the death chamber, which the rabbi had passed under many times. It said SILENCE.

The same dynamic, I realized, was at work for correction officers. You didn't have to be flaying an inmate's back with a cat-o'-nine-tails to be wounded by the job. That was simply its nature, a feature of prison work as enduring as Sing Sing's cellblock design. "In its application the familiarity it causes with suffering destroys in the breast of the officer all sympathetic feeling": The words of the Auburn physician seem to me to express a timeless principle.

When I was first looking into the lives of guards, somebody at Council 82 suggested I speak with the union's chaplain. I was surprised to learn about Father James Hayes, and I liked him immediately. He said that he counseled members over the problems the job seemed to cause—alcoholism, divorce, wife and child abuse, ill health. He also mentioned counseling a guard who had put his finger on a sad truth that priests seem to understand better than doctors or social workers.

The CO was retired, said Father Hayes, but his retirement was troubled by the thought of what his life's work had amounted to. "Father," he said. "I spent thirty-three years of my life depriving men of their freedom."

The priest told me he had nodded, listened, and prayed. There was nothing more to do.

———

Amos Squire's tenure at Sing Sing coincided with that of two of its most famous wardens, Thomas Mott Osborne and Lewis Lawes. Osborne stayed only a few months; Lawes, more than twenty years. Osborne was at heart a politician and reformer; Lawes was a firm but sympathetic warden several cuts above the rest, a passionate believer in doing the job right. Both were from upstate prison towns. Both—though they oversaw Sing Sing's executions—were against the death penalty.

A life-size bronze statue of Osborne stands, anomalously, in the foyer of the Albany Training Academy. Draped over one outstretched hand is a set of cuffs and chains; in the other is an open book. I say anomalously because to Osborne, guards were not people to be admired. In fact, he envisioned a prison system that would dispense with them altogether. New York's prison system in the early twentieth century, to his concerned eyes, was in need of complete overhaul. "Prisoners are treated now like wild animals and are kept in cages," he said in a lecture in 1905. "The system brutalizes the men and the keepers. [The inmates] are forced to work, and this is not reformatory. It does not create in the criminal a desire to work and respect the law. . . . I would propose a system [wherein] the prisoner's sentence would be indeterminate. He would work for a living or starve, and if diligent would be allowed to save up and purchase luxuries and possibly freedom. He would be self-governing and learn to respect law."

Osborne grew up in a wealthy household in Auburn, and, after attending prep school and Harvard, became mayor of Auburn, a newspaper publisher, and a manufacturer. A patron of young Franklin Delano Roosevelt, he held other state appointive offices before getting himself named chairman of the new State Commission on Prison Reform. He succeeded in having a political ally appointed as warden of Auburn prison and then had a brainstorm: He would enter Auburn for a week as an "inmate" and use the experience and publicity to launch a campaign for fundamental prison reform.

Osborne's original plan was to enter the prison population anonymously, but he was soon dissuaded: Inmates would figure out his identity, he was told, and he would be taken as a deceiver, a spy, never to be trusted. So instead, he addressed all the inmates of Auburn in September 1913, a day before joining them. "I am curious to find out," he said,

> . . . whether our Prison System is as unintelligent as I think it is; whether it flies in the face of all common sense and all human nature, as I think it does; whether, guided by sympathy and experience, we cannot find something far better to take its place, as I believe we can.
>
> So, by permission of the authorities and with your help, I am coming here to learn what I can at first hand . . . I am coming here to live your life; to be housed, clothed, fed, treated in all respects like one of you. I want to see for myself what your life is like, not as viewed from the outside looking in, but from the inside looking out.

Anticipating criticism by observers outside prison, if not those within, he added,

Of course I am not so foolish as to think that I can see it from exactly your point of view. Manifestly a man cannot be a real prisoner when he may at any moment let down the bars and walk out; and spending a few hours or days in a cell is quite a different thing from a weary round of weeks, months, years.

Still, he argued in *Within Prison Walls,* a book recounting his experiences, our inability to ever put ourselves precisely in the place of another should not keep us from "constantly studying and analyzing the human problem. It still remains true that 'the proper study of mankind is man.' "

Osborne openly adopted the nom de guerre Tom Brown for the duration of his imprisonment, and began his voluntary stay. His first-person narrative, written diary-style, attempts little dispassionate observation and, somewhat embarrassingly, reveals him ill prepared for prison life. He complains about having to sleep in underwear instead of pajamas—why couldn't the state provide those?—about the gristle in his hash, about a feeling of claustrophobia in his cell ("If I were just to let myself go, I believe I should soon be beating my fists on the iron-grated door of my cage and yelling."). The inmates around him seem generally to be a swell bunch of guys, and he shows only faint recognition that his prominence may affect their behavior toward him.

Yet despite his sentimentality and preconceptions, he came away with some shocking stories, particularly his description of Auburn's "jail" or Box, and some keen insights. "Rigid discipline," he decided, ". . . increases disrespect. . . .

I believe every man in this place hates and detests the system under which he lives. He hates it even when he gets along without friction. He hates it because he knows it is bad; for it tends to crush slowly but irresistibly the good in himself.

By the same degree that he was popular among inmates, he appeared to alienate the guards. They mocked him, according to his inmate confidants, and considered him naive. He tried to evince some empathy for them in his book. ("I can conceive no more terribly disintegrating moral experience than that of being a keeper over convicts," he wrote. "However much I pity the prisoners, I think that spiritually their position is far preferable to that of their guards. These latter are placed in an impossible position; for they are not to blame for the System under which their finer qualities have so few chances of being exercised.") Still, beneath it his disdain was evident. "I should not like to be understood as asserting that all keepers are brutal, or even a majority of them," he wrote. "I hope and believe that by far the greater number of the officers serving in our prisons are naturally honorable and kindly men, but so were the slave-owners before the Civil War."

Upon his "parole" from Auburn, Osborne was praised in some circles and, as he expected, mocked and jeered in many others for "playing at" prisoner, for thinking it "necessary to wallow in a mud hole to know how a pig feels." But it served his purpose of getting prison reform on the public agenda and strengthening his hand for the next phase of his campaign.

At the core of Osborne's crusade was a belief that nothing inmates learned in prison really helped prepare them for independent lives outside. "It is liberty alone that fits men for liberty," he liked to say, and with the thought that they needed to do more for themselves, he undertook the next phase of his work, helping Auburn inmates establish a form of self-government. The Mutual Welfare League, which slowly grew from this effort, was an administration-supervised means for inmates to run their own lives, from administering a system of discipline to organizing sports to starting a commissary where inmates could buy goods with a special League scrip. To the consternation of his many political enemies, and certainly Auburn's guards, Osborne used his charisma and the credibility earned as an "inmate" to put this system into effect.

Osborne, increasingly a national figure, was appointed warden of Sing Sing on December 1, 1914. The previous warden had left after a corruption scandal, and such was Osborne's renown that the Republican governor was willing to give him a try. Osborne began to institute familiar reforms but found Sing Sing more complicated than Auburn. Mutual Welfare League–style reforms threatened the entrenched power of certain inmates. His transfer of powers of self-determination to inmates provoked loud and repeated charges of coddling. The governor himself began to get irritated with Osborne over his repeated attacks on capital punishment—the warden made a point of being out of town whenever an electrocution was scheduled. Plots were hatched to discredit him, and before his first year was over, one finally snared him: a raft of charges alleging violation of prison rules, including one count that warden Osborne "did commit various unlawful and unnatural acts with inmates of Sing Sing Prison, over whom he had supervision and control."

A main source of the sodomy testimony was an inmate whom Osborne had previously identified as a spy for the superintendent of prisons—one of his political enemies—and had transferred out. This man, Fat Alger, claimed to have drunk claret on the warden's porch one night till 2 A.M. and then stayed in his bedroom till 3 A.M. Despite what some saw as the transparent falsity of the charges, Osborne was indicted by a Westchester grand jury. The sensational legal battle that followed utterly consumed him until, several months later, all the charges were finally dropped. He resumed his job as warden, only to resign three months later.

Though his profile was never again so high, and the institutions of reform he began were attenuated over the years, Osborne succeeded in shifting the course of American penal practice and modified the seemingly set in stone operations of two of the country's biggest rock piles.

Thomas Mott Osborne's inspirational tenure as warden of Sing Sing was typical only insofar as it was short. Until the 1950s, when it became a civil service post, the job was a political appointment, often bestowed on men who knew nothing whatsoever about running a prison. "The quickest way to get out of Sing Sing is to come in as warden" was a popular joke. Thirty-one Sing Sing wardens had lasted only little over a year; they included a steamfitter, a coal dealer, a horseman, a postmaster, a customs revenue collector, a millionaire and philanthropist, and "assorted ward-heelers." Four years after Osborne left, however, a former guard from Elmira named Lewis Lawes took the helm and in twenty years on the job became America's most famous and admired warden.

Lawes had started his career as a guard at Clinton prison and then returned to his hometown of Elmira, where he rose to the post of chief guard. And yet this guard's guard was highly literate and open-minded. To him, Osborne had been an inspiration. "Of all the array of incoming and outgoing wardens in the century of Sing Sing's history, [Osborne's] name stands out in bold relief," Lawes wrote in 1932. "To him must be given the credit for a more enlightened policy that, while not entirely complete, pointed the way toward the new penology."

Though not primarily a reformer, Lawes had strong opinions about the possibilities of prisons. Osborne's shortcoming, as Lawes saw it, was that he gave prisoners too much self-government too fast—and that some of what he gave should never be given at all. "There can be no democracy within prison walls," Lawes wrote. "A group of men who have quarrelled with the law cannot be expected to set up a government patterned after the one they antagonized."

Sing Sing's Mutual Welfare League had quickly become the domain of gangs and cliques, Lawes said—an officially sanctioned Darwinian power structure. The more talented individuals who should have figured prominently would have nothing to do with it. The proper role of the League, Lawes believed, ought to be as a "moral force," not an actual mechanism of self-government.

Gradually, Lawes shut down the League. In its place he established an administration distinguished by its humaneness and intelligence. Prison administration couldn't help being a despotism, but it could be an enlightened one. "It quickly became apparent to me," he wrote,

> that . . . the prison warden, to be effective, would have to constitute himself not as an instrument of punishment but a firm, frank friend in need. He would have to stretch humanitarianism to the limits of the law, with a stiff punch always in reserve. . . . My job is to hold my men and, as far as possible, to win them over to sane, social thinking. And I judge the effectiveness of that job not so much by obedience to rule, for rules can be enforced, but by the humor of the general prison population.

Like Osborne, Lawes believed that increasing public knowledge of prisons could only be good. Osborne had brought prisons to the public eye through his spectacular deeds; Lawes had other methods. The crime wave of the 1920s and 1930s, the great gangster era, increased public interest in prisons and punishment, and the interest of Hollywood in particular. Lawes obliged the industry by allowing Warner Bros. inside his prison. The film *Angels with Dirty Faces* (1938), starring James Cagney and Humphrey Bogart, was filmed partly inside Sing Sing, as were *Each Dawn I Die* (1939), with Cagney and George Raft; *Castle on the Hudson* (1940), with John Garfield and Ann Sheridan; and others, including two based on Lawes's books *Twenty Thousand Years in Sing Sing* and *Invisible Stripes*. A recurrent theme was of "hard-boiled, but not incorrigible inmates who somehow came around under the compassionate, but firm hand of the warden." The title of his book *Invisible Stripes* referred to the stigma that continued to hobble criminals after they'd done their time and left their striped uniforms for the streets.

Lawes wrote five nonfiction books in all; he also did radio broadcasts and contributed articles to magazines. Time and again he tried to drive home the idea that crime really begins in the slums, and that prison itself can't cure it. For one Hearst Metrotone newsreel he sat in his office, young inmates around him wearing masks to preserve their anonymity.

> From my desk within the walls of Sing Sing, I see daily the constantly increasing numbers of boys and young men who are committed to prison. A very great proportion could be made into law-abiding, resourceful citizens. . . . You may be shocked by their youth, yet they are typical of the small army of young men that make up a major proportion of the population of our prisons. . . . We have come to the aid of our savings banks, we have organized to save our forests, why haven't we some plans for youth that will take our young people off the road, that road that leads them, year after year, in a constant procession, to the gates of our prisons . . . ?

Lawes also invited major league baseball teams into prison to play against the Mutual Welfare League team, the Black Sheep. During one such game, Babe Ruth hit what has been purported to be his longest home run ever, 620 feet, over the prison wall.

When Lawes arrived in 1920, Sing Sing had a population of slightly over one thousand, all housed in the original cellblock. But the crime wave led to more inmates, and by 1927 there was serious overcrowding in all of the state's facilities. Construction of all the main Sing Sing buildings in use today began in the early twenties: a new Hospital Building, a new Death House, 5-Building, and 7-Building. In 1926 it was decided to build A- and B-blocks on the hill, and in 1929 they were completed, along with the chapel and mess hall. Laundry and administration buildings followed shortly, then the school building and a new power plant. Lawes hired the first black guard in 1925 and endorsed plans to institute a six-day workweek for prison officers, down from seven.

Lawes ran his prison in a paternalistic way that had a warmth we would not recognize today. He met daily with representatives of inmate groups. Lawes's children knew the inside of the prison from movies they watched there, and the inmates who worked in his house as cooks, cleaners, and handymen knew his family. When his wife died, in 1937, every single inmate is said to have filed out through gates past her casket in the warden's house and then back into prison. In 1940, Lewis Lawes finally retired.

One thing had not changed while Lawes was at Sing Sing: the old cellblock. Amidst the controversies and corruption, the many wardens, and the advent of "penology"—including progress in prison architecture and conditions elsewhere—the massive structure sat immobile, barely altered in a hundred years except for growing more crowded (six hundred cells were double-bunked in 1909) and losing a floor and a half in a 1917 demolition bid that was halted after the state realized it still needed the space. Diseases like cholera, dysentery, and scarlet fever had haunted it from the start; in 1892, the same year twenty-seven inmates died there from tuberculosis, Dr. R. T. Irvine observed that the building offered "unusual opportunity for diffusion of this disease." A 1905 State Prison Improvement Commission found the cells damp, too small, and badly ventilated, concluding, "verily, this is far worse than living in a sewer." Yet, as the official department history put it, the cellblock "continued to hang like a millstone around the neck of the institution . . . continued to swallow thousands of inmates into its malevolent, malodorous maw"—over a hundred thousand men in its first century alone. Finally, in 1943, the last of the original cellblock's inmates were moved out. Parts of the structure were used as a vocational shop until the roof burned down in 1984, when the building was permanently closed—boarded up and fenced in though, inexplicably, not removed. The prison continued to grow and operate around its historical core.

The 1950s and 1960s brought what has been called the professionalization of corrections—the idea that prison was something the working person might make a career of, whether as a "correction officer" or as a college-educated warden. Prison jobs became civil service jobs; prisons within the states became more standardized and centrally controlled; and unions in a few states, particularly New York and California, became important players. For officers, professionalization meant more training and implied a higher standard of on-the-job conduct. The self-image of the corps was remade, partly in the hope that a "professional" could command higher pay. As Sergeant Bloom had told us at the Academy, "If you want to act like a guard, go ahead—that's easy. But if you want to be a correction officer and get paid like a CO, then pay attention."

Professional administrators came to replace the politically appointed wardens of old. Though the change was long awaited, the advent of bureaucratic administration seemed to guarantee that the visionary tendency of an Osborne and the humane one of a Lawes were things of the past. The same qualities of imagination that the institutions seemed to require so badly were less available than they had ever been before.

Sing Sing moved in some ways into the future, incorporating a small number of vocational programs, a few school courses, a counseling staff, and expanded opportunities for inmate recreation. But this development was limited by a lack of space. The town of Ossining was now firmly packed around the prison's great walls, which meant there would be no funds forthcoming for the modern industrial education shops that other maxes enjoyed, no room for a prison farm, such as the one run by inmates at Green Haven. In the meantime, as the prison aged, newer facilities looked that much better by comparison. The town of Ossining grew frustrated that it could collect no taxes on fifty-five acres of prime shorefront land. Throughout the 1970s and 1980s, repeated calls were made to close Sing Sing down.

A slow push was under way to reemphasize the rehabilitative possibilities of prison in New York State when, on September 9, 1971, the Attica prison uprising began. It was a tumultuous time in American politics—sixteen months earlier, the Ohio National Guard had killed four students at an antiwar rally at Kent State University. Barely two weeks before the Attica revolt, the California tower guard had shot to death Black Panther George Jackson, and the next morning Attica inmates refused to eat breakfast and wore items of black clothing in solidarity. Throughout the summer of 1971, Attica was jumpy; it took only a small confrontation in the yard between two inmates and three officers to spark the violent inmate takeover that would make history. But the rebellious inmates wished to get one thing straight at the beginning of their written statement of five demands: "The incident that has erupted here at Attica is not a result of the dastardly bushwacking of the two prisoners Sept. 8, 1971," they wrote, "but of the unmitigated oppression wrought by the racist administration network of the prison, throughout the year."

Governor Nelson D. Rockefeller refused to negotiate directly with the inmates, and on September 13, worried that the inmates were harming their hostages, the state police launched a bloody battle to retake the prison. Two hostages, it turned out, had been seriously injured by the inmates, but ten hostages and twenty-nine inmates were then killed by police in the attack. Three hostages, eighty-five inmates, and one state trooper were wounded.

With one hand Rockefeller continued to implement some of the previously approved reforms—drug-rehabilitation programs, college-degree classes—but with his other, he pushed through the Assembly a raft of strict antidrug laws. One effect of these laws was an increase in the prison population, over the next twenty-five years, of 560 percent. This explosive growth resulted in the building of fifty new prisons and the transformation of the Department of Correctional Services into the state's second-largest employer, after Verizon. With all the new construction upstate, and the suspension of executions in 1963 due to legal challenges, Sing Sing was no longer where the public attention—or the cutting-edge practices (such as shock camps for teenagers or, in other states, privately run prisons)—was focused.

Its long history and gradual marginalization made Sing Sing increasingly different from the state's other prisons. Lewis Lawes wrote of being wary of his appointment there in 1920, in part because when he had visited a few years earlier, as chief guard at Elmira, his recollection of it "was not altogether satisfying." He went on: "There was, at that time, little attempt at cleanliness. The yard was littered with debris." The air of neglect gradually if inexplicably returned after Lawes left; something about the place seemed to invite it. Around 1969, B-block, only forty years old, was condemned due to structural problems and abandoned. In 1973 Sing Sing itself was changed by the state from a maximum-security prison into a "reception center"—a place where new inmates would arrive to be tested and classified and then sent to the prison where they would ultimately serve their sentence. Then, due to a lack of cells in New York City because of the closing of the

Tombs jail, it also became a stopgap holding pen for some of New York City's overflow during the city's financial crisis.

By 1982 Sing Sing had been reclassified once more as maximum-security. B-block was refurbished and reopened as a "transit block," supposedly holding inmates for limited times. Shortly after this reopening came the 1983 incident in which Sergeant Wickersham and sixteen others were held hostage. Looking back for the reasons behind the B-block takeover, a state report commented that Sing Sing was by then "to most of the outside world . . . a relic from musty books and old movies, which many people were surprised to learn was still in use after 157 years." It

> had become a place where no one had any idea what was supposed to occur . . . increasingly unmanageable. Senior departmental staff invested negligible effort to correct operational deficiencies at the facility. . . . In spite of the lack of interest . . . Ossining continued to function without any "serious" incidents. It had its own way of life which was perceived by many to enable the facility to function in spite of departmental guidelines. Accordingly, senior staff were reluctant to disturb what appeared to be Ossining's equilibrium.

By the late 1980s, Sing Sing's status as a de facto training facility was well established. Its reputation for being loose and wild was ascendant. Four guards and a sergeant were indicted in 1982 on corruption charges, such as being paid to smuggle marijuana and cocaine into prison. Nineteen eighty-three brought the B-block takeover and hostage crisis. In 1986 a burglar and two murderers, having distracted officers with smoke bombs, escaped through a window of the school building onto the train tracks below, using wire cutters and a thirty-foot-long rope made of shoelaces. All this was followed in 1988 by the mortifying headline on page one of the New York *Daily News* that read SING SING SEXCAPADES and the banner inside that read SWING SWING:

> ALBANY—Sex, drugs and gambling have been rampant in Sing Sing prison over the last two years under the protection of a clique of rogue correction officers, according to guards and a former ranking prison official.
>
> The sexual escapades in the maximum-security prison

allegedly include trysts between male inmates and female guards—including two suspected of prostitution—in the prison-chapel projection room and a cell.

Guards who tried to crack down on inmate drug use were subject to death threats—purportedly by corrupt officers, according to one guard.

The story said that random urine tests had shown that 21 percent of Sing Sing inmates were on drugs, compared to a statewide prison average of 6 percent.

———

Upon assuming the wardenship of Sing Sing, Lewis Lawes sat down with a stack of "musty reports and records that had not been looked at in decades." As he traced the prison's history, he saw progress, the "puritanical" practice of the nineteenth century evolving into the "more enlightened social thought" of the twentieth. But if you compare the state of America's prisons at mid-twentieth century to their condition today, it is hard to make the case for any further progress at all.

As a former officer looking back into Sing Sing's history, I was struck by lost institutions of the old prison, such as the bands that played as prisoners marched to chow. Early in the twentieth century, inmates who prized special bars sewn onto their uniforms for time served were humiliated when, as punishment, these symbols of accomplishment were removed. During World War II there were wildly successfully inmate blood drives—1,106 pints were donated in 1943. These all look like signs that inmates, though segregated in prison, still considered themselves a part of mainstream society in some way. As recently as twenty years ago, old-time officers told me, it would be exceptional to find more than ten B-block inmates on keeplock. Nowadays, the number is nearer a hundred, and the Box is always full.

Almost unarguably, prisoners' attitudes about their punishment have worsened. Few seem to feel that the exchange of their time and liberty for their commission of a crime is a fair one, and many if not most continue to insist upon their innocence. And race has entered the equation, on the side of the inmates. Eldridge Cleaver, writing from Folsom prison in the sixties, observed:

One thing that the judges, policemen, and administrators of prisons seem never to have understood, and for which they certainly do not make any allowances, is that Negro convicts, basically, rather than see themselves as criminals and perpetrators of misdeeds, look upon themselves as prisoners of war, the victims of a vicious, dog-eat-dog social system that is so heinous as to cancel out their own malefactions: in the jungle there is no right or wrong.

Rather than owing and paying a debt to society, Negro prisoners feel that they are being abused, that their imprisonment is simply another form of the oppression which they have known all their lives. Negro inmates feel that they are being robbed, that it is "society" that owes them, that should be paying them, a debt.

The essential relationship inside a prison is the one between a guard and an inmate. Any true progress in the workings of a prison ought to be measurable in changes in the tenor of that relationship. The guard is mainstream society's last representative; the inmate, its most marginal man. The guard, it is thought, wields all the power, but in truth the inmate has power too. How will they meet, with mutual respect or mutual disdain? Will they talk? Will they joke? Will they look each other in the eye?

The course of this central relationship is one that is hard to tease out of official investigations and even prisoner memoirs, but my sense is that it has evolved little, if at all. Nineteenth-century inspectors' reports show that while guards as a mass were feared, individuals among them were liked and hated; in reports of punishments, it can be ascertained that some guards meted out a huge number, others, very few. Some guards were honest; others, clearly on the take. According to a legislative report from 1851, "The amount of compensation allowed to the officers is so small, that a high order of talent cannot be pressed into the service of the State. . . . We cannot expect all the virtues in the world for $1.37 a day." That hasn't changed much, either.

Even so, the author of the report saw how guarding could be done either poorly or well.

To become a good officer requires much more knowledge and experience than is generally supposed; and it is a long time after a new officer enters upon his duty, before he becomes, even under the most favorable circumstances, fully competent to discharge it. It is not like a man's driving a herd of oxen or working a piece of machinery, the whole mechanism of which he can learn in a short time. But it is controlling the minds of men, no two of which are alike—it is curbing their tempers, whose manifestations are infinitely various—it is directing their motives which are as diverse as their personal appearance or physical conformation. And it requires an intimate knowledge, if not of human nature at large, at least of the habits, tempers and dispositions of the men immediately under their charge . . . under such circumstances, the most gifted man would be the better for experience, and the less gifted would be more valuable than him, if he had experience enough.

This consideration, so evidently the dictate of good sense, seems to be entirely overlooked in the government of our prisons, and changes occur, among the officers, from whim, caprice, or political motives, with a frequency that is utterly subversive of good government.

At Sing Sing, the century-old warning is still unheeded.

One day, after I finished my shift, a deputy superintendent gave me permission to look through two manila folders in which he kept a lot of old newspaper clippings and prison memorabilia. In one of them I saw a HELP WANTED poster published by the state in the 1950s to attract new guard applicants. It listed as job duties the usual supervision and custodial work, but there was also a line about helping to counsel and reform the prisoner. Nothing like that was ever presented to me during training. I think the Department is smart enough to know that today's COs would only laugh.

But in their hearts, I think the officers wish it weren't so. I think they'd rather chat with an inmate and reinforce his connection to the outside world than dodge missiles of shit and piss. I think the statue of Thomas Mott Osborne in the foyer of the training academy is there because, somehow, Elam Lynds won't do. Osborne, the inmates' friend, chains in one hand and book in the other, is the only hero corrections can possibly have. He is perhaps best known for this quote: "We will turn this prison from a scrap heap into a repair shop." The presence of his statue, I think, speaks to an idealism that is never openly discussed by guards, the hope that prisons might do some good for the people in them, that human lives can be fixed instead of thrown away, that there's more to be done than locking doors and knocking heads, that the "care" in *care, custody, and control* might amount to something beyond calling the ER when an inmate is bleeding from a shank wound.

Instead, the most recent trend in corrections is the advent of the "supermax" prison, of which there are now roughly three dozen in the United States, including New York's newest facility. A supermax is like a huge SHU, with 100 percent segregation cells. The inmates in them have minimal contact with each other and practically no relationship at all with their guards. "If you ask me, that's a recipe for a junkyard dog," an Academy instructor opined to us. I think she was right. And the odd thing is, the idea for a supermax is not new. Solitary confinement around the clock, with idleness during the day: Elam Lynds, before he hit on the congregate system, tried it back in 1821.

CHAPTER 6

LIFE IN MAMA'S HOUSE

I went to do a film in a penitentiary, and I was up there six weeks—Arizona State Penitentiary—it was, like, 80 percent black people . . . I was up there and I spoke to all the brothers, and it made my heart ache, you know? All these beautiful black men in the joint, goddamn warriors, they should be out there helping the masses. And—I was real naive, right?—six weeks I was up there, I talked to the brothers, and I talked to them, and—[in a low, grave voice] *thank God we got penitentiaries!* I mean, murderers, do you hear me, real live murderers!
—Richard Pryor, *Live on the Sunset Strip,* 1982

The cop who had been an Alcatraz guard was potbellied and about sixty, retired but unable to keep away from the atmospheres that had nourished his dry soul all his life. Every night he drove to work in his '35 Ford, punched the clock exactly on time, and sat down at the rolltop desk. He labored painfully over the simple form we all had to fill out every night—rounds, time, what happened, and so on. . . . If it hadn't been for Remi Boncoeur I wouldn't have stayed at this job two hours.
—Jack Kerouac, *On the Road,* 1957

"Take your shirt off, please. Show me your hands, both sides. Now, arms away from your body. Turn around. Okay."

A nod when we're finished, and we move on to the next cell. He's heard us coming and wants to know why.

"You can probably guess. Just do it, please."

"And what if I don't?"

"The sergeant will come, and they'll write you up." The man sighs, shrugs, pulls his T-shirt over his head, does the dance. We move on to the next cell.

B-block is locked down, and we're looking for knife cuts. It is May. For the third day in a row, the Latin Kings have been attacking the Bloods, and vice versa. Not en masse—just stealth encounters, stabbings without warning. One incident provokes the next; we're told that the cycles of retaliation began at Rikers Island earlier this month. Each time we let the inmates back out, someone else is attacked, violence flaring up like one of those trick birthday candles.

The sergeant wouldn't say why we were conducting these "upper-body frisks," but it doesn't take a genius: The white-shirts think that at least one participant in the latest cutting exchange, though wounded, escaped undetected. So we're looking for blood, skin that needs stitching, a gash from a homemade blade.

At the next cell, the inmate is lying on his bunk. "R-63, take off your shirt, please." He sits up bleary-eyed, then stands, removes the shirt. Like many inmates, he's in excellent shape from weight lifting. And like many inmates, he has scars: three inches long on his waist below the ribs, about one inch long on his arm, penny-size circles that look like two bullet wounds on a shoulder blade.

"Nothing fresh," says the officer I'm with, more to himself than in dismissal. He's an old-timer who doubts we'll find anything and acts like he's seen it all before. I'm not so world-weary. The huge number of scars surprises me. Half the inmates seem to have been stabbed or shot at some point in their lives. Often, the scars are on their face: a pale, thick line across the back of the skull where no hair grows, a sliced nostril imperfectly healed, a gash along a cheek that ended when the blade passed through a lip. The most ghastly wound is on a man who looks about nineteen: a ragged cicatrix that winds from one corner of his mouth to beneath his left ear, then all the way around his head, under the right ear, and back to the other corner of the mouth, as though the assailant intended to peel off the top: a sadist's trophy.

We continue down the line. Gash after gash after gash. But nothing fresh.

———

There are drawbacks, but overall lockdowns are a pleasure. When the inmates are all locked in their cells, most of what is stressful in the life of a block officer goes away. The galleries are clear, at least until trash begins to accumulate. The gates stay closed. The PA system stays quiet, because there is nothing the inmates need to be told.

Lockdowns follow what are officially known as unusual incidents. Besides gang-related violence, that can mean attacks on guards, problems with the count (an inmate missing from his cell), or even the discovery of especially scary contraband, like the stash of bullets, zip gun, and bags of marijuana that were found in the basement of the mess hall later that year, all inside Styrofoam boxes sealed with clear tape. The commissioner of corrections has to approve all lockdowns, because they are stressful to inmates, essentially turning them all into keeplocks.

I was surprised to hear B-block was still locked down when I came to work the next day, but not upset about it. I walked over to Mama Cradle, the B-block OIC, with my old classmate Bella.

Bella had distinguished himself in our training class by being the only person to flunk the first-aid course, a requirement for graduation. It wasn't for lack of trying. A thirty-something father of two, he badly wanted this job, but he had barely passed his other exams, and first aid had stumped him. Of course Nigro had let him take the test again; I and a couple of others helped him study before he did, because he was a nice guy, hapless but good-natured. Everyone applauded when Nigro announced that Bella had finally passed.

We became friendly after that. Bella told me he'd had problems at a New Jersey detention facility for minors, where he'd been a counselor/guard—some of the kids had escaped during his watch. He was exonerated, because two other employees who were supposed to be supervising the kids with him had not turned up for work. Bella had grown up in the Bronx and attended a tough high school near where I lived; his brother was a cop. He missed his kids a lot during our weeks at the Academy, as I missed mine, and we talked about that. He had an application in for a New Jersey road-maintenance job, but nothing had come of it yet.

Mama Cradle told us there was nothing for us to do just then, but we shouldn't stray far—and should not venture out onto the flats. This was because, to relieve their boredom and express their contempt, inmates were occasionally tossing items out of their cells in hopes they might hit one of us. Alcantara, in fact, had been drenched with what appeared to be water and was sent off to change his uniform. So we hung near Cradle's office, where there was a ledge over our heads, then migrated to the gym and used some of the inmates' exercise equipment until Cradle called us back to her office.

"I want you guys to do the feed-up," she directed a group of us new officers. "Then later you'll pick up the trays." She pointed us to a pile of large garbage bags.

That was the downside of lockdowns: having to do the inmates' scut work. But Bella never seemed to complain, and with him as my partner, I didn't mind, either. We joined other new officers in the mess hall, where I held a tray and Bella stacked it high with Styrofoam "clamshells" full of beef stew and rice. Maneuvering with this load took skill. I descended a narrow staircase from the mess hall to R-gallery very carefully, because with the trays stacked high, I couldn't see in front of me. It got worse on R, where no one had swept or picked up in many hours. The floor of the narrow gallery was an obstacle course—littered with chicken bones from dinner the night before, toast from breakfast, jam packets and scrambled eggs, spilled coffee and juice, covered by a layer of Styrofoam cups and clamshells. I waded slowly, blindly, determined not to fall and entertain the inmates. Bella handed out meals, amazingly upbeat. Something about this assignment cheered him.

"He-e-e-re's lunch!" he announced at cell after cell, undaunted by silence and surliness. "Why don't they send up some chicks instead of you ugly motherfuckers?" was the nicest thing we heard. "The beer's coming," Bella would say in return, or simply, "Have a nice day!" I took little steps forward.

We made a second round, passing out juice and coffee, and then killed time on the south-end staircase. He'd put in for a transfer to Bedford Hills, Bella said. I didn't have to ask why he was transferring to a prison farther from home, but did so anyway. "For the calmness," he answered. "And because of some of the officers here." More than the inmates, Bella was put off by the way the more senior officers treated us. They issued orders, neglected to explain procedures, were eager to lay blame, and tried to humiliate us.

We gave the inmates twenty minutes or so to finish their meals, then set back down the gallery wearing latex gloves and bearing huge trash bags. A dismal assignment, I thought: garbagemen to the inmates. Bella was unfazed and, in fact, began to sing the theme from *Mr Rogers' Neighborhood*:

> *It's a beautiful day in the neighborhood,*
> *A beautiful day for a neighbor. . .*

He sang it again and again, smiling when the inmates stared at him as if he were crazy and smiling when I stared at him in admiration. Forget his test scores: Bella knew a secret way to handle all the crap, and I envied him.

————

Part of maturing into a regular officer at Sing Sing was deciding whether you were an A-block person or a B-block person. Somehow, Sergeant Holmes formed an idea of where you belonged and then tended to send you there. This was not always accomplished through intuition. Some guards would start out at A-block, then lock horns with Sergeant Wickersham, and thereafter be sentenced by mutual agreement to B-block. Others would begin at B-block, get turned off by the greater chaos factor—the younger, more transient inmates or the higher incidence of gang violence—and head back to A-block. The deciding difference for some officers appeared to be architecture. Though the two buildings were quite similar, some felt—as I did—that A-block's longer galleries (eighty-eight cells long) were that much more unmanageable than B-block's (sixty-eight cells long). Others preferred A-block's modernized though undependable electronic locking system to B-block's ancient, manually operated brakes and levers. There tended to be more white officers bidding A-block and more officers of color bidding B-block, but there were many exceptions. Though I spent more time in A-block early on, I turned into a committed B-block person and eventually bid it myself. And I would have to say the main factor behind that for me was Mama Cradle.

There are some people in this life that you mysteriously like the moment you see them, and Mama was that way for me. I had no good reason to like her. She would sometimes reassign me from easy jobs that Holmes had given me to hard ones, and in the beginning, especially, she had a low opinion of me. But I liked her. I liked her aura, her toughness, her . . . shape. The novelist Jim Harrison once wrote of dancing for five hours in Mexico with "a maiden who resembled a beige bowling ball." ("She was, in fact, shaped rather like me," he wrote.) I'm married to a slender woman, but Mama was that appealing round girl to me—spherical but solid—and I always pictured us together on a dance floor, my hands in no danger of meeting behind her back.

Inexplicably, I wanted to *please* Cradle. At the beginning, I always failed. She assigned me to the center gate and Q-south, the gallery next to her office and told me, "I don't want to see nobody out where they ain't supposed to be." I ran them as strictly as I could but confronted the limits of my ability when the keeplocks returned from their rec. Two of them ran past their cells and, despite my commands to stop, past me, up to the gate, where they hollered for Cradle.

"Mama got to help me with this form," said one.

"I'll help you with the form after you lock in," I told him. "Direct order."

He ignored me and kept hollering for Cradle, who eventually walked over, telling one of the men to go into his cell and the other to come see her. When she ignored me as he had, I knew I'd messed up. I was new, and they didn't respect me. I wondered what it took, and in hindsight, I wished I'd knocked down or tackled the little one. It might have been seen as an overreaction, but at least I would have gotten everyone's attention.

Later in the day Mama replaced me on the gate with a larger, more senior officer and sent me to patrol the gym. I felt she was sending me a message, and at the end of the day I told her I'd do better tomorrow. If Mama wanted me to run, I'd run.

I did fare a bit better the next day, and the day after that, Mama sent me to V-gallery, at the back, where Officer Smith had taught me so well during my training. Smith was gone for a while, she explained. "And it ain't V-Rec today—remember!" she warned, meaning, nobody out when they weren't supposed to be.

Without Smith there, of course, that was easier said than done. Inmates asserted privilege in time-tested ways that were difficult to deny ("I'm the head yard porter, CO, so I've got to get out there before they drop rec—Smitty always just lets me wait by the door down there."). And inmates from other galleries dropped by, some of them for legitimate reasons (the law library porter was supposed to be walking around picking up and dropping off books) and some not (errant gallery porters from other floors who parked themselves in front of their buddies' cells were a constant problem).

Aragon was working Q-south, a short gallery that I handled the paperwork for, and, probably unlike any of his predecessors, he thought it important to turn in mental-health referrals on a couple of his inmates who seemed in need of help. While we were in my office looking for the forms, two or three unauthorized inmates apparently appeared on the gallery and were noticed by some wandering senior officer, who, knowing we were new and vulnerable, tattled to Cradle. Soon we heard ourselves summoned over the PA system. We walked over and squished ourselves into Cradle's office, where she chewed us out.

"What did I say about keeping your galleries clear?" she demanded. "Can you do it, or do I need to find someone else?"

We said we could do it, and I thought Aragon felt the same respect and grudging affection for Cradle that I felt. But as soon as we were out of earshot, he said, "I can't stand that bitch! I'm running that gallery better than at least ninety percent of officers do."

Inmates also had somewhat polarized reactions to Cradle. Seeing her anywhere in the block besides the OIC office provoked comment, because Mama's physical stature seemed to keep her from venturing very far. Not that she was frail. I was on a gallery upstairs one day and after she ambled by, two inmates started talking about her in terms I can only describe as admiring: "Mama gonna kick you in the nuts, and you gonna start to fall. Then she gonna get you with an uppercut and knock your head back. You think you bad, but Mama gonna show you who's toughest."

Another day, I saw her infuriate some inmates on R-gallery north, just above her office. She was in the middle of dropping runs when she stepped from her office out onto the flats to gaze up at the front-side galleries. What she saw was a lot of inmates out of their cells when they weren't supposed to be, hanging out mainly in anticipation of rec.

"Officers, clear your galleries!" she called into the PA microphone. "I'm not calling another run until all those inmates are in their cells! Clear your galleries!"

That day was the commissary run for R-gallery, and the inmates right above her office put their faces to the chain-link fence and started yelling at her. The issue wasn't really Mama herself but Sing Sing's poor administration: The commissary didn't always have room for all the inmates who were allowed a buy, and often those who weren't at the front of the line downstairs didn't get to go. Mama, however, with her loud voice and take-no-lip approach, was their lightning rod. The inmates started getting abusive, and Mama, of course, yelled right back. She wouldn't budge. Pretty soon, with countless inmates from other floors joining in, it sounded like Mama against the world. I quickly joined a group of officers who marched upstairs to get the R inmates to lock in. It was a fight for Mama's dignity! We spread ourselves out, made our presence known to the main instigators. I stood right next to one man who was directing a particularly abusive string of epithets toward Mama. He ignored me, so I told him to stop. Still he ignored me, so I asked for his I.D. He gave it to me, but then, like a true knucklehead, kept on swearing. I wrote him up (106.10, direct order; 107.10, interference with staff; and 107.11, verbal harassment). I did it for Mama.

Though Mama seemed aware of my shortcomings, Sergeant Holmes kept assigning me to V-gallery, and somebody finally told me that Mama must be requesting me. "You're kidding," I said, truly amazed. It was the first hint of praise I'd received, however indirectly, from anyone at Sing Sing. I didn't think Cradle even knew my name. Others confirmed that Mama had daily conversations with Holmes about whom she wanted back and whom she didn't. They had a warm relationship. I answered her phone one day when she was away from the desk, and Holmes said, "Is L.B. there?"

"L.B.?"

"Cradle," he said. "Is Ms. Cradle there?"

"It's for you, L.B.," I told her a moment later, and when she hung up, I asked what that stood for.

"Oh, L.B.?" she said with a wide smile. "Little Bitch."

Officers who weren't assigned to galleries had time at the end of the shift to laze around and chat a bit. One day I heard Cradle advise one whose two weeks of vacation were coming up that he "shouldn't just sit around at home, like all the other COs do on vacation. Go somewhere."

"Like, what do you mean?"

"Like Colonial Williamsburg." Cradle mentioned an officer friend who had just returned from a package tour to the Virginia attraction and sang its praises. The officer gazed into the distance. "Colonial Williamsburg," he said. He'd never go.

Another time little Baez, the front-gate officer, was talking about what he'd do when he got home—the cold beer, the game on TV, the relatives coming over. He asked Cradle about her evening.

"Cook dinner, wash my hair, set it," she said.

"Set your hair?" asked Baez. "You sleep with rollers, Mama?"

He was intrigued. Cradle didn't wear her hair natural, but in a wavy do. It took some time. She put up with the officers asking tongue-in-cheek questions about her procedures.

An officer like me hadn't been there long enough to see the change, but older ones clued me in to the upsetting news: Cradle was burning out. After seventeen years on the job, fourteen of them in B-block, she was showing signs of stress. A couple of these signs I recognized, such as the way she'd press her left hand to her forehead and close her eyes when some officer, usually a new one like me, committed an error like losing a keeplock or dropping a run at the wrong time. Or she would get into loud arguments with inmates. I'd taken it all as just part of her style, but apparently it wasn't. Rumor had it she was exploring transfer options and might be headed on to Fishkill or Downstate. Of all times, I thought. Just when I'd arrived.

———

8/24/97 7:05 a.m. CO T Conover on duty with census of R-63 and W-64 and 4 sets of keys, PAS #831, 2nd officers Corbie and Cespedes, and the following K/L's: R-3, 6, 11, 12, 20, 26, 28 (adj.), 42, 51, 52, 60, 63, 64, 65, 66, and W-10, 23, 28, 46, 47, 55, 60, 61.

———

A new page in the logbook began each of my shifts as a gallery officer. Like untold numbers of officers before me, I acknowledged receiving the equipment of the previous officer (keys and PAS, or Personal Alarm System—the radio with the emergency pull-cord) and the essential numbers regarding inmates. The activity was half brain-dead ritual and half Cover Your Ass ("I didn't know he was a keeplock, Lieutenant—the list I was given didn't have him on it!"). I didn't mind the logbook as much as the officers who cringed at paperwork of any kind did. But I was depressed by what it represented—the hours measured, the boredom of inmates and irritation of officers, the ticking of the clock, the niggling accountability. What the upstate union rep had told me years earlier about an officer's career amounting to "a life sentence in eight-hour shifts" seemed to be encapsulated in that big red-bound ledger.

Still, I always scanned previous days' entries for moments of excitement. This Sunday morning—8/24/97—there was a wad of bloodstained inmate clothing and sneakers stuffed into a corner of the office. It was probably related to something that Miller, who had filled in here a couple of days earlier, had mentioned to me at lineup. As W had headed to chow, Miller said, he'd noticed an inmate, W-9, holding his face, trying to hide blood that was coming out from under his hand. The inmate claimed his cut was an accident, but clearly he'd been attacked. The next day, someone else on W had been beaten up—a reprisal, from the looks of it—and was taken to the ER. I liked to look up these things in the log to see how the officers, who were generally taciturn, had described the dramatic events: "7:57 A.M., W9 seen bleeding, sgt. called, gallery locked down" was Miller's whole story.

They said that at some prisons upstate, guys with seniority *wanted* to be gallery officers, that the galleries were small and tightly run and relatively peaceful. I could see liking that: You'd get to know a small group of men, their characters and foibles, and they'd get to know you. Maybe there wouldn't be the constant testing or rudeness or invective, because you'd know you were going to be together the next day. But not in B-block. These reverberations of gangland strife at Rikers, plus the huge size of the galleries, the constant turnover of inmates and, especially, officers, ensured there was no chance of cozy community developing. I dreaded the job.

But I wanted to like it, because gallery work was the essential job of jailing. Forget running a gate or being an escort or doing construction supervision or transportation or manning a wall tower—a good robot might almost do those. The real action was on the gallery looking after inmates. To do this job well you had to be fearless, know how to talk to people, have thick skin and a high tolerance for stress. Nigro had told us that whenever prison administrators wanted to know what was really going on in a prison, what the mood of the inmates was, they asked the gallery officers. We were like cops on a beat, the guys who knew the local players, the ones who saw it all.

I thought I could do it. I *wanted* to do it, to satisfy myself that the toughest job was not beyond my capacity. But there were days when I wasn't so sure. And at the end of those days, when my head was pounding and my feet ached and I contemplated the meliorative effects of alcohol or a joint, I was always haunted by that mental image of Mendez, the officer who had cracked under the strain of a string of bad days in A-block. I felt his presence on the crowded gallery, saw him in the parking lot—my dark brother, a quivering ghost.

———

"Gallery officers, send down your Early Meds. Early Meds at this time."

This announcement over the PA always signaled the first inmate release of the day, and it was a small and easy one. Early Meds were a handful of diabetics and others, usually old or weak, who had to visit the emergency room for medication before breakfast. They were seldom any trouble, and usually numbered only two or three per gallery. If you were new to the gallery and didn't know who they were, you just looked down the cells for a waving hand. Having let out my three guys, I closed the brakes, took the cells off deadlock one at a time, and sat in the office to await the call for morning chow, the first mass release of the day.

Holmes had assigned me several days in a row to R-and-W gallery, dispelling any thought I had entertained that he was starting to like me. The night officer I'd taken over from was Sims, who had once said to me of the inmates, "I don't care, I don't like them, they're not my friends." She was always leaving signs around the office like PLEASE CLEAN UP YOUR MESS. THE ROACHES LIKE IT BUT I DON'T. I would have sympathized (I tied my lunch sack shut to keep the roaches out, having seen what happened if you didn't) except that she herself usually left the desktop littered with crumbs and half-finished cans of soda. As I was straightening up, I opened the top drawer of the battered old desk, the only one that would open, and found a bar of state soap with a two-inch heart shape carved out of its center.

Soap carving was a time-honored jailhouse art. I'd known about carved pistols from the movies, but inside Sing Sing I had also seen carved mini-radios and animal sculptures. I even had an idea who had made this heart. He probably made it for Sims, as a stand-in for chocolates or a date to the movies. In their deprivation, inmates would grasp at anything. The mystery to me was how it had made its way into the office. Despite her professed antipathy, Sims must have accepted it. But significantly, the heart hadn't made it from the office to Sims's home. Leaving it here was some sort of middle path, and I thought I understood that middle path, because I was coming to understand the paths on either side: Completely tune the inmates out, as Sims professed to do, or else let them in, at your peril. What, I wondered, if she didn't have anybody at home? What if he had told her he loved her? What might she be tempted to do?

"R-gallery, on the chow!"

I walked from the office and pulled the brake on the north side, then the brake on the south side. Many cell doors opened immediately; inmates had been leaning on them. There followed percussive thumping as they stepped out and swung the doors shut. I stood next to the big garbage can in the center of the gallery, blocking the short passage to the W side—this would ensure that the inmates walked to the chow hall, not over to W-gallery to visit their pals.

"Morning, CO," said a few, and a couple nodded and said, "Conover." Most passed without acknowledgment.

These were the guys, the source of my pain, the source of their own pain; the source of their victims' and of their families' pain. My first few days, they had seemed like one big green-clad undifferentiated mass. Now, of course, they all had faces to me. Of the sixty-odd men on each side of the floor, I knew maybe half by name—sometimes their real last name or sometimes just a nickname I'd picked up.

There went Jones. There was Itchy. There was Twin, and Cameron. Moultrie, McClain, and Savarese. Stuckey and Buddy. Not that I really knew them. But I recognized them, and was getting to know those who would let themselves be known.

What officers understood about inmates varied widely. The ghetto-reared officers from New York City surely knew the most. The typical north-country kid knew very little. With my experiences, I was probably somewhere in between, but I was also caught between two warring impulses: the incuriosity that made the job easier and an anthropologist or social worker's fascination with the twists of life that created a criminal and led him to such a place.

The Department gave conflicting messages about how much we should know. The main feeling was that inmates were like a contagion—and the more you kept a professional distance, the better off you'd be. It wasn't good to know inmates' crimes, because then you might treat them unequally. It wasn't good to know their personal lives, because they might try to drag you into them, which would compromise security. On the other hand, it helped security to be aware of their alliances, of gang unrest, and so forth.

In practice, this was nearly impossible. Information about gangs was never casually revealed to officers. It was generally known among us that the Latin Kings, a Puerto Rican gang originally from Chicago, was the most powerful group in B-block and that the rival Bloods, originally from Los Angeles, were in disarray. The Ñeta gang, born of Puerto Rican jails, was the only one to include members from outside a single ethnic group; some Asians were tied to the BTK (Born to Kill) gang. White supremacists weren't much of a factor in B-block. Black Muslims came in many stripes, from mainline Nation of Islam to the splinter Five Percenters. This hard-line faction, born of New York prisons and ghettos, believed that 85 percent of black people were like ignorant cattle, 10 percent were bloodsuckers (politicians, preachers, and others who profited from the labor and ignorance of the docile 85 percent), and an anointed 5 percent were the poor, righteous teachers of freedom, justice, and equality. R-and-W had its Five Percenters, I knew, and plenty of the others. But as inmates swirled past on their way off the gallery, they looked to me, in terms of their gang allegiances, as undifferentiated as a great school of fish.

In another area, however, I had a bit more insight, and that was mental illness. The psychologist at the Academy had spoken about the high number of mentally ill inmates mixed in with the "normal" ones: psychotics with poor hygiene ("You smell 'em before you see 'em") or odd associations (Bill Clinton, they'd believe, was in charge of the Clinton Correctional Facility); hallucinators who thought that football players in the huddle were talking about them or that the state had implanted microchips in their brains. R-and-W had all of these, and the worst cases were loners, shunned by the mass of inmates.

The psychologist had conceded that the single largest group of unwell inmates—those suffering from so-called antisocial personality—was harder to pick out of the crowd. People with this syndrome, he said, were exasperating individuals who were "hard to cure through therapy." Their calling card was "a history in which the rights of others were violated." They couldn't sustain relationships. Their parents had been irresponsible. These inmates didn't obey rules and laws. They failed to honor obligations. They had no sense of loyalty or guilt. They were incapable of love—"others have no more value to them than a car or a pen." They had a low frustration level; they didn't plan, and when they broke the law, they got caught.

Maybe a quarter of all inmates had antisocial personality, the psychologist at the Academy had said, and I was ready to believe it. But then he admitted that there was uncertainty on this point; the number could be as low as 15 percent or as high as 80 percent. *Antisocial personality,* though it described plenty of guys on R-and-W, seemed also to serve as a catchall for problem inmates who couldn't otherwise be categorized. That was disheartening, just another suggestion that psychology, admittedly far from curing inmates, even had trouble describing what was wrong with them.

Psychotics, schizophrenics, and people with antisocial personality—I tried to sort them out, but to most officers, they were all just bugs. We were more likely to classify them as murderers, drug dealers, or child molesters. But since the system actively discouraged us from thinking in those terms, prison work was an exercise in the massive erosion of distinctions, the lumping together of disparate kinds, the suppression of the mind's ability to perceive difference.

All you could see for sure was that Sing Sing was the ending, at least for a while, to 2,300 sad stories. It was staggering to contemplate the accrued tales of dysfunction, pain, and violence that had preceded these prison terms—and, frankly, easier not to. The past seemed like so much noise when you were trying to deal with the difficult present.

———

That morning in August was not so different from many others. When the inmates returned from chow around eight-thirty, I saw several more I was familiar with. Marshall was thirty years old, sentenced to 150 years to life for taking part in a robbery of a Brooklyn bodega in which his partner had killed the owner. The case was somewhat famous, because the partner had been a New York City policeman. Marshall, normally quiet, had told me that the guards respected him because he hadn't testified against the cop to save his own skin. Six feet tall and two hundred pounds, Marshall had permission to take extra "medical" showers because, he explained, he was bothered by a bullet lodged near his shoulder.

Less physically imposing and more approachable was Astacio, one of my porters, known to everyone as Buddy. Buddy couldn't have weighed much more than a hundred pounds, and I worried that he had AIDS. But he was energetic. As one of a small number of inmates—maybe three in the block—who drew custom-made greeting cards for other inmates, he spent many hours in his cell using a vast collection of felt-tipped pens to create cards with intricate designs and a personalized message ("Thinking of you this Christmas, love you forever, Curtis"). Other inmates paid up to five packs of cigarettes for one of these little works of art.

"What are you in for, anyway?" I'd asked Buddy one day, after he showed me a few cards.

"Murder," he said, forming his hand into the shape of a pistol and pulling off a few rounds. "Three counts." I must have looked skeptical; he didn't seem the type. "Gang stuff," he explained.

I went home and looked him up on the Web. There was a new site sponsored by a New York victims' rights group, and DOCS had passed to them an entire inmate database of names, crimes, and parole dates. The website said he wasn't a murderer at all, that he was doing twenty-four-to-life for two counts of burglary and a grand larceny. (And he had prior felonies.) Everyone, I suppose, wanted to be known as a murderer in prison.

Including Van Essen. Initially, I was sympathetic toward this mouselike, fifty-five-year-old white man. He was always friendly but never imposed on me, and I could tell he had it tough in here. Guys hit him up for his commissary, he admitted to me, and he was stressed by all the noise. I could picture him hunched over ledgers. He brushed off the question when I asked what he was in for—an argument, a misunderstanding, he muttered. Then I checked the Web: sodomy first degree, sexual abuse first degree, sentence of eleven to thirty years. According to statute, someone convicted of the sodomy charge has engaged in "deviate sexual intercourse with another person: 1. By forcible compulsion; or 2. Who is incapable of consent by reason of being physically helpless; or 3. Who is less than eleven years old." I wished, then, that I hadn't checked, because, thinking of my own kids, I couldn't talk to Van Essen after that.

I assigned a nickname to another of my inmates. He had been engrossed in a book entitled *Cartel: Historia de la Droga* one day when I walked by. Saenz was Colombian, I knew, so I nicknamed him Medellín, after the original cocaine cartel, and he seemed to like it. Medellín was always trying to get me to do illicit favors for him—take a message to someone he knew on the outside, buy him some gloves (for the cold weather? he wouldn't explain), get him a new watch battery (he wore a Rolex).

"CO, you got change?" he asked me one day, pulling out his wallet, then laughing when I pretended to reach for mine. This was an old inmate joke, as they were forbidden to have cash.

"How come you keep trying to turn me, Medellín?" I asked him. "How many times do I have to tell you, I—"

"CO, because you can do better than this!" he said, gesturing at the block. "You can make big money. You want a girl? I can get you a girl—pretty one, man, what do you say?"

"Not this year, *compa*."

I locked up Marshall, Buddy, Van Essen, Medellín, and all the others and waited for the morning programs to be called.

———

Inmates not only often referred to each other by nickname, they amused each other by coming up with nicknames for officers, too. In the months I worked in B-block, inmates offered up the following nicknames for me:

Italiano: A Dominican on W-gallery had heard me speak Spanish and decided that I had probably learned it because I was Italian, and Italian was similar to Spanish.

Boy George: The inmate who thought this up couldn't stop laughing.

Huck Finn: My college roommate had called me that, too.

Stress Agent: An inmate I was always having to shoo off the gallery would announce me with this nickname whenever he saw me coming. (Another inmate I was always chasing called me Robocop.)

Christopher Walken: I probably hadn't slept much the night before I reminded someone of this gaunt actor.

Ferris Bueller: Actor Matthew Broderick played this teenager in a comedy film.

R2D2: The amusing, short robot in the original *Star Wars*.

Rob Lowe: Probably an attempt to flatter.

Three's Company: The inmate associated me with John Ritter, the actor on this sexually suggestive 1970s sitcom.

Conman: "Don't get conned by Conover the Conman. He knows a conman 'cause he's a conman," said a friendly inmate with rapper inclinations.

125th Street: I overheard an inmate discussing this main thoroughfare in Harlem with his neighbor and volunteered that I'd been there the past weekend. Assuming I was from upstate, he thought I was lying. "Martin Luther King Boulevard, the other name for it," I said.

"What, you were goin' to the peep shows?" he asked me.

But the nickname I heard the most often was, unfortunately, dreamed up by one of my mentally ill keeplocks. I did something to annoy him, and he shouted it out that first day for perhaps an hour, nonstop—and thereafter, whenever his off-kilter brain told him to, which was pretty much daily. He was black, but he shouted it with a broad white-guy accent like Eddie Murphy's. The name he shouted was that of the TV character most synonymous with the archetypical skinny, ineffectual, small-town policeman. He shouted it over and over, day after day: *Barney! Barney Fii-i-i-ife! Barney!*

Come over here, Barney! Barney, where'd you go?

Let me out of jail, Barney!

Hey, Barney! Hey, Don Knotts!

With my programs dropped, and out of the block at a little past 9 A.M. that morning, my main job was to keep the galleries clear until about 10:30 A.M., when inmates began returning for the 11 A.M. count. Porters mopping the floor and new arrivals moving into empty cells were the only ones who were supposed to be out of their cells. I patrolled to make sure the work got done and no one was loitering. Almost always, I had to stop at the cell of Larson.

"You chasin' away my company again, Conover?" Shooing inmates away from the cell of my most popular keeplock was a never-ending job. All sorts of inmates liked to lean on the bars of R-29 cell and talk, talk, talk. Larson was, as I liked to tell him, an "attractive nuisance."

"What do you mean?"

"It's lawyer talk—like a swimming pool with no fence around it; little kids come by and fall in."

"Conover!" Larson feigned offense.

"I know—nobody's drowning here. But why does everybody want to talk to you?"

Larson, tall and slope-shouldered, with long, braided hair, was sitting on his bunk as usual. Except for one hour of rec per day and a shower on Mondays, Wednesdays, and Fridays, it's where he was all the time. According to a printout in Cradle's office, he was the block's longest-term keeplock, having spent the past seventeen months in his cell, with three more to go, a sentence within a sentence. But instead of seething with anger like so many other keeplocks, Larson had an aura of beatific calm. A stoner's calm, I had thought at first, given the slow, spacey way he spoke and blinked. And a friend in the disciplinary office lent credence to this speculation, telling me that Larson was keeplocked mainly for the repeated use of marijuana in prison.

But there was more to him than that. I had at first suspected Larson of being a conduit for contraband—and I never ruled this possibility out—because he was always exchanging everything from magazines to M&M's with the inmates who stopped by. But that was too cop-brained. Larson was also, clearly, a sort of spiritual figure, and one with a head on his shoulders. His inmate nicknames were Powerful, Powwow, and PW.

"They come to me because . . . I'm like family to them," he said to me that day, as one of my porters stopped to listen. "Most of these guys didn't have a father, and I can be that." It was only a partial explanation. But I had connected with Larson better than I did with most inmates, and I wanted to know more.

Our friendship, if you could call it that, had started a couple of months before with his mocking me, but in a way that I deserved. I was running keeplock showers and came to his cell to take him to his. Though my floor had seven shower stalls (regular cells, with shower heads and drains), B-block's decayed plumbing and incredibly poor water pressure meant that usually, only three or four were usable. "Word on the street," I said to Larson as I unlocked his cell, "is that the W-36 back-side shower is the best today."

Slipping his feet into flip-flops and reaching for his towel, Larson paused to laugh. " 'Word on the street'? Where'd you hear that? How about, 'Word on the avenue'? 'Word on the street' is like 'chill out'—dig what I'm saying?"

"Yeah, you the upstate homeboy, CO," chimed in his neighbor.

I was embarrassed. I felt the same way I had when I heard my parents say "Groovy!" sometime around 1970.

"Okay, what should I say, Larson?" I asked, trying to save face. " 'Rumor has it'?"

He laughed again. "That's it, CO. 'Rumor has it.' "

After that he looked at my name tag for the first time.

"Conover," he said slowly, committing it to memory. He preceded me to the shower, and I locked him in for his ten or so minutes of allotted bliss.

Larson's cell decor reflected his difference. Like so many other inmates, he had a dozen or so girlie pinups on his wall, but his were conspicuously clothed. And they weren't white but African-American, like him. He had a pile of cassette tapes, mostly hip-hop, but he had a much taller stack of books. His *Dictionary of Evolution,* he told me, he had bought from another inmate for a pack of cigarettes. There were volumes of Afrocentric history like the ones that are sold on the sidewalk in downtown Brooklyn, social science primers, and an academic survey of perceptions of race over the years.

I had stopped at his cell another day after he knew me a little and asked what he was reading.

"Here," he said, passing the book through the bars. "Read this page." The book was an old work of physical anthropology, and the passage was about the classification of *Homo sapiens* into different racial strains.

"Ah, yes," I said. "They used to worry about this stuff a lot."

"Who?"

"Anthropologists."

Larson stared at me. "What's your story, Conover?" he asked a moment later. "You're not like the other COs here."

"What do you mean? You mean because I'm not from upstate?"

"No. It's something else. The way you think and the way you walk."

My heart rate rose a bit. Except for Dieter, back at the Academy, my passage through the Department of Correctional Services had been blissfully free of anyone, officer or inmate, with the slightest interest about my background. Prisons were full of people who liked to talk more than they liked to listen, and lack of curiosity had been my friend. But Larson was smart and uncannily observant. "You went to college?" he asked.

"Yeah."

"And what did you study?"

"Anthropology."

"Anthropology? That's a hard and deep subject, man. I respect that." He stared at the wall for a moment. "What are you doing here? You should be a teacher or something."

I paused and swallowed. It was my feeling exactly, and I wanted to tell him so. Instead, I evaded by saying, "Life takes funny turns, Larson. You probably know something about that. How did you end up here?"

It was his third bid, he said. After doing time for assault in Alabama, where he grew up, and a second sentence for weapons possession, he had been in New York, dating a woman who was also dating a CO. He and the man had gotten into an argument in the lobby of her building. The CO had drawn his gun but Larson had shot him first—"too many times," he said—and Larson had been sent back to prison, with a sentence of eight years to life.

"Conover, when I came into prison the first time, I couldn't read or write." Apart from prison literacy courses, he said, he was entirely self-educated. Instead of wasting so much of the inmates' time on rec, Larson thought, Sing Sing should put a small library on every gallery so that inmates could sit in their cells and read.

Over days and weeks, I found myself, like his fellow inmates, stopping by to talk to Larson fairly often. Sometimes I had to wait my turn, as one of my porters, or another person authorized to be outside his cell, would be deep in discussion already. One day it was my porter known as Itchy, for all the time he spent scratching his scalp. "What kind of God lets people suffer?" Larson was demanding of Itchy as I approached. Itchy, a short, middle-aged murderer, wasn't used to my being party to his conversation and went silent.

"He's a Christian," Larson explained to me.

"Well, excuse me for butting in, but don't all gods let people suffer?" I asked. Helping people deal with suffering was a large part of most religions, I ventured, and suggested that none of them promised complete happiness. "What god makes everybody happy?" I asked Larson.

"Me—my own," he said, smiling, a little smugly, I thought.

"If everybody's his own god, that's different from a religious God," I answered, then was called to the gate. The next time I came near, Larson was demanding of Itchy, "Who *is* your God, anyway?"

I stood by. Itchy, who usually seemed lighthearted and funny, looked a little mad, and I said so.

An inmate I couldn't see from two cells down was listening and chimed in. "He's mad because Powerful tell him the truth and he ain't ready to hear it." Later, I offhandedly asked Itchy if he was still mad. No, he said, he wasn't. He liked talking to Larson no matter what he said, "because he's interested in history and where we all came from and what we're supposed to do."

Larson, sounding a bit like the Savior, once said to me of those who came to talk to him, "They can't love me like I love them because they don't love themselves. They don't know who they are." These two deprivations, he maintained, along with a third one—that of "a good model of a decision maker to look up to" when they were growing up—were behind most of their criminal careers. They made bad choices, and most had been taught since they were young that they wouldn't amount to much. His own mother, he said, made comments that "dulled" his "potentials and capacities."

Apart from the excitement of meeting a thinking person in prison, I liked talking with Larson because it gave me hope that the inmate-officer gap had some chance of being bridged. Then one day, a few cells down the gallery from his, I got into something of a shouting match with an inmate named Curry, who was angrily refusing to leave the slop sink despite repeated requests. Larson, to my surprise, started adding to the noise with calls of, "Anthropology! Anthropology!" Under the circumstances, it sounded a bit mocking.

"What's up with that?" I demanded the next day.

"What's wrong, Conover? You don't want people to know?"

Larson, I already knew, had talked about me to other inmates; twice in the past week inmates I didn't know had asked me whether it was true I had a Ph.D.

"Yeah, there's that. But maybe it's also the tone. You didn't sound exactly . . . friendly."

"And we're friends, right, Conover?"

"You tell me, Larson."

He sat silently. His question went right to the heart of the matter and left us at . . . an impasse. But I had a feeling he wouldn't mock me again, and he didn't.

It may be that I was a bit paranoid, given my secret mission, but paranoia was nothing foreign to B-block. Even the seemingly steady Larson suffered from this prisoner's disease. The fear that if you agitated too much you might disappear on a transfer to another prison or suddenly come down with AIDS was common among black nationalists, he told me. And I soon realized that he himself suspected that the system could probably just do away with you if it wanted to.

"What about relatives reporting you missing?" I asked.

"You ever hear about the new gym at Clinton?" he responded. I said I hadn't. "When they were digging the foundation, they found the bodies of a lot of old inmates."

"You mean, like an old prisoners' graveyard? I think Sing Sing used to have one of those, long ago, up by Wallpost fifteen."

"No, not skeletons—*bodies*," he said.

I let that sit for a moment. "Hmm. For what it's worth, I haven't seen or heard anything that makes me think that could happen."

Larson nodded knowingly, as if now convinced of my naïveté. He told me I must not have met the backwoods clans of guards who run Attica, Clinton, or Comstock—"people who could do anything and hide anything."

But conspiracies weren't his main interest—redemption was. Race and color were his great obsession. He wanted to learn the true meaning of blackness and thereby conquer the stigma; anthropology intrigued him as the study of where humankind began. But his mind was also full of pseudoscience.

Black, he said, was the color of carbon, the element that was present in all life. Therefore, we were all inherently black. Black, also, was the color of fairness; why else were the robes of judges black? He told me about an article he had read, by a white researcher who couldn't deny the truth, about the amazing properties of melanin, the source of pigment in the skin. Japanese bullet trains actually ran on it, he'd read. Early hominids with an abundance of melanin in their skin could absorb energy from the glare of the sun or the sound of the wind and convert it into calories if they ran short of food. And they lived longer because of it—up to 150 or 200 years, in bygone days. Again I told him I doubted it, but I felt somehow honored to hear the off-kilter theories of this isolated autodidact, because I knew he wouldn't tell just anyone, especially not COs.

"Do you think I'm inferior?" he asked.

"What do you mean? Because you're black? Of course not."

"But don't you think other COs do?"

That one I didn't want to answer, so I tried to make a joke. "Maybe a few of them, but not the black ones."

"Don't be too sure," Larson replied. He thought that even successful black men were insecure. "Look how they go and marry white women, want to hang out with white people. They're trying to prove something to themselves."

"Not you, though," I said.

Larson pointed through his bars, across the gallery walkway, through the chain-link fence, and down to a cluster of white OJTs chatting on the flats. "Nope. Not to one of those *peasants*."

―――――

Though deprivation had warped Larson's vision in a couple of areas, it seemed crystal-clear in another: new prison construction. He passed me a couple of dog-eared photocopies from radical journals that decried the huge social resources being devoted to imprisonment—$35 billion a year in the United States and growing, despite the drop in violent crime. By the time I was writing this book, a cover story in *The Atlantic Monthly* had made the same points in greater detail. Though the rate of violent crime in the country is down 20 percent since 1991, the number of people in prison or jail has risen by 50 percent. California, with the Western world's biggest prison system (40 percent larger than the federal Bureau of Prisons), predicts that at the current rate of expansion, "It will run out of room eighteen months from now [December 1998]. Simply to remain at double capacity the state will need to open at least one new prison a year, every year, for the foreseeable future."

Is it possible that violent crime has decreased *because* so many people are being locked up? Apparently not. Studies have shown that most of the new inmates swelling the system are nonviolent drug offenders subject to mandatory sentencing laws. Though nobody knows for sure, experts think that the real reasons behind the decrease in violent crime are, most likely, the expanding economy, which offers potential criminals more chances for a job, and demographic trends—the number of young men in the United States has been declining since 1980, due to the tapering off of the baby boom.

Even so, prison construction in the United States seems to have developed an unstoppable momentum. One element of the growth is the rise of for-profit prisons. We don't have them yet in New York—the unions have kept them out—but many states have been tempted by the prison companies' promises of cost savings. Larson asked whether I didn't think it was wrong when companies had something to gain by seeing people sentenced to prison—in other words, when they had a stake in their failure. Cast in that light, it did seem wrong, I answered.

You could feel the rush of prison growth even in the forgotten backwater of Sing Sing, where the superintendent had said that getting money to build new and bigger vocational shops was his number-one priority.

"I'd die to stop that," Larson said, to my surprise.

"You don't want to see this place improve?"

"No. The money should all be put back into the poor neighbor-hoods, back into education for children, to change the things that send people here." He held out the articles he had loaned me. "You read these, right?"

I nodded.

"Then tell me, Conover, if I understand correctly. It says here in this article that the government is planning right now for the new prisons they're going to need in ten or twelve years. I got that right?"

Again I nodded.

"That's wrong."

"What's wrong about planning ahead?"

"Because, dig this. Anyone planning a prison they're not going to build for ten or fifteen years is planning for a child, planning prison for somebody who's a child right now. So you see? They've already given up on that child! They already *expect* that child to fail. You heard? Now why, if you could keep that from happening, if you could send that child to a good school and help his family stay together—if you could do that, why are you spending that money to put him in jail?"

I had no answer for Larson. He had made me feel dumb in my uniform, like a bozo carrying out someone else's ill-conceived plan. But he didn't act as if I were to blame.

"Hey," he said by way of good-bye. "Next time you're back, bring me a couple of theories to talk about."

———

Around 10:30 that morning, inmates began returning to the block in escorted groups from their morning programs—mostly chapel, yard, and gym on a Sunday, but also school, library, commissary, package room, and hospital on weekdays. After glimpsing them on the flats, I pulled open the brakes to release the cell doors and then waited till they made their way up the end stairs to the gallery. They were supposed to go directly to their cells and lock in for the 11 A.M. count, but many stopped to talk with friends, to trade magazines (including pornography, known universally as "short eyes"), or to distribute items they'd bought at the commissary. Many also stopped to talk to me, as it was one of the few times during the shift when they had unfettered access.

A consequence of putting men in cells and controlling their movements is that they can do almost nothing for themselves. For their various needs they are dependent on one person, their gallery officer. Instead of feeling like a big, tough guard, the gallery officer at the end of the day often feels like a waiter serving a hundred tables or like the mother of a nightmarishly large brood of sullen, dangerous, and demanding children. When grown men are infantilized, most don't take to it nicely.

That morning, I decided to count the number of times I said no before lunch.

"CO, you give me a shower? I ain't goin' to lunch. I got a visit coming, today or tomorrow." The request was from Rodriguez, a Puerto Rican with striking green eyes who could have been a fashion model if he hadn't gone into robbery and murder.

"Well, which is it, today or tomorrow?"

"I don't know, Papi. Just let me have a shower this once."

"As I recall, you didn't lock in around this time yesterday when I asked you to lock in, isn't that right?"

"Yesterday? Oh, man, that's ancient history. I won't cause you no more trouble, Conover, you do this for me."

"Not today. Try me another time."

His friend, standing at the periphery, had been listening and now asked me the same thing. "How about it, Conover. One for me, too?"

"No!" I said impatiently, turning away.

The next fifteen were:

—CO, *would you call to check the money in my commissary account?*

—CO, *can you find out when my disciplinary hearing is?*

—CO, *can you call to see why my laundry bag didn't come back?*

—CO, *can you take this over to W-46 for me?* (The inmate held out a paperback book by Danielle Steel.)

—CO, *do all you guys get your hair cut in the same place?* (a joke)

—CO, *do you have an extra roll of toilet paper?*

—CO, *you got any more state soap?*

—CO, *can I go on the W side and borrow a belt from my homey? I got a visit.*

—CO, *will you call to see if they got a new package list?*

—CO, *can I have some soap balls to mop out my cell?* (These were cellophane-wrapped packets of powdered soap that dissolved in water.)

—CO, *can I use the slop sink?*

—CO, *you got any Tylenol?* (Sometimes there was a box of it in the office.)

—CO, *will you let me out when they call for the movie?*

—CO, *did you find my clothes in the shower?*

—CO, *can you find out where R-7 moved to?*

Not all of these were improper requests; but the others were mainly favors, to be done when I had spare time, which was seldom. You had to get good at saying no, and learn a couple of rules about it. One was to never say, "Sorry, but . . ." That was pure self-defense. It kept the aggrieved inmate from responding, "You ain't sorry, CO—don't give me that bullshit," or, "Yeah, you *are* sorry—you a sorry-ass excuse for an officer, you know that, CO?" Another was not to get angry, even if it was the one thousandth annoying request, because sometimes they were just baiting you, hoping to make you mad.

There were, of course, times it was important to say yes.

—CO, *can you give me a State Shop form?*

—CO, *can you sign this form for a new I.D.?*

—CO, *you got a light?*

—CO, *I need a plumber, man—my toilet won't stop running and it's gonna overflow.*

Inmates were always messing with their toilets, and early on I tried to find out what they might have done to cause the problem. Some inmates, for example, would try to flush something huge, like a bedsheet, in hopes it might foul up the entire block's plumb-

ing or allow them to flood the gallery. But I seldom asked anymore; there wasn't time.

"What cell?"

"W-forty-two."

"I'll try to get a plumber this afternoon."

"Thanks, CO."

A keeplock was waving his mirror at me from inside his cell, so
I stepped down the gallery to talk to him.

"Officer Conover, did you check that out, what I told you?"

This inmate had transferred a couple of weeks before to
R-gallery from the Box, but they had not yet returned his personal
property. All he wanted was his watch back. The shaved-headed
man, of Indian or Pakistani descent, had been unfailingly courteous to me, which was the only reason I was trying to help him with
this problem. Box time probably meant he'd assaulted an officer,
and the Box was so full that he might technically still be serving
Box time even though he was now on a gallery and therefore might
still not be entitled to have his personal property back. Trying to
get his watch could have turned into a wild-goose chase, in which
I'd spend a long time on the phone with obscure clerks, only to
learn that the inmate couldn't have his watch yet, anyway. Finally,
in the event, after two phone conversations, I learned that he *was*
supposed to have his watch by now; somebody had fucked up.

"You have to write down in a letter your name and number and
the date you were supposed to get the watch, and then I'll sign it
and have a sergeant sign it and maybe before 2000 you'll see your
watch," I said, smiling.

"Thank you, CO!" he said, beaming, and I felt I had made a
friend, which was a good thing. (Two weeks later, when this inmate's arm—with the watch on it—waved me over again, this
hope was confirmed. "CO," he whispered. "Have this one take the
drug test." He handed me a scrap of paper with a cell number
written on it. The inmate being ratted out was difficult and disre-
spectful, so I didn't mind passing the tip along to a sergeant. Still,
I was puzzled. "I won't tell who gave it to me," I whispered back.
"But aren't you worried he'll come after you?" I wondered how he
could trust me enough. He shook his head in a way that said,
"Don't worry about it." He had clout or connections, I supposed;
he felt his armor was in place.)

On my way back to the office, I saw escort officers arriving on
the gallery to do the count and go-rounds, and glanced at my own

watch. "Five minutes till the count, gentlemen," I called loudly. "Please step into your cells."

The cell adjacent to my office was one of two on the gallery that were double-bunked. Overcrowding in the Department had led to the start of double-bunking in maxes a few months before. The newest arrivals went in there, usually guys straight from Rikers, and the typical wait for a single cell to open up was around eight weeks. But they all complained loudly: "Can't you do something for me, CO? This guy snores like a motherfucker." I could sympathize—there was barely room for two men to stand in there, with the extra locker—but there was nothing I could do. Unless . . . Two weeks earlier, I had discovered that Department policy let guys who were 300 pounds or over get out of their double-bunked cells, for obvious reasons, and I had been able to alleviate the misery of a 350-pounder and his squeezed-in roommate. And today's complaint looked promising.

"I got the top bunk, CO"—the newest guys always did—"but I still got a bullet in my knee and I can't really get up there." The forlorn-looking young man showed me the bullet hole near the patella; there was no exit scar.

"How about you guys just swap?"

His roommate shook his head. "No way, CO. I waited a month to get down here on the bottom bunk."

"I'll see what I can do."

Two or three minutes till the count. Suddenly, an angry-looking Puerto Rican murderer named Olivero appeared, glaring at me. "Well?"

"Okay, be right there."

Olivero made belts and wallets in his cell and had permission to use a special class of leather-working tools, so he wanted to make sure his cell was deadlocked every instant he was away—a reasonable request that he demanded unreasonably. He would glare at me—a glare so overdone it was stagey but so intense it sometimes scared me—if I wasn't right there to lock his cell behind him when his run was called. He would often shout, *Get over here! Do your job!* He pronounced it "yob."

"Patience!" I would say to him. "My yob involves locking more cells than just yours." I had trouble believing that anybody could be as angry as he appeared to be with me all the time, and so, hoping for the flicker of a smile, I would say, *"Yes, sir!"* ironically, or beg, *"¡Discúlpeme, maestro!"* as I came over to let him in or lock him out. He would swear at me in Spanish, occasionally smiling, but more often thinking, I imagined to myself, how much he'd like to rip my head from my body or slowly disembowel me with his tiny leather-work tools.

Lunch that day began like any other: a ten- or fifteen-minute window starting at count time when I had no immediate demands to satisfy other than those of my stomach and could wolf down the sandwich and chips I'd brought. But just as I lifted my sandwich and opened my mouth, an announcement came over the PA: "Gallery officers, secure your galleries and report to the flats. All gallery officers." My annoyance yielded to excitement as I realized what was happening: This was Mama Cradle's last day. There was about to be a send-off for her downstairs.

In my admiration for Cradle, I hadn't paid attention for a while to what people were saying about Mama. I had heard the burnout rumors as just the kind of complaints that always swirl around strong personalities. Then Sergeant Murray had canvassed the more senior B-block officers about Cradle. There seemed to be a lot of discontent. She was too often overwrought, and increasingly prone to abusiveness. I began to reassess her a bit. She was a great figure, but things did seem to run better when she was away.

Finally, the rumors were confirmed: Cradle was leaving. She planned to transfer, probably to the Downstate Correctional Facility, about forty-five minutes north, as soon as a good post opened up for her. With all her seniority, people said, she ought to be able to bid something good—meaning easy.

I hadn't, until that morning, heard anything for weeks. And now suddenly it was upon us: Cradle's last day. I stepped onto the flats just as they were taking out a big chocolate cake, upon which was written WE'LL MISS YOU, L.B.—B-BLOCK. Anywhere but prison, there would have been somebody snapping photos—Sing Sing forbade it. Cradle was beaming and a little bit choked up. There were cans of soda and a lot of paper plates and forks and presents. Somebody gave her a bottle of massage oil called Boob Lube.

"It's only enough for one!" quipped Cradle's likely replacement as OIC, a tall bodybuilder named Chilmark.

"Should have got the forty-ounce size," Ebron chimed in.

There was raucous laughter. Another officer pretended to give

her a good spanking. It was all very raunchy and fun, not sentimental. Somebody dropped an entire piece of cake on the floor
and, it being Sing Sing, didn't bother to pick it up. It was left for
Cradle to plant her boot heedlessly in the middle of the dropped
cake.

Our party was delaying the inmates' lunch, but strangely there
were no complaints: The departure of Cradle, which they now
must have apprehended, was an occasion of moment. As things
quieted down, the veteran OIC hugged everyone—it was only the
week before, I found myself thinking, that Cradle had put her arm
around my shoulders and assured me that I'd make a good officer
someday. On the periphery, senior officers speculated that she
might be back, and I could see what they meant. Cradle enjoyed
such authority in B-block, it was hard to imagine the place without her.

"Remember that time she chased Sergeant Murphy out of her
office?" I asked D'Amico, and we laughed. Whatever idea Murphy
had been putting forth had not met Cradle's test of reasonableness,
and that was the end of it. Many sergeants and officers, and certainly most inmates, were glad she was going. The strong personality that was so useful in running a block could easily cross over
the line into abusiveness—look at Rufino in A-block. But Cradle's
chewing outs always seemed to me to be born more of exasperation than meanness.

She didn't come back. We heard she got a job at Downstate sitting in a little booth and flicking a switch that opened and closed
a gate—in other words, that she'd gone from one of the most
frontline, demanding, and interactive posts to one of the most
brain-dead. It was the CO version of early retirement, and I hope
it was what she needed.

———

The cake was my lunch that day. Returning upstairs, I released my
feed-up workers—inmates who delivered meals to the keeplocks—
and then, finishing a log entry, was interrupted by an officer I
didn't know, who handed me a copy of the go-round sheet.
"W-twenty-nine needs to go to the emergency room," she said.

"Is that right? What for?"

"Something about his ear."

"Oh. The ear guy."

I had forgotten the cell number, but I knew W-29. A couple of weeks before, as an escort officer, I had taken the kid to the ER for the exact same complaint. On the way, we had chatted. Often, the younger guys, the more recent arrivals, were more talkative. He wasn't from the city, like most other young inmates, but from near Poughkeepsie, where he had held up a supermarket ("stuck a Grand Union") with a couple of friends a year or so before. His dad was a CO, he told me, his uncle a policeman, his sister a scientist. "I'm the only one who's no good." I was thinking: the projects, special ed/learning disability, juvenile offenses. There was something kind of open and appealing and needy about the kid. He told me he was twenty-one, but I would have put money on him being younger. "I think there's a cockroach stuck in my ear," he had told me. I'd peered in there as we waited for a gate to open, expecting to spot a couple of wiggling antennae, but couldn't see anything.

I'd stayed in the room while the nurse examined him, as we were required to do. There was no cockroach, she announced, just a lot of wax. She gave him something to pour in there to loosen it.

"Was this an emergency?" I'd asked her as we left, and she gave me a look like, Are you nuts? Normal procedure was to put in for sick call the night before, but we had to respond if inmates claimed there was an emergency—a rule, it only later dawned on me, that was open to interpretation. That day, as I was eating my lunch, I just thought, okay. I called downstairs and got him an escort, thinking all the time to myself that this is a kid who never got any attention—no, this is a man who is really a kid who never got any attention, and now he's stuck with COs and inmates and we can't give him enough attention so he wants some from the nurses.

On my way out of the prison at shift's end, I had to wait at a gate. Through the bars, I saw an escorted group of B-block inmates coming back from the hospital, among them the young man I had sent again that afternoon.

"Hey, CO!" he said to my surprise. He sounded almost desperate. He put his face up to the bars.

"You okay?" I asked.

"Yeah," he said. "But where you goin'?"

"I'm going home."

"You're going home?" He looked like a kid who had learned

that his father was leaving when he saw him headed out the door; nobody had warned him in advance.

"Yup, home," I said, giving a little wave as the gate opened and thinking, God, you poor knucklehead, why didn't anybody take care of you? Where were your parents?

CHAPTER 7

MY HEART INSIDE OUT

Ninety-five percent of the guards I've met are doing their job simply because they need the money.
—Mumia Abu-Jamal, *Death Blossoms*, 1997

If the inmates are failures, at least they were reaching—most in very small ways, but some reach is certainly preferable to no reach at all. The cop, as I've stated before, is a guy who can do no other type of work, who can feed himself only by feeding upon this garbage dump.
—George Jackson, *Soledad Brother*, 1970

The publicity has shifted to the trial, and to the sentence; the execution itself is like an additional shame that justice is ashamed to impose on the condemned man; so it keeps its distance from the act, tending always to entrust it to others, under the seal of secrecy. . . . Those who carry out the penalty tend to become an autonomous sector [which] relieves the magistrates of the demeaning task of punishing. In modern justice and on the part of those who dispense it there is a shame in punishing, which does not always preclude zeal. This sense of shame is growing: the psychologists and the minor civil servants of moral orthopaedics proliferate on the wound it leaves.
—Michel Foucault, *Discipline and Punish*, 1978

If prison were constructed to make any living thing happy it might have been cats.
—John Cheever, *Falconer*, 1977

"Leave it at the gate," you hear time and again in corrections. Leave all the stress and bullshit at work; don't bring it home to your family. This was good in theory. In reality, though, I was like my friend who had worked the pumps at a service station: Even after she got home and took a shower, you could still smell the gasoline on her hands. Prison got into your skin, or under it. If you stayed long enough, some of it probably seeped into your soul.

I had thought that being only a visitor to the world of corrections, I would be immune to this syndrome. My whole project, after all, was to keep one foot in and the other out, to be self-consciously aware that what I was doing was an *experience,* not my *life.* It's called participant observation, this research method of anthropology. Every afternoon upon arriving home, I sneaked in the back door so that my two young kids wouldn't hear me and planted myself in front of the computer for an hour or so, taking notes and settling into my real skin. I breathed in the smell of the books on my shelves and counted the days until I had a weekend off, counted the weeks until I could take a vacation, counted the months until the year was over.

Between the time I emerged from my study and let the baby-sitter go and the time my wife came home, I had about two hours. Two hours, it sometimes seemed, to get healthy, because the kids were pure and I was dirty. My daughter, one, and son, now three, would be thrilled to see me, and I treasured this time together. But it could also be the worst time of the day, because in a way, I'd been dealing with difficult children all day long.

That August evening on the day Cradle left, we played in the yard and, when it got dark, went inside and played with Lego blocks. One of the accessories we had inherited from a neighbor was a little jail. It came with a policeman (badge, cap with visor, uniform) and a bad guy (five o'clock shadow, eye mask, thug's cap).

My son asked me about it. "Who goes in jail?"

"That burglar," I said, pointing him out.

"Then what does the policeman do?"

"He puts him in jail."

My son looked puzzled. "Then he's the bad guy."

"What do you mean?"

"He's the bad guy because he puts the other one in jail."

"No, no," I began, trying to explain. "The burglar has to go to jail because he did something bad first. The policeman puts him there to keep us safe."

"Then the burglar's bad, and the policeman's bad."

"No," I said, "only the burglar's bad."

But my son didn't quite get it. And by that time he wasn't the only one.

As usual, playing with Lego lasted only so long. My son wanted to wrestle. His sister was tired. I gave them a bath. Then she was ready for bed, but my son still wanted to wrestle. "Why don't we read a book instead?" I suggested.

His sister pooped out during the reading of *Horton Hears a Who,* and I laid her in her crib. But my son, too tired and too excited, began to act up. He knocked things over. He climbed onto the back of a chair. He grabbed for things—scissors—that he wasn't supposed to have. As I took a phone call from Margot, who had to work late at her job in Manhattan, he announced that he was going to go wake up his sister.

"No you're not," I said.

"Yes I am!" he cried gleefully.

"A—, don't do that," I repeated.

"Okay!" he said, but he shot up the stairs toward her room.

Something in me sort of snapped. All day long I was disrespected by criminals; I felt that home should be different. I ran up the stairs and picked him up by his pajama tops outside her door. "When I say no, you will listen!" I whispered angrily, giving him a spank, surprising myself.

I had never done that before, and it surprised him, too. He burst into tears. This woke his sister. I was furious, and I ordered her to go back to sleep. She didn't obey, either. The house filled with sobs. "Into your room," I ordered my son, and carried him bodily when he "refused to comply."

A use-of-force on my own son, I realized the moment after it happened. There were better ways to handle the situation, I knew, but none that I seemed capable of at the time. I asked him to lie down with me in his bed so I could read him another book, and eventually he did. Then he held on to my arm, kind of tight. I felt like crying into his shirt, breaking down, sobbing for a good hour. I turned my head and read the story.

That night started a trend. Margot and I had seen others take hours to get their kids to bed, and had vowed we'd be relatively firm about it: We would read a story, kiss them good night, turn off the light, and leave the room.

Only now, I'd started fudging. I'd read my son the book on his bed and then lie down next to him for a minute. I only had to do it once or twice before he started requesting it. Then it became a part of our routine: my arm around him, his little hand on my arm, and soon his sonorous breathing. It was, truly, the sweetest thing in my day, and often I would fall asleep, too, out of exhaustion and the feeling of peace.

When I woke up and staggered into our bedroom, Margot, normally the more softhearted of the two of us, would look at me skeptically.

"I know, I know," I'd say. "I really don't mean to fall asleep in there, but I'm so tired."

It was an excuse, an evasion, a way not to examine the fact that I'd never been meaner or more vulnerable.

―――

The next morning, I listened to a news station on the car radio as I drove to work. It was still dark outside. There was a story about the murder of a New York City public school teacher, Jonathan Levin, by one or two former students who wanted money. Levin, like me, was a son of privilege (big privilege in his case; his father was the chairman of Time Warner), and evidently beloved by his students. The killers were two more fucked-up inner-city teenagers, who in a few months would be moving into a place like R-and-W gallery.

The story reminded me of another from just the week before: The emotionally disturbed grandson of Dr. Betty Shabazz, the widow of Malcolm X, had been arrested and charged with setting the fire that engulfed her in the apartment they shared.

Young black men killing the people who loved them. I felt I'd never heard sadder stories in my life. And as a CO, I knew something the newspapers didn't: the next step, the kinds of lives these boys would lead from here on in. I felt sad for them, sad for me, sad for the world.

I sat for a while in the Sing Sing parking lot to collect myself. You couldn't walk into work this way, upset about things. It made you vulnerable. In the locker room I searched around for my game face, found it around the time I strapped the gear onto my belt: baton, latex-gloves holder, key clips—the tough stuff, the accoutrements of guard identity. They were a help, at times like this. I put the emotions away, and punched in.

―――

Margot had agreed to my project almost as blindly as I had pursued it. Generously and supportively, she adjusted her schedule and cut back on other commitments to accommodate mine. We have a strong marriage that thrives on our mutual curiosity about the world. Even so, the strains grew. Our social life suffered, sometimes because of my schedule, sometimes because mentally I just couldn't handle certain kinds of Manhattan parties or dinner dates after a day of work in the prison. Ambitious people, mannered people, neurotic people, high-society people—the kind of people who make life in the city so interesting—became unbearable to me. I was overwhelmed. I just wanted plain vanilla, down-to-earth.

The secrecy of my project took a different kind of toll on our relations with friends: Nobody knew about it; nobody could know. The world was too small, and both my safety and my livelihood were at stake.

Also—and this was probably a mistake—I didn't want to tell Margot everything I knew or had seen. Back at the Academy, Sergeant Bloom had recommended that we all discuss with our families the possibility of being taken hostage. I didn't want to scare her with that kind of stuff, didn't want to alarm her any more than necessary. And in a different way, I didn't want to sully the kitchen table with the kinds of things I'd seen and heard during the day; it just seemed best to keep it inside.

But inside is a bad place for stress. This is very obvious in retrospect, but it wasn't obvious on those nights after we got the kids to bed. I wouldn't volunteer details of my day, and when she tried to update me on her life, often I would just tune her out. I found myself impatient in a way I couldn't explain. I didn't want to hear about the minutiae of her day. There wasn't room in my brain for what seemed trivialities. Black moods would come from out of nowhere and envelop me. I tried to hide them by acting civil, but "civil" came off as chilly and robotic.

One day we were driving back to the city from a visit with friends upstate. I'd had the weekend off for a change—a chance to relax, be with Margot and the kids. But in the middle of the Saw Mill River Parkway, with all of them asleep, I was seized with the closest thing I've ever had to a panic attack. What if I got assigned to R-and-W tomorrow? I thought. The feeling of dread was a dense cloud that blocked my view of everything around me. I slowed down, tried to repress it. I'd been away from R-and-W for a couple of weeks now. There was no reason Holmes would stick me over there again. The odds were ten to one, twenty to one. I turned on the radio, tried listening to the news.

It was a beautiful evening, and when we got home, Margot suggested that we all take a walk around the neighborhood. We put the baby in the stroller and set off. Relaxed, Margot started telling me about her friend's visit to her sister in Colorado and her sister's critiques of her and her friend's critiques of the children and her mom chiming in and . . . and suddenly I couldn't bear to listen to it right now, I thought—or did I say it out loud? I probably did; something had to give. Who cared about the friend when I might have to work R-and-W tomorrow? Margot got mad. I had no time or patience anymore for any of them, her or the kids, she charged. I had never been in a harder situation in my life, I responded. Couldn't she see? There was no room in my head for it! You're not just oblivious, she responded, you're ridiculously rigid and prickly. And with that, I got hostile. You have no idea, I answered, no idea what this is like. And I thought, How dare she complain when I'm working so hard to hold myself together, to maintain a calm exterior?

Maybe that's because you don't tell me what it's like! she shot back. Four more months, I answered, wearily. Can we just hang on four more months and then it will be over. Can you deal with it for that long?

————

Many mornings as I returned to Sing Sing—leaving home at the gate, in this direction—I asked myself the same question. Could I make it until the end of the year? Most often (though not always) the answer was yes. Despite the problems, work still intrigued me on many levels. There was the existential level: A young inmate's bitter statement that he was going to be in here "till the sun burns out" got me wondering about the torture of time, the strange practice of "doing time." There was the human-behavior level: The character played by Woody Allen in his current film said that whenever he met a woman, no matter how young or how old, somewhere in his mind he was thinking about having sex with her. My take on it, working in a place where physical confrontation was always possible, was that most men, meeting other men, instantly asked themselves: Could I beat him in a fight?

But also I had been assessing myself as a prison guard and was bothered by my conclusions. Up in Albany, Nigro had given me an overall evaluation of excellent—rare in the Department, he assured me. Here at Sing Sing, I had dropped a notch—my first evaluation by the sergeants was "good." No complaints offered; just nothing stellar.

What vexed me was that I knew it was true, that despite my exertions and desire to do well, despite my college degree, I wasn't better at the actual job of being a guard than anybody else. Too often I lost my cool, wavered in emergencies, forgot details of the ninety-nine rules (how many magazines could they have in their cell?), failed to use force when it might have been a good idea to do so. Several officers around me—I thought of Miller, Smith, Stone, Singleton, Stickney—seemed much more effective. And I would have trouble in areas where they had no trouble at all.

A good example was the laundry run. A gallery's laundry was done a couple of times a week. One day was sheets and towels; another was clothing. Volunteer porters went cell to cell in the morning collecting the dirty laundry, they carried it about a quarter mile through tunnels and down a prison drive to the Laundry Building, and later in the day, always escorted by an officer, they picked it up.

One rainy September afternoon I was the officer escorting four R-gallery porters back from the Laundry Building. It was a sheets-and-towels day, and the loads were heavy; four porters really weren't enough to carry it all. I walked at the end of the procession, as was customary, and could see that the last porter in the file, a slight jokester inmate known as Beezle, was barely making it. Beezle was hardly over a hundred pounds, and his enormous, unwieldy bundle of sheets and towels had to weigh fifty or sixty pounds.

One of the things I had learned at Sing Sing was, as it had been put to me, "an officer never helps an inmate carry his shit." This rule was unwritten but hard and fast. An inmate moving from one cell to another often had big garbage bags full of property to carry; you didn't help him with it. An inmate who had received your permission to swap his sagging bunk with a firmer one in the empty cell next door usually needed a hand, but it couldn't be yours—it had to be that of another inmate. Officers who lent their strength to help an inmate were openly mocked.

Still, Beezle was seriously overmatched. He staggered under his load like an ant carrying a jelly bean. We had gone only fifty yards and already the inmates in front of him had turned a corner and were waiting at the 5-Building gate; he and I were alone on the paved drive that led to the building. Still, I resisted the urge to help. I was an officer. I knew the rules.

From around a corner appeared a young black man in slacks and glasses, a civilian. He had probably come from the School Building; he looked like a teacher, maybe of one of the GED classes. As he approached, he glared at me.

"Why don't you help the man?" he demanded angrily as he passed us.

I ignored him, but the remark stung. It was exactly what my conscience was asking. Once we turned the corner and he couldn't see me, I caught up with Beezle and helped him support the teetering load.

Of course it was only about ten seconds before we passed an officer. "Get one of those other porters to carry that!" he chided.

"Their hands are full, too," I answered, trying to look a little embarrassed.

Four more officers weighed in before we had made it back to B-block:

"He-e-ey," in a disapproving tone.

"What, you need some exercise?"

"You shouldn't be doing that."

"Oh, how nice."

————

Back at the Academy, more than one instructor had said it took four or five years to make a good CO. I had wondered why. There seemed to be no difficult concepts to master; the rules were all straightforward. In terms of civil service, you were only on probation for a year. The easiest way to get in trouble, everyone said, was to arrive at work late or call in sick too often. The four or five years thing had sounded like self-flattery.

But after five months at Sing Sing, I understood. Experience mattered. Or, more precisely, it took time (and confrontations) to decide (or to discover) what kind of person was going to be wearing your uniform. A hard-ass or a softie? Inmates' friend or inmates' enemy? Straight or crooked? A user of force or a writer of tickets? A strict overseer or a lender of hands? The job was full of discretionary power and the decisions about how to use it were often moral.

I envied my classmates who had been penciled in to easy posts: patrolling the parking lot, guarding the sally port, perched atop a wall tower. With a job like that, you could go home with your peace of mind intact. But moving into the fall, with the end in sight, I wanted to squeeze as much of the four or five years it took to make a good CO into my single rookie year. I wanted to deepen my experience, achieve as much mastery as I could in the time I had. And with that end in mind, I did something that would have been unthinkable a short while before: I bid B-block. I would be there every day.

With my meager seniority, the choice of steady posts was limited. My first choice was V-gallery, the single gallery on the flats that Smith once had. I didn't get it, but I did get my second pick— a regular rotation, every couple of days, between R-and-W, V-gallery, and escort. For better and worse, my daily fate was thenceforth sealed, and I was freed of the awful unpredictability of Sergeant Holmes.

———

Escort officer was, actually, a bit of a misnomer. On the day shift, an escort officer usually spent about half his day supervising in the mess hall, during breakfast and lunch. A relatively large number of officers—eight to a dozen—were assigned to each meal because of the prison mess hall's well-known reputation as a place where inmates can "go off." There was a variety of duties. The mess hall OIC stood on the bridge and decided when a gallery would be called to eat and when it would be excused. Another officer locked and unlocked the gates that controlled inmate movement off the galleries. Two or three others monitored the metal detector and pat-frisked inmates as they passed through the short tunnel between the mess hall and the bridge.

But the worst job, and the one I was usually assigned because I was new, was overseeing the steam table. At this post—one of the several spots in Sing Sing where sheer boredom and the potential for sudden mayhem existed side by side—your feet got tired and your authority was questioned constantly. Standing at the steam table, watching as the population of B-block shuffled by, each inmate receiving his plate from the servers, I always thought of an assembly line in a poorly run explosives factory. Tedium, tedium, tedium, then—*bang*—you'd be missing your hands.

And never did the stakes seem higher than on waffle day. *Waffle day*! The news was passed to the knot of officers outside the mess hall by one who worked in the kitchen. It was a morning in October. Alcantara, the mess-hall OIC, got on the phone with the B-block OIC downstairs.

"Chilmark?" he said. "It's waffle day. You got any extras to send me?" Extra officers, he meant, because waffle day presented an enforcement challenge on the food line. The inmates loved waffles and sometimes went to great lengths to acquire more than their share. It was not as bad as the situation on fried chicken day, but still it was bad—a little worse than, say, fish-stick day.

Chilmark said he'd see what he could find but that in the meantime Alcantara had better get started. Running the ten galleries of B-block through the 226-seat mess hall sometimes took nearly two hours.

"Okay, send me Q-and-V," said Alcantara. There was a pause of a few seconds and then we heard, echoing through the cavern of B-block, the voice of Chilmark bellowing over the PA system.

"Q-and-V galleries, on the chow!" he cried. "X on standby!"

In a minute or two the inmates from the flats would be streaming up the stairs, over the third-floor bridge, and into the mess hall. It was important for us to assume our posts first.

Alcantara made the assignments. "Ruane, you got the north-end gates? Bailey on the split. Baker, Smith, Singleton on the pat-frisk." He paused to see who remained. "Conover, steam table. Goldman, you take the other steam table."

The mess-hall building, in the shape of a plus sign, is centrally situated; A-block, B-block, 5-Building, and the Sing Sing storehouse each back up to one of its four sides. There is a central kitchen, and a separate mess hall for each of the three cellblocks; the busy crossroads between them all is known as Times Square. The officer doing the "split" divides incoming inmates into two contingents that line up on either side of the room's periphery and wait their turn on the serving line. The three mess halls vary only slightly in size and configuration. All have tall barred windows on two sides, with loud exhaust fans at the top. All have long steel tables with stools bolted to the floor in pairs and an aisle down the middle. The rooms are loud, with no decoration. Steel I-beams span the ceiling. White-clad mess-hall workers mill around the steam tables, walk back and forth wiping off the tables with rags, tie up bags of garbage, and mop up spills.

Security precautions are fairly elaborate. The two heavy gates that block the route between the B-block shell and the mess hall proper, for example, are locked whenever a gallery has passed in or out; every officer inside knows that if rioting erupts, the gate officers are instructed to lock us in with all the inmates so that the riot is contained. (During the hostage crisis of 1983, inmates broke down the single gate that then separated the mess hall from B-block and might have spread the riot to the rest of Sing Sing if they hadn't been stopped at Times Square.) Newer maximums and mediums and many older ones have ceiling-mounted chemical agent dispensers in case of riot, and often an officer in an observation booth who can activate them. Sing Sing, for reasons no one could ever explain to me, has never been retrofitted with gas.

The tunnel between the two gates is the pat-frisk area. If an inmate misbehaves in the mess hall, every newjack learns, you don't take him to task in the mess hall itself: That could inflame his friends and start a riot. Instead, you notify the officers in the tunnel. They'll pull the inmate aside when his gallery leaves and talk to him when his friends are far beyond the locked gates.

Waffle day. I said hello to the two inmate servers behind the steam table, as usual; one nodded in response. I thought the best position for me was four or five feet behind them and slightly to the side. This gave me a view of their area, where they passed out the three allotted toaster-size waffles, syrup, butter, and bacon, as well as of the juice dispenser, where inmates were supposed to help themselves to one small plastic cupful. The server who hadn't acknowledged me had a round, shaved head and, like many food workers, had grown a bit pudgy from the practically unlimited opportunity he had to filch food.

I watched as he gave four waffles apiece to two inmates in a row. My first test.

"Excuse me," I said. "It's three, right?"

He turned and glared at me before placing three waffles on the next plate. It seemed only a few minutes later that he passed a large fistful of sugar packets to another friend of his, instead of the prescribed six.

"Hey," I said, this time stepping up next to him. "Are we going to have trouble today?"

He took a step away from my disagreeable presence. "What—you gay, right, CO? That's why you paying so much attention to me?"

"You flatter yourself," I said. "Just do the job you're supposed to."

He muttered as he went back to serving. "Motherfucker's gay," I heard him say to the next inmate in line. It was an unfortunate way to start the day, since sometimes one inmate's hostility seemed to spread, through a form of osmosis, to those who hadn't even witnessed any altercation.

And on a waffle day, of all things. Like pieces of fried chicken, waffles found ways to fly out of the serving pan and into the hands and pockets of inmates. Only the most obsessive surveillance could prevent this. During the exit frisks, we'd find waffles stuffed inside pants and shirts. Servers would sometimes tuck a couple into the loose disposable serving gloves they wore and slide them around the edge of the steam table to friends on the other side. If the servers lined up just so—which my two occasionally did—they would obstruct my view so I couldn't see their hands. Once, when I saw this alignment about to occur again, I shifted suddenly to the side and caught the servers in the act of waffle-gloving. I grabbed the glove and lofted it into the trash without comment.

Cueball gave me a look of pure hatred. "Anyone ever tell you you look like Mark Fuhrman?" he asked. "No," I said.

An hour or so later, when I made an inmate return an extra helping of bacon that Cueball had bestowed, he glared at me anew and pointed at the inmate I had stopped.

"On the street, you probably wouldn't even *look* at that brother," he charged. "You probably afraid he gonna rob you or something."

So now I was a racist homosexual who feared all young black men. In this case, though, the fear would have been justified—the man, after all, was a violent con.

I smiled, then grinned. "He probably *would* be about to rob me," I said. The more I thought about that, the funnier it seemed.

"Shut up, man!" he said. "You look better when you ain't talking."

———

I had worked my first steam tables acting as rigid as that server was hostile. Letting inmates get away with things struck me as letting leaks spring in a dike—the other inmates would notice, and would be encouraged the next time I was on the steam table to try for extras. The massive pilferage that ensued would make me look powerless, ridiculous.

"Juice cup!" I would insist to an inmate who'd given himself the larger, milk-size cup of juice, as though he had shorted me ten dollars in change for a twenty.

"But I already poured it, CO!" the man might protest.

"So pour it out," I would say.

"Pour it out?"

"Pour it out."

Or I'd demand to count the sugar packets of an inmate who, I was sure, had taken too many. Or I'd say an inmate couldn't have an extra plate for his salad, that he had to fit everything on one plate. It was petty stuff in a transaction that was already law enforcement at its most utterly trivial level. The inmates' protests, though they had a patina of moral force, only hardened my resolve.

"Why, CO? It come outta your paycheck?"

"You denying a man his *food*? That's low, CO, that's as low as it gets."

"You gonna think back on this in twenty years, CO, and you gonna be *ashamed* of yourself."

I looked at it this way: If there was only a set amount of food available at a given meal, we had to control the portions. And the inmates were not badly fed—only slightly worse than we had been at the Academy. Of most entrees, whether spaghetti and meatballs or chili or chicken fricassee, they were allowed larger portions than most people could eat. They just couldn't get as much of certain things as they wanted—waffles, fish sticks, cups of juice, or cookies. This is when they tried to make us feel like the bastards who ran the workhouse in *Oliver Twist*.

"I'll say a prayer for you, Officer," said one pious Muslim whom I had stopped from taking extra coffee cake early that summer. Right behind the Muslim was an inmate I knew a little bit. He looked at me sort of pityingly, and I wondered if he was about to join the prayer campaign for my soul. "In a few days, CO," he advised me, "you won't give a fuck anymore."

He wasn't completely right, but I did realize I was wearing myself out with zeal. Other officers, though they would uniformly deny it, let the servers give away much more food than was allowed. Who really gave a damn about two extra cookies? I looked again at Officer Smith and liked what I saw.

Smith had a certain presence as he stood there near the tiny packets of ketchup, arms crossed in front of him. You could tell he cared, but you could also tell it wasn't a personal thing for him.

We were there to enforce the rules, that was all. He looked be-mused, not angry, when he saw an infraction, and his look said to the inmate, "Did you really think you were going to get away with that?"

I tried to relax. To an inmate with the extra juice, I began to say, "Drink it here."

"Here?"

"Just don't leave the steam table with it."

That way, we could both win. No sergeant or other inmates would observe him with a big cup of juice on his tray, but I could show I didn't mind if he drank it, that it was appearances that mat-tered to me. I nodded at the servers to allow porters I had worked with an extra helping—that was a traditional consideration. And at the end of the day, when the last house was being served the last portions, I basically told the servers they could divide the food up equally, because we all knew that what wasn't eaten would be tossed into the trash.

Still, there were some transgressions I just couldn't abide. One day I worked the steam table at breakfast. My counterpart on the neighboring steam table was Thurston Gaines, an Ossining local who had been in my training class. An hour or so into the serving there was a commotion at Gaines's table, and the mess hall grew silent. Gaines, a black officer so big that he seldom seemed to have to raise his voice, had traded words with an inmate who tried to cadge extra juice from under his nose. The inmate then tossed all the juice at Gaines, drenching his uniform. He was relieved by an-other officer so that he could change into a clean shirt and wipe off his glasses.

On my side of the room, two inmates caught the spirit of this in-cident and utterly ignored my warnings to take only the allowed amount of juice. They just pretended not to hear me. One I had had trouble with before, and I advised the officer at the gate to get his I.D. card on the way out. Then, with the meal finished, I wrote up my first mess-hall ticket. A stolen cup of juice was good for: 106.10, direct order; 124.16, mess-hall procedure; and 116.10, theft of state property.

To my surprise, however, the sergeant who signed the ticket did not have the inmate keeplocked pending his hearing. Later, I would learn that the disciplinary committee, inundated with more serious offenses, had essentially thrown this one into the circular file. That really made me feel like Barney Fife.

I was sitting in the gym with Thurston Gaines later that day, and he was philosophical about our respective humiliations. He had known some of Sing Sing's officers and white-shirts his whole life. "They say it's a lot different upstate," he said wistfully. "COs don't have the kind of power here that they do up north—we're too close to the media, to their [inmates'] families, to lawyers."

"Like, what goes on upstate that we don't do here?" I asked.

"If the tiniest thing goes down in the mess hall in Attica?" he said. "They march them outside." In the winter. Literally to chill. At Attica and Clinton, he said, inmates didn't even talk to female officers. It was flat-out forbidden.

"And if they do?" I asked, knowing that every jailhouse rule was eventually violated.

Gaines paused and smiled. He was a soft-spoken, gentle-tempered man.

"They get the fucking shit beat out of them," he said.

The possibility no longer bothered me as it once had.

————

The second-worst mess hall job was seating. Until a year or two before I arrived, inmates could sit more or less where they wanted to. Now, to fill the room more efficiently, they had to sit next to the last person who had come off the line. But sometimes, through reluctance or obtuseness, they seemed to have a hard time figuring out which seat was theirs. One or two of us stood in the middle of the room to direct traffic and make sure seats weren't skipped.

This wasn't a good job for a brand-new officer, in part because even this new, strict seating plan had its exceptions. I was told about the first ones during my early tries at the job: The outermost seats at every table, for example—those next to the men in line at the room's perimeter—were left empty. This was because a fight could start around those seats, with the accidental bump of a diner by an inmate standing in line or a deliberate act, such as a clandestine stabbing. The seats nearest the trash can where inmates scraped off their plates were left empty, too, so that no one would get splashed. Two tables at the very back of the room were reserved, mainly for kitchen workers. And then there were the seats left dirty or wet by previous inhabitants that the kitchen workers had failed to wipe clean. We didn't try to make anyone sit in those.

The hardest part for a new officer, though, was inmates' love of testing a newjack. If three friends wanted to sit together and there was one seat remaining in a row, the first inmate might refuse it, since that would separate him from the others. The officer's job was to insist—though, as a fallback position, an experienced officer might simply see whether the fourth inmate in line would take the seat. Sometimes inmates would intentionally spill something on a seat they did not wish to occupy or tell the officer that a friend in line was coming to take it "in just a second."

Over time these challenges to authority tended to diminish. The inmates came to recognize me from my time in B-block. I realized how much that familiarity was worth, and felt that in bidding my job, I'd done a smart thing.

———

By late October I was feeling a bit like an old-timer: fewer surprises on a given day, and correspondingly fewer problems. But in fact I was still quite new, a fact driven home to me one day as I was seating inmates in the mess hall.

At first it looked like a routine hassle: An inmate refused to sit next to the one adjacent to his assigned seat.

"What's the problem?" I asked.

"I won't sit there."

"Why not? What's the reason?" I repeated.

"He stinks, CO! The dude stinks!" Some at the table laughed, and the alleged stinker looked up at me. I felt bad for him, and thought the inmate with the tray in his hands was perhaps being oversensitive.

But a senior officer saw what was happening and came up to me. "Let him skip a seat," he said.

"Really?"

"Sure. You ever smelled that guy?"

I recognized the inmate, but I didn't realize he smelled worse than everyone else.

"The guy really smells bad. Usually he sits at the back table there. I don't know why he didn't today."

That was when I realized that one of the back tables, or at least one end of it, was not just for workers but for the B-block untouchables. Even among the stigmatized—criminals—there were social distinctions, and here was a big one. Several people back there stank so badly that it was unappetizing to eat next to them. The more time I spent in my new, permanent assignment, the clearer it became that prison sociology was more complex than it first appeared. It wasn't long, for example, until a new arrival in the block pointed to another kind of untouchable: "the ugly transsexual."

B-block had, at the time, five transgender inmates that I was aware of, and between R-and-W and V-gallery, I supervised three of them. Though all three seemed to feel they were actually women, they had very different styles.

First there was Rivera, known also as Baywatch. Baywatch was slender, with plucked eyebrows and center-parted, shoulder-length hair bleached a shade of light auburn. He had a boy's figure but a girl's walk, and a scared-doe look. Of all of them, he seemed the most sought after by inmates. Baywatch wouldn't talk to officers, but his presence was widely accepted by inmates. He was no untouchable. On the contrary, he was the "girlfriend" of a member of the Latin Kings gang, who, I was told, regarded himself as heterosexual. Baywatch was his prize. I would see them nuzzling in the yard like a pair of junior high school lovers. When the two of them were caught in the same cell in flagrante delicto, both were keeplocked—101.21, contact between inmates; 109.10, inmate out of place; 118.22, unhygienic acts. (Officers even had to break up a necking session while they were waiting in the disciplinary office bull pen.) But these measures didn't end the affair. It was said that later, when Baywatch was off keeplock but the boyfriend was still on, a rival for the transvestite's affections got himself intentionally keeplocked in order to be able to try to stab the boyfriend during keeplock rec.

Behind Baywatch on W-gallery was a black inmate named Sam. A big-boned guy with breasts, Sam would probably qualify as a transsexual, but that seemed to be the least of his differences with Baywatch. Sam was catty, and a vamp. He wore his state pants tight and exaggerated his hip movement when he walked. His hair was short and upswept, close on the sides and poufy on top. He put a hand on his hip and swung the other limply in front of him when he stopped to talk to me. And I had to talk to Sam a lot: He was chronically tardy, in everything from leaving his cell at chow time to getting back in it after a meal. I began to get fed up, but he would always shrug and apologize and, sounding like a can't-be-bothered-heiress on a soap opera, sigh, "I just cahhhn't seem to get myself together, cahhn I?"

Once, when I escorted some inmates to the commissary and we were all hanging around in the hall waiting for a gate to open, two female officers fixed their attention on Sam. "Is that lipstick you're wearing?" asked one. It looked like one of the trendy dark shades, meant to convey a ghoulish look, à la Morticia Addams.

"No, doll, it's not. I made it myself." He giggled. "It's ground-up pencil lead. But it works, doesn't it?"

The two officers looked at him in amazement. Then the three of them chatted some more. The commissary was taking forever to open. Sam suddenly pressed his knees together.

"I've got to pee so bad!" he exclaimed, then asked me, "Could you take me to the State Shop, please, officer?" I said I would see, and headed to a wall phone to ask if the State Shop was willing to let him use the bathroom. As I dialed, he added, "You could watch. I bet you'd like that. You'd be surprised what you see."

"No doubt I would," I agreed.

Sam had admirers, and sat at mess hall tables like anyone else. But that did not seem to be true about the third sexually ambiguous personality I supervised, a transsexual in his forties whom the other black inmates called Grandma. Of the three, Grandma was by far the most freakish. Under his sagging, mango-size breasts protruded a potbelly. A bun, which he had fashioned out of an uneven coif and tried to angle forward, did not hide the fact that his hairline was in full retreat. His teeth were long and yellow; behind black-frame glasses, you could see he had plucked and then redrawn his eyebrows. He was short and slightly swaybacked. I had spoken to him a couple of times, and he was unfailingly courteous, even charming. Clearly, though, he was the "ugly transsexual." And, as no one could consider him an object of desire, he was ostracized.

Soon after he arrived on V-gallery, I noticed that Grandma often didn't go to the mess hall. When he did, he usually sat at the untouchables' table. One day, though, when I was assigned seating duty, I saw Grandma head out of the service line with his tray and aim straight for the regular tables. I seated him normally.

There was an immediate uproar. The man who had sat down before him stood up and said something like, "Don't you put your rat ass down on that stool." Grandma slammed down his tray. I felt sorry for him and angry at the inmate and told the inmate to sit down.

"There is no fuckin' way I'm going to eat next to this freak!" he pronounced loudly.

I started feeling righteous. "Don't act like an asshole. He's a human being. He won't hurt you." Numerous inmates shouted back their disagreement at me, but rising over them all was the roar of Grandma.

"The problem here is all you silly young black men!" he cried with vehemence.

"Fuck you, faggot!" came the response, followed by a fusillade of further insults.

"Come on, sit in back, where it's calm," I suggested, and Grandma came with me to the untouchables' table.

After that, Grandma became one of my regular chat buddies on the gallery. There was something sympathetic about him; and both of us, though in different ways, were outsiders in B-block.

He was also, strange as it is to say, a refreshing sort of female presence in a place where macho was the rule. One day, for example, I made a special phone call for him because, instead of going to the hospital, he had somehow ended up at the School Building and missed a medical appointment. "I just have no sense of direction!" he said with exasperation, placing a hand on his cheek like a befuddled belle.

To reschedule his appointment, I'd had to take his I.D. card to the office. It was full of surprises. "Edward?" I asked when I gave it back, not sure, perhaps, what I had expected his real name to be.

"My friends call me Janice," he said with a smile.

"But why do you have a beard in this picture? It's only two years old! Were you, um . . ." I didn't quite know how to ask how long he'd "been a woman."

"Oh, I've had *breasts* a long time, if that's what you mean," he said, reading my mind. "But what happened was, they took that photo when I was keeplocked. Sometimes when you're keeplocked, you just can't be bothered to shave, you know?"

"Sure," I said, smiling.

The birth date on the card showed that "Janice" had been born just two years before me, though from his appearance, I would have guessed that he was at least ten years older than that. Prison had that kind of effect on many men. He had been in and out of it for most of his adult life, he told me—mostly arrests for prostitution. But now he was maxing out on a four-to-twelve bid for second-degree murder. He'd been paroled not long before but had fallen immediately back into old bad habits.

"I'm an alcoholic, you see, and I was sitting in a park in Chelsea drinking vodka when I heard a car horn honking. I turned around and thought, My, that's a familiar face . . . and it was my parole officer!" No drinking was a condition of his parole; by getting caught, he had earned a ticket back to prison. So now he was waiting to finish his sentence, of which less than two years remained. He had spent earlier parts of it in Auburn, Clinton, and Attica. His victim was his ex-lover, but he claimed to have been falsely convicted—"because I just happen to be poor, black, and gay," he said. "They didn't have my prints on the knife or anything." Though Janice seemed sweet, I had no trouble imagining him capable of murder. The longer I spent in Sing Sing, in fact, the easier it was to imagine anybody, anywhere, committing practically any crime.

I had thought there might be some solidarity between Grandma and the other gender-benders until the day I heard him being hectored by a new queen, who was getting lots of attention in the block.

"The boys in here don't want an old lady!" the pretender proclaimed. "They want a sexy young man!"

Did Janice feel persecuted inside prison because of who he was? I asked one day. "Oh, not really," he said. "It's not fair that other gay men can hug sometimes, like during V-Rec or something, but if I hug anybody, people talk.

"The main thing, you know, is they're all hypocrites. Just last week a boy said, 'Janice, show me your titties.' I said, 'Okay, but I'm going to tell everyone.' He said, 'No!' I mean, really. Be yourself!"

Not even macabre interest made me want to catch a glimpse of Janice's titties. But I'm not sure I could vouch for my desires if I were imprisoned for a long time in a densely packed world without women and at the peak of my sexual vigor. With its raucous sounds and smells of sweat and threat, B-block virtually seethed with testosterone. Some of it was channeled into bodybuilding; much more found its outlet in masturbation. Jerking off is the main sexual activity in any prison. Sometimes you'd catch a glimpse; occasionally you'd catch a whiff. The cumulative daily output of these 636 men was probably huge, a sad symbol of their thwarted energies.

It must have always been so in prison, though it cannot be said that earlier generations looked upon it with today's tolerance. A state prison inspectors' report of 1845 showed that masturbation had been considered far from benign:

> J.S.—sent to the asylum in March, 1844; we cannot ascertain what is his real name, nor by what name he was received in the prison, nor how long he is to continue; he is a confirmed lunatic; brought on him by onanism.
>
> W.H.—sent from New-York 15th December, 1843, for two years, for grand larceny; nineteen years old; native born; became addicted to onanism three or four years before he came here, and was in a shocking state of *dementia* when he came in; he is now in a fair way of being cured, but is still very stupid and idiotic.

Truly, long-term autoeroticism probably does have ill effects, though of a different nature than was thought in the nineteenth century. The Minnesota hatchet murderer I wrote about earlier, imprisoned for seventeen years starting at age nineteen, still had a pretty girlfriend when he was paroled and I met him. But even after a few months with her, he confided, intercourse took a backseat to the familiar pleasures of his own hand.

The next-most-common type of prison sex, after the autoerotic, is certainly consensual. My classmate Dimmie had pulled down a sheet hung across bars one day to find two inmates having sex. Baywatch and his beau had been caught in the act, as well. John Cheever, who wrote from his home in Ossining, has a consensual affair take place between two otherwise straight inmates in *Falconer*, his prison novel, and such a relationship—between the transvestite Molina and the guerrilla Valentin—is the very gist of Manuel Puig's magnificent *Kiss of the Spider Woman*. But consensual sex is something that the authors of most novels and scripts about prison can't seem to acknowledge.

Most common in drama, by far—and least common in real life—is forcible sex. The rape of the white middle-class inmate is a staple of contemporary prison movies, from *American Me* to *Midnight Express* to *The Shawshank Redemption*, and it even takes place in the supposedly hyperrealistic TV prison series *Oz*. It is such a fixture of how middle-class America thinks about prison that people who hear I worked in Sing Sing always bring it up within a few minutes—if they dare bring it up at all.

The rape-of-the-white-guy trope has roots in a 1967 play, *Fortune and Men's Eyes,* by John Herbert, in which a friendly, essentially noncriminal newcomer to a Canadian boys' detention facility is raped by a predatory roommate. It was further developed in a play called *Short Eyes,* written at Sing Sing by an inmate named Miguel Piñero and turned into a critically acclaimed feature film by Westchester filmmaker Robert Young in 1977. *Short Eyes* tells the story of a skinny white guy, thought to be a child molester, who is raped and then murdered by his fellow inmates with the tacit complicity of his guards.

Certainly, prison rape still occurs in New York and elsewhere. Phelan told me that two of B-block's long-term keeplocks had been caught exiting the cell of a distraught inmate who lay face-down on his bunk with his pants around his ankles. But the famous punk-protector system of popular lore seems to be outdated or exaggerated. Several longtime inmates I spoke with thought it was almost a thing of the past—for several reasons. One is the willingness of courts to hear inmates' lawsuits against states. This trend, which began in the early 1970s, is said to have forced states to make the protection of vulnerable prisoners a high priority. Protective custody (PC) is now a big deal. Inmates who ask for protection but fail to get it can make expensive claims.

Another factor is the decline, to some degree, of the cons' code of ethics. Longtime inmates seem to agree that in the old days, rape victims would never speak up, because that would mean informing on a fellow inmate. Now, however, though the code of silence is still nominally in place, inmate lips seem looser and officers' use of snitches more widespread.

I would even guess that, at least at Sing Sing, sex between (female) officers and inmates is presently more common than forcible sex between inmates. Certainly, I heard more about it. A young woman I had trained as an OJT on V-gallery was fired about a year after I left for having had sex with an inmate in Tappan. (According to the story officers told, another inmate, who had guarded the bathroom door while the officer and her boyfriend were inside, demanded his own piece of the action, and then blabbed when she turned him down.) And just a few weeks after I left Sing Sing, another female officer was apparently fired for having had sex with one of my most macho and obnoxious keeplocks on R-gallery.

Sing Sing's one female sergeant, Cooper, who was in charge of housekeeping, warned female officers several times at lineup that they were not to wear makeup or engage in any flirtatious behavior with inmates. Obviously, there was a reason for that: Sex was just so much in the air.

And perhaps the sex was not only between inmates and *female* officers. A young inmate who arrived on V-gallery after I'd bid it kept finding reasons to ask me questions. He was a light-skinned black man with a shaved head, and he was always trying to make eye contact with me. He was very outgoing, using any excuse to start a chat. Like everyone else, he began in one of the two double-bunked cells but after six weeks or so was moved to his own cell. One day during afternoon rec, when I was deadlocking all the cells, he called me back to his.

"Conover," he said excitedly, waving to me.

"Yeah?"

"Come over here."

"What do you want?" I asked from several cells away. I was going to have to change direction and interrupt my chores to go talk with him. But he was insistent.

"Just come over here."

I did.

He asked, "Anyone else out there?"

"Where?"

"On the gallery!"

I looked around warily. It was one of the few times in the day when the gallery was practically empty; mainly, it was keeplocks who were still in the cells. "Nope."

"Mirrors?"

"Why?" I demanded. I could not imagine these questions as anything but a prelude to violence—not only did he plan to strike me or throw something but he also wanted me to help him make sure there would be no witnesses. He looked very excited.

"Conover," he whispered. "You know I go both ways?"

"What?"

"Shhh! I go both ways!"

"Yeah, okay, so you go both ways," I said quietly.

"Come in here!"

"What? Why?"

He was frustrated that I still didn't get it. "I want to blow you!" He opened his mouth and pointed at my crotch. I was surprised—first, that he would declare his desire, and second, that he would believe there was any chance in the world that I would take him up on it, even if I were gay.

"Sorry, not my thing."

"Come on! Nobody will see!"

"I'm the wrong guy!" I said. "Not into it!" I started walking away. But again he summoned me, in a loud whisper.

"Conover!"

"What!" I answered, annoyed. I turned around and, frowning, stood back in front of his cell.

"Conover, don't tell anyone, okay?"

It was just as Janice had said.

"Okay, man. Don't worry. I won't."

After that, he never looked at me again.

———

R-and-W was my adrenaline challenge and stress test; V-gallery, by virtue of being half the size, was a place where I could be a better officer and have more of a chance of feeling, at shift's end, that some of the inmates were actually human. Though inmates still tested and tried to intimidate me on V, they did so without knowing that after the pressures of working R-and-W, I felt almost impervious to their lesser demands. I caught more glimpses of the humanity of inmates on V-gallery than anywhere else at Sing Sing.

———

Perch struck me as the kind of guy who probably had acted badly since he was about nine. He was an unfortunate combination of mental disability (my guess) and rage. And he was also big and strong enough to do real damage. Though keeplocked, he got a special escort to the psych floor twice a day to take his meds. I was surprised the morning I saw him, unescorted, walking by me on the flats with a group of inmates headed for the gym. I had figured he was keeplocked for a good long time.

That afternoon—it was early in my experience on V-gallery—I was using my go-round sheet as a guide for pulling the brake to release the runs. When the OIC called out, "Law library," for example, I would check the sheet to see if anyone had put down law library when the officer doing the go-round came by his cell. If nobody had, I wouldn't pull the brake. If three had, I would pull the brake and count off the three. If four came out, I'd know who was out of place. Most officers didn't use the sheets for this, but I saw no reason not to.

The OIC called for the hospital run. I checked. Nobody on

V-north had put down hospital. Two on V-south had, so I let them out, closed the brake, then walked into my office to answer the phone.

When I came out, someone down on V-north was waving his arm madly out of his bars. I walked down to see what he wanted and heard the voice of the OIC as I did, announcing that the run to the hospital building had been "terminated"—it had left the block, in other words. The arms belonged to Perch.

"CO, I been waving to you for five minutes!" he shouted, greatly agitated. "Why the fuck you don't let me out for hospital? Let me out now!" He shook his door.

I checked the list. "I didn't let you out because you didn't put down for hospital," I said, showing him. "You put down for yard."

"CO, I don't know what the fuck I put down. I just know I got an appointment in the hospital! Let me out!"

"Hospital run's over," I told him. "That's what the go-round's for—to let us know where you're going."

"What? You telling me I can't go to the hospital?" he cried.

"Right."

The OIC was calling another run, but over Perch's yelling I couldn't hear what he said. I began to walk back toward my office. "CO, come back here!" His shouting continued. A couple of inmates advised me that Perch really did need to go to the hospital, that I should find a way. I saw Smith passing by.

"You were right not to let him out, technically, but this guy's a bug," he said. We noticed that Perch was now in the process of trashing his cell and was throwing things—clothing, paper, toiletries—across the flats. "Let me see if I can find somebody to escort him to the hospital."

Perch showed no signs of recognizing me the next time I worked the gallery. He had gotten keeplocked again, and I made a point of treating him courteously. It was keeplock shower day. I gave him the second shower. A keeplock officer appeared and asked me to let out another inmate just as Perch told me he was done.

"Hang on a sec," I told Perch. "I've got to let this other guy out."

Perch flipped. I heard him yelling at me from the shower cell as I went to unlock the other inmate. He was angrier than ever when I came back.

"You pussy-ass motherfucker!" he shouted. "Let me out of here now, you cocksucker!"

Though Perch was no doubt imagining how he'd like to tear me limb from limb, I felt strangely calm, fatalistic. I went through the center-stairway passage and asked another officer to accompany me while I unlocked Perch's shower cell. Perch didn't stop cursing me as he walked to his cell, but he didn't swing at me, either. I locked him in and breathed a sigh of relief.

Weeks went by. Perch appeared to have forgiven or forgotten me. Then a sergeant came by and asked me to do a psych referral on a new inmate on V-gallery and paused to check his notepad for the cell number.

"V-forty-eight?" I asked. I already knew the one. He was next door to Perch, a toothless old guy who had asked me to read his commissary account statement for him so that he could learn whether he had enough money to buy "grease," by which he meant Chapstick—his lips were cracked, and he kept touching them when I asked what he meant.

"Sorry," I had explained. "You've only got four cents."

The sergeant told me that the man had been found wandering in A-block, having signed up for law library (you would get in trouble for this if you were sane); that he had arrived back in B-block holding his dick, he had to pee so badly; and that he had told the gate officer that his cell was the little cage we used for monitoring telephone use. I said I'd be happy to do the psych referral.

The psych-referral form required me to get the old man's responses to some simple questions.

"Do you know what prison this is?"

The man paused for a moment. "Downstate, right?"

"Do you know what day it is?"

At this point, Perch started to heckle me. "Stop asking him that shit, man!"

I tried to continue. "Do you know your name?"

The man looked confused. Perch, meanwhile, was working himself up into a lather equal to his previous ones.

"Fuck you, man! Leave that motherfucker alone! Can't you see he's crazy?"

With that last question, I stopped trying to conduct my interview. I turned and looked at Perch. I was glad to see he recognized insanity and could appreciate, on some level, his hostility toward my amateur psych-testing. What could we really do for this guy, anyway? Even after I submitted the report, the only thing that appeared to change for the old man was that he got transferred, for reasons unknown, to a cell upstairs on R-gallery.

Crazier than Perch or the old man, however, was the day a woman from the Department of Parole came to interview Perch. I stood next to her as she talked to him—standard procedure when a civilian was on the gallery. Perch, to my amazement, was to be released on Friday. "Did you know he's still keeplocked?" I asked her, disbelieving, as I walked her back to the gate.

She shrugged. "It doesn't matter. He's still getting out."

"I've got to tell you, that seems like a big mistake," I said, trying to imagine what would happen on the first day Perch forgot to take his meds and somebody bumped into him on the subway.

"Don't worry. They all come back," she said offhandedly.

"Run, Forrest, run!"

Inmate Nolen enjoyed calling that out whenever I walked by, particularly when I was in a hurry. I reminded inmates of many different actors and the characters they played in movies, but he was the first one to see a resemblance to Forrest Gump. At first it didn't bother me, but then I saw the movie. Forrest had some kind of disability in his legs and looked foolish running. Nolen yelled it for weeks, and finally I asked him to stop.

"Sure, Forrest, why not?" he said, grinning. But he didn't stop. He did it more. He was just that kind of person: annoying, exasperating—you wanted to pop him in the mouth. The closest I ever got was one day when he was escorted down from the mess hall after an argument with the disputatious Officer Colon, who was always stirring things up. Nolen was loudly announcing that he was going to charge her with sexual harassment and that he wouldn't go into his cell until he could speak with "at least a captain." The officers all thought that was hilarious. Even Sergeant Murray, who watched three of us form a threatening ring around Nolen, which finally induced him to enter his cell, later commented to Colon, "Tell Nolen if you wanted a stupid white man, you'd find one who made more than fifty-three cents a day."

Apparently, he had been a plumber on the outside. For a while he was keeplocked, but it was the most ineffectual keeplock I ever witnessed. Sergeants and OICs kept getting him out, to deal with one of B-block's chronically overflowing toilets or stuck basin valves or nonfunctioning showers.

The only other white man on V-south at the time was Elliot Markowitz, a decaying old murderer who smoked too much, got pushed around by young gangsters, and was prone to depression. He was sallow and overweight and had a style of kvetching that got under the skin of many officers. But I kind of liked Elliot. I called him by his first name and could persuade him to do things when other officers failed.

Nolen apparently noticed this. One day he told me that I should read some of Elliot's poetry, that it was "really good." Elliot sorted through a deep box full of pages and passed me a few with his yellowed fingertips. I sat down at one of the picnic tables on the flats outside his cell and read. The first one was entitled "Seagulls":

> Long hours
> waiting waiting
> to see the
>   flying
>   seagulls
> to really see them
> I waited around all day
> Keeping peace with in
>   as best I could
> Trying to grow and
>   accept the truth
>   of reality
> To see flying seagulls.

Another one I liked was called "Singing in the Shower":

> I get a lot of pussy
> heh heh men's talk
> honey, pass the soap
> put it deep in me baby
> ooh ahh
> pass the shampoo
> fuck the shampoo
>   let's fuck
> we are fucking
>   ooh
>   aah

Nolen, out of his cell and supposedly doing work as a plumber, saw me with the papers, came by, and tried to grab them. I would have sooner died than have Nolen reading my poetry, but Elliot said, "Okay, sure."

"Singing in the Shower" didn't interest Nolen much. But he fixated on "Seagulls" and mocked it loudly, declaiming it in his pseudo-retard voice. An hour later, on his way to chow, Nolen was still chortling about it and cracking himself up.

" 'Waiting to see,' " he chanted, " 'the flying seagulls.' "

———

Perhaps even more than people on the outside, inmates appreciate pets. Though forbidden, living contraband kept finding its way into cells. The most common were probably the sparrows that nested in B-block, often atop small utility boxes high on the outer walls, next to the long windows that were open at least a crack to the outdoors. Inmates would carry bread back from chow, stuff it into the chain-link fence along the gallery, and watch from their cells as the birds came to feed.

Some were experts on bird life: I saw a Pakistani on U-gallery, way up at the top, peering down through his bars into a nest where a mother was feeding her babies. "The second set this year," he told me in early summer. He directed me to the cell of a friend of his, who had fit a square of cardboard into the bottom of one of the mesh laundry bags that inmates put their underwear in, placed a sparrow in the bag, and hung it from his ceiling.

My walk along the flats was interrupted one day when I noticed a long string stretched out from the front of an inmate's cell and then saw that the far end was tied around the leg of a tiny sparrow. The inmate started to reel the bird in, but I put my foot on the string. It reminded me of a town where I had lived in Mexico, where boys used to stun birds with slingshots, tie strings to their legs, and, when they revived, fly them tethered like kites. The birds almost always died of exhaustion. One day I had seen it happen to a baby owl. I took out my small pocketknife and cut the string. The inmate howled.

"No bird torture," I explained.

"No, CO, he can't fly!" the Spanish-speaking inmate protested. "He fell down from the nest. I feed him, else he die!"

"Oh." I saw that I might have acted prematurely. I walked over and cupped the bird in my hand; to my surprise, he perched on my finger. I handed him back to the inmate.

Another day, a baby sparrow was chirping loudly on the flats as we officers left the mess hall one morning after breakfast; its mother, perched on a nearby trash can with food in her beak, looked ready to feed him. The baby opened its mouth and vibrated its wings, as a hungry baby will do. This time an inmate porter intervened. He chased the mother away with a broom, then kept trying to shoo the baby in the other direction.

"Why are you doing that?" I asked.

"I want her to know she can't save it," he said. *I want her to know she can't save it.* Was this part of a conversation he'd been having with himself about his own life? Make mother admit the truth? The phrase stuck in my mind for days after.

Finally, another inmate had gone after the baby sparrow—it almost hopped onto his finger, but then got spooked and went fluttering into somebody's cell. A passing officer looked in and, turning to a colleague, said, "Sparrow soup."

And there were furry animals. Back in the 1930s, warden Lewis Lawes had upset the inmate population by prohibiting the popular practice of tending rabbits. These days, there were no rabbits about, but within the walls of the prison lived a large colony of wild cats. You'd notice them stretched out on grassy slopes on a sunny day or milling beneath the windows of certain buildings where inmates dropped food for them.

Somehow, one of my inmates on V-gallery had gotten one of the kittens into his cell. He was a big Italian-American from Bensonhurst, Brooklyn, and someone had sent him a matching set of linens for his cell: burgundy sheets, burgundy pillowcase, burgundy mat beside the bed, burgundy handkerchief over the basin light, which produced a burgundy glow in the cell. He kept cardboard alongside the bottom bars to keep the animal from getting out, though often she did anyway and he'd have to find her on the gallery when he returned. Though it was probably against the rules, I thought having a pet was healthy, and occasionally asked him about it.

"Only pussy I'll ever get," he quipped.

That made me nervous for the cat.

———

There was another pet on V-gallery that I didn't notice until I had worked there several weeks. I must have looked into the cell of Medina, chief of the block's painting crew, twenty times during my morning go-round before I realized that, inside a clear pyramid he had constructed from plastic wrap, masking tape, and sticks, a large spider was suspended in her web.

"Is that what I think it is?" I asked, peering into the dark cell.

"Yeah, but I don't know what kind of spider," he said.

"What do you feed it?"

"Mostly roaches. Though there ain't so many in here since I caught her. She's getting bigger, too, you know. Want to see her eat?"

I nodded. He pulled his bunk away from the wall and tipped up a box he kept on the floor; soon, wriggling between his thumb and pinky was a small cockroach. He opened a hatch and popped the bug into the pyramid. The reaction was swift.

"She'll be happy for a week or two on that," he said.

Kindergartens have their gerbils, firehouses their Dalmatians. Of all possible pets, that spider seemed right for Sing Sing.

At the end of the day shift, the OIC often dispatched three or four or five of the departing officers on a final sweep of the flats. The sweep was an almost leisurely circumnavigation of the block on ground level, to check that all inmates were in and all gates were locked, that everything was in order. The sweep officers were generally keeplock or escort officers who otherwise would be idling near the front gate, waiting for their earliest chance to head down the hill. I liked being part of the sweep whenever I was an escort officer; the five or ten minutes of measured steps, conversation, and—what else to call it?—esprit de corps were a good way to end the day.

One day I set off on the sweep with Smith, Phelan, Phelan's sidekick Pacheco, and Chilmark. Somehow as we left the front gate heading north on Q-gallery, the conversation turned to the last big unrest Sing Sing had had. It had taken place in B-block just a month before my arrival, when I was training at the Academy. In those days, following breakfast, the B-block inmates bound for programs in various other parts of the prison were allowed to congregate on Q-north prior to being released from the block in smaller, escorted groups. It was no longer done that way, and the events of that morning were the reason.

Suddenly all hell had broken loose on Q-north. The 150 or so inmates gathered there were suddenly shouting, running, in disarray. It was later determined that only seven or eight inmates were fighting, but at the time it had seemed like a full-scale riot. Smith had been around the corner on V-gallery, and the first he knew of what was going on was the strange thuds that issued from under the north stairs—the sounds, he later learned, of an inmate being thrown against a metal wall. By the time he got to the scene, one inmate was lying with his head on the north-end stairs while another inmate, the size of "a moose," was jumping up and down on it.

"I saw it go squish, bounce back, squish, bounce back—it actually changed shape," he said. Having been in the block just a few months, Smith said, "That's the first time I really understood where I was."

Chilmark said that he had been standing near the front gate, ten feet away and on the other side of the fence from an inmate who was getting the shit beaten out of him by two others. A third inmate waited until the beating was done and the victim was motionless before reaching down with a knife and cutting his face from ear to ear, right across his nose. Even though I had only a verbal description, it affected me deeply, somewhat like the video footage of the truck driver, Reginald Denny, who was dragged from his cab at a stoplight in riot-torn Los Angeles in 1992. While a helicopter filmed from above, man after man kicked Denny in the face, dropped rocks and bricks on his head, abused him far beyond the point of helplessness. Pure atavistic hatred and butchery from people who moments before might have said, "Good morning, Officer."

The group of us rounded the corner onto V-gallery. I had never witnessed mass chaos, but just the weekend before I had seen the precursor. I was one of probably four officers assigned to supervise the hundred-plus inmates at V-Rec on a Sunday afternoon. A visitor wouldn't have noticed anything strange: three TVs on, as usual (showing NFL football, Spanish-language drama, and *Xena: Warrior Princess*), chess, checkers, and dominoes being played, general milling about. Only, for some reason, something made the hair stand up on the back of my neck. Something was palpably weird. As I made my way to the center gate, searching the crowd for another gray uniform, I was tremendously relieved to spot Miller, an unusually competent officer from my class, whom I really liked. Just as I was about to open my mouth, Miller took me to the side and said, "Does it seem kind of creepy to you in here today?" We sought out a third officer, who had felt the same thing, and he went to get the sergeant. More officers started dribbling in; soon there were maybe a dozen, as well as the sergeant. He came to talk to me.

"Well?" he said.

"I don't know, Sarge. Something's not right."

"They had told us something might be going on between the Muslims and the Latin Kings," he said, never once questioning our fear.

Nigro had described this phenomenon at the Academy, and he was absolutely right: Somehow you just knew. The sergeant, after a couple of minutes, knew too. He called the lieutenant. The lieutenant arrived and told us to lock the two middle gates, which effectively divided the group in half. Then he got on the PA system and announced that V-Rec was over. Once everyone was back in their cells, he terminated rec in the gym and the yard for good measure. There was loud grumbling, and even shouts of protest, but his actions—though nothing was ever proven to be in the air—struck me as totally sensible.

Some officers fed on the violence, I knew. Phelan and Pacheco were probably two of them. Pacheco had been talking the day before about how many new uniforms he'd had to buy because of all the blood he got on them. He'd made it sound like a complaint, but I knew it really wasn't. A new uniform was a CO's Purple Heart.

We rounded the last corner, nodded at the officer at the gym door, and headed toward the front gate and freedom. But there was music—an inmate was playing a tape loudly from his cell. This was forbidden: Inmates had to use headphones. "Turn that down," said Phelan, the biggest of us.

The inmate only pretended to turn it down. "Hey," said Phelan, and we all stopped.

The inmate looked up at Phelan defiantly. "The gallery officer don't care. What's it to you?" he demanded. "You're just talking big 'cause you're on the other side of those bars."

The gallery officer was standing just a few cells down. Phelan grabbed the keys from the guy's belt, strode over to the inmate's cell door, unlocked it, and flung it open with a bang. He reached over, yanked the tape player out of its plug, and stood in the door-way holding it like a club.

"Now I'm not," he said fiercely. "You want to come out?"

I had never seen an inmate cower so, and for good reason: Phe-lan's stance said he was ready to take the man's head off. The show was gratifying to watch; Phelan was not afraid to put his massive physical presence to work. The little touch of Elam Lynds was good for our morale.

Violence and the potential for violence were a stress on inmates and officers, but not on all of them, and not all the time. There were moments when, due to the constant tension of prison life and the general lack of catharsis, violence and the potential for vio-lence became a thrill. It had been a long, hot summer in B-block—a long, low wave of attacks and reprisals, and then lockdowns to let everything cool off. Following almost every series of incidents, officers would search the yard, the gym, and other places inmates congregated and prepared for battle, looking for weapons. Usu-ally, we would find scores of them—in trash cans, under rocks, on ledges, or just beneath the dirt. Sometimes our efforts seemed to forestall the next wave, sometimes not.

I remembered the day I'd been standing outside the commissary, waiting to escort my inmates back to B-block, when the gate officer told me there'd be a delay—some kind of fight had broken out in the block. Frustrated that I'd missed it, I paced the floor, locked my in-mates behind another gate, and waited for some news. Then, up the tunnel from B-block, a long succession of officers and handcuffed inmates came into view. The first three inmates were bleeding badly around the head; the officers wore latex gloves. The inmates I was in charge of shouted out encouragement and support.

"Did you get the motherfucker?"

"Yo, Smiley!"

"Ernest, my man!"

The handcuffed, injured inmates looked not despondent but electrified. Regardless of their wounds, they looked utterly thrilled by what had just happened.

Finally we got to return to the block, which by now was locked down. I helped make sure my group of escorted inmates got locked into their cells, then went down to the flats. My friend Scarff was working Movement and Control, next to the OIC's office. A group of us asked him to tell us what had happened.

Apparently, three or four inmates had chased and beaten two

others as they were leaving the gym. The pursued inmates headed toward the OIC's office, where officers were congregated. When the officers realized what was happening, several of them, including Scarff, chased the attackers back down toward the gym. There had been pileups of officers and inmates; Scarff had recovered a shank. One of the assailants, as his victim was marched by in handcuffs, his shirt bloodied, had gleefully taunted him, "I got you! I got you!"

Scarff wasn't a newbie like many of us others; he had worked corrections in Maryland before coming here. But he now seemed as excited as the inmates had been.

"It was the first time in five years that I've been involved in a major incident," he said. "And I loved it! I wanted to hit somebody!" It seemed that Scarff had experienced some of the same intoxicating rush that the inmates had felt. It made all kinds of sense. There were so many unresolved angry exchanges in Sing Sing, so much that never got settled. How many times had I heard an inmate or an officer say, semi-facetiously, "I'm gonna set it off!" Light a fuse! Start a little chaos! In some warped and exaggerated form, it seemed like the same kind of impulse as getting wild on a Saturday night, letting off steam after a week of tension or boredom.

Our sweep was done, the shift nearly over. I walked down to the time clock with everyone else, then noticed on the chalkboard that a meeting of the union local was to begin in about half an hour. Officers had been injured in a melee in the B-block yard the week before, and it seemed likely the matter would come up. As much as I preferred to go home, I thought it would be a good thing to attend.

———

Sportiello, head of the local, thought maybe he should have advertised the fact that the union meeting would have free food. The twelve of us that showed up had been able to put away only two or three feet of the pair of six-foot-long grinders wrapped in blue cellophane. The remainder just sat there, reminding everyone how far short we had fallen of the 10 percent of the membership—about seventy people—required for a quorum. There was talk of amending the constitution to take this apathy into account. There was fond remembrance of the meeting a few years back when hundreds had attended because the state was proposing to end COs' traditional privilege of carrying concealed firearms off the job. (The state had backed down.)

After an hour of two of endless-seeming discussions of how to elect delegates to the big state union meeting in Albany, of why the disability insurer had been changed, and of whether the local should support a Little League team, I began to see why no one came. Then, as though it had been planned, the door to the room swung open slowly and a young officer hobbled in. He had one arm in a cast, one leg bandaged and held off the floor, and bruises on his face, including a black eye. Discussion stopped and hands came together in applause. The wiry man in his late twenties was Harper, an evening-shift officer who had been injured by inmates in the yard during an incident the week before.

Though few had seen it, the incident was well known to most officers at Sing Sing. It had led to the lockdown of B-block for three days, a small article in *The New York Times,* promises of change by the administration, and the rounds of recriminations and second-guessing that were so common in corrections when things went seriously wrong. Harper, who worked in the B-block yard, was the main victim by most accounts, but other versions of the incident made him out to be a hapless error-maker.

It had started when Harper and other officers were doing random pat-frisks of inmates headed out the yard door. One inmate, in the middle of being frisked, took his hands off the wall and dashed out the door. Harper and the other officers took off after him.

The B-block yard was as long as the block, with twelve-foot-high chain-link fence on two sides, B-block itself on a third, and the mess-hall building and storehouse on the fourth. Most of it was a sandy wasteland, but on its northern edge, along the mess-hall building, there were crumbling concrete terraces that inmates liked to sit on, a horseshoe pit, a boccie ball court, a couple of televisions under plywood roofs, an open-air toilet, and a bank of cold-water showers. It looked like a decrepit, overused park in someplace like Haiti. Into this area, which generally had the greatest concentration of inmates, ran the inmate fleeing the pat-frisk.

At the time, I was told, there were some three hundred inmates in the yard and four officers. Worried about losing their man, Harper and the others pursued him to the area of the terraces and Harper tackled him. But their troubles were just beginning, because the yard is, in many ways, like the mess hall: a place where many inmates come together, and passions are easily inflamed. The rules for pursuing inmates there are not hard and fast, but the conventional wisdom says that it's smarter to wait for the pursued to leave. Handcuffing the man who fled was not a straightforward matter, and apparently, as the officers worked to subdue him, inmates gathered around to complain that the officers were being too rough. Following the shouts came projectiles: rocks (of which there are many in the yard), horseshoes, and boccie balls. Harper was knocked out when a horseshoe hit him in the back of the head. Another cracked his elbow. The three other officers were wounded, too. Harper was carried out on a stretcher.

As Harper no doubt knew, Sing Sing's Monday morning quarterbacks had decided that he should never have pursued the inmate into the crowded yard. But when the union meeting's agenda finally reached new business, he stood up and made it clear matters were a bit more complicated than they at first appeared. Why hadn't the officer in Wallpost 17 stepped outside and fired a shot or two into the air? he wanted to know. Why, several days after the incident, hadn't the administration removed the boccie balls and horseshoes from yards other than B-block's? Why didn't yard officers on his shift have more than one radio among them?

The union leadership seemed nervous about getting too squarely behind Harper. For one thing, the wallpost matter was also complicated, and criticizing that officer was something they weren't sure they wanted to do. The problem was that the incident took place probably 250 to 300 yards away from the post. This, again, was a quirk and shortcoming of Sing Sing. There was a second wallpost closer, but it was situated in such a way that the terrace area was in a blind spot. The Department authorized use of the AR-15 rifle only up to a distance of about a hundred yards, because accuracy deteriorated so much with the additional distance. At most other facilities these questions would never arise; the wallposts would be situated where they would do the most good.

It was even worse in the A-block yard, where certain areas were invisible to *any* tower. Construction of a new tower there had long ago been okayed, the union president explained, but no funds were available to build it. Harper bitterly asked why a new parking lot was being built up the hill if "no funds were available," then again brought himself angrily to his feet, or foot.

"There's still stones out there bigger than my hand!" he protested. "The yard still has blind zones, like the one we were in. How many of us will have to get hit in the head with a horseshoe before this changes?"

The council ground its wheels. A resolution was finally passed urging the administration to address the pressing security problems in the yards.

———

I often drove between home and work with Officer Rob Saline. Visually, Saline and I were a study in contrasts. At more than three hundred pounds and well over six feet tall, he was easily twice my size, probably the largest person in B-block. Bronx-bred, he kept his head shaved and wore designer tortoiseshell glasses. He had played football for the Air Force and, briefly, for the New York Jets. His feet hurt a lot—I suppose because they carried such a massive burden.

Saline and I had met on a transportation detail, escorting inmates to appearances at the Westchester County Courthouse in White Plains. Sergeant Holmes had sent us together, possibly as some sort of joke. The transportation sergeant had greeted Saline with delight: "Now, that's a correction officer!" I recall him saying when Saline lumbered into the room. The sergeant ignored me completely. As Saline and I sat around the courthouse, we realized that his girlfriend lived and worked not too far from my home. He didn't have a car, he told me, due to financial problems, and was spending a lot of time in my neck of the Bronx. Would I ever be willing to give him a lift?

So Saline pitched in for gas, and at 6 A.M. many mornings and 3:15 P.M. many afternoons, he squeezed himself into the front seat of my Toyota. The car's driving dynamics totally changed with Saline aboard. Aragon, in fact, complained that Saline had ruined his shocks in the days when they carpooled, but to me it was worth it for the window into the big man's world.

He was about my age and had daughters in "Carolina." He moonlighted as a security guard for a jewelry company. Often after work I'd drop him off at an intersection near the Cross County Mall, where he'd visit his girlfriend at work in the Fashion Bug store. He was rather touchy, and rubbed many people the wrong way. A few guys, I knew, refused to give him a ride anymore. (Sergeant Wickersham was among those with whom he maintained an avoidance relationship.) He carried an alphanumeric beeper and consulted it often; his plans were subject to constant change. Our rendezvous might be set up at 11 P.M. the night before or 5:15 A.M. the morning of. Once, when I'd been away a few days on a vacation I hadn't told him about, he left this message on my machine, like a rap: "Yo, Teddy Ted, this is Rob. I just calling 'cause I thought you was dyin'. I didn't see you at the job so I hope you feelin' better. Tell your lady and your kids I said hi, and I hope you feelin' well, man. If you need me call me, man, you know, if you need me to do somethin' for you. Ciao."

We talked mostly about the circumstances and personalities at work—often I got gossip from Saline sooner than from anyone else. And one morning, late in September, he shared some breaking news, additional details of which were passed quietly around B-block for the next few days.

Four B-block officers—Pitkin, De Los Santos, Garces, and Lopez—had gone out drinking. At a Queens strip joint called the Playhouse, Pitkin—a short, pugnacious, extroverted officer who some felt had a Napoleon complex—ran into an ex-con in the men's room. The man had been a B-block inmate with, apparently, a long-standing grudge against Pitkin. He recognized the guard and, possibly as a prank, held a ballpoint pen to his neck. The two tussled, and the fight spilled out into the main room, where the three other officers joined in, not only subduing the man but, according to the stories, handcuffing and then *continuing* to "subdue" him, all in full view of the other customers. One officer, during this final phase, apparently drew his gun to keep other patrons at bay. The police were called and, upon arrival, arrested the officers on assault charges.

All were released pending an investigation, but we learned the next day that Sing Sing had demanded their badges. They were suspended without pay until the matter was resolved. Soon, investigators from the Department's Office of the Inspector General were interviewing them, and, not long after, we learned that the district attorney had decided to bring felony assault charges to a grand jury.

All the information was passed around piecemeal, but this consistent story emerged and pieces of it were confirmed to me by superior officers; one lieutenant, while signing my logbook, told me, sotto voce, that he had been the one to accept their badges. Most jailhouse gossip quickly makes its way to the inmates, but officers were uniformly insistent about keeping them ignorant about the story of the Playhouse Four, as the group had come to be known. We'd whisper about it in stairways or around the OIC's office.

"You heard?" I asked one officer from Yonkers—Camacho—who had been away on vacation. We were standing alone by the yard door. I told him.

"Payday" was his first reaction, and for the first time I realized that, yes, it had happened on one of the alternate Wednesdays when we were paid. Payday was party day. The story also seemed to reinforce one of Camacho's most strongly held convictions: "Don't ever hang out with COs!" he said vehemently. "When they're together, they think they're like—" He held his hands out as though to indicate an extremely big head. In other words, like the whole world is their cellblock.

Feliciano, as we stood next to each other in lineup one day, murmured, "You know that inmate who attacked Pitkin? Turns out he's the cousin of my friend's girlfriend." The lesson for him was: When you are from the big city, it's a very small world.

Another officer, Riordan, brought the matter up with me when we were near the center staircase during the morning count; no one could see or hear us. Any of the four would lose his job if convicted of a felony, he said. De Los Santos was especially vulnerable because, like me, he had worked less than a year as a guard and was still on probationary status—not afforded all the protections of union members, in other words.

"What I don't get is why they had to handcuff him first," said Riordan. "Just beat him up without handcuffing him!"

"I think it's just lucky they didn't shoot him, too," I replied. Riordan took out his little two-inch knife, the maximum size we were allowed to have, and, seemingly on a whimsy, sliced up all the notices on the inmate bulletin board. One of them had to do with the upcoming inmate Jaycee rap contest. Riordan extemped his own rap: "I live in B-block, I'm in for life. / This big guy is Wally, he's my wife."

I wasn't exactly sympathetic to the Playhouse Four, but I did find myself hoping they didn't make it into the news. Around this same time, tabloids and local TV news shows were full of revelations about the abuse of a Haitian immigrant, Abner Louima, by New York City police officers who had shoved a broomstick up his rectum. Any further incident of police brutality would be tinder for this media fire. But, maybe because the Playhouse incident involved minorities on both sides, it got no press.

In late November, two months after the event, I arrived at work to find the following message written on a chalkboard: PLAYHOUSE 4—NO TRUE BILL—JUSTIFIABLE FORCE. In other words, the grand jury had decided not to indict the officers. I felt myself breathe out a little of the collective sigh of relief. The guys, as other officers had noted, were just doing what we'd been taught to do inside prison when one of us was threatened: respond en masse. The handcuffs, pistol, and continued beating were unfortunate but, hey, when you all shared the same difficult circumstance— prison work—you tended to give each other the benefit of the doubt.

Still, the idea that there is a current of brutality in corrections work is hard to deny. Anyone who follows the news knows that you don't have to look far to see correction officers at their worst. In New Jersey in 1995, jail guards processing inmates who had rioted at an immigration detention center ran them through a punching and kicking gauntlet, and later placed at least one of their heads in a flushing toilet and pulled out the pubic hairs of another with pliers. In Florida in 1999, nine guards armed with a stun gun conducted a putative cell extraction of an inmate that left him dead; they have refused to talk, and the state has classified it a homicide. (It seems relevant that the inmate was on Death Row for having killed a CO.) On Long Island in 1997, an inmate who annoyed his guards by calling out for methadone died of a ruptured spleen after two of them beat him in his cell. Before he died, it was alleged, they tried to get him to sign a statement saying that his injuries were accidental. (A joke I heard from a CO in a bar upstate: How many COs did it take to push the inmate down the stairs? None—he fell by himself.)

Every single story about guards seems to reinforce the brutal stereotype. When I see accused officers on television or read the remarks of union reps in the papers, what disappoints me is the universal denial that the events ever took place as alleged, or any admission of the obvious, that among the many good officers there are also a few bad ones. Even as what journalists call background—remarks made without attribution—guards don't dare admit that all of us at times feel like strangling an inmate, that inmates taunt us, strike us, humiliate us in ways civilians could never imagine, and that through it all the guard is supposed to do nothing but stand there and take it. This information wouldn't excuse the crimes, but it might chip away at the stereotype by making a few of the incidents more *understandable*. Instead, guards adopt a siege mentality—a shutting up, a closing of ranks—that is law enforcement at its stupidest.

———

Abusive guards are out there, no question. They were not, by and large, the newer officers at Sing Sing, the ones I worked with in B-block. I think the constant turnover worked against the news-making brutality: B-block officers lacked the solidarity, the shared experience and mind-set of an upstate prison that could allow bad things to happen and be successfully covered up. But I could sense the potential for abusiveness in a couple of officers from outside the block whom I'd come into contact with or heard stories about.

In the early fall, I was working V-gallery, on the flats, just downstairs from W, when above me I heard a commotion. "House nigger!" an inmate shouted angrily. "Doing the white man's work!"

"Bitch!" an officer shot back, along with some other things I couldn't hear.

The action was taking place two floors up, on X-gallery. I stopped to watch, as did the officer working the yard door and another. We stood next to each other, and ascertained that the yelling officer, the one the inmate had called "house nigger," was up there doing a cell search, probably as a result of a tip that the inmate had drugs or money or a weapon. He was a senior officer with a reputation for being tough; he sometimes came over to B-block on an assignment like this. Probably near fifty, he was built like a tank and always seemed to have his jaw clenched.

The inmate whose cell was being searched was a tough-looking guy in dreadlocks. Typically during a cell search, one officer did the searching while another stood with the inmate outside the cell. But in this case, there were two big officers assisting the search officer; they probably had expected some trouble.

The officer was pissed off and in the guy's face, repeatedly calling him a bitch. The two other officers, one of them from my class, held their hands off their sides as though they expected action any instant.

"Fuck you, man, I'll see you in New York!" said the inmate.

"Is that a threat?" asked the officer, now *very* close.

The inmate said something else, and the officer spit in his face. The inmate tried to retaliate but was brought down in an instant, crunched by the three big guys. As they subdued him, the inmate next door started screaming out, berating the tough officer.

"You a low creature, man! I can't believe you done that! You lower than dirt." Inmates down below called up to ask what had happened.

"He spit on the brother."

"Who did?"

"That officer from the hospital, the same one that snuffed Mad Dog when he was in the Visit Room."

Then an inmate called out to us on the flats: "You all were witnesses!"

It was true, though we all knew it meant nothing. We'd never act as witnesses for an inmate. We hadn't seen a thing. Then an inmate yelled out: "Plummer, how would you feel if that was your little brother or cousin?"

Plummer was one of the officers I was standing with. Like the tough officer upstairs, he was black. Plummer said nothing.

I wondered how the paperwork was going to be handled on this one. The next day at lineup, I asked Officer Z, the one I knew from the Academy, who had been standing there, about that part of it.

"Well, we all sat down in the sergeant's office and talked about it," he explained.

"And what did you say about the spitting?"

"Well, he didn't spit at him. What happened was, he was yelling at the guy and some spit came out of his mouth—you know how it is when you're yelling." Ah. It was interesting to watch Officer Z maintain this story even though he knew that I knew it was made up. A time-honored law enforcement ritual, one of the few creative acts the job demanded: remembering an incident, revising it so that it happened as it should have, and then repeating that story until it sounded real.

When I thought back on the altercation, though, what stuck with me wasn't the cover-your-ass part so much as the inmate calling down to Plummer and asking how he'd feel if it were his little brother. "My little brother wouldn't have called him a house nigger," I imagined Plummer saying to himself. But it went to the heart of the complicated situation for minority officers. They were working for the Man in an unequal, sometimes unjust society—I doubt that many would quibble with that description. It didn't mean their position was untenable; it just meant they had to put up with a lot of shit that white officers did not.

House nigger was the leading epithet. As one inmate on R-gallery had explained it to me, "In the old South, you had your house Negroes and your field Negroes. The house Negroes were the maids and the cooks and the butlers and such. And the field Negroes were the brothers and sisters out there with dirty hands. And even though slavery's gone, technically, you still got your house Negroes and your field Negroes. And the difference between them is that the house Negro's gonna be sad when the house burns down. And the field Negro ain't."

It wasn't just the black officers who were compromised. In June, an escort officer up on T-and-Y had marched with a law enforcement contingent in New York City's annual Puerto Rico Day parade. I was listening the next day when other officers asked him how it went. He shrugged. "Lot of people watching give you shit, man. They don't cheer. I'm not going to do it next year." It took no more explanation than that; his listeners all understood. "But I'm, like, Hey, at least I've got a job," he added.

Outside the mess hall another day that fall, I spoke with Brown, a young black woman officer from the Bronx whom I respected, about the same general conflict. When inmates gave her trouble about her job, she said, she told them, "Do you know right from wrong? Then what's the problem? Why you talking about the system, the man? There's you and there's me."

But surely minority officers' allegiance to the system was constantly tested in ways that white officers' was not. Alcantara, for example, told of one day double-parking his van in Harlem so that he could drop off something at a relative's apartment. With his wife waiting in the passenger seat, he had jumped out of the van and begun to jog down the sidewalk to the building's front door. His wife watched in horror as two undercover cops appeared, trained their pistols on him, and told him to freeze. Alcantara said he did exactly as told, lying on the sidewalk, and then asked the officers to remove his wallet so they could see his badge. The crisis was over in a moment, but these kinds of things happened all the time. Smitty, who drove a Lexus with tinted windows, said he was pulled over in lower Westchester every month or two. As a young black man in a nice car, he took it for granted that he fit a police profile.

"I don't even take my hands off the steering wheel till I can talk to them," he said. "I look straight ahead and say, 'Officer, I am a New York State peace officer, and you'll find my identification next to me on the seat.' I wait for them to tell *me* to move my hands, and then I do it *very* slowly."

I, meanwhile, hadn't been pulled over for years. I was even kind of looking forward to it so that I could beat a ticket by showing my badge. But it didn't happen.

———

Then there was the complicated matter of minority officers recognizing new inmates. More than once, I'd heard a colleague tell a sergeant that a new inmate was somebody he had known in high school or in the old neighborhood and the sergeant then asking if that was going to be a problem. ("No, I just wanted you to know" was the typical answer.) In some cases, maybe this led to officer and inmate being too close. But just as often—or even more often, it seemed to me—it led to them keeping a greater than normal distance.

My most impressive lesson on the lives of minority officers came on the mess-hall bridge with Smitty and Brown. In between patfrisking inmates as they entered or exited the mess hall, there was time to just stand around and gab. The subject turned to the Internet. I asked whether either of them had heard about the website that listed all New York State prison inmates, along with their crimes, their dates of birth, the date of their first eligibility for parole, and so forth. All of it was information we weren't supposed to have, and I thought they'd be intrigued by this new situation, particularly Smith, who had learned so much about the individuals he was in charge of during his days on V-gallery.

"But what about privacy?" he asked. He had learned whatever he knew by just asking the inmates.

"Well, think of it as a way to check what you've been told," I said.

Smith shook his head. Brown, too, looked deeply skeptical. I didn't see why, and she tried to explain. "Look, I'm from the Bronx," she said. "There are six of us kids and I'm the youngest. My older brother was riding the subway one day. Guy across from him drops his gym bag by mistake, and there's an automatic in there and it goes off. It hits my brother in the leg. The leg had to be amputated. Now, can you imagine what I would have done if I caught that guy?"

"I don't know you well enough to know."

"Well, I would have hurt him, or even maybe killed him if I

could. I'm a person who respects the law, but . . . sometimes there's things you can't help, right?"

Smith agreed: There were things you just couldn't help. Anyone could get caught up in the heat of the moment.

Their point was that anyone could end up inside. The black officers I knew, especially, seemed to feel this—that the line between straight life and prison life was a very thin one and that sometimes the decision about which side you were on was not yours to make.

———

Prisons reconvene old neighbors as well as people with even deeper connections. Shortly after I left Sing Sing, there was a story in *The New York Times* about a man named Baba Eng, who had been at Sing Sing for twenty-two years. He was "serving a life sentence for murder, when a new inmate walked into the shower room one day and stared at his face.

" 'Dad!' the stranger finally exclaimed.

"The man was his son, whom Mr. Eng had not seen since his arrest, and who now was in prison himself for armed robbery. 'It was the worst moment of my life,' Mr. Eng recalled. 'Here was my son; he had tried to imitate my life.' "

Prison life creates its own pathologies. Experts are increasingly worried about the effect of a parent's imprisonment on children—both the increased likelihood that a child of a criminal will become a criminal himself and the idea that prison itself may become a twisted rite of passage for young men. But can *rite of passage* possibly be the correct term for a kind of suspended animation that leaves you older, weaker, less sexually attractive, and less connected to community than before you went in?

Stone told me that when he had worked at Green Haven, among the inmates had been a father, his grandfather, and his son. On W-gallery, we had an uncle and his nephew. On R-gallery, we had Twin, a murderer, whose twin brother was imprisoned upstate. My wife and I were mugged in the eighties in Brooklyn Heights; the criminal was a crack addict who was finally apprehended after robbing several other people. His three brothers, detectives told us, were already imprisoned upstate.

I knew no story stranger than that of Foster. The tall, troubled black woman from my training section, a single mother and former Rikers guard, had wept openly from the pain of Defensive Tactics, had made us late and gotten us in trouble with her chronic

tardiness, and had, according to rumor, been chastised at Sing Sing
for falling asleep on the job and, of all things, for speaking in
tongues during chapel services for inmates. She had transferred up
to Bedford Hills, the maximum-security prison for women in
Westchester County. There, according to my classmate Buckner,
who preceded her to the women's prison, an older woman inmate
was in the habit of bragging to officers about her daughter, the correction officer. He and other transfers from my class recognized
from snapshots the daughter of whom the older woman was so
proud: Foster.

To have a mother in prison and become a guard there yourself—
that was the strangest bond I heard all year.

———

Early in my V-gallery days, one of my double-bunked new-arrival
inmates got keeplocked. This was a big bother for me and his cell-
mate, because it meant I had to keep the bolt on the cell deadlocked all the time. His roommate had to get my attention every
time he wanted in or out.

"How'd you manage to get keeplocked so soon?" I asked him.
"Most guys, it takes at least a few weeks."

The inmate smiled somewhat sheepishly. Unlike many
keeplocks, he had no problem with authority—or no problem
with me, at any rate.

"Just a hassle with another inmate, CO," he said. "Something I
had to do."

He was unremarkable enough to me at that point that I never
even bothered to check further about what he was keeplocked for.
He remained a face in the crowd until one sweltering day in July
when he was no longer keeplocked. B-block could get hot and
sticky if there was no breeze outside, and on this day, many of the
inmates who went to the yard after midday chow peeled off their
shirts before heading outside. Delacruz, as I'd learned this inmate
was called, was one of these. As he did, I noticed the large tattoo
spread across his chest like a banner: ASSASSIN! it read. That was
fairly interesting, but then I noticed his back, which was almost
entirely covered by a long poem in Spanish, tattooed in a flowing
script. That was fascinating, and in my surprise I said something
like, "Whoa, what *is* that?"

Delacruz gave a little smile and said, "It's a poem," and continued on his way out to the yard.

When he returned I tried to find out more. He brushed off my question about what poem it was, but he did explain how he'd gotten it. A white guy at Rikers Island was the artist, he said. The "ink" was made by burning plastic—a pen or a toothbrush—under a metal surface, like the bottom of a bunk. You wiped off the thick soot, mixed it with toothpaste and soap, and there was your ink. Your pen was a pencil with two needles tied to the point with string. The string soaked up the ink. The artist's many jabs left its residue under the surface of the skin.

Five days later, Delacruz finally told me about the poem. It was from a book in the Rikers library that "really meant a lot to me," he said, though he didn't like to talk about it.

"But who wrote it?" I asked.

"Oh, it was a Jewish girl during the Second World War. I translated it into Spanish."

"You mean Anne Frank? The one who wrote a diary?"

He looked surprised. "Yeah, I think that's it," he said. "Anne Frank."

On my next day off, I took Anne Frank's *The Diary of a Young Girl* off my shelf and reread it. The parallel between a prison cell and the tiny space where Anne and her family had hidden from the Nazis in 1942 was immediately clear, as was the way that Anne, at thirteen, was imprisoned by her Jewish identity, by the very fact of who she was. There was no poem in my version of the diary, however, and I assumed it must have been included in a different edition.

The next time I saw Delacruz, I told him about my rereading the book. I even let him know that I had visited the Anne Frank house on a trip to Holland and had seen the rooms where she had hidden. Delacruz didn't really react with the interest I had expected, and I worried I'd gone too far, maybe sounding like a braggart or claiming a personal interest in this story that was greater than his or seeming to pry. Or maybe the thought of a CO who had been to Europe and was into Anne Frank was just too fucking strange. So I laid off for a while.

Delacruz, in the meantime, graduated to his own cell, but it was way upstairs on U-and-Z, not on V. So we'd acknowledge each other in the mess hall or wherever else our paths would cross. Then, months later—December—I was back on V preparing to let my keeplocks out for their daily rec when I discovered that among them was none other than Delacruz. He'd been locked up two days before, he explained, and then moved downstairs.

"Hey, you want to read that book again?" I asked him.

"Yeah!" he answered enthusiastically. "I *loved* that book."

Thus our acquaintance was reestablished. I brought the book in—smuggled it, technically—and peeked in on Delacruz as he savored it. He skipped rec and read it cover to cover. Then over the next few days he read it again, slowly. I saw him discussing it with the inmate next door (another robber, named Perez) and I worried he'd tell the man I'd brought it in—I didn't want inmates to have anything on me, no matter how minor. That's why I let Delacruz return the book, accepting it back with a measure of relief. He parted with it like an object of love.

"It's the best book I ever read," he said this time. "I cried all the way through."

I asked him if he'd seen the poem in there. No, he said. But the book he'd read the first time hadn't looked exactly like this one. Another edition, I again figured.

After that we talked often and easily. I liked Delacruz initially because of the poem, and then later because I didn't think he bullshitted me or tried to get anything from me. He was keeplocked this time, he said, for extorting from another inmate in the commissary.

"Hmm, sounds bad," I said.

Delacruz didn't pretend to be ashamed. "What can I tell you, Conover? It's what you do to survive."

Delacruz was short, fit, handsome, and dark-complected, with brown eyes and thick eyebrows. He was in for robbery—his fourth prison term, he said, after three in Virginia (two for a period of months, and a third for four years). He had entered Virginia's most famous prison, nicknamed the Wall, at age sixteen, he said, because the state believed he was eighteen: His mother had brought him into the United States from Puerto Rico using the birth certificate of his older brother, who had died at age two.

"That was the worst time, man, being sixteen, sitting in that bus, looking out the window at the Wall."

Prison now, at age twenty-six, didn't seem so scary, and time didn't weigh on him as it once had, though he was serving a sentence of ten years. In fact, he told me, he was lucky that it was only ten years. The immigrant victims of two of the robberies he had been charged with most recently had refused to testify against him. (I knew that this kind of reluctance was one reason that immigrants were often muggers' targets.) He said he didn't even know the exact date he was keeplocked until but thought it was later that month. "And it's a good thing it doesn't bother me, Conover, because it isn't the first time, and it won't be the last."

About ten days before Christmas, it snowed overnight. Delacruz and his neighbor, Perez, were two of several keeplocks who reasonably opted against recreation in the yard the next day: Inmates had no waterproof footwear. When I peered into his cell later that morning, after my other inmates had all gone to their programs, I saw Delacruz dozing. Perez, who had started acting friendly toward me since my dealings with Delacruz, was staring straight ahead. I had a few moments of free time.

"So," I said, leaning against the bars and letting a moment of silence pass. "What's up?"

For a few moments, Perez didn't answer. He may have been deciding whether to tell me. "Thinking about the robberies I'm going to do when I get out," he finally said, with the candor of his neighbor. "A year you plan. You think I'm not going to pull it off?"

I raised an eyebrow. Delacruz, I noticed, had sat up on his bunk and was rubbing his eyes.

"I know it's not a positive thing, but what else do I have to do here?" Thinking through the robberies in advance, he reasoned, ensured their smooth execution. His preferred targets were pharmacies and "numbers joints." The planning involved considering every contingency: what to do if they reached for a gun (shoot them, of course, even though you wouldn't want to), what to do if someone else entered the store, where to go afterward, and so on.

"You're thinking about specific places when you do the planning?"

"Sure," he said, as though it were obvious.

"They're in poorer neighborhoods?"

"Yeah."

"Tell me something I've always wondered. Why don't you ever rob people in richer neighborhoods? They probably expect it less and are carrying more. You wouldn't have to rob as many times then."

Here, Delacruz joined the conversation, explaining that you might get more cash robbing a rich person on the street but that you'd have to be in their neighborhood, and judges would hit you harder for that: They would know the victim was white because of the name, the address, etc. It was much safer, obviously, to rob less prosperous people of color.

Still, spur-of-the-moment jobs could land you in trouble. Like the last one. Perez had robbed somebody his first day out from a previous bid, he told me, using a gun borrowed from a friend. He hadn't gotten caught, but it had made him feel reckless.

"It's like I'm addicted," he admitted. "I'm not into drugs. I don't like hanging out with other criminals," he told me. "I always do the jobs alone." His friends didn't even know where he got the money. "They probably think it's from selling drugs." And money was the sole reason for them.

I didn't want to argue with Perez, and entertained no illusions that it was within my power to change his ways. But I had to ask: "You know robbery, um, hurts people. Scares the shit out of them. Makes them poorer. I've been robbed, so I know. How do you justify that?"

"Conover, you know if you got a felony record you can't even get a job at McDonald's? Plus, you'd need a GED. You can't get any job."

I said I didn't believe that you couldn't get any job, that I knew people who had. Here, Delacruz jumped in again.

"Okay, maybe, but it's going to pay shit and it's going to take a couple months. And what are you going to wear while you're waiting? In the ghetto you get no respect if you don't look right, have a car, a Mercedes-Benz—those things. No woman will go out with you. Don't get me wrong, Conover—*I'm* going straight this time. But it's gonna cost me. That's reality."

To me it was a weird contrast: the urgency about getting money on the outside versus the seeming lack of urgency about getting out of prison. But then I decided that his blasé attitude about serving time might be a pose. I saw Delacruz that afternoon checking a dictionary, making sure to spell correctly all the words in a legal appeal to get his sentence reduced.

I'd been working up to asking Delacruz about his poem again, to see if now he'd tell me the exact words tattooed on his back. But as I walked into B-block one afternoon, I saw Sergeant Murray escorting him out of the block with all his belongings. Murray later told me he'd been taken to 5-Building after the superintendent received an anonymous letter claiming that when Delacruz got off keeplock, he'd be stabbed over money he owed. I wondered what Delacruz hadn't told me. I remembered how often he did not take advantage of keeplock rec, and realized now that he might have been afraid. I wondered whether he himself might have written that letter.

I left Sing Sing before I found out the answers to my questions. But months later, when I had become a civilian and Delacruz had become an inmate at a medium-security prison, I wrote him a letter, with my post office box as a return address. I gave him some news about myself, then closed with a question: "What were those lines of poetry on your back, anyway?"

To my delight, he sent them to me in Spanish. I began my detective work. The library had plenty of editions of Anne Frank's diary, but not one included a poem. I consulted a couple of experts. Anne Frank had written some poetry, but nothing like the lines Delacruz had sent me, they said. I wondered if Delacruz was somehow mistaken. But then I decided that, addiction to robbery aside, he seemed like a together enough person to keep straight the source of a poem he had inscribed on his own back. I sat down and read the diary one more time, looking for a clue, a reference, a snippet of something that I might have missed. I found it on the last page, in the very last words—not poetry in stanzas, just Frank's prose.

Delacruz had translated into Spanish from an English translation of Anne Frank's original Dutch. But the gist was still there. It was unmistakable.

> When everybody starts hovering over me, I get cross, then sad, and finally end up turning my heart inside out, the bad part on the outside and the good part on the inside, and keep trying to find a way to become what I'd like to be and what I could be if . . . if only there were no other people in the world.

It was easier to stay incurious as an officer. Under the inmates' surface bluster, their cruelty and selfishness, was almost always something ineffably sad.

———

The signs were few and sporadic: Perry Como carols played over the PA system in the waiting room of the commissary, seemingly to piss off the inmates; the wilting, Charlie Brown–type tree on Hospital, fourth floor; the memo, read to us at lineup several days in a row, about how this was a tough time of year for inmates, about how we should be on the lookout for signs of depression and encourage inmates who needed it to seek counseling "or the companionship of their fellow man." This last line, with its homoerotic undertone, provoked smirks the first time it was read and unabashed laughter by the third or fourth. Even the sergeant reading it had to suppress a laugh.

And then there was another memo, read for several days beginning around December 20, about how anyone who even *thought* about "banging in" (calling in sick) between now and New Year's would need a separate doctor's note for every single day and even then would have his records subject to disciplinary review. I had been considering that very thing, the thought of Christmas in prison being so depressing, but the memo pretty much torpedoed the idea.

On the day of Christmas Eve, I supervised the distribution of little holiday "gift boxes" containing useless toiletries and a few snacks, compliments of a charity. And then I watched inmate representatives figure out how to distribute to every inmate the "holiday cheer" they had chosen: a can of Coke and two bags of chips. The cognitive dissonance grew. Standing on the mess-hall bridge, two sergeants waited for inmates to get out of earshot and then wished us all a Merry Christmas. The officer I was with disapproved of this well-wishing.

"This is the time of year when a lot happens, and it's because officers let their guard down," he warned.

Certainly it was true that a lot happened this time of year. Anecdotal evidence indicated there was an increased appetite for drugs and alcohol. Just the month before, an inmate on C-gallery had killed another by stabbing him in the heart—apparently, right in front of an officer ("there were gallons of blood," I was told)—the first murder in a New York State prison that year. A deputy superintendent whose office I passed on my way out told me he was staying late because two years earlier there had been a Christmas Eve homicide on M-gallery. And just as there is said to be a jump in wife beatings on Super Bowl Sunday, so it was true that suicides in prison often occurred around the holidays.

Though it fell on a Thursday, Christmas was handled like a weekend day at prison: no programs and few runs. This should have meant an easier-than-normal day, but I think that for most of us, the relative inactivity just meant more time to feel shitty about being in prison on Christmas. Everyone's mood seemed subdued, inmates and guards alike. It wasn't just because we couldn't participate in Christmas (though a few inmates had visitors); it was because, as an officer, you mainly had to deny it. Christmas spirit—generosity, forgiveness, goodwill toward men—ran pretty much counter to what we were supposed to be doing. Prison was for punishment; it wasn't ours to forgive. Kindness, as Nigro had said back in the Academy, was taken for weakness and exploited. Goodwill didn't enter the picture. This job was about maintaining power, and goodwill could erode that power.

Unless, I thought, it was surreptitious. This idea came to me when I took some men on a package run—the package room was open because of the potential for late-arriving Christmas presents. While the inmates milled around, waiting their turn at the window, I got the package room officers to let me inside, where I sat in a comfortable chair. They were pretty swamped. Bags with inmates' names on them filled practically every available space. An extra officer was in there, X-raying new boxes and then going through them, throwing out things that weren't allowed. The discard box was large, and it was quickly filled with toiletries that contained alcohol; clothing colored blue, black, gray, or orange; packages of food that hadn't been factory-sealed; and . . . cigarettes.

Cigarette packages that lacked a New York State revenue stamp—cigarettes purchased out of state, for example, or on Indian reservations—were not allowed to be distributed to inmates, and were apparently thrown away. I thought of the inmates I knew whom nobody was likely to remember at Christmas. There were lots of them. My heart went out to the most pathetic. When no one was looking, I stuffed about a dozen of the cigarette packs into my jacket.

Mainly, I gave them to the bugs. One was Addison, a tall, middle-aged black man on W who for weeks had sported a Mohawk; he seemed like a furtive Manhattan homeless person, which perhaps he once had been. I'd had to escort him a few places, after which he didn't seem as scary as he had initially. He was fearful of other inmates, not of officers, and spent half his time looking over his shoulder for would-be attackers. He spent the other half scanning the floor for cigarette stubs. He was an inveterate collector of these, which, in prison, tended to be extremely short. As I had paused for him to add to his handful one day, he sang a verse from "King of the Road":

I smoke old stogies I have found
Short, but not too big around

I told him about an old hobo I'd met who claimed you could tell the state of the economy by the length of butts on the ground, and Addison laughed and said, "Maybe so."

He was just starting his second "state bid," he told me, having done numerous "skid bids" for turnstile jumping, etc. His nephew, he told me, was locked on the same gallery.

He came from a fucked-up world. I gave him three packs.

I gave Larson a pack. I didn't think he smoked, but cigarettes were like money.

I gave Cameron ("Don't get conned by Conover the con man"), who for days had been asking me what I was going to bring him for Christmas, two packs and a slice of spice cake from my lunch bag.

I gave three packs to a bug on R who was forever cadging cigarettes and also had an incredible body odor problem.

I did it all quietly, placing the packs on the cell bars as I walked by, trying not to let the recipients see me and get something on me, though I was planning to resign soon after the new year. When I walked back by the cell of the stinky bug, he was handing a fresh Newport to his neighbor, who was asking him quizzically, "Hey, how'd you get these?"

I gave a pack to the Colombian.

I gave a pack to the old bug who'd wanted Chapstick. Maybe he could trade the pack for some.

I gave a pack to the young guy who thought he'd had a cockroach stuck in his ear.

I gave packs to three guys I had keeplocked. No hard feelings.

———

At lineup the next week I was feeling a bit giddy, trying hard to repress the joy that was gathering in my soul: I had turned in my resignation papers, and today, though not quite my last day at Sing Sing, would be my last one on R-and-W.

There was a symmetry in this, as R-and-W had been the place where I'd spent my first, awful day as a Sing Sing trainee more than eight months before. Maybe it was naive, even reckless, to expect it, but I had a premonition that today's shift could be the best yet. With each succeeding month, I'd learned how to run a gallery more smoothly. It wasn't clear what this ability would count for in the outside world—maybe the complaints desk at a department store would be a breeze—but at least, I thought, I would enjoy this hard-earned expertise on my last day as the R-and-W officer.

I sat down in the gallery-office cell, started a new page in the logbook, and then leaned back to savor my coffee and catch up on recent events on the gallery. Stone, the regular officer, had been on duty the day before. Most of his log entries were just a few words—"7:10 A.M., R chow"—but midday, he'd written a whole paragraph. He'd stopped an inmate from another gallery who was on R without permission and asked him what was in his paper sack. The inmate had sprinted for the gate, but Stone had caught him and found . . . a "16 in. shank."

Sixteen inches? I thought. That wasn't a shank, that was a sword. Why the hell would anyone have a weapon that length? What mayhem did he contemplate? There was no indication that Stone had been hurt in the confrontation, but still, it seemed a bad omen.

I had a zillion keeplocks—approximately one out of every five inmates—and today, alas, was keeplock shower day. My second officer, as usual, had disappeared after doing his go-rounds, leaving me to move all these guys through the showers myself. I thought I could do it if I got an early start.

Minutes into this process, I found that of seven shower cells, only two were operable. Normally, there were three or four working. B-block's plumbing was unbelievably dismal, I thought as I locked an inmate into the second shower.

"Hey, CO!" he hollered after about five minutes. I walked over to the shower cell and looked through the bars. He was covered head to toe in suds. "The hot water went off!"

It was true. It had suddenly gone off throughout the block. I could hear the complaints from other floors. "Guess you're out of luck," I told him, thinking, as I said it, that I was the one who was out of luck: The hot water never went off all day, which would have allowed me to cancel showers. Usually, it was off for just an hour or two, long enough to make it plain that not all the keeplocks would get their showers and that they'd have to compete with the porters for showers in the afternoon.

Just then I had an unwelcome visitor to the gallery—one of the tough transportation officers with a reputation for meanness. Apparently, they didn't have any work for him this morning, so they'd sent him to "help" in B-block. I'd seen how he acted around inmates, and now I'd get a taste of his attitude toward young officers.

"What are these inmates doing out?" he demanded of me, sounding like some asshole sergeant.

"I believe they're cleaning the floors."

"You have *five* porters cleaning the floors?" He was counting two he'd seen on the other side.

"One of those is my clerk. This other guy is just out for a second." Why was I defending myself to him?

He stood there looking disgusted. W-gallery inmates began to return from chow. I gave them a couple of minutes to lock in, then stood near the brake and hollered, "Step in, gentlemen!"

"You shouldn't waste your breath yelling," he said after a moment of watching me. "You should just pull the brake and then, anybody who didn't get in, lock 'em up."

"I know," I sighed. "In a perfect world."

"If you know, then why don't you do it?" he demanded.

He was starting to bother me. I came to work prepared to do battle with inmates, not fellow officers, and I felt I wasn't handling it quite right.

"Listen," I said to him. "I'm a regular here. I know these guys. This is how I want to do it today." Pathetic, I thought after I'd spoken. I should have fired a louder shot over his bow.

"How you want to do it," he said in a mocking tone.

"That's it," I said, looking him in the eye.

"Fine," he said, and descended the stairs to the flats.

Good riddance, I was thinking. Then I heard his announcement come over the PA system.

"All inmates out on the gallery on R-and-W without a reason, return to your cells!"

That fucker. He was trying to embarrass me. No doubt he had been badmouthing me to all who would listen downstairs.

"Hey, Blaine!" I shouted down through the mesh, suddenly angry. "What's your fucking problem?" He was somewhere under the overhang near the OIC's office, and I couldn't tell whether he'd heard me. What, I wondered, would be the penalty for punching a fellow CO? I got back to work, decided to try to let it slide.

To my surprise, he was back a couple of hours later when the R side returned from lunch. I thought he must be trying to mend fences, because he asked for the south-side keys—he was actually going to help me lock my guys in, not just stand there and criticize. He had a hard time getting the brake closed—you had to know which doors tended to jump out and get in the way—but finally succeeded, a little bit winded.

Then, one of my gym porters appeared. The gym OIC had let him out, he explained, so that he could take a crap in his own cell. He was on some kind of medication for diarrhea. He locked on the row of cells that Blaine had just secured, and whether to let him in was entirely up to me.

"That okay, Conover?" the inmate asked.

"Have you already told him no?" I asked Blaine.

The officer shook his head.

"Then you can," I told the inmate, opening the same brake Blaine had so labored to close moments before. Blaine, despite my gesture of respect, gave me a look of pure disdain and with a laugh of disgust left the gallery. I felt I'd handled it just the right way.

Just a few minutes later, as I was regaining my composure, I noticed the smell of smoke, an acrid odor I couldn't quite place. And then heard Blaine's voice again. *What the hell,* I was thinking when I realized he and others were banging on my center gate—the red dots were responding to an emergency on the top floor. It turned out to be an inmate's bedding and mattress on fire. Saline, on U-and-Z, had seen smoke billowing out of a cell and, unsure if there was anyone inside, had pulled his pin on his way to the fire extinguisher. It turned out nobody was at risk. But the unsettling fumes that accompanied this kind of arson—which was usually started by a small Molotov cocktail, and almost always gang-related—persisted and unsettled me for a long time, nudging out the last possibility of a sentimental journey on this last day on the gallery.

And in fact the afternoon took the form of an ever-growing pile of aggravations. One of my keeplocks began shouting at me that lunch had never been brought to his cell. (On his wall he had posted a bit of dyslexic Christian cheer: "This is day the God made.") When I called the mess hall, they said I needed a request form from the OIC; when I called the new OIC, he said he didn't have one. An inmate on the other side—Addison, to whom I'd made the gift of cigarettes just a couple days before—was furious with me because when he'd declined breakfast, I'd deadlocked the door to his cell on his request (he was afraid of intruders) but had then forgotten to unlock it at lunch. Lacking any help, I had to escort him to the north gate personally and get the attention of officers on the mess-hall bridge. By the time I got back, half a dozen officers were waiting on my center gate—impatient, in a couple of cases, to the point of anger. Over the PA system, the OIC instructed me to pick up my phone, then asked why I hadn't heard it ringing: The Adjustment Committee was about to call me to do a disciplinary hearing over their speakerphone. (Officers often testified this way in absentia.)

Three inmates, W-3, W-10, and W-22, said they needed to go to the Emergency Room. Two keeplocks, R-55 and W-59, wanted to know what they were charged with; they claimed they'd never been issued a ticket. A new inmate arrived on W from the psych unit with one arm and no mattress—I'd have to make a few calls to straighten that one out. Another new inmate arrived on W and rightly observed that his cell was a mess. Though I was under no obligation to do so, I thought it would encourage the right habits to let him mop it out. This was a mistake. He turned the cleaning into a big production, making separate requests for the tiny bags of powdered soap we kept in the office, for a toilet brush, for garbage bags. He made a huge pile of his personal shit on the gallery that was hard to walk around. And each time I was about to call an end to the chaos, I got sidetracked by exigent cries of "R-and-W, center gate!"

In the meantime, the hot water was back, and the keeplocks were clamoring for their showers. One of them, Henderson, who was about my height but with seventy-five more pounds of muscle, told me I'd better get him in before I left or else.

"Don't be an asshole," I told him.

"What?" he said, surprised. Officers normally tried to avoid inflammatory talk like that, but I'd had it.

He challenged me with the line that had pushed Phelan to action on the flats. "You wouldn't talk like that if I weren't in the cell," he charged.

With memories of Phelan's bravado, and a giddy recklessness, I turned around, opened the cell door, and repeated myself with no intervening bars.

"Don't be an asshole, Henderson," I said. "It just slows me down."

I don't know what I was thinking. Henderson pushed the cell

door open and walked out past me. In that moment I could have jumped him. But I didn't want to start a fight and lose it. Pull my pin or call for help? It would be too embarrassing to have to describe how I'd arrived in this situation. Instead, I tried to reason with him.

"Listen, nobody's going to get a shower if you don't go back in."

"Just a second. I got to have a word with my friends," said Henderson, walking a few cells down.

"Hey," said an officer on the flats, who could see Henderson and knew he was supposed to be in his cell. Henderson looked over his shoulder and waved at the officer.

"Come on, give me a break," I pleaded with Henderson, humiliated. Three or four minutes later, he went back in.

There was still time, I thought, to try to get a couple of other keeplocks into the shower before my gym porters came back and demanded theirs. But no sooner had I unlocked one of the cells and turned the corner than a gym porter who shouldn't have been there tried to beat me to it. To my amazement, he actually tried to open the shower cell door as I held it closed. It was a total meltdown! We were in the middle of this little power struggle when another gallery officer appeared from downstairs and shifted the balance of power to my favor. I locked the porter in his cell, prefatory to keeplocking him, and tried to come to grips with the splitting headache that had crept up on me. Though I disliked the pushiness of my gym porters, the other officer counseled me that things would probably go more smoothly if I just announced that keeplock showers were dead and let the gym porters figure out for themselves who would shower in the remaining half hour of my shift.

I had just a few minutes to write my Misbehavior Report. The phone rang: a sergeant, telling me that members of the executive team might be making a spot inspection soon, and to let out my porters for a quick cleanup straightaway.

"Right, Sarge," I said, hanging up. I locked up the office and hustled down the gallery to see who was available.

"Conover!" called Larson, laughing, as I walked madly by. "Calm down! You're gonna have a heart attack!"

If it had been anyone else, he would only have succeeded in pissing me off. But in that moment, I finally got it. Fuck getting the porters out. Fuck writing up one last Misbehavior Report. Fuck the executive team. Given my lame-duck status, none of it really mattered.

I stopped, turned around. I took a deep breath and went back to Larson's cell, leaned against the bars. A problem I'd had from day one, I knew, was taking it all too seriously. Perfectionism was unattainable on a gallery in B-block. Getting yelled at now and then—whether by sergeants, other officers, or inmates—was just life, especially in Sing Sing.

For a minute I just stood there, incapable even of making conversation.

Larson passed over an old *National Geographic* that showed the architectural detailing of some ancient Mesoamerican temples. He was particularly interested in the inscriptions on the stelae.

"Look at those," he said.

"Yeah," I agreed, taking the magazine. "I'd like to see them. It would be cool to know what they meant."

"I'd like to touch them," said Larson.

I took more deep breaths, trying to calm myself.

"This is it for me today, Larson," I told him. "No more R-and-W. I'm leaving the service. I'll be back New Year's Eve, though, filling in on S-and-X."

"Is that right, Conover?" he asked. "What are you going to be doing? I mean, you got another job lined up?"

"You'll hear from me about that," I said.

"R-and-W, center gate!"

Back to work.

———

I closed out the logbook and just sat. Fifteen minutes into the evening shift, I still had not been relieved. Wouldn't that be perfect? I thought to myself. Stuck for overtime on my last day on the gallery . . . With a growing feeling of disgust at the prospect, I waited for the phone to ring, for Holmes or some other sergeant to give me the bad news.

Finally, half an hour late, an officer arrived—but, he was quick to explain, he wasn't my relief, only an OJT. Then another OJT. They couldn't run the gallery by themselves—they were useless! Five minutes later, another officer appeared. No, he told me, he wasn't an OJT. He had finished training three days before. And, yeah, this was his gallery tonight.

"How's your day been so far?" I asked him.

"Not so good," he answered.

"Well, it'll get worse," I assured him.

He hadn't even known to bring up a fresh radio battery with him from the OIC's office. He had no clue how to do anything on the gallery. I sent an OJT to fetch one. I explained how the keys worked, or didn't work—how some cells wouldn't open with the key that was supposed to open them, so you had to go try the other set . . . but then I saw how hopeless it was. The basic lesson was at least an hour long. And now the OIC was on the PA system, telling all gallery officers that inmates were on the go-back, and to open their end gates.

"Where's the end gate?" the officer asked.

"Your immediate problem," I answered, "is that all the cells are still on deadlock. You've got to get them off right away, while the gallery's still clear and you have some elbow room."

"Hey, thanks, man."

Thanks, sure, I thought sardonically. Unlocking all the cells was a five- to ten-minute procedure, and within a couple of minutes, returning inmates from R-and-W would be clogging the north-end stairs, creating a huge traffic jam for inmates headed higher as they waited at the gates. I could have been a great guy and stuck around to help with the impending chaos. But my head was about to split open.

Fuck it, I thought. And in the true, not-my-problem spirit of Sing Sing, I fled.

THE FIRES OF THE NEW YEAR

Something there is that doesn't love a wall, that wants it down.
—Robert Frost, "Mending Wall," 1914

Sing Sing at night felt like a catacomb. The parking lot and locker room were deserted. In the lineup room, the skeleton crew barely filled a single file. I recognized the B-block contingent from having relieved them on galleries or passed them in the tunnel on many mornings. There were only five of them.

"Nice way to spend New Year's Eve, huh?" said Greene, sarcastically. He was the R-and-W guy. I'd first tried to swap shifts with him, but he wasn't interested. Instead I'd swapped with Tracy Scott, just upstairs on S-and-X. My wife had to work tonight at her job, I'd told Tracy, so I'd decided I might as well, too. In fact, I'd been wondering whether the stories about B-block on New Year's Eve were true or exaggerated and wanted to find out first-hand.

Greene joked with me as we walked the tunnels to B-block. I was obviously a day-shift guy; he could tell by my baton. I looked around and realized that nobody else was wearing his.

"It's because no inmates are out at night—you'd never be standing next to one," he explained. "They only can leave their cells in an emergency, and in that case you've got to have a supervisor standing there."

The main duty of the shift, he reminded me, was just making sure that the inmates weren't dead. "If they're dead and hard, you're gone" was the way the white-shirts put it. Dead and warm, on the other hand, showed you were doing your job.

I'd had a recurring dream about Sing Sing that took place in this tunnel at night. In the dream, I was turning the corner that led to the B-block front gate. The way had been only faintly lit, but once I turned that corner I found myself in complete darkness. A light-bulb had burned out, I figured. I'd have to make it to the gate on intuition. In the silence, then, I realized I wasn't alone: There were inmates sprawled across the floor, sleeping. I toed my way tentatively forward, shuffling so as not to step on them. Reaching out for the wall to keep myself oriented, I touched an inmate's shirt and recoiled. Men were standing along the wall, too, I realized, on either side of a gate that had been inadvertently left ajar. I could make out vague outlines. Suddenly, instead of the guy in charge, I was the one at risk, and I tried to slip by silently, not even stirring the air.

I was surprised, in real life, by how dark the block was when we walked in around 11 P.M. All the main lights were off; only the center-stairway landings were illuminated. Besides this, scattered inmates had on the short fluorescent lights over their basins, so standing on the flats, looking up at all the galleries, reminded me of being on a dark street near some hulking apartment building where only a few tenants were still up.

But the lights didn't really tell who was awake. I was a bit taken aback when, at eleven-thirty, simultaneous whoops broke out from all over the building. The cue, I realized, must have been the in-house radio station, tuned to 97.1 FM ("Hot 97—blazing hip-hop and R&B"), probably part of the countdown to midnight. Behind all the dark and quiet was a certain electricity, an expectancy I wasn't used to feeling in B-block and didn't fully understand. What did New Year's Eve mean here?

I made my rounds. Greene had advised me not to shine my flashlight into inmates' faces while they slept but rather just to aim it at the ceiling or the floor. That would cast enough light over the cell to make sure the inmate hadn't hung up or slit his wrists. ("Just check for blood on the floor," the officer had advised.) I stood for a few moments in front of each cell, checking whether an inmate was breathing by the rise and fall of sheets and blankets. Some sleeping inmates had left their lights on. Some wakeful inmates had turned their lights off. I was disconcerted by the cells with lights still on and inmates standing up, because they were invariably backlit and I couldn't see their faces or what their hands were doing. Many of those awake were holding their mirrors out and chatting with their neighbors. I had to tell several to quiet down—there was supposed to be no talking at all at this hour.

Occasionally, I could eavesdrop. Turning the corner from S to X, I heard one inmate say to another wistfully, "Another year."

"Yeah, another year closer to goin' home, you heard?"

Unlike my friends, they weren't celebrating the arrival of the New Year so much, it seemed, as closing the book on the old.

The other officers seemed jumpy. I heard my office phone ringing as I finished my rounds at about 11:45 P.M. The sound was much more audible at night, I realized. The OIC downstairs told me to quiet down whoever it was that was speaking so loudly on X—a silly request, I thought, so close to midnight. Even so, I told her I'd go check on it. Then, as I walked away from the office to do so, the ringing phone summoned me back again.

It was her again. "And don't go out on the gallery after this," she warned.

"Okay, why not?" I asked, though I had a pretty good idea already.

"Just don't," she repeated. "You'll see, if you haven't already heard about it."

As I walked, I heard the big windows in the outer wall being cranked open by somebody downstairs. A cool breeze started blowing through the block on this winter night. Somebody was anticipating the events to come so that they wouldn't have to walk out on the flats again for a while.

The first fires started maybe ten minutes before midnight. I saw them flickering way down the gallery on either side of my office, one a pile of magazines, one maybe a roll of toilet paper. Turning the corner to X-gallery, I saw three more, one of them larger, like a small campfire, sending bits of burning embers flying into the dark space beyond the fence. Smoke was suddenly everywhere, like the air in a living room where someone forgets to open the flue before starting a fire.

I looked across the open space to the outer wall, which was now a wall of reflections. In its windows were a series of twinkling flames from floor to ceiling. Every gallery, apparently, was like mine. Then began a sixty-second countdown, with maybe a hundred voices jumping in by the end: ". . . nine, eight, seven, six, five, four, three, two, one." Then whoops and shouts pealed from every quarter, and howls and even a trombone blasting. Everyone rattled the gates and the block literally shook.

Meanwhile, down on the flats, three or four big fires were getting going. From small starter fires, inmates had been throwing out boxes and sheets of newspaper and Lord knows what else, trying to achieve the fuel density necessary for a real blaze. And in at least two spots, they were succeeding. Flames from these fires were leaping some five feet into the air, producing a lot of cheers.

The fire alarm went off. It was a bell that, given the block's acoustics, echoed loudly off everything and lent an aura of nightmare to the surreal scene. It sounded for about five minutes, and then, I guessed, was shut off manually. Less than a minute later, though, it began ringing again. One last time it was shut off, and then, apparently, the OIC gave up: The bell just rang and rang, unanswered, jangling my nerves and no doubt many others'. It put me in mind of those nuclear power plants where blasé technicians had grown so weary of false alarms that they'd begun to miss the real ones, with profound consequences.

Meanwhile, the block filled with smoke. This was not like the smoke from the mattress on U-and-Z a few days before but a thick, eye-burning, lung-choking smoke. The air moving through the windows—it was getting cold in the block—didn't seem to diminish it at all. Under the stairway lights, you could see the dark smoke billowing, moving by in clouds.

CO Greene came up the stairs from R-and-W to take a look at my gallery. "Got any marshmallows?" he asked with a grin.

I slipped down the stairs to look at his gallery; the picture was the same. I walked over to chat with Larson. He had a blanket pulled over his head, was apparently asleep, absenting himself from the whole affair.

Back to my gallery. Twelve-thirty now. The officer on T-and-Y came downstairs and sniffed around disapprovingly. He was an old-timer and apparently had thought of a way to assuage his own irritating feelings of loss of control.

"You should put these out and write them up!" he said sternly.

"Probably," I said. "But don't you have your own fires to worry about?"

"Mine are all out."

I looked at the windows on the outside wall, saw reflections of flickering flames just overhead. I pointed. "I don't think so," I said.

He left. It was hard to know how seriously to take the fires. The contents of individual cells could burn, and wood in the catwalk area between the galleries could burn, but not the block as a whole. I didn't know about the roof. Smoke inhalation was a concern, but with the windows open there was some air circulation. Just to have something to do, I got out a fire extinguisher and blasted the smoldering toilet roll nearest the office. It didn't put out the flames, just sent it spinning down the gallery. Inmates nearby immediately complained about the smoke. I walked down and tried to stamp it out with my boots, but it smoldered all the more.

"Tough luck," I said over their complaints.

I passed another fire on my way back to the office. The inmate who had probably set it appeared to be having second thoughts. He was trying to seal off the front of his cell by hanging plastic bags and blankets all over the bars—the smoke was that dense.

I sat in the office chair and closed my eyes, trying to get some of the smoke sting out. The phone rang. It was an officer outside the locked front gate of the block, wondering why nobody was answering the bell. He said he'd been standing there for fifteen minutes.

"I think it's the same bell the fire alarm uses," I told him. "As you can probably hear, the fire alarm bell is ringing." I told him I'd go downstairs and let him in myself.

"Christ," he shouted, stepping into the block and standing a little too close to the bell. We looked in both directions down the flats. The fires were as high as our heads. The sight, I thought, would give Sergeant Bloom a heart attack. "B-block's out of its mind. I just came from A-block, and there's no fires at all over there."

"It's because it's so young here," said the OIC, whose nerves seemed frayed.

I thought about the day I'd been helping another officer search a cell on Q-south. We'd taken an inmate's junk outside his cell, piled it on the flats, and were searching the remaining contents one piece at a time. Unbeknownst to us, an inmate from some nearby cell—we never found out which one—was tossing lighted matches at the heap. Maybe he hated us, maybe he hated that inmate, maybe he didn't know what he hated, but eventually the pile caught fire. We felt the heat from a sudden inferno on our backs and leaped out of the cell. Dragging corners of things that weren't yet alight, we pulled the bonfire apart. It took a long time to burn out. Tonight's would take longer.

"Guess they just need to let off some steam," said Greene with a grin as we stood on R-and-W, still gazing at all the little fires as the clock approached 1 A.M. 1998.

"Huh," I said. That explanation seemed a bit thin. I thought about the photograph I'd stood next to in the basement hallway of the Academy countless times as we waited for chow, entitled something like *Smoldering Ruins of Auburn Prison*. There had been a massive riot there in 1929. I thought about my anger and frustration after I'd been slugged in A-block, my fantasy of the building and all its contents going up in flames. An incident later in B-block had called my bluff: I'd discovered a fire in the service area that ran down the center of the block; welders upstairs had unwittingly ignited a length of PVC pipe. When I'd blasted it with water from the fire extinguisher, the burning plastic had simply scattered and the fire spread, and for a moment I'd been terrified—the service area was full of old wood. The thing had finally gone out by itself, but not before an image of a stable full of burning horses had flashed through my mind.

Above all, though, I thought about the inmate I had spoken to on R-and-W who had explained to me the essential difference between the slave who worked in the field and the slave who worked in the house: The former, he said, wasn't sad when the house burned down.

In fact, I thought, the slave who worked in the field, in a certain frame of mind, might even be happy to see the house burn down. I only wondered how bad things would have to get before he could see it burning down with himself inside.

It's now three years since I last walked out of Sing Sing, and seven months since *Newjack* came out in hardcover. Many readers have asked me what happened since I quit: How did the state respond to my book? What were the reactions of my fellow officers? How did the experience change my life? And many people want to know what we should do about what can fairly be called our prison problem.

Predictably, the New York Department of Correctional Services (DOCS) was not happy about *Newjack*. By getting hired as a CO I effectively circumvented their prohibition on visiting the training academy and the prisons. A couple of months before publication, I called Charles Greiner, who was still the superintendent of Sing Sing, and told him about my project. I thought he might already have heard—I'd started telling officer friends—and I expected stony silence. But he appeared to know nothing of it, and listened long and carefully with what seemed to me great interest. He asked only whether I thought I'd gotten everything right, and I told him I'd done my best. There was no anger in his response; he said he looked forward to reading it.

But, by the time *The New Yorker* called DOCS to fact check a story I adapted for them from *Newjack*, word had spread. "He didn't ask us for help with his book and so we're not going to help him check his facts," a spokesman snapped at the researcher, perhaps unaware that I *had* asked for help back in 1994, but was turned down. That attitude was a sign of things to come. Soon after *Newjack* was published, I learned that it had been declared contraband: New York State officers were not allowed to bring it into prisons, and inmates who received copies in the mail or through visit rooms had them confiscated. An acquaintance of mine who went to Sing Sing on an official visit had to leave his copy at the gate.

Thinking maybe Albany was unnecessarily equating me with the devil, I sent a signed copy to the commissioner of corrections, which he acknowledged with a curt note; I never heard from him again. An official from another state would later tell me he was with the commissioner at a corrections conference and sat next to him as he read it near the swimming pool, moaning. A spokesman for DOCS, however, insisted later that neither he nor the commissioner would bother to read the book. "Who cares?" he said to a reporter for the *Albany Times Union*. "Why would I be interested in the view of a newjack?"

Three months after the book came out, DOCS decided that inmates *could* see *Newjack* after all—after their copies had been censored. In other words, any inmate who received *Newjack* had to surrender it immediately, on penalty of receiving a ticket for contraband. The prison would then forward the book to Albany, where somebody would physically tear out six pages that, according to officials, were "a potential source of injury or conflict among violent and predatory offenders within our system." The press release wouldn't say exactly which pages they were, but said they had to do with "issues of deployment of chemical agents, use of pressure points and holds taught to Officers to control inmates, control of emergency equipment in the event of a potential staff hostage situation, descriptions of Officer actions and duties during a mass incident, escape procedures, the effective range and use of certain firearms, and the local issue of descriptions of security issues in Sing Sing yards." Mainly Academy stuff, in other words, along with what to do during a red dot emergency and the ways in which officers were made vulnerable by the antiquated configurations of Sing Sing's exercise yards.*

Were these legitimate security concerns? I don't believe so. Riots have almost always been the result of poor prison administration or operation, not inmate knowledge of our top secret aikido grips. I had thought carefully about whether anything in *Newjack* could conceivably endanger my fellow officers before I included it in the book, and no officer has yet complained to me about those revelations. Indeed, when this was all playing out in the summer of 2000, *The New York Times* quoted an official of the correction officers' union as saying, "We have no problem with the book. What he did was admirable." No other prison system I know of limits inmate access to *Newjack*.

The atmosphere of controversy did give me some trepidation about a reading I was scheduled to give at the Ossining Public Li-

*I have since learned that the redacted pages are 39–40, 49–50, 51–52, 81–82, 277–278, and 279–280.

brary in June of 2000. Of the half dozen officers whom I had told about the book prior to publication, none had seemed angry or concerned, but I knew that *Newjack* wouldn't please everybody. I worried that an appearance in Ossining might present some malcontent with an opportunity to come after me.

The library is about a mile from Sing Sing, and twenty minutes before the reading, the room was already packed. One hundred and twenty folding chairs were taken, and the forty or so people standing near the entrance were told to move near the podium and sit on the floor. I squeezed through the mob, noting the crew from C-SPAN's *Book TV* and then the fact that the front rows of chairs were filled mainly with gray uniforms. As she clipped on my microphone, the head librarian told me that some of the officers had arrived two hours early. She added that the local policemen had been invited simply as a precaution.

"What local policemen?"

"You didn't see them? They're out front." Somebody from Sing Sing had called the week before, she explained, and "frightened our reference librarian" by telling her that "some people" at the prison were angry about the book and "might cause trouble" at the event. I had a sense of foreboding much like the one that had suffused so many of my days at Sing Sing—a feeling of imminent confrontation, of badness just ahead. But if there was one thing I had learned inside prison, it was how to repress fear. I clipped on a microphone and stepped to the lectern.

I've never enjoyed giving formal speeches, and so I spoke without notes about why I did the book: how prisons have gotten too numerous to ignore, how officers are so stunningly stereotyped, how the state has unfairly reserved the right to keep prison operation away from public scrutiny, how there's no substitute for understanding a life like living it yourself, and how secrecy is a last resort for researching a story, but how once in a while, circumstances demand it. As I spoke I tried to read the faces of the officers and others in the room, scanning them for sympathy or anger or derangement. I saw glimpses of many reactions, but could draw no conclusions.

The range of questions asked after my talk was similarly inconclusive: there was the anti-prison activist who launched into a speech that I had to cut short, the tall bureaucrat (I guessed) who gruffly asked whether I'd announced my intentions to my coworkers, the woman interested in how my family handled the

experience, the black man who wanted to know about white su
premacists in the system (I took him to be asking about inmates,
but it turned out he wanted to know about officers).

Disconcertingly, people were seated all around me, and some of
the questions came from behind; a television sound man waded
carefully among those on the floor. The overcrowding lent a sense
of chaos and volatility. I took a last question, received applause,
and prepared to sign books at a table to my left. My wife, Margot,
who knew nothing about the threat received by the librarian,
stopped me as I was about to sit down. "I don't like the feel of
this," she said, clearly rattled.

In the absence of an open space to form a line, people pressed in
on me all around the bookseller's table. At one point I stopped
looking up to see where the book in front of me had come from; I
simply said to the arm that put it there, "Would you like me to sign
this to you?"

"Sign it to Perlstein," a deep voice growled.

"Uh, Perlstein," I said absently. "How do you spell that?"

"You should know," came the reply. I looked up, followed the
arm to the bicep and then finally to the face of . . . "Perlstein,"
the huge white man who worked in the Special Housing Unit, or
the Box, with Sing Sing's worst inmates. He had raked his baton
down my shin during my training there to demonstrate its power
to inflict pain. In *Newjack* I had given him that pseudonym and
described him as a "shaved-headed monster."

Which still fit. Perlstein looked, if anything, even larger than I
remembered him; his skull was shinier, his eyes smaller. But here,
in a library and in his civvies, he wasn't so frightening, was somehow . . . denatured. And then as the crowd shifted I noticed that *in
his other arm he held a little girl.* Perlstein was a parent! I couldn't
think of a thing to say, except, "So, uh, did you like the book?"

"It was all right."

Officers I didn't know asked me to sign their books, too. A
couple of them referred to the menacing sergeant whom I had also
given a pseudonym. "Hey, Sergeant Wickersham is waiting for you
outside," said one. "He's greasin' his baton. He's gonna drop a
quarter, then tell you to bend over and pick it up."

CO humor.

Nurses from the prison's emergency room came by, as well as
the prison's "recreation director" and a bevy of sweet older ladies

from town. Half an hour later, the only people left were my wife and I—and about a dozen officers.

Three of them took out cameras. They wanted their pictures taken with me. They wanted their pictures taken with Margot. I knew a few of them: Aragon, Loachamin, McCall. . . . I was finally daring to believe that this was a good thing, that danger did not lurk. As she folded up chairs, the librarian said she'd heard the town policemen had enjoyed my presentation.

"Security? What'd they need security for?" CO McCall asked ingenuously. He gestured at the gathered officers. "They got all the security they need right here!"

Aragon had both a Polaroid and a regular camera, and he gave me a print of us shaking hands. I had portrayed him on the first page of *Newjack* as a guy who was a bit lock-obsessed: he put The Club on his car even though it was parked right beneath a wall tower and had affixed a tiny hasp on his lunch box to keep out pilfering officers.

"So you're not sore at me?" I asked him.

"Naaa." If anything, he seemed apologetic. "I have a different lunch box now that doesn't have a lock on it."

For all the time I spent in an officer's uniform, one poignant reality of the life had only begun to sink in, and that was the depth of the stigma they felt, the pain of society's disregard. The antidote was recognition and an appreciation of the job's unique difficulties. This *Newjack* seemed to provide—"I saw you on TV, you told it like it is, man!" said an officer I'd never met—and in light of that recognition, it appeared that many things could be forgiven.

This was the first book I've written since the advent of e-mail, and more than 300 officers and their family members have sent me feedback in these eight months since publication, almost all of it enthusiastic. Among them were Vinny Nigro, my jolly trainer, who wrote, "Thanx for my 15 minutes and the history." A fellow newjack who bought *Newjack* the week it came out wrote, "It's about time the public finds out about us. You tell the true story. Reading your book was like reading about myself." Mendola, Goldman, Scarff, DiPaola, Smith, Saline, and others have all been in touch; I even had a spirited exchange with a writer who finally admitted to being Sergeant Wickersham's sister and felt I'd been unfair to him. The biggest surprise has been the number of responses from officers' spouses, many of whom say things like, "I didn't really know what my husband did at work until I read your book." The occasional dissenter accuses me of betraying my fellow officers and being a rat, asserting that "what goes on in corrections should stay in corrections." Since I hope *Newjack* constitutes an argument against that sort of thinking, I don't imagine I'll ever win those people over.

The response from inmates is coming in more slowly. Almost none of the ones I described in detail are still at Sing Sing. Larson wrote me that he's doing a long term in the Box at a prison upstate; he hasn't written back since I mailed him the book, which probably means the state is taking its time tearing the pages out. Delacruz was transferred to a new prison soon after I mailed him a copy, and I have no idea when it will catch up to him. Sadly, I was told that Elliot Markowitz, whose poetry I quote in Chapter 7, is now in the state mental hospital in Marcy, New York, and not allowed to receive books. A woman who is involved with a Sing Sing inmate got an early copy to him through the visit room and told me it was being passed around enthusiastically. When people ask me if DOCS has changed anything as a result of my book, I share the tidbit that he told her: soon after publication, the inmate said, the filthy windows in B-block were washed for the first time in memory.

Maybe that's DOCS' idea of reform.

———

I've traveled across the country doing interviews about my experience, and the surprising thing—compared to other book publicity I've done—is that I don't get tired of it. One reason is the long time I had to keep the experience a secret. Any ordeal benefits from being talked about, and I was denied that by the route I chose. Writing the book was sometimes therapeutic in the same way, though just as often the prospect of sitting down at my desk on a sunny morning and mentally transporting myself back to Sing Sing for the day was painful.

I had dreams about Sing Sing while I was there and since, though oddly I never had nightmares until the book was published and I was talking about it every day. These really bad dreams have usually involved scenarios in which I—and sometimes my family—get attacked by inmates or other criminals, usually with a knife. I happened to recount this to a group of medical professionals at a convention of the American Public Health

Association, and a psychiatrist suggested it was probably post-traumatic stress disorder. That seems like rather a grand name for it, and I don't want to suggest that I went through anything like what soldiers who saw combat in Vietnam did. But I do think that if you repress something regularly (in my case, fear), it's going to come back to haunt you.

My wife, Margot, is of course asked all the time how she put up with me working at prison, how the household endured it. I'm proud of her generous answer, which is that thousands of people married to correction officers do the same thing every day, often for years at a time, and she only had to put up with months. I try to keep my own experience in the same perspective.

In radio and television interviews, many of the same questions come up again and again. For a while last summer, I thought I'd heard them all, the natural questions of someone who hadn't read the book. ("Why would you do a thing like that? Is there a lot of rape in there? Are many of the guards really brutal?") But then I was interviewed over the phone from Detroit by Mitch Albom, who wrote the book *Tuesdays with Morrie*. His third question, which seemed simple, caught me off guard: How did you feel on your last day? "I felt great," I began almost reflexively, but then paused—there were complicated feelings there that I hadn't examined—and finished, "but maybe also a bit sad."

In the weeks since, I've thought about that question a lot. My last visit to Sing Sing was not the New Year's Eve described in the epilogue; it was the day, about a week later, when I drove back up to Ossining to turn in my badge and I.D. and uniforms. My mood was bright as I entered the prison wearing blue jeans for the first time ever, uniforms on hangers slung over my shoulder. Near the gate was a young Latino officer from the Bronx whom I had helped train and whom I liked.

"Hey, where you going?" he asked me, uncomprehending, as I headed up the stairs to the personnel office. The answer was obvious, of course, but I could see he was surprised. He told me he'd learned more working with me than with several veteran officers who hadn't taken much time with him. I'd been part of his induction, his *teacher*, for chrissakes—and here I was, bailing? The look on his face reminded me of the look on the face of the inmate I'd taken to the ER when he thought he had a cockroach in his ear. "Where are you going?" the inmate had asked when he saw me on the gate at the end of my shift. Back home, was the answer, back to my life. And yet, and yet—work in so many ways *becomes* our lives. Here I was so needed, and there was so much to be done.

My step was lighter as I returned to the car where my wife was waiting. But I felt an unmistakable regret. It was as though I'd spent a year as an exchange student in some chaotic Third World backwater, I'd tell a friend later. I'd been there long enough to learn some of the exotic language, survive some of its brutal customs, become fond of many of the locals—and now I'd never be back, would never need that hard-won knowledge again. And so I felt strangely wistful. It was a realization, a passage, that probably would have found a way into the original *Newjack* if I'd had it sooner.

———

Some readers will leave this book wondering what we should do about our prisons. We pay billions of dollars a year in this country to run institutions that few would argue leave the people who go through them—inmates and officers alike—worse off in many ways than they were when they went in. It is a huge problem, but there are a few simple changes that I think would make a great difference.

First, states need to repeal mandatory sentencing laws for drug offenses. Prisons should be for violent criminals, not mainly poor men from rough neighborhoods who get caught selling or using drugs. I think that most prison time for drug possession does more harm—to families as well as to offenders—than good. New York and California are just beginning to give first-time drug offenders treatment instead of prison sentences, and that's a positive development.

Second, studies have shown again and again that nothing lowers recidivism rates like education. Refusing to consider postsecondary education as a frontline attack on crime is a terrible mistake. Prisons should start teaching again, and with officers justly resentful at inmates being offered for free what ordinary citizens have to pay for, it makes sense to me that officers should be allowed to take part in these same classes, off duty.

Along these same lines, I think we should take the lead of European countries in trying to blur the sharp line that exists in our prisons between guards and other employees. The term "correction officer" is imbued with the promise of reform and assistance. I think it would help to rehabilitate prisons themselves if officers taught some of the classes, did some of the counseling, were allowed to engage their own hearts and minds on the job, instead of just having to pretend they don't have any.

A researcher I admire, Kelsey Kauffman, has written that "prisons are perhaps the most racially divisive institutions in America today." I think she makes a good case. Prisons in our country sow a lot of racial hatred, both inmate-to-inmate and between inmate and officer. And almost everyone in prison eventually comes out, spreading this hatred. We should work hard to improve the prisons in our society—take up the unfinished work of Thomas Mott Osborne and transform these scrap heaps into repair shops, to paraphrase the great reformer. Not all inmates can be helped, but some can, and it's foolish to let them languish. And, because prisons are the unhappy symptom of our violent and grossly unequal society, we should recall the words of inmate Larson: stop planning for the incarceration needs of today's children, and instead begin reducing their poverty and increasing their opportunity. It's now 175 years since Sing Sing was built—way past time we tried some new ideas.

Ten years after its first publication, *Newjack* is still very much alive for me. I give frequent talks about it and readings from it, and hear every week from readers who have discovered the book for the first time, or read it for the second or third.

I was torn, in the months following publication, over the question of whether to write another book about prison. It was a reflection, I think, of the same ambivalence I felt as I left Sing Sing for the last time. *Good riddance!* said one part of me, while another part countered, *Wait—after all you've learned here, and all that remains to be done?* For a time I pursued some stories around extreme punishment and around the idea of parole and prisoner re-entry into the community. But nothing coalesced into a book.

Then came the morning of September 11, 2001, which began for me with an appointment for my daughter at an eye doctor in Manhattan. As we drove home toward the Bronx, I wondered why there was no inbound traffic on the highway – I imagined there was a big accident ahead, with southbound cars somehow blocked. Not until I reached the northern tip of Manhattan did I see that police weren't letting any more traffic over the bridge and realized that in fact, the big accident was in my rearview mirror, beneath the plume of smoke down at Manhattan's southern end.

From that morning, the American prison story took an interesting turn. My country began its "war on terror," with surprising developments. America's prisons, it turned out, were headed overseas. Harsh incarceration was key to the American military response to 9/11, most notably in the prison camp at the US naval base at Guantánamo Bay, Cuba, but also in places with other names that would become widely known, and not in a good way: the Iraqi prison at Abu Ghraib where leaked photos showed American soldiers abusing Iraqi prisoners; the prison at Bagram, Afghanistan, plagued by escape and attacks and two incidents of prisoners being murdered; and the network of black site prisons to which the CIA spirited high-level "unlawful enemy combatants" under its "extraordinary rendition" program, which remains cloaked in secrecy.

The specialized knowledge which I gained at Sing Sing suddenly appeared to have broader applicability. At a time when very few journalists had been allowed to visit Guantánamo, the *New York Times Magazine* sent to me see its Camp Delta. This was the second prison camp on the base. Camp X-Ray, which received the first prisoners, was mostly tents, but Camp Delta had more of an air of permanence: the mini-cell blocks were modified shipping containers, with windows and doors cut out and yellow arrows spray-painted on the floor pointing to Mecca. At the last minute a reporter for National Public Radio and I were shown something the outside world didn't even know about: a separate facility for "juvenile enemy combatants". In other words, some of the prisoners at Guantánamo were not even 18. Among the three young men detained in the special unit was a 15-year-old Canadian citizen who has since been convicted in a military court of killing an American soldier with a grenade in Afghanistan.

Military handlers were with me practically every second, and at pains to limit what I saw and heard. But happily, I discovered that many of the people who actually ran Guantánamo worked in corrections and police departments in the United States – they were National Guard reservists seconded to Gitmo for stints of a few months at a time. The camp superintendent ran his own prison in Illinois. Several had heard of *Newjack,* and the experiences we had in common gave us things to chat about when I got to sit with them in the mess tent or tour their housing and the cellblocks. The visit helped me to understand that with Guantántamo and other prisons that kept inmates in extreme isolation, the American military was in effect exporting the American practice of supermax incarceration.

I had an unfruitful conversation with Captain James Yee, the Muslim chaplain (and West Point graduate) who would be accused (but later exonerated) of spiriting classified information out of camp on his laptop computer. And I spoke at length with Major General Geoffrey Miller, whom President George W. Bush had appointed to oversee the operation. The mechanism by which our prison practice was exported grew clear for me when I read, a few months later, that the person in charge of Iraq's Abu Ghraib, during the time that its operations sullied our reputation around the world, was none other than the same Major General Geoffrey Miller. He'd been sent there after doing a good job at Guantánamo.

I wrote about Guantánamo for the *New York Times Magazine* and about Abu Ghraib for the *New York Times*. But I have not yet written another prison book. My most recent book, *The Routes of Man*, is, on the contrary, about roads, and the kinds of difference they make in various countries around the world. The book had many inspirations, but one of them, I am quite sure, was the afternoon Sergeant Holmes assigned me to transportation detail. On that day, you'll recall, another officer and I took a prison van and drove a young gang member who had been involved in a brawl to another prison upstate, and brought a different inmate back to Sing Sing with us. When we stopped for fast food on the highway, I chatted with the new guy. He was staring at all the big semi-trailer rigs parked nearby. "That's what I want to do when my bid's done," he murmured, "drive one of those things."

As an officer, I wrote in my journal, "It made all the sense in the world to me." And I wasn't just saying it: working in a prison made me want to *move*, to cross a lot of space, to be on the road. And, since I wasn't a prisoner, that was pretty much the first thing I did after I turned in my badge.

———

My life, in other words, has moved on. The son who I described playing with Lego after I returned home from work one day is in now in high school, and will soon take his college entrance exams. The daughter who was an infant in her crib is very much a teenager, and taller than her mother.

Recently, a student emailed me on behalf of her class asking whether there was any part of *Newjack* that I wish in retrospect that I had omitted. I pondered the question for a while and then replied that no, there was not ... but there were a couple of things I wished I could have added.

One was an incident regarding the prisoner I call Larson. Larson, you'll remember, was a thoughtful, well-read man whom some inmates seemed to regard as a seer, and with whom I discussed anthropology. The story I couldn't find a place for in the book begins on a day I attended a fancy wedding after work. I'd brought a suit to Sing Sing and left it in my car; after work I changed into it stealthily, so nobody would ask questions. I was headed to wealthy, northern Westchester County, and friends of my wife whose lives had minimal intersections with a place like Sing Sing. At the wedding I had a great time. I didn't get home until two in the morning, and then had to get up at 5 A.M. for work. As I walked down the gallery, bleary-eyed and headachey, taking cells off deadlock, Larson was evidently watching me with his mirror. As I drew even with his cell he called out, "Hey, Conover!"

"Morning, Larson."

"Let me ask you a question."

"Okay."

"How come you're walking like you should be wearing a tuxedo today?"

I think my heart skipped a beat. Naturally, I told him I didn't know what he was talking about.

The other tale, which came together too late to make the original Afterword, has to do with an older inmate named Warith al Habib (his pre-Muslim name was Vincent Jenkins). He had been shot in the Attica riot and still had a bullet in his hip. It had caused some arthritis, which was just one reason he was irascible and hard to get along with, sometimes yelling at me like a crazy homeless person ("ID card? You want to see my ID card? Why don't you just ask for my transit pass, officer, and call it what it is: apartheid! This is South Africa, and you're trying to keep me in the bantustan!"). Another reason he was angry, according to him, was that he'd been falsely convicted of his latest crime, and done five years for nothing, with a couple more to go. He'd been convicted of rape. That was probably pretty unusual for a man in his mid-60s, but I didn't doubt it – inmates were always insisting to me that they were innocent.

Anyway, I went to visit Habib after we'd both left Sing Sing – I to write my book and he to a prison with a geriatric unit. Once again, he brought up his innocence and told me that his lawyer was working with Barry Scheck, an attorney famous for exonerating inmates through the use of DNA evidence. Scheck and his other lawyer, Eleanor Piel, were going to get him out any day now. Yeah, yeah, I remember saying. But what else is new with you?

Fast forward about six months to a hot summer night. I was watching the local newscast from bed. The exterior of a forbidding prison filled the screen and the news anchor said that today Barry Scheck and the Innocence Project had freed another prisoner on DNA evidence ... and cut to video of Habib walking out of prison with Scheck. I was truly shocked, and the implications took a while to sink in: not only had I disbelieved him, but I'd been part of his wrongful incarceration. That's something I imagine I'll never forget. Exoneration-by-DNA has shaken the criminal justice system to its roots over the past ten years, injecting a needed note of uncertainty into the correctional enterprise.

———

Sing Sing, in short, remains a part of me even though I've left my job behind. It was a personal proving ground of sorts: *could I survive in there?* And in a larger sense, as I've written, it was a dark window into the failures of society. Finally, though, I remember it as a collection of people, one group who failed an important set of measurements, and another group charged with looking after them. I spent a piece of my life with these people and find myself thinking back mostly fondly, even to some of the awful ones. The good and the bad, I see myself in them all.

Chapter 1: Inside Passage

9. **It plainly derives:** Norman Johnston, *The Human Cage: A Brief History of Prison Architecture,* p. 40.

Chapter 2: School for Jailers

15. **an annual budget of $1.6 billion:** According to Robert Gangi, executive director of the Correctional Association of New York, the DOCS budget figures do not include the cost of pensions and other benefits; a more accurate figure, as of 2000, would be $2.3 billion. (Personal communication, 21 January 2000).

19. **California, where prisons are already at double capacity:** Eric Schlosser, "The Prison-Industrial Complex," *The Atlantic Monthly,* December 1998, p. 52.

19. **Since the dismantling of apartheid:** Comparisons of international rates of incarceration are periodically published by The Sentencing Project, 1516 P Street, NW, Washington, D.C. 20005.

19. **By mid-1998:** Allen J. Beck and Christopher J. Mumola, "Prisoners in 1998," Bureau of Justice Statistics, U.S. Department of Justice, 810 Seventh Street, NW, Washington, D.C. 20531.

19. **In the 1990s:** The Sentencing Project and *New York Times* editorial, 13 March 1999.

20. **highest rates of divorce:** I was unable to independently verify Puma's claims.

41. **Concomitant with the rise of imprisonment:** *The Corrections Yearbook 1982,* Pound Ridge, N.Y.: Criminal Justice Institute, 1983, p. 33, and *The Corrections Yearbook 1988,* Middletown, Conn.: Criminal Justice Institute, 1999, p. 133.

50. **It reminded me of Philip Zimbardo's famous experiment:** C. Haney, C. Banks, and P. Zimbardo, "Interpersonal dynamics in a simulated prison," *International Journal of Criminology and Penology,* 1973, pp. 69–97.

50. **Zimbardo has since accepted some criticism:** "Zimbardo's Prison—Renowned professor calls 1970s prison experiment unethical," *The Stanford Daily Online,* 14 May 1996.

54. **He pointed out, entirely correctly:** *The Green Mile,* a movie starring Tom Hanks that was released in 1999 after my period of prison employment, broke new ground by portraying at least one prison guard as humane and beset by moral dilemmas.

57. **In 1995, the average two-bedroom rental:** *The New York Times,* 28 December 1995, p. B1.

Chapter 5: Scrap Heap

171. **The prison's most famous warden:** Lewis E. Lawes, *Twenty Thousand Years in Sing Sing,* p. 239.

172. **without a place to receive:** *Report of the agent of the Mount-Pleasant State Prison, relative to the government and discipline of that prison.* New York State Senate, 14 March 1834, p. 8.

172. **The inmates and their keepers:** "Keepers," in the terminology of the time, were the staff members in direct charge of prisoners; "guards," usually armed, patrolled a prison's perimeter.

172. **As James S. Kunen has written:** "Teaching Prisoners a Lesson," *The New Yorker,* 10 July 1995, p. 35.

172. **In England:** Amos O. Squire, M.D., *Sing Sing Doctor,* p. 260.

173. **The period between:** Michel Foucault, *Discipline and Punish: The Birth of the Prison,* pp. 7–8.

173. **Auburn Prison, meanwhile:** "These Are Your N.Y. State Correctional Facilities: 7. Auburn Prison, Part I," in *Correction,* a monthly publication of the New York State Department of Correction, Vol. XIV, No. VI (May 1949), pp. 7–8.

173. **From this experiment:** *Report of the agent . . .* p. 6.

175. **Their first sight:** George Wilson Pierson, *Tocqueville in America,* p. 100.

175. **they labour assiduously:** Ibid., p. 101.

175. **All strength is born:** Ibid., p. 101.

175. **Tocqueville and Beaumont heard a story:** Ibid., p. 99. Also see Gustave de Beaumont and Alexis de Toqueville [*sic*], *On the Penitentiary System in the United States and Its Application to France,* p. 203, note.

175. **The practical art:** Gustave de Beaumont and Alexis de Toqueville [*sic*], *On the Penitentiary System in the United States and Its Application to France,* p. 203.

176. **We have seen 250 prisoners:** quoted in George Wilson Pierson, *Tocqueville in America,* pp. 101–102.

176. **One cannot see:** Ibid., pp. 102–103.

176. **whilst society in the United States:** Gustave de Beaumont and Alexis de Toqueville [*sic*], *On the Penitentiary System in the United States and Its Application to France*, p. 47.

176. **I am completely convinced:** quoted in J. P. Mayer, *Alexis de Tocqueville: Journey to America*, New Haven: Yale University Press, 1960, p. 25.

177. **Two iron rings:** James R. Brice, *Secrets of the Mount-Pleasant State Prison, Revealed and Exposed: An Account of the Unjust Proceedings Against James R. Brice, Esq., by which he was convicted of the Crime of Perjury, Accompanied by Affidavits to Prove His Innocency: Also an account of the Inhuman Treatment of Prisoners by some of the Keepers; and an authentic statement of the officers and salaries, with other curious matters before unknown to the public*, p. 32.

177. **Levi Burr, an inmate imprisoned for perjury:** Levi S. Burr, *A Voice From Sing Sing, giving a general description of the state prison, a short and comprehensive geological history of the Quality of the Stone of the Quarries; and a synopsis of the Horrid Treatment of the Convicts in That Prison*, pp. 17–18.

178. **More than a hundred blows:** *Report of the Select Committee* [to examine prisons] *of the* [New York State] *Assembly of 1851 . . . transmitted to the legislature, Jan. 7, 1852*, p. 26.

178. **Bank robber Willie Sutton:** Willie Sutton, with Quentin Reynolds. *I, Willie Sutton*. New York: Farrar, Straus and Young, 1953, p. 92.

178. **There are daily:** Levi S. Burr, *A Voice From Sing Sing, giving a general description of the state prison, a short and comprehensive geological history of the Quality of the Stone of the Quarries; and a synopsis of the Horrid Treatment of the Convicts in That Prison*, p. 44.

179. **Several men grab a chain:** Ibid., p. 30.

179. **A report from 1839:** These extracts of the 1839 report are reprinted in *Annual Report of the Inspectors of the Mount Pleasant State Prison*, January 6, 1848, pp. 8–11; italics original.

180. **The local coroner:** "These Are Your N.Y. State Correctional Facilities: 7. Auburn Prison, Part II," in *Correction*, a monthly publication of the New York State Department of Correction, Vol. XIV, No. VI (June 1949), p. 4.

180. **His rule was never to forgive:** letter to General Aaron Ward from John W. Edmonds, "one of the inspectors of the State Prison at Sing Sing," 1844, in SLT pamphlet volume 19, p. 7, New York Public Library.

180. **there is evidence:** letter from Assistant Keeper Requa in SLT pamphlet volume 19, New York Public Library.

181. **[the cat-o'-nine-tails]:** letter from Blanchard Fosgate, M.D., to

members of a legislative committee "to inquire into the financial affairs, discipline, and the general management of the different prisons," included in *Report of the Select Committee of the* [New York State] *Assembly of 1851*, p. 74.

181. **I think that not one man:** included in *Report of the Select Committee of the* [New York State] *assembly of 1851*, p. 225.

182. **cut off the fingers of one hand:** Ibid., pp. 227–228.

182. **Auburn physician Blanchard Fosgate:** Ibid., pp. 70–71.

183. **the first social worker:** Roger Panetta, professor of history at Marymount College, interviewed on C-Span special, "Tocqueville Town Meeting: Penal System," June 6, 1997.

183. **much more depends:** John Luckey, *Life in Sing Sing State Prison,* p. 17.

184. **A big business enterprise:** *New York Herald Sunday Magazine,* 14 December 1919, p. 2.

184. **James Brice:** James R. Brice, *Secrets of the Mount-Pleasant State Prison,* pp. 65–66.

185. **In Buffalo in 1881:** James E. Penrose, "Inventing Electrocution," *American Heritage of Invention and Technology,* Vol. 9, No. 4 (Spring 1994), p. 36.

185. **Roxalana "Roxie" Druse:** *The New York Times,* 28 February 1887, p. 2.

186. **The hanging did not go well:** *The New York Times,* 1 March 1887, p. 2.

186. **Worried by the plans:** James E. Penrose, "Inventing Electrocution," p. 40.

187. **Public excitement:** *The New York Times,* 7 August 1890, p. 2, and Th. Metzger, *Blood and Volts,* pp. 151 ff.

188. **At the following execution:** Th. Metzger, *Blood and Volts,* p. 171.

188. **Experimentation continued:** Ibid., pp. 171–173.

189. **the method of execution:** "These Are Your N.Y. State Correctional Facilities: 8. Sing Sing Prison, Part II," in *Correction,* a publication of the New York State Department of Correction, Vol. XIV, No. VIII (August–September 1949), p. 16.

189. **In New York and New Jersey:** Squire, *Sing Sing Doctor,* p. 201.

190. **He describes Hulbert:** Ibid., pp. 201–202.

190. **Shortly before the time:** Ibid., p. 203.

191. **According to the 1929 obituary:** *Ossining Citizen Sentinel,* 23 February 1929.

191. **Next, he sat with the condemned:** The hand signal, given on the ex-

hale, was Squire's idea—a personal refinement of methodology. "While I was chief physician . . . we felt it was desirable to apply the first jolt when the lungs were empty. When the current hits the body, the glottis contracts, imprisoning any air that might be in the lungs. With the breaking of the current, the chest collapses. Air escaping then would make a loud and horrible sound and cause foaming at the mouth." (Squire, pp. 198–199.)

192. the only member of the prison staff: Squire, *Sing Sing Doctor*, p. 199.

192. I have been so overwrought: Ibid., p. 1.

192. Even though I had the respect: Ibid., p. 200.

193. Each time a person is executed: Ibid., p. 279.

193. When I got back home: Ibid., p. 220.

194. Having confided in a friend: Ibid., p. 221.

194. a historical documentary: History Channel, "The Big House," 24 May 1998.

196. Prisoners are treated: Rudolph W. Chamberlain, *There Is No Truce: A Life of Thomas Mott Osborne*, p. 237.

196. I am curious: Thomas Mott Osborne, *Within Prison Walls*, pp. 16–17.

197. Still, he argued: Ibid., p. 8.

197. If I were just to let myself go: Ibid., p. 42.

197. Rigid discipline: Ibid., p. 188.

197. I can conceive no more terribly: Ibid., p. 136.

198. I should not like to be understood: Ibid., p. 135.

198. necessary to wallow: *The Bridgeport* (Connecticut) *Standard*, quoted in Chamberlain, *There Is No Truce: A Life of Thomas Mott Osborne*, p. 262.

198. It is liberty alone: Chamberlain, *There Is No Truce*, p. 237.

198. The governor himself: Frank Tannenbaum, *Osborne of Sing Sing*, pp. 194–195.

199. did commit various unlawful and unnatural acts: Westchester County grand jury indictment, excerpted in Chamberlain, *There Is No Truce: A Life of Thomas Mott Osborne*, p. 329.

199. Until the 1950s: Lewis E. Lawes, *Twenty Thousand Years in Sing Sing*, pp. 109, 290.

199. Of all the array of incoming: Ibid., p. 105.

200. There can be no democracy: Ibid., p. 118.

200. It quickly became apparent: Ibid., p. 111.

201. A recurrent theme was of "hard-boiled": *The New York Times*, 21 October 1977.

201. **For one Hearst Metrotone:** A portion of this newsreel appeared in the History Channel's "Big House" documentary, 24 May 1998.

202. **One thing had not changed:** "These Are Your N.Y. State Correctional Facilities: 8. Sing Sing Prison, Part II," in *Correction,* a publication of the New York State Department of Correction, Vol. XIV, No. VIII (August–September 1949), p. 4.

202. **Dr. R. T. Irvine deduced:** Ibid., p. 4.

202. **A 1905 State Prison Improvement:** Ibid., p. 4.

202. **the cellblock "continued to hang":** Ibid., p. 3.

204. **The incident that has erupted:** Tom Wicker, *A Time to Die: The Attica Prison Revolt,* p. 319.

204. **Lewis Lawes wrote:** Lewis E. Lawes, *Twenty Thousand Years in Sing Sing,* p. 66.

205. **Looking back for the reasons:** "Report to Governor Mario M. Cuomo: Disturbance at Ossining Correctional Facility, Jan. 8–11, 1983," by Lawrence T. Kurlander, Director of Criminal Justice, State of New York, September 1983, p. 224.

205. **It had become a place:** Ibid., pp. 25–26.

205. **Five guards and a sergeant:** *The New York Times,* 29 July 1982, p. B3.

205. **In 1986 a burglar:** *The Citizen Register* (Ossining, New York), 14 December 1986, p. 1.

205. SING SING SEXCAPADES: New York *Daily News,* 30 January 1988, pp. 1–2.

206. **Upon assuming the wardenship:** Lewis E. Lawes, *Twenty Thousand Years in Sing Sing,* pp. 68, 74.

207. **One thing that the judges:** Eldridge Cleaver, *Soul on Ice,* p. 58.

208. **According to a legislative report:** *Report of the Select Committee* [to examine prisons] *of the* [New York State] *Assembly of 1851 . . . transmitted to the legislature, Jan. 7, 1852,* pp. 5–6.

209. **We will turn this prison from a scrap heap:** Rudolph W. Chamberlain, *There Is No Truce: A Life of Thomas Mott Osborne,* p. 412. The quote adorned a tablet set into the wall at 114 East 30th Street in New York, once the home of the Osborne Association, a nonprofit organization providing services to ex-offenders.

Chapter 6: Life in Mama's House

232. **the number of young men:** according to estimates of the number of resident males age eighteen to twenty-four. Population Estimates Program, Population Division, U.S. Census Bureau, Washington, D.C. 20233.

Chapter 7: My Heart Inside Out

261: **A state prison inspectors' report of 1845:** "Report of the Committee appointed to examine the condition of Insane Convicts," in *Annual Report of the Inspectors of the Mount-Pleasant State Prison*, January 10, 1845, pp. 16–20.

287: **Shortly after I left Sing Sing:** *The New York Times*, 7 April 1999, p. A1.

Abbott, Jack Henry. *In the Belly of the Beast: Letters from Prison*. New York: Random House, 1981; reprint ed., New York: Vintage Books, 1991.

Abu-Jamal, Mumia. *Death Blossoms: Reflections from a Prisoner of Conscience*. Farmington, Pennsylvania: The Plough Publishing House, 1997.

Beaumont, Gustave de, and Alexis de Toqueville *[sic]*, *On the Penitentiary System in the United States and Its Application to France*. Translated by Francis Lieber. Philadelphia: Carey, Lea & Blanchard, 1833; reprint ed., New York: Augustus M. Kelley, 1970.

Bergner, Daniel. *God of the Rodeo: The Search for Hope, Faith, and a Six-Second Ride in Louisiana's Angola Prison*. New York: Crown, 1998.

Brice, James R. *Secrets of the Mount-Pleasant State Prison, Revealed and Exposed: An Account of the Unjust Proceedings Against James R. Brice, Esq., by which he was convicted of the Crime of Perjury, Accompanied by Affidavits to Prove His Innocency: Also an account of the Inhuman Treatment of Prisoners by some of the Keepers; and an authentic statement of the officers and salaries, with other curious matters before unknown to the public*. Albany, New York: 1839.

Burr, Levi S. *A Voice From Sing Sing, giving a general description of the state prison, a short and comprehensive geological history of the Quality of the Stone of the Quarries; and a synopsis of the Horrid Treatment of the Convicts in That Prison*. Albany, New York: 1833.

Chamberlain, Rudolph W. *There Is No Truce: A Life of Thomas Mott Osborne*. New York: Macmillan, 1935.

Cheever, John. *Falconer*. New York: Knopf, 1977.

Christianson, Scott. *Condemned: Inside the Sing Sing Death House*. New York: New York University Press, 2000.

Christianson, Scott. *With Liberty for Some: 500 Years of Imprisonment in America*. Boston: Northeastern University Press, 1998.

Cleaver, Eldridge. *Soul on Ice*. New York: Dell, 1968.

Earley, Pete. *The Hot House: Life Inside Leavenworth Prison.* New York: Bantam, 1992.

Foucault, Michel. *Discipline and Punish: The Birth of the Prison.* Translated by Alan Sheridan. New York: Pantheon, 1978; reprint ed., New York: Vintage, 1995.

Frank, Anne. *The Diary of a Young Girl: The Definitive Edition.* New York: Doubleday, 1995; reprint ed., New York: Bantam, 1997.

Gilligan, James, M.D. *Violence: Reflections on a National Epidemic.* New York: G.P. Putnam's Sons, 1996; reprint ed., New York: Vintage, 1997.

Jackson, George. *Soledad Brother.* New York: Coward-McCann, 1970; reprint ed., Chicago: Lawrence Hill Books, 1994.

Jacobson-Hardy, Michael. *Behind the Razor Wire: Portrait of a Contemporary American Prison System.* Photographs and text by Michael Jacobson-Hardy; foreword by Angela Y. Davis; essays by John Edgar Wideman, Marc Mauer, and James Gilligan, M.D. New York: New York University Press, 1999.

Johnson, Robert. *Hard Time: Understanding and Reforming the Prison.* Belmont, California: Wadsworth, 1996.

Johnston, Norman. *The Human Cage: A Brief History of Prison Architecture.* New York: Walker & Co., 1973.

Kauffman, Kelsey. *Prison Officers and Their World.* Cambridge, Mass.: Harvard University Press, 1988.

Lawes, Lewis E. *Twenty Thousand Years in Sing Sing.* New York: Ray Long and Richard R. Smith, 1932.

Liberatore, Paul. *The Road to Hell: The True Story of George Jackson, Stephen Bingham, and the San Quentin Massacre.* New York: Atlantic Monthly Press, 1996.

Luckey, John. *Life in Sing Sing State Prison, as seen in a twelve years chaplaincy.* New York: N. Tibbals, 1860.

Metzger, Th. [*sic*] *Blood and Volts.* Brooklyn, New York: Autonomedia, 1996.

Mitford, Jessica. *Kind and Usual Punishment: The Prison Business.* New York: Knopf, 1973.

Morris, Norval, and David J. Rothman, eds. *The Oxford History of the Prison: The Practice of Punishment in Western Society.* New York: Oxford University Press, 1995.

Nelson, Victor. *Prison Days and Nights.* Boston: Little, Brown, 1933; reprint ed., Garden City, New York: Garden City Publishing Co., 1936.

Newman, Christopher. *Killer.* New York: Dell, 1997.

Number 1500. *Life in Sing Sing.* Indianapolis: Bobbs-Merrill, 1904.

Osborne, Thomas Mott. *Within Prison Walls: Being a Narrative of Personal Experience During A Week of Voluntary Confinement in the State Prison at Auburn, New York.* New York: D. Appleton, 1914.

Pierson, George Wilson. *Tocqueville in America.* New York: Oxford University Press, 1938; reprint ed., Baltimore: Johns Hopkins Paperbacks, 1996.

Puig, Manuel. *Kiss of the Spider Woman.* New York: Knopf, 1979; reprint ed., New York: Vintage, 1980.

Reich, Ilan K. *A Citizen Crusade for Prison Reform: The History of the Correctional Association of New York.* New York: The Correctional Association of New York, 1975.

Shakur, Sanyika, aka Kody Scott. *Monster: The Autobiography of an L.A. Gang Member.* New York: Atlantic Monthly Press, 1993; reprint ed., New York: Penguin, 1994.

Sing Sing Prison: Its History, Purpose, Makeup and Program. Albany: New York State Department of Correction, 1958.

Squire, Amos O., M.D. *Sing Sing Doctor.* Garden City, New York: Garden City Publishing Co., 1937.

Tannenbaum, Frank. *Osborne of Sing Sing.* Chapel Hill, N.C.: University of North Carolina Press, 1933.

Wicker, Tom. *A Time to Die: The Attica Prison Revolt.* New York: Quadrangle/New York Times Book Co., 1975; reprint ed., Lincoln, Nebraska: University of Nebraska Press, 1994.

Wideman, John Edgar. *Brothers and Keepers.* New York: Holt, Rinehart and Winston, 1984; reprint ed., New York: Vintage, 1995.

Wines, Frederick Howard. *Punishment and Reformation: A Study of the Penitentiary System.* New York: Thomas Y. Crowell, 1919.

Yates, J. Michael. *Line Screw: My Twelve Riotous Years Working Behind Bars in Some of Canada's Toughest Jails.* Toronto: McClelland & Stewart, 1993.